Praise for NO CONTEST, recipient of
the American Psychological Association's 1987
National Psychology Award for Excellence in the Media

"Superbly researched, lucidly written, and delineated with admirable clarity."

— *Los Angeles Times Book Review*

"A sophisticated book . . . [that] cuts to the bone, paring away our false beliefs in competition as the backbone of U.S. superiority in the world, in sports, production, happiness, whatever. Alfie Kohn, scholarly, scolding, and eloquent, demolishes all the myths."

— *Minneapolis Star-Tribune*

"One of the most thought-provoking books of this or any other year . . . [It] truly engages a reader from first page to last."

— *West Coast Review of Books*

"NO CONTEST is must reading for educators."

— *Phi Delta Kappan*

"Kohn makes a sound argument against competition as a healthy approach to social behavior . . . [A] penetrating and convincing study."

— *Boston Herald*

"Well-researched and thought-provoking . . . Alfie Kohn's book about the ill effects of competition will cause arguments at the dinner table and heated debate amongst educators."

— *United Press International*

"Kohn . . . persuasively demonstrates how the ingrained American myth that competition is the only normal and desirable way of life — from Little Leagues to the presidency — is counterproductive, personally and for the national economy."

— *Publishers Weekly*

No Contest

THE CASE AGAINST COMPETITION

Revised Edition

▾

ALFIE KOHN

HOUGHTON MIFFLIN COMPANY

Boston   New York

Library of Congress Cataloging-in-Publication Data

Kohn, Alfie.
    No contest : the case against competition / Alfie Kohn.
    — Rev. ed.
        p.   cm.
    Includes index.
    ISBN 0-395-63125-4
    1. Competition (Psychology)   2. Cooperativeness.
    3. Aggressiveness (Psychology)   4. Social interaction — United
    States.   I. Title.
    HM291.K634   1992
    302'.14 — dc20   92-26141
                        CIP

Printed in the United States of America

HAD 10 9 8 7 6 5 4

The author is grateful for permission to use excerpts from:
    "Success Anxiety in Women" by Georgia Sassen in *Harvard Educational Review*, February 1980, 50:1. Copyright © 1980 by the President and Fellows of Harvard College. All rights reserved.
    "Mama Told Me Not to Come" by Randy Newman. Copyright © 1966 by January Music Corp. Assigned to Unichappell Music, Inc. International Copyright Secured. All Rights Reserved. Used by permission.
    Books and articles quoted or cited in the text under the usual fair use allowances are acknowledged in the notes and references.

ACKNOWLEDGMENTS

◁ ▷

For almost every person who writes a book, there is a circle of friends, relatives, and (if the author is sufficiently preoccupied with the project) even casual acquaintances who have been subjected to conversation about it. A well-known writer once turned me down for an interview, claiming he didn't like to talk about whatever he was working on at the time lest his energies be drained. This still baffles me. For the last ten years, I've been eager to talk about competition with anyone who spoke English. The many discussions that resulted have refined my thinking on the subject immeasurably, and I'm grateful to those who have listened and questioned and argued. The same goes for those who spoke up after more formal talks I've given in the Boston area and for my students at Tufts University and the Cambridge Center for Adult Education who wrestled with the topic for an entire semester. No one had to put up with more than those who live (or have lived) in the cooperative house I lived in for five years: Carol Hetrick, Phil Korman, Ellen Carlino, Marianne Takas, Jeb Brugmann, Claudia Cahan, Bob Irwin, Carol Dirga, Don Bishop, and Lynne Weiss.

My interest in competition can be understood in this context: I am fascinated by questions that seem basic to being human, that address us as whole persons rather than just as disembodied intellects, and that cannot be dealt with adequately within the confines of a single academic discipline. That I have such an orientation is due largely to two people: Rob Beneckson awakened it, prodding me to start reading in psychology and helping me to read critically. George Morgan shaped it, becoming for me a mentor in the best sense of that word — and, later, a treasured friend.

My original plan was to edit a collection of essays on competition, but it wasn't long before I realized I had a lot more to say than could be contained in an introduction. While I was trying to say it, I pressed drafts of chapters on people whose judgment I valued, hoping for critical readings. I was not disappointed, and I am pleased to thank Laura Schenk, Claire Baker, Phil Korman, Stewart and Estelle Kohn,

Susan Hewitt, Marianne Takas, and Georgia Sassen, all of whom
helped me to reach a much-needed sense of perspective in addition
to suggesting revisions large and small. I've learned about cooperative
learning from a number of people since the first edition of this book
was published; if I mention only Eric Schaps and David Johnson, it's
because they were kind enough to read and comment on my new
chapter that deals with the topic. (Alisa Harrigan did so, too, but she
has my gratitude for a lot more than that.)

Bill Greene's contribution merits a separate paragraph. In view of
his agile intelligence, I would have been happy with even a small
helping of his help. I was lucky enough to receive more hours than
I can count: he read every chapter, said a great deal about them — all
of it useful — and forced me to rewrite and rethink much of what
follows. Whatever you think of this book, it is far better than it would
have been without his help. The legal profession is lucky to have him.

With all of this advice and guidance, it would have been a shame
to keep the final product all to myself. This is where Larry Kessenich
and John Ware came in. Their enthusiasm for the project is responsible for turning it into a published book. I have not only Larry but
also Ruth Hapgood, Lois Randall, and Gerry Morse to thank for
editing, as well.

Let me note, finally, that most of the research for this book was
done in the libraries of Harvard University, the size of whose holdings
is matched only by the school's determination to restrict access to
them. I am delighted to have been able to use these resources, and
it hardly matters that I was afforded this privilege only because the
school thought I was someone else.

CONTENTS

◁▷

At every quarterly examination a gold medal was given to the best writer. When the first medal was offered, it produced rather a general contention than an emulation and diffused a spirit of envy, jealousy, and discord through the whole school; boys who were bosom friends before became fierce contentious rivals, and when the prize was adjudged became implacable enemies. Those who were advanced decried the weaker performances; each wished his opponent's abilities less than his own, and they used all their little arts to misrepresent and abuse each other's performances.

— Robert Coram, *Political Inquiries* (1791)

1

◁ ▷

The "Number One" Obsession

Life for us has become an endless succession of contests. From the moment the alarm clock rings until sleep overtakes us again, from the time we are toddlers until the day we die, we are busy struggling to outdo others. This is our posture at work and at school, on the playing field and back at home. It is the common denominator of American life.

Precisely because we are so immersed in it, competition can easily escape our notice. A fish does not reflect on the nature of water, Walker Percy once remarked, "he cannot imagine its absence, so he cannot consider its presence."[1] Even those who think and write for a living have paid surprisingly little attention to the subject. In the last fifty years, for example, no one has written a book that explores the very idea of competition and the way it plays itself out in all the varied arenas of human life. I do not mean a lament about what has happened to sports today or a recipe for being a winner in business or a statistical operation performed on abstractions that issue from experimental games. These roll off the presses regularly. I mean a look at what it really means to try to beat other people, a careful investigation of this arrangement that requires some people to fail in order that others can succeed.

If such an analysis is long past due, the need for it is nowhere more urgent than in this country. Different cultures depend on competition to different degrees in structuring their economic system or schooling or recreation. At one end of the spectrum are societies that function without any competition at all. At the other end is the United States. Here is social psychologist Elliot Aronson:

> From the Little League ball player who bursts into tears after his team loses, to the college students in the football stadium chanting "We're number one!"; from Lyndon Johnson, whose judgment was almost certainly distorted by his oft-stated desire not to be the first American President to lose a war, to the third grader who despises his classmate for a superior performance on an arithmetic test; we manifest a staggering cultural obsession with victory.[2]

Others have used similar language. "Competition is almost our state religion," says one observer.[3] It is "an American cultural addiction," remarks another.[4] "Resistance to competition is viewed as suspiciously un-American," notes a third.[5]

This does not mean that competition is found only in the United States. The examples offered in this book will likely seem familiar to readers elsewhere. But what may be merely familiar in other places has reached exaggerated, often ludicrous, proportions in this country. We can see this both in the pervasiveness of competitive activities and in the fervor with which we approach them. Our economic system is predicated on competition, while our schooling, from the earliest grades, trains us not only to triumph over others but to regard them as obstacles to our own success. Our leisure time is filled with highly structured games in which one individual or team must defeat another. Even within the family there is rivalry — a muted but often desperate struggle that treats approval as a scarce commodity and turns love into a kind of trophy.

Not only do we get carried away with competitive activities, but we turn almost everything else *into* a contest. Our collective creativity seems to be tied up in devising new ways to produce winners and losers. It is not enough that we struggle against our colleagues at work to be more productive; we also must compete for the title of Friendliest Employee. The only way we can think of to socialize with the people who work for another company is to try to beat them in a competitive game. If we want to escape all of this by, say, going out dancing, we find that even here we are involved in a contest. No corner of our lives is too trivial — or too important — to be exempted from the compulsion to rank ourselves against one another. Even where no explicit contest has been set up, we tend to construe the world in competitive terms. Several years ago, to cite one small illustration, the *New York Times Magazine* featured a profile of Placido Domingo that declared he had "challenged Luciano Pavarotti — and, many say, surpassed him — for the title of the world's leading tenor."[6] Opera, too, cannot be enjoyed without our thinking in terms of who is number one.

Thus it is that Vince Lombardi's famous comment — "Winning isn't everything; it's the only thing" — must be understood not merely as the expression of one football coach's fanaticism, but as a capsule description of our entire culture.[7] Our lives are not merely affected by, but structured upon, the need to be "better than." We seem to have reached a point where doing our jobs, educating our children, and even relaxing on the weekends have to take place in the context of a struggle where some must lose. That there might be other ways to do these things is hard for us to imagine — or, rather, it *would* be hard if we were sufficiently reflective about our competitiveness to think about alternatives in the first place. Mostly we just accept it as "the way life is."

The current celebration of business competition makes these issues particularly timely. Bookstores have been deluged with guides to winning in the marketplace largely because of the rhetoric spilling out of Washington over the last few years. The competition that has been indiscriminately encouraged actually has the effect of shifting power from elected representatives to private corporations, from those who are theoretically accountable to all citizens to those who are, at best, accountable to only the tiny fraction of people who stand to make a profit. (Half of all corporate stock is owned by one percent of the population, while 81 percent of all families own no stock at all.)[8] But even if the mystique of corporate success becomes less fashionable after a few years — even if public officials no longer see themselves chiefly as cheerleaders for private industry — our economic system is fundamentally grounded in competition, and an exploration of the subject will continue to be relevant. Moreover, I am concerned in this book with far more than the machinations of the business world. Competition is a deeply ingrained, profoundly enduring, part of our lives, and it is time to look more closely at what it does to us.

·   ·   ·

Let us begin with a more precise formulation of the topic. I think it is useful to distinguish between what might be called *structural competition* and *intentional competition*. The former refers to a situation; the latter, to an attitude. Whereas structural competition has to do with the win/lose framework, which is external, intentional competition is internal; it concerns the desire on the part of an individual to be number one.

To say that an activity is structurally competitive is to say that it is characterized by what I will call *mutually exclusive goal attainment* ("MEGA," for short). This means, very simply, that my success requires your failure. Our fates are negatively linked. If one of us must lose exactly as much as the other wins, as in poker, then we are talking about a "zero-sum game." But in any MEGA arrangement, two or more individuals are trying to achieve a goal that cannot be achieved by all of them. This is the essence of competition, as several social scientists have observed.[9]

The same phenomenon sometimes has been described as a situation of scarcity. This does not explain competition but simply restates it: If I must try to defeat you in order to get what I want, then what I want is scarce by definition. We need to be careful not to confuse this sort of scarcity with the kind that refers to an objective shortage of some commodity. It is possible, of course, for two hungry people to compete for a single bowl of stew. But in most contests, the goal is simply a prized status. Structural competition usually involves the comparison of several individuals in such a way that only one of them can be the best. The competition itself sets the goal, which is to win; scarcity is thereby created out of nothing.

Structural competitions can be distinguished according to several criteria. Competitions vary, for instance, with respect to how many winners there will be. Not everyone who applies for admission to a given college will be accepted, but my acceptance does not necessarily preclude yours (although it will make it somewhat less likely). On the other hand, only one woman in a bathing suit will be crowned Miss America each year, and if Miss Montana wins, Miss New Jersey cannot. In both of these competitions, notice that winning is the result of someone's subjective judgment. In other cases, such as arm wrestling, pre-established and reasonably straightforward criteria determine who wins.

Beauty contests and college admissions also share another feature: neither requires any direct interaction among the contestants. The success of one simply rules out or reduces the chances for success of another. There is a stronger version of structural competition in which one contestant must *make* the other(s) fail in order to succeed himself. War is one example. Tennis is another. Whereas two bowlers competing for a trophy take turns doing the same thing and do not interfere with each other, two tennis players actively work at defeating each other. Which of these postures is in evidence depends on the rules of the game, the type of structural competition that is involved.

Intentional competition is much easier to define — although its nuances are quite complex indeed, as we shall see later. Here we are simply talking about an individual's competitiveness, his or her proclivity for besting others. This can take place in the absence of structural competition, as all of us have observed: someone may arrive at a party and be concerned to prove he is the most intelligent or attractive person in the room even though no prizes are offered and no one else has given any thought to the matter. The psychoanalyst Karen Horney described as neurotic someone who "constantly measures himself against others, even in situations which do not call for it."[10]

The reverse situation — structural competition without intentional competition — is also possible. You may be concerned simply to do the best you can (without any special interest in being better than others), yet find yourself in a situation where this entails competing. Here it is the structure rather than your intention that defines success as victory. Perhaps you are even averse to competing but find yourself unable to avoid it — an unhappy and stressful state of affairs known to many of us. The most extreme case of structural competition without intentional competition is a circumstance in which individuals are ranked and rewarded without even being aware of it. Students may be sorted on the basis of their grades even if they are not trying to defeat each other. (The distinction between the two varieties of competition is especially useful in allowing us to make sense of such a scenario.)

Finally, let us take note of the rather obvious fact that competition can exist among individuals or among groups. The latter does not rule out the former: even as two corporations or nations or basketball teams are competing with each other, it is possible that the people within these groups can be vying for money or status. Competition among groups is known as *intergroup* competition, while competition among individuals within a group is called *intragroup* competition. These distinctions will prove important in later chapters.

.   .   .

Competition is not the only way to organize a classroom or a workplace. This is hardly a controversial observation, but because we have come to take competition for granted, we rarely think about alternatives. In this book, following the lead of most social psychologists, I will be considering three ways of achieving one's goals: *competitively*, which means working against others; *cooperatively*, which means working with others; and *independently*, which means working without regard to others. Although we sometimes speak of an individual or a culture as being both competitive and individualistic, it is important to realize that they are not the same. There is a difference between allowing one person to succeed only if someone else does not, on the one hand, and allowing that person to succeed irrespective of the other's success or failure, on the other. Your success and mine are related in both competition and cooperation (though in opposite ways); they are unrelated if we work independently.

We sometimes assume that working toward a goal and setting standards for oneself can take place only if we compete against others. This is simply false. One can both accomplish a task and measure one's progress in the absence of competition. A weightlifter may try to press ten pounds more than he did yesterday, for example. This is sometimes referred to as "competing with oneself," which seems to me a rather unhelpful and even misleading phrase. A comparison of performance with one's own previous record or with objective standards is in no way an instance of competition and it should not be confused with it. *Competition* is fundamentally an interactive word, like *kissing*, and it stretches the term beyond usefulness to speak of competing with oneself. Moreover, such sloppy usage is sometimes employed in order to argue that competition is either inevitable or benign: since nobody loses when you try to beat your own best time, and since this is a kind of competition, then competition is really not so bad. This, of course, is just a semantic trick rather than a substantive defense of competition.

The third alternative, cooperation, will play a more important role in the pages that follow. The word refers to an arrangement that is not merely noncompetitive but requires us to work together in order to achieve our goals. Structural cooperation means that we have to coordinate our efforts because I can succeed only if you succeed, and vice versa. Reward is based on collective performance. Thus, a cooperative classroom is not simply one in which students sit together or talk with each other or even share materials. It means that successful completion of a task depends on each student and therefore that each has an incentive to want the other(s) to succeed.

When we think about cooperation at all, we tend to associate the concept with fuzzy-minded idealism or, at best, to see it as workable only in a very small number of situations. This may result from confusing cooperation with altruism. It is not at all true that competition is more successful because it relies on the tendency to "look out for number one" while cooperation assumes that we primarily want to help each other. Structural cooperation defies the usual egoism/altruism dichotomy. It sets things up so that by helping you I am helping myself at the same time. Even if my motive initially may have been selfish, our fates now are linked. We sink or swim together. Cooperation is a shrewd and highly successful strategy — a pragmatic choice that gets things done at work and at school even more effectively than competition does (as I will show in chapter 3) and can serve as a basis for creating challenging and enjoyable games that do not require us to compete against one another (as I will show in chapter 4). There is also good evidence that cooperation is more conducive to psychological health and to liking one another.

Even in a competitive culture there are aspects of cooperative and independent work. In fact, a single day at the office can include all three models. The most common mix consists of intragroup cooperation and intergroup competition: working with others in a group in order to defeat other groups. Football players cooperate in order to win and employees pull together in order that their company can earn higher profits than another company. It should be clear, however, that these orientations do not appear with the same frequency. Notice how often cooperation in our society is in the service of competition — and how often we must compete without being able to cooperate at all. As Robert Bellah and his colleagues put it, "The world of individualistic competition is experienced every day; the world of harmonious unanimity is fully realized only in sporadic flashes of togetherness, glimpses of what might be if only people would cooperate and their purposes reinforce, rather than undercut, one another."[11]

.   .   .

That most of us consistently fail to consider the alternatives to competition is a testament to the effectiveness of our socialization. We have been trained not only to compete but to believe in competition. If we are asked about it, we unthinkingly repeat what we have been told. Unfortunately, the case for competition, as most of us have learned it, does not stand up under close scrutiny. It is a case that relies on rhetorical gambits, such as the insinuation that people who oppose competition are simply afraid of it, or on a lack of conceptual precision, such as the confusion of competition with conflict or with success. It is a case that sometimes misrepresents itself, such as by disguising the impulse to compete as a simple need to survive. Long ago, Bertrand Russell pointed out that what is often meant by "the struggle for life is really the [competitive] struggle for success. What people fear when they engage in the struggle is not that they will fail to get their breakfast next morning, but that they will fail to outshine their neighbors."[12]

Most of all, the case for competition is based on a great deal of misinformation. Specifically, it has been constructed on four central myths, and these myths, in the order of their popularity, form the basis of the next four chapters. The first myth is that competition is an unavoidable fact of life, part of "human nature." Although this assumption is made casually (and without evidence), it demands a considered response; if it were true, arguments about competition's desirability would be beside the point since there is nothing we can do about our nature. The second myth is that competition motivates us to do our best — or, in stronger form, that we would cease being productive if we did not compete. This assumption is invoked to explain everything from grades to capitalism. Third, it is sometimes asserted that contests provide the best, if not the only, way to have a good time. All the joys of play are said to hinge on competitive games. The last myth is that competition builds character, that it is good for self-confidence. This claim is not heard quite so often as the others — probably because it contradicts not only empirical evidence but our own experience of the psychological impact of competition.

I mean to refute each of these myths by looking at all the arenas of human life where competition is present and by reviewing the relevant evidence from such diverse fields as education, social psychology, sociology, psychoanalysis, leisure studies, evolutionary biology, and cultural anthropology. Contributions from philosophy and literature will be included for good measure. Investigating a topic like competition really seems to require this kind of interdisciplinary approach; the territorial inclinations of most scholars have often limited their effectiveness at exploring this and other important questions. These questions sprawl rudely across the boundaries that divide academic specialties.

Beginning with a definition of terms, as I have done, is fairly standard. But in this case, being clear about what competition means not only helps to keep the issue in sharper focus; it actually forms the basis of a critique. Strip away all the assumptions about what competition is supposed to do, all the claims in its behalf that we accept and repeat reflexively. What you have left is the essence of the concept: mutually exclusive goal attainment (MEGA). One person succeeds only if another does not. From this uncluttered perspective, it seems clear right away that something is drastically wrong with such an arrangement. How can we do our best when we are spending our energies trying to make others lose — and fearing that they will make us lose? Can this sort of struggle really be the best way to have a good time? What happens to our self-esteem when it becomes dependent on how much better we do than the next person? Most striking of all is the impact of this arrangement on human relationship: a structural incentive to see other people lose cannot help but drive a wedge between us and invite hostility.

Again, all of these conclusions seem to flow from the very nature of competition. As it happens, they also are corroborated by the evidence — what we see around us and what scores of studies have been finding. One may not be inclined to consider this evidence, though, until the elemental question has been asked: What do we *mean* when we speak of competing?

The more closely I have examined the topic, the more firmly I have become convinced that competition is an inherently undesirable arrangement, that the phrase *healthy competition* is actually a contradiction in terms. This is nothing short of heresy because only two positions on the question are normally recognized: enthusiastic support and qualified support. Broadly speaking, the former can be called the conservative position and the latter, liberal. Conservatives champion competition of all kinds, often coming close to Lombardi's dictum about winning's being the only thing. Liberals are typically more restrained, granting that *excessive* competition is to be avoided and lamenting that our culture now encourages winning at all costs. Competition itself, however, if it is kept in its "proper perspective," can be productive, enjoyable, stimulating, and so on.

The latter is the view of most of the critics of competition whom I will be quoting throughout this book. It seems to me, however, that they are unwilling to see their intuitions — and, in some cases, their data — through to their logical conclusion. Perhaps this is because these writers assume that they would lose all credibility if they took the extreme position that competition simply makes no sense, and thus they feel compelled to say that the problem is not with competition, per se, but only with the *way* we compete or the *extent* of our competitiveness. Despite the fact that such moderation confers respectability, my conviction that the problem lies with competition itself (and that the extent of this problem is in direct proportion to the degree of competitiveness in a given activity) has been strengthened as I have looked at each of the spheres where it appears. I believe the case against competition is so compelling that parenthetical qualifications to the effect that competing can sometimes be constructive would be incongruous and unwarranted.

What follows is an elaboration of this radical critique. After addressing the four central myths of competition — that it is inevitable, more productive, more enjoyable, and likely to build character — I examine its interpersonal consequences in chapter 6. This is followed in chapter 7 by a discussion of whether such ugly things as cheating and violence represent the corruption of true competition or its very consummation. Chapter 8 considers the current movement on the part of many women toward becoming competitive in the same way men are, chapter 9 reviews the prospects for replacing competition with cooperative alternatives, and the final chapter, new to this edition, focuses on one particularly promising such alternative that allows schoolchildren to learn with each other instead of against or apart from each other. Finally, in a new afterword, I describe how this book has been received and offer some reflections on signs of change (and of stasis) in our culture since the first edition was published.

2

Is Competition Inevitable?

THE "HUMAN NATURE" MYTH

> Of all the vulgar modes of escaping from the considera-
> tion of the effect of social and moral influence on the
> human mind, the most vulgar is that of attributing the
> diversities of conduct and character to inherent natural
> differences.
>
> — John Stuart Mill,
> *Principles of Political Economy*

PLAYING THE "HUMAN NATURE" CARD

Those who argue most vigorously that competition is desirable are
often the same people who assert that it is part of human nature: it is
not only good that we try to best each other; it is inevitable. Strictly
speaking, of course, the second contention cancels out the first. There
is little point to debating whether we should be what we unavoidably
are. From the perspective of a critic of competition, though, it is
necessary to demonstrate that we do not *have* to be competitive before
showing why we *ought* not to be.

This chapter's task, then, is to scrutinize the widely accepted but
rarely defended claim that competition is inevitable. In doing so, it
makes sense to begin with the larger issue of inevitability itself. What
is involved in the claim that a given attribute is part of "human nature"? Can such a claim be substantiated? Who benefits from this
position? After addressing these questions, we can go on to consider
the particular issue of competition.

There are two versions of the human nature argument. The first
claims that differences among particular groups of humans are innate. For instance, if women and men (or whites and nonwhites) are
treated differently in a particular society, this is said to be a function

of biology. This position purports to show that various findings in evolutionary biology and genetics prove that sexist and racist practices are unavoidable if not positively adaptive.

The second kind of human nature argument — the one with which this chapter is concerned — says that particular characteristics are an unavoidable part of being human. These characteristics are said to be inborn rather than learned, part of "nature" rather than "nurture." This debate has been going on for some time, and in each generation a new crop of scientists arises to carry the torch for biological determinism. A generation ago, Cyril Burt offered "proof" that intelligence was chiefly a function of genes. His evidence turned out to be fabricated, but it is interesting to note how long he was able to get away with his claims and how many of his conclusions continue to be accepted long after his data were proved worthless.[1] Today, biological determinism is championed primarily by certain neurobiologists and psychiatrists on the one hand, and by the school of sociobiology that has grown up around Edward O. Wilson, on the other.

Most often, though, "human nature" is invoked in a casual way to account for various behaviors we encounter. Almost anything that we regularly come across is assumed with a shrug to describe the human condition. Interestingly, the characteristics that we explain away in this fashion are almost always unsavory; an act of generosity is rarely dismissed on the grounds that it is "just human nature."* Apart from the empirical grounds for defending such claims, though, it is important to remember that the burden of proof falls heavily on someone who asserts that a given characteristic is part of our nature. It is he or she who must provide compelling evidence to substantiate such a belief, and not the rest of us who must prove it is not so. Anyone who offers an assertion for our consideration has such a burden, but it is that much more formidable when the claim is absolute: to say that a given characteristic is in our nature is to assert that it is a feature of all human beings, across all cultures and throughout human history. Moreover, it is to propose its inescapability for all humans in the future.

---

*There are exceptions, however. Humanistic psychologists such as Abraham Maslow and Carl Rogers contend that human beings are fundamentally good — that is, that what we think of as healthy, productive, ethical behavior is the natural tendency of our biological natures. This approach hearkens back to the neo-Freudian tradition that includes Erich Fromm and Karen Horney, and, for that matter, all the way back to Jean-Jacques Rousseau. More recent evidence from developmental psychology conceivably could be used to support the hypothesis that altruism is inborn. See p. 201, note 24.

Has the human nature argument actually been proved? It is hard to tell because there *is* no single argument. "Human nature" really is an expression of commonality among many different schools of thought as applied to many different characteristics. It is a full-time undertaking to determine whether even a single attribute is an inescapable feature of human life. It would appear that the empirical evidence does not begin to support most such claims, but I cannot hope to rehearse this evidence here. Fortunately, others have done so and have shown the weaknesses of biological determinism in its many incarnations.[2]

In fact, it is difficult to know how one could *ever* prove decisively that something is part of human nature, given the theoretical complexity of such disputes. Many of us assume that all questions to which scientists address themselves admit of a definitive answer once the evidence has been assembled. If we want to know whether schizophrenia has a genetic basis, for example, we assume we can simply collect the data, see what they say, and move on to the next question. This commonsense view of how science works probably comes from high school science courses, which represent the field about as well as civics courses represent what actually goes on in politics. We were never taught about controversies over how a scientific dispute is to be framed, the various uses to which certain terms are put, the debates over the applicability and significance of particular findings. Data are not simply collected but interpreted, and how they are interpreted depends on what is counted as evidence as well as one's positions on other theoretical questions.

If in contemporary physics — the hardest of sciences — one rarely settles a question to everyone's satisfaction by performing an experiment, this is all the more true when humans are the subject matter. Even the sociobiologists admit that the idea that there are certain genes which determine our behavior is merely fanciful speculation at this point. (Critics ask whether such genes in principle could ever be found; if human behavior results from a complicated interrelationship among genes — and then again between genes and social forces — the enterprise of sociobiology is misconceived from the start.)* Let

---

*This matter of interrelationship is noteworthy with respect to the nature/nurture disputes because the critics of biological determinism typically do not subscribe to a *tabula rasa* environmentalism. If these critics are sometimes represented as doing so, it is because this simplistic version of environmentalism has been thoroughly discredited by now and attributing it to one's adversaries makes it easier to dismiss them. Moreover, to us say, for example, that someone sought to demonstrate that it is "human nature" to be aggressive.[4] How could this be done? Providing evidence that aggression is universal would be a necessary, but not sufficient, step in such a proof. Even here, moreover, people of good faith might well disagree about what constitutes aggression and whether it really exists in a given culture.

These considerations have to do with the truth or falsity of claims about human nature. But we should not ignore the uses to which such claims are put. It is true that an empirical dispute is not resolved by illuminating the functions served by one argument or the other. Still, it is altogether appropriate to ask of any argument: *Cui bono?* (Who benefits?)

Arguments to the effect that something is unavoidable — and claims about human nature, in particular — are typically offered in defense of the status quo.* Now one may question whether advocates of biological inevitability *intend* to retard change; one may even question whether findings in support of this position enjoy acceptance largely because of their political implications. What is beyond dispute, however, is the practical consequence of such a perspective. Who benefits from the belief that unregulated capitalism is "natural" — or the belief that *any* feature of the status quo follows from something intrinsic to our make-up? Clearly it is those who are well served by that status quo.

The human nature argument has the effect of blunting change and it is played for all its rhetorical advantages. Ideals and reforms are opposed on the ground that they are impossible to attain, that they fly in the face of the "givens" of life. "Your idea is charming, but unfortunately It's Just Human Nature To Be greedy/aggressive/competitive/territorial/lazy/stubborn, so it hasn't much chance to succeed." While undesirability (a matter of value) is debatable, impossibility (a matter

---

insist that we are not merely "survival machines — robot vehicles blindly programmed to preserve the selfish molecules known as genes"[3] is not necessarily to cast our lot with the equally deterministic premises of, say, Skinnerian behaviorism. We can also challenge biological determinism from the vantage point of an affirmation of human freedom.

*This is not always the case. An emphasis on inevitability sometimes is found on the part of people who do not oppose change. Twenty-five hundred years ago, Heraclitus argued not that change is desirable, but that it is inexorable. Orthodox Marxists, too, with their talk of historical inevitability, are preoccupied with what is bound to happen.

of fact) is not. In the name of realism, uncounted ideas have been dismissed and their creators along with them — a phenomenon that we will consider again in the last chapter.

Finally, I should observe that the human nature position is also an appealing one for psychological reasons. When we are criticized for an attitude we hold, it is tempting to respond, "Look, this is the way I was brought up." This is sometimes an appeal to cultural relativism, whose subtext is: "Who are you to judge?" but it is more often an appeal to determinism that argues, "I cannot choose to believe otherwise." If I cannot change, there is no point in arguing that I should.[5] There is no shortage of putative causes for our behavior (or values) that can be used to deflect criticism. The almost limitless range of behaviors currently being tied to neurotransmitters offers a new set of excuses to supplant those provided by psychoanalysis. "[People] used to say: 'It's not my fault. My parents did it to me . . .' Now they say: 'It's not me. It's a biochemical disorder in my brain.' "[6] Far more attractive than such rationalizations, however, is the claim that *no human* could be expected to act otherwise.

Even when we are not directly challenged to defend our behavior, the prospect that our actions or attitudes may be inevitable is attractive. Freedom can be unsettling if not positively terrifying[7] — and scientific determinisms are, psychologically speaking, the contemporary counterpart to theological doctrines of predestination. To be relieved of responsibility can, paradoxically, be experienced as freeing. Finally, the discomfort contemporary Americans have with value judgments can create a strong incentive to resort to arguments that certain things *must* be. In several respects, then, the human nature argument — which is virtually impossible to substantiate — is very seductive indeed: it fortifies social arrangements, offers a rhetorical advantage in disputes, and makes life easier psychologically. These are considerations well worth keeping in mind as we proceed to consider the specific issue of competition.

ON ARGUMENTS FOR
THE INEVITABILITY OF COMPETITION

Competition is cited as part of "human nature" as often as any other characteristic, so one might expect that there is quite a bit of argument and evidence to substantiate this claim. Amazingly, a careful examination of the literature turns up virtually nothing. The inevitability of competition is either tacitly assumed or simply asserted as if it were obvious. I want to examine these assertions in the writings of people who are favorably inclined toward competition before going on to review the evidence against its inevitability.

Among those thinkers who believe competition is unavoidable are the authors of two of the classic works on play: Roger Caillois and Johan Huizinga. Both take it for granted that we are unavoidably competitive creatures. "Games discipline instincts and institutionalize them," Caillois wrote;[8] that these competitive tendencies merit the status of instincts he did not bother to defend. For his part, Huizinga treated play and competition as virtually interchangeable. The possibility of noncompetitive play literally would not occur to someone who believes competition is part of our nature.

In their 1917 essay on the subject, John Harvey and his co-authors observed that, for many people, "in games the pleasure comes from the competition itself . . . and not from success." From this they quickly concluded that "there is therefore in human nature an instinct of pure competition which finds satisfaction in the very act of striving to do something better than other people, even though the attempt is not successful."[9] This is rather like claiming that because many people prefer the car ride to the arrival at their destination, humans must have an instinctive attraction to automobile travel. The sociologist James S. Coleman, in his investigation of American high schools twenty-five years ago, employed equally dubious logic. He declared, "The removal of scholastic achievement as a basis of comparison does not *lessen* the amount of competition among adolescents; it only *shifts* the arena from academic matters to non-academic ones." He illustrates the latter with "the competition between two girls for the attention of a boy."[10] That competition is not restricted to the academic arena is surely true, but this hardly substantiates Coleman's implicit assumption that a set level of competitiveness exists in us willy-nilly and the best we can do is to rechannel (displace) it to this object or that.

One of the very few recent book-length treatments of competition is Harvey Ruben's self-help manual, *Competing*, the first sentence of which is, "Competition is an inescapable fact of life."[11] This, we later learn, is because "we indeed have a competitive 'code' in our chromosomes"[12] — an astonishing claim that is not substantiated or even explained. Ruben evidently believes we are genetically programmed to compete on the grounds that competition is very widespread and that we begin competing very early in life.

Although they are not defended, these, at least, are reasons one might suppose competition is part of human nature. Somewhat more common, however, are rhetorical tricks and even name-calling as a way of justifying this assumption. Ruben's chief *modus operandi* is to define a wide range of behaviors as indirectly competitive and thus effectively define a noncompetitive orientation out of existence. For example, "Whether the child realizes it or not, learning to wait for a feeding while mother attends to another sibling is one of the first competitive lessons."[13] And again, people who "seem the *least* competitive of all types actually have only adopted more circuitous strategies to get what the others strive for more obviously."[14] In subsequent chapters, we are told that all acts of comparison, as well as the act of joining a group, are intrinsically competitive behaviors. This model tells us more about its creator than about the world he purports to describe.[15] It also sets up an unfalsifiable argument. Whereas any example of a noncompetitive individual or culture should be sufficient to disprove the idea that competition is part of human nature, Ruben has arranged things so that even many such examples will not suffice: He has denied the very *possibility* of acting noncompetitively and so "proved" its inevitability.

Because Ruben frames his argument at such length, it is easy to see what he is doing. More commonly, though, a writer will make a brief comment about competition that seems persuasive but actually rests on the same conceptual sleight of hand. "Sometimes people are inclined to hide their competitive instincts and drives," writes Harold J. Vanderzwaag, "but when they participate in sport, their competitive nature is usually revealed."[16] Translation: People are competitive on some occasions and not on other occasions; therefore, the former is real and the latter is an instance of disguise. Here, too, the argument is laid out so no amount of empirical evidence can possibly disprove the hypothesis that competition is inevitable.

Some writers have resorted to *ad hominem* attacks on those who question the naturalness of competition. "I think we're all scared to face the competitive side of our nature," comments Mary Ann O'Roark in an article entitled, " 'Competition' Isn't a Dirty Word."[17] This neatly puts anyone who challenges the inevitability of competition in the position of being frightened, of lacking the courage to grasp a difficult but obvious truth. The well-known biologist Garrett Hardin goes further, becoming rather snide, in fact:

> We are not surprised to note that young people whose needs are taken care of by their elders often fail to appreciate the inevitability of competition. What is surprising is that adults whose specialty is the behavior of human beings in groups — sociologists — should hold competition in such low esteem.[18]

Besides blurring the issues of inevitability and desirability, Hardin pronounces himself unwilling to consider that these upstart social scientists may be on to something. The slam at privileged youth, however, is actually more interesting than it first appears. Put plainly, Hardin's point is that people who have not had to compete believe that competition is avoidable. But what if such people are correct? If we generalize the meaning of having one's "needs . . . taken care of," we are left with the provocative suggestion that competition exists not because it is in our nature but because of economic or psychological deficits that are, in principle, remediable.

I have not carefully selected these examples of unjustified assertion, rhetorical trickery, and name-calling as straw men. They virtually exhaust the available literature. I have not been able to discover any other explicit arguments for the inevitability of human competition.[19] Let me therefore turn to the opposing position. There are, broadly speaking, two general responses to the claim that competition is an inevitable feature of human life: (1) cooperation is at least as integral to human life as competition, and (2) competition is a learned phenomenon. I will begin with the first and return to the second later in this chapter.

The respects in which other species (and "nature" as a whole) are cooperative will be examined in the next section. But there is a good case to be made that we regularly underestimate the role that cooperation plays in human life. We attend instead to the far more visible instances of struggle. "The truth is that the vast majority of human interaction, in our society as well as in all other societies, is not competitive but cooperative interaction," according to educational psychologists David and Roger Johnson.[20] Ashley Montagu has been arguing this for quite some time: "Without the cooperation of its members society cannot survive, and the society of man has survived because the cooperativeness of its members made survival possible . . ."[21] Arguably, the ubiquity of cooperative interactions even in a relatively competitive society is powerful evidence against the generalization that humans are naturally competitive. Our lives are "promotively interdependent," to use Morton Deutsch's language, by the very fact of living and working together. This is true in every society; it is inherent in the very *idea* of society. If not simply false, the claim that we are unavoidably competitive is therefore a truth so partial as to be utterly misleading.

This tendency to cooperate, to work actively with rather than against others, has been found among toddlers and even infants. So-called "prosocial behaviors" — cooperating, helping, sharing, comforting, and so on — occur in almost every child, even though research in this area has been practically nonexistent until very recently.[22] Regular examples of children under three years of age giving their toys to playmates, spontaneously taking turns in games, and so on must give pause to anyone who assumes competitiveness is the natural state of the human.[23] I am not trying to suggest by this that it is "human nature" to help others. The problems with such claims have been raised earlier, and what is good for the competitive goose is good for the cooperative gander. One pair of researchers explicitly disavows this conclusion, in fact, arguing that "prosocial behaviors result from experience; they are learned."[24] But from wherever such inclination to help derives, it exists literally from the beginning of life. While we may not be unavoidably cooperative, we are, at worst, not unavoidably anything at all.

THE REAL STATE OF NATURE

In considering the relative prevalence of competition and cooperation, we now turn to the natural world. In doing so, we find ourselves in what seems unfriendly territory. In fact, competition in the animal world is often cited as powerful evidence that competition is part of our nature, too. Before looking more closely at the evidence, however, we need to challenge the assumption that the proper study of mankind is animals. Even if other species were as competitive as some people think, this, like any fact about other species, has at best a very limited relevance to ourselves. As Marshall Sahlins, Richard Lewontin, and other critics of sociobiology have shown — and it should not be necessary to rehearse here — the mediating force of culture puts our species in a class by itself. Only humankind manipulates symbols, reflects upon the fact of its reflecting, questions, makes value judgments, appreciates absurdity, creates institutions and then considers their limitations. Because of this, the historian Richard Hofstadter was absolutely correct to insist that "judgments as to the value of competition between men or enterprises or nations must be based upon social and not allegedly biological consequences."[25]

But let us, for the sake of the argument, grant some relevance to the question How does nature operate? From my own exposure to documentaries and popular conception, a series of images has lodged itself in my mind. Two powerful and deliberate males of an uncertain species are locked in mortal combat while the feminine prize coolly sits on the sidelines. A huge fish swims up behind a smaller version of itself, jaws wide open. A fierce feline gracefully turns its less swift-footed cousin into steak. Some ignominiously vanquished species lies collectively rotting, while the victors are just off camera having lunch. This, I had always assumed, was the real state of nature: somewhere just beyond the tranquil loveliness of a spring day in the forest, all was red in tooth and claw. At this very moment, animals from paramecia to hippopotami are vigorously organizing themselves into winners and losers.

As a humanist (in one sense of the word) I was dismayed at this picture of the natural world; as a humanist (in another sense) I was in no position to challenge its accuracy. Of course, the picture is not without its element of truth. Obviously the scenes I saw on television actually happened; I was not, after all, watching highly paid stunt wolves. Still, as some biologists have been pointing out since the turn of the century, the animal world is not what many of us assume.

To understand why this is so, let us consider the idea of "natural selection," one of the greatest conceptual advances in the history of human thought. This theory states that the better adapted a species is to its environment — and, specifically, to changes in that environment — the greater the probability of its being around in the future. To adapt is to be able to procreate; to procreate is to survive. So much is uncontroversial. For many years, though, some biologists and ethologists have encouraged the widespread conception that natural selection is tantamount to competition. "Survival of the fittest" (to use the term coined not by Darwin but by Herbert Spencer) seemed to connote a struggle. Winners live to fight another day.

In fact, there is no necessary relationship between natural selection and competitive struggle. As Stephen Jay Gould put it recently:

The equation of competition with success in natural selection is merely a cultural prejudice. . . . Success defined as leaving more offspring can . . . be attained by a large variety of strategies — including mutualism and symbiosis — that we could call cooperative. There is no *a priori* preference in the general statement of natural selection for either competitive or cooperative behavior.[26]

Gould's point is that there is nothing about evolution that *requires* competition. And, indeed, Darwin himself made clear that he was using the term "struggle for existence" in a "large and metaphorical sense, including dependence of one being upon another."[27] But what do we find in practice? Surprisingly, natural selection usually occurs without any discernible struggle, those exciting documentaries notwithstanding. According to the late George Gaylord Simpson,

Struggle is sometimes involved, but it usually is not, and when it is, it may even work against rather than toward natural selection. Advantage in differential reproduction is usually a peaceful process in which the concept of struggle is really irrelevant. It more often involves such things as better integration into the ecological situation, maintenance of a balance of nature, more efficient utilization of available food, better care of the young, elimination of intragroup discords (struggles) that might hamper reproduction, exploitation of environmental possibilities that are not the objects of competition or are less effectively exploited by others.[28]

Natural selection does not require competition; on the contrary, it discourages it. Survival generally demands that individuals work with rather than against each other — and this includes others of the same species as well as those from different species. If this is true, and if natural selection is the engine of evolution — the central theme of "nature," as it were — then we should expect to find animals cooperating with each other in great numbers. And so we do.

It was Petr Kropotkin, in his 1902 book *Mutual Aid*, who first detailed the ubiquity of cooperation among animals. After reviewing the habits of species ranging from ants to bison, he concluded that

competition . . . is limited among animals to exceptional periods. . . . Better conditions are created by the *elimination of competition* by means of mutual aid and mutual support. . . . "Don't compete! — competition is always injurious to the species, and you have plenty of resources to avoid it!" That is the *tendency* of nature, not always realized in full, but always present. That is the watchword which comes to us from the bush, the forest, the river, the ocean. "Therefore combine — practise mutual aid! . . ." That is what Nature teaches us.[29]

Fifty years later, W. C. Allee reaffirmed this principle in his book *Cooperation Among Animals*.[30] Montagu, meanwhile, accumulated an impressive bibliography of other scientists who were coming to the same conclusion.[31] Zoologist Marvin Bates is representative of these writers: "This competition, this 'struggle,' is a superficial thing, superimposed on an essential mutual dependence. The basic theme in nature is cooperation rather than competition — a cooperation that has become so all-pervasive, so completely integrated, that it is difficult to untwine and follow out the separate strands."[32] It is in the interest of both individuals (or species) if they do not compete over, say, a watering hole; migration is one of many strategies that will allow both parties to survive. Notice, though, that these writers are saying not only that animals tend to avoid competition, but that their behavior is overwhelmingly characterized by its opposite — cooperation.

A question suggests itself at this point. If the accuracy of this view is so widely accepted in the scientific community, if Kropotkin wrote so early and is still recognized as having been on the right track, what accounts for the widespread acceptance of the Hobbesian-Spencerian picture? Why does the idea of a cooperative nature seem surprising to so many of us?

There are several answers. First, cooperation is "not always plain to the eye, whereas competition . . . can readily be observed," as Allee put it.[33] Lapwings protect other birds from predators; baboons and gazelles work together to sense danger (the former watching, the latter listening and smelling); chimpanzees hunt cooperatively and share the spoils; pelicans fish cooperatively. Indeed, the production of oxygen by plants and carbon dioxide by animals could be said to represent a prototype for the cooperative interaction that becomes more pronounced and deliberate in the higher species. None of this, however, makes good television. It is easy to ignore an arrangement that does not call attention to itself.

Second, there is some ambiguity about the language involved. Following Darwin, some biologists and zoologists[34] use "competition" in its metaphorical sense, referring to nothing more than natural selection. If we find only one species remaining in a given area where there once were several, we might describe the winnowing process as "competition." In itself, this is unobjectionable, provided that we keep in mind that this is not a matter of observation or even inference, but rather of definition: we are using the word in such a way that this scenario *is* competition. But this becomes problematic when we confuse the two meanings of competition — this broad, almost trivial sense, which describes all living things, and the narrower sense that refers to an intentional attempt to best another. Such a confusion can be exploited, as I suspect Garrett Hardin does, to argue for the inevitability of competition in human life. It's an ingenious syllogism, of a type that often has been used to draw fallacious conclusions:

1. The natural world is inherently competitive (sense one).
2. Humans are competitive (sense two).
3. Therefore, human competition is also inherent.[35]

There is a third explanation for why we consistently regard nature as competitive and overlook the compelling evidence of mutual aid. This lies in the common tendency of the observer to project himself onto the observed, a tendency that explains the remarkable similarities between gods (Hebraic, Hellenic, and otherwise) and the people who wrote about them. John A. Wiens, a biologist, lays out considerable evidence to suggest that "competition is not the ubiquitous force that many ecologists have believed" and asks, "Why, then, have [they] been so preoccupied with competition?" His answer: "Competition . . . occupies a central position in Western culture — witness its expression in sports, economics, space exploration, international politics, or warfare. Little wonder, then, that community ecologists expected . . . that the primary factor organizing communities would be competition."[36] The very transmutation of natural selection into competition, of differential reproduction into exploitation, reflects a tendency to shape biological theories according to socioeconomic biases. (Unconsciously, we understand nature to be just like ourselves.) Then these biological theories — congealed into an account of how the natural world really is — are used to legitimate cultural practices. (Consciously, we use nature to justify ourselves.) Several thinkers have caught on to this,[37] but the clearest statement was offered in 1875 by Frederick Engels:

> The whole Darwinist teaching of the struggle for existence is simply a transference from society to living nature of Hobbes's doctrine of *bellum omnium contra omnes* [a war of all against all] and of the bourgeois-economic doctrine of competition together with Malthus's theory of population. When this conjurer's trick has been performed . . . the same theories are transferred back again from organic nature into history

and it is now claimed that their validity as eternal *laws* of human society has been proved.[38]

.   .   .

I began this section by noting that data concerning animals have a limited relevance for humans. Let me close with this qualification: if we are concerned about our own collective survival, the natural world may have something to teach us after all. Its lesson is that cooperation generally has far more survival value than competition. This, as Darwin recognized, is *particularly* true for human beings. Montagu summed up the case:

> In so far as man is concerned, if competition, in its aggressive combative sense, ever had any adaptive value among men, which is greatly to be doubted, it is quite clear that it has no adaptive value whatever in the modern world. . . . Perhaps never before in the history of man has there been so high a premium upon the adaptive value of cooperative behavior.[39]

Such a prescription, however, anticipates later chapters simply by virtue of being a prescription. Here our task is only to consider whether competition is inevitable in human life, and the very idea that we *ought* to minimize it rests on the assumption that we can — hence, that it is not inevitable.

LEARNING COMPETITION OR COOPERATION

From the prevalence of cooperation, we turn now to the other major argument against claims of inevitability: the contention that competition is learned. A tour of the literature through many disciplines makes it clear that the great majority of theorists and researchers who have investigated competition have concluded that the competitive orientation is indeed learned. Theoretically (and, as we shall soon see, practically, too) what is learned can be unlearned.

The first comprehensive investigation of the topic was the 1937 study sponsored by the Social Science Research Council. Mark A. May and Leonard Doob reported 24 specific findings based on "the existing knowledge represented by the survey of the literature of the field," the first of which was this: "Human beings by original nature strive for goals, but striving with others (co-operation) or against others (competition) are learned forms of behavior."[40] Neither of these two, they continued, "can be said to be the more genetically basic, fundamental or [primordial]."[41]

This conclusion has withstood half a century of study across several fields. The father of modern research on competition in social psychology, Morton Deutsch, of Columbia University, wrote in 1973 that "it would be unreasonable to assume there is an innately determined human tendency for everyone to want to be 'top dog.'"[42] Sports psychologists Thomas Tutko and William Bruns agreed, basing their opinion on considerable experience with athletes of all ages:

> Competition is a learned phenomenon . . . people are not *born* with a motivation to win or to be competitive. We inherit a potential for a degree of activity, and we all have the instinct to survive. But the will to win comes through training and the influences of one's family and environment. As the song in *South Pacific* says, "you've got to be carefully taught."[43]

In the United States, we *are* carefully taught, and the result is that, excepting the kind of invisible cooperation that is required for any society to run, Americans appear to be uniquely uncooperative as a people. David Riesman, the eminent sociologist, found an interesting irony in "the paradoxical belief of Americans that competition is natural — but only if it is constantly re-created by artificial systems of social roles that direct energies into it."[44] First we are systematically socialized to compete — and to want to compete — and then the results are cited as evidence of competition's inevitability.

Consider the dimensions of that socialization:

> For two centuries [writes psychologist Elliot Aronson] our educational system has been based upon competitiveness. . . . If you are a student who knows the correct answer and the teacher calls on one of the other kids, it is likely that you will sit there hoping and praying the kid will come up with the wrong answer so that you will have a chance to show the teacher how smart you are. . . . Indeed, [children's] peers are their enemies — to be beaten.[45]

The message that competition is appropriate, desirable, required, and even unavoidable is drummed into us from nursery school to graduate school; it is the subtext of every lesson. The late Jules

Henry, who turned his keen anthropologist's eye to our own culture, made this strikingly clear:

> Boris had trouble reducing "12/16" to the lowest terms, and could only get as far as "6/8." The teacher asked him quietly if that was as far as he could reduce it. She suggested he "think." Much heaving up and down and waving of hands by the other children, all frantic to correct him. Boris pretty unhappy, probably mentally paralyzed. . . . She then turns to the class and says, "Well, who can tell Boris what the number is?" A forest of hands appears, and the teacher calls Peggy. Peggy says that four may be divided into the numerator and the denominator. Thus Boris' failure has made it possible for Peggy to succeed; his depression is the price of her exhilaration; his misery the occasion for her rejoicing. This is the standard condition of the American elementary school. . . . To a Zuñi, Hopi, or Dakota Indian, Peggy's performance would seem cruel beyond belief.[46]

Something far more significant and lasting than fractions is being taught here. Boris will likely grow up despising the Peggys he encounters, perhaps fanning that wrath until it takes in all women or some other group that seems to include too many winners. Perhaps he will be unequal to the demands of active rage and will simply slink through life a confirmed failure. In any case, he and Peggy will take from this classroom a common lesson: other people are not partners but opponents, not potential friends but rivals.

In a hypercompetitive society, it is never too early to begin such training. Most recently, "readiness programs" have appeared to prepare infants for "the feverish competition at the better nursery schools."[47] By the time of elementary school, the pressure to be number one is nothing new, but it has just begun to be codified and quantified. A first grader may be crushed, for instance, if her homework assignment is stamped with a smile face while others receive a smile face *and* a "VERY GOOD." Eventually this ranking takes the form of grades. "Educational achievement," writes Morton Deutsch, "is measured so as to conform to an assumed underlying distribution. The social context of most educational measurement is that of a contest in which students are measured primarily in comparison with one another rather than in terms of objective criteria of accomplishment."[48] Where in this carefully designed laboratory of competition can a child even sample cooperative achievement? In fact, most teachers misunderstand the very word *cooperation;* they use it to refer to obedience. To "cooperate" is to follow instructions.[49] We have another word for genuine cooperative effort, as several writers have pointed out: It is *cheating*.*

When class is over, the lesson continues. Children are taught that all games must have a winner and a loser. As Peter and Brigitte Berger have written, "It is only very young children who sometimes wish, wistfully, that 'everyone should win'; they soon learn that this is 'impossible' — in American society, that is, for there are other societies in which children actually play games in which 'everyone wins.' "[50] The idea that everyone can win evokes condescending smiles, and it doesn't take long before these children come to accept the naturalness of competition. Here is Jean Piaget, in his classic work *The Moral Judgment of the Child*, questioning six-year-old Mar: " 'Who has won?' 'We've both won.' 'But who has won most?' "[51] Piaget is not only learning from his young informant, but also teaching him.

The inculcation of competition in the classroom and on the playing field is a source of unending frustration to some parents. Fathers and mothers who would prefer that their children learn to work *with* rather than *against* others can do only so much to foster this value since they do not raise their children in a vacuum. Even determinedly liberated parents must contend with an elaborate competitive structure outside the home that will frustrate their best efforts at education. "Out there," doing one's best means triumphing over others. (This is the same struggle that defines parents' attempts to steer their children away from sexism or violence or mindless obedience or unhealthful foods or any number of other things sanctioned by our society.)

Such a clash between the parents and the rest of the culture is exceptional, however. The family generally is an efficient vehicle by which societal norms are transmitted, not a holdout against these norms. Most parents raise children according to the values by which they were raised, and this process perpetuates the larger culture in which it occurs. From our very earliest days, we are busily absorbing an uncritical acceptance of competition. We are being primed for the classroom and the workplace. As we grow, the socialization in the home continues to work hand in glove with the socialization outside

---

*Of course, just because all cooperation may be called cheating (because we have no legitimate place for it in American classrooms) does not mean that everything we call cheating is genuinely cooperative or otherwise admirable.

the home. There is pressure to make our parents proud — by being not merely good, but better than others, at schoolwork, sports, and almost any other activity in which we take part. If Dad, in his day, had the highest batting average in school, then we must do likewise. If Dad was *not* a superlative athlete, then we must distinguish ourselves anyway: our task is to provide vicarious gratification. If our parents never got very far in school, we must not merely take advantage of the chances they never had — we must be the very best of students. Examples of such pressure can be multiplied indefinitely. Of course some parents, who sport newly raised consciousnesses, may proudly declare to any who will listen that they "ask of Bobby only that he do his best." But this official posture surely does not fool Bobby. He is fully aware that "doing his best" is a code that means beating his peers. As a result of their own training, most parents, even if sincere, still communicate subliminal messages of disappointment with anything other than victory.

But the family does not merely encourage and sustain competition in the outside world — it manufactures its very own brand. This is particularly true in the nuclear family, which, let us remember, is not the only possible arrangement for child-rearing. One series of field studies in the South Pacific found that "greater rivalrous responses . . . occurred in children brought up in Western-type small nuclear families rather than the traditional extended families."[52] How does this happen? First, many parents carefully (though often unconsciously) direct a drama of sibling rivalry on the stage of their own homes. Even competition booster Harvey Ruben is appalled by the " 'divide and conquer' theory of parenting" whereby children who are set against each other are easier to discipline. Setting up an insidious race to become Mommy's favorite mostly benefits Mommy. It gets the dishes dried, for one thing. But far more important are the emotional rewards for parents, who are "every bit as much in need of approval, affection, and support as their children, and in many cases, unfortunately, they are able to get this most easily by nourishing divisiveness within the home."[53]

In some homes, it is the parents who compete for their children's love. "Whom do you love more?" is seldom asked aloud, but parental behavior often seems motivated by this concern. The intrinsic sickness of this family pattern, like the terrible consequences for all concerned, will not be considered here. My point is only that such dynamics foster competition. We grow up thinking of love as a scarce commodity — the prize in a desperate contest that we will enter again and again. We associate being loved with winning a race, and this happens partly because of the very language with which we have heard affection expressed ("Who's the best little girl in the whole wide world?"). Beyond love, we will generalize the need to be number one, taking competition with us to any and all arenas.

The process of socializing children to be competitive is sometimes tacit. Few parents, for example, sit their child down and say, "Now, Steven, it's time you learned that you can't have a good time unless you set things up so one side wins and the other loses." This attitude is taught by example. On the other hand, the idea that people attain excellence exclusively in a competitive setting — that no one would be motivated to work in a noncompetitive economic system — is something we often hear in just so many words. Even more common are expressions of the belief that one has no *choice* but to be competitive: competition is an unavoidable feature of human life, so you might as well get used to it right away. Some parents may sincerely believe this, but others feel conflicted and vaguely guilty about their own competitiveness. If they convince themselves (and teach their children) that one can't help being competitive, they can live more easily with themselves. This belief in competition's inevitability may be insupportable for all the reasons discussed in this chapter, but it soon takes on the shape of a classic self-fulfilling prophecy. By teaching children to act in a way that is said to be inevitable, we *make* the practice inevitable and so make the proposition true. This may well be the heart of the socialization process.

To complicate matters further, competition seems to be self-perpetuating. In his long career of studying conflict — and, more generally, social interaction — Deutsch has found that any given mode of interaction breeds more of itself. Specifically, "the experience of cooperation will induce a benign spiral of increasing cooperation, while competition will induce a vicious spiral of intensifying competition."[54] Quite a bit of research on the so-called Prisoner's Dilemma (PD) Game, in which players choose whether to cooperate or defect,* has confirmed this. Moreover, Harold H. Kelley and An-

---

*The game, such a favorite of researchers that one writer called it the "*E. coli* of social psychology,"[55] is set up so that the two players are more highly rewarded if they both cooperate than if they both defect, but that an individual stands to gain even more if she defects while her opponent cooperates. The paradox, to which I shall return in the next chapter, is that while the traditional paradigm of the social sciences (particularly economics) is predicated on rationality from the individual's perspective, in PD what is rational for the individual is irrational for the pair.

thony J. Stahelski's PD experiments found that people who generally are cooperative tend to resemble competitive individuals when they must deal with them. Competition, we might say, cannibalizes cooperation.[56]

And what of those who already incline toward competition? Why do they persist in their ways? Kelley and Stahelski found that whereas cooperative individuals realistically perceive that some people are cooperative like themselves while others are competitive, competitive individuals believe that virtually everyone else is also competitive.[57] Thus we have another self-fulfilling prophecy: competitive people (falsely) assume that all others share their orientation — and, indeed, those who declare most vociferously that "it's a dog-eat-dog world out there" usually are responsible for more than their share of canine consumption — which impels them to redouble their own competitive orientation. This finding has been replicated by several other researchers.[58]

Both the desirability of competition and the strategies for implementing it, then, are taught to us from our earliest days. This orientation then reproduces itself. What is peculiar, as Riesman pointed out, is that we should have to contrive such a thorough program of socialization if competition really were part of human nature. (Typically it is those who argue most strenuously for the latter who are, at the same time, vigorously promoting this training process.) Far more plausible is the hypothesis that all of this training is *not* superfluous: we compete only because we have learned to do so.

In order to prove this hypothesis correct rather than simply arguing for its plausibility, one would need some evidence that children can be taught to cooperate. If they take to this approach — learn it easily, enjoy it, continue using it — it would be evident that competition is not inevitable. Longitudinal studies of this kind have not been performed, to my knowledge — unless one regards cross-cultural data as naturalistic evidence along these lines. However, some work in early childhood education comes close.

A few years ago, Gerald Sagotsky and his colleagues at Adelphi University successfully trained 118 pairs of first- through third-grade students to cooperate in a series of classroom games. This was done through a combination of direct instruction and modeling (having them watch someone else be reinforced for engaging in the desired behavior). About seven weeks later, a new experimenter tried a new game with these children and found a significant retention and generalization of the cooperative approach, particularly among the older children. "Overall, the study indicates that a relatively brief and straightforward intervention can effectively train cooperation."[59] Similar generalization has been reported on the part of fifth graders[60] and, in still another study, third graders.[61] Earlier and more primitive research found that children continued behaving cooperatively even when reinforcement was briefly withdrawn.[62] More recently, Aronson not only had remarkable success with a cooperative learning technique but also discovered that teachers continued to use it years after the experiment was over.[63] Deutsch reported that adults, too, taught themselves to cooperate when the game they were playing rewarded such behavior.[64]

A somewhat more anecdotal account of this effect is provided by David N. Campbell, who reports on his visit to an unnamed British elementary school. When another American teacher on the tour asked these children who was the smartest among them, they "didn't know what he was talking about. They had evidently never thought about it. . . . There were no put-backs, grades, tests, gold stars. *All* stories and drawings were displayed on the walls. Children were not placed in failure situations, forced to prove themselves, to read at 'grade level' every week." When he returned home, Campbell resolved to make his own classroom less competitive.

> It required only about three weeks for the changes to emerge [he continues]. The first was an end [to] the destruction of others' work. Later a spirit of cooperation and help began to be common. Finally there was what I look for as the real measure of success: children talking freely to every adult and stranger who walks in, leading them by the hand to see projects and explaining their activities, no longer afraid, suspicious, or turned inward. Such changed attitudes developed because we stopped labeling and rank-ordering.[65]

Some of the most interesting work with recreational cooperation has been done by Terry Orlick at the University of Ottawa. After leading children from preschool age to second grade in cooperative games, he found a threefold to fourfold increase in the incidence of cooperative behavior when the children were later left to play by themselves. Control groups, meanwhile, tended to become more competitive as the year progressed.[66] Orlick also found that children reported being happier playing cooperative games: "Given the choice, two thirds of the nine- and ten-year-old boys and all of the girls would prefer to play games where neither side loses rather than games where one side wins and the other side loses."[67] In the classroom, meanwhile, 65 percent of a group of sixth graders said they preferred a cooperative learning structure. The total sample here was divided evenly between those who tended to attribute their successes or failures to themselves ("internalizers") and those who attributed consequences to fate or other people ("externalizers"). Significantly, a majority of both groups preferred cooperative learning.[68] As of 1984, a pair of researchers were able to cite seven studies showing a preference for cooperative over competitive or independent experiences.[69]

I am aware of no studies that found a preference for competition over cooperation — providing the subjects had experienced the latter in some fashion. This qualification is critical: it is not unusual for people to say they prefer to compete but then to change their minds when they see at first hand what it is like to learn or work or play in an environment that does not require winners and losers.[70] This, incidentally, has been found to be true of college students, too.[71] The evidence seems persuasive, then, that children can learn to cooperate and, when given a choice, seem to prefer this cooperative arrangement.

The evidence is far less clear, however, on the question of how old children must be in order to learn to cooperate. The traditional position, following Piaget's developmental schedule, is that children cannot cooperate *or* compete in any meaningful way until they are about six or seven years old and have reached the "operational" stage.[72] This position is compatible with the usual movement of children toward increasing competitiveness. What precedes competition, it is argued, is not positive cooperation but merely the absence of competition (two very different things) — or, for that matter, the absence of any sophisticated goal-directed activity. The ability to cooperate and to compete are said to develop around the same time.[73]

The fact that very young children do not compete, then, is not terribly significant. Young children do not have body hair either, but that doesn't mean that body hair is a learned phenomenon. On the other hand, the fact that children normally become more competitive as they grow older[74] also means very little because most children have not been exposed to models of cooperative interaction.

Yet not everyone is agreed that young children cannot cooperate. Spontaneous pro-social behavior takes place in infants, as we saw before.[75] Anna Freud observed nineteen-month-old toddlers building a tower together, taking turns adding blocks.[76] This could mean that Piaget and his followers are wrong. But even if we insist that such collaborative or helping behaviors do not qualify as genuine cooperation, there is evidence that children of only four or five — past the toddler stage but not yet "operational" — can indeed be taught to cooperate. In fact, Orlick has found "young children to be most receptive to cooperative ventures and cooperative challenges." He proposes that this is true because "the younger the child, the less time he has had in the competitive mainstream of our society and therefore the more willing he is to accept cooperative games."[77] Millard C. Madsen's research seems to support Orlick's view, at least within this country. In presenting an experimental problem that required a cooperative solution, he found that "more younger than older children are successful in solving the problem in such a way as to maximize reward."[78] Sagotsky, on the other hand, found that older children (seven- or eight-year-olds) learned to cooperate more readily than younger ones, which is what Piagetian theory would predict.[79] But all of these researchers agree — and the whole of this section confirms — that cooperation can be learned; thus, competition is by no means inevitable.

LIFE IN OTHER CULTURES

Even in the era of the "global village," as Marshall McLuhan characterized the interdependence of the modern world, ethnocentrism remains. It is present in two forms: as a value judgment that unfamiliar cultural practices are *ipso facto* inferior ("if it's different, it's worse"), and as an empirical belief that what is present in one's own land must be universal ("if it's here, it's everywhere"). I am concerned with the latter, and specifically with the assumption, usually unstated, that because competition is so pervasive in these parts it must be pervasive everywhere. If this assumption is wrong, then competition is learned and it is not inevitable.

In chapter 1, I suggested that the United States appears to be uniquely competitive. This observation also has been made by researchers who have observed other cultures and/or tested their inhabitants. Anthropologists Beatrice and John Whiting recorded the frequency of such acts as touching, reprimanding, offering help, insulting, and so on, in six cultures, one of which was in the United

States (a small New England town). As a proportion of total acts observed, the latter scored lowest on offering help.[80] Another researcher compared the way people in four Scandinavian countries, England, and the United States described child-rearing orientations and norms of masculinity in their respective nations. On both subjects, she found a far greater emphasis on competition in the United States.[81] In experiments with Anglo-American and Mexican children, two psychologists discovered that the former "tended to remain in conflict even when to do so prevented them from getting as many toys as possible" — a tendency that was rightly characterized as irrational competition. When permitted to do so, these children also took away another child's toy even though they had nothing to gain from this act.[82]

These data concerning the competitiveness of Americans* are particularly useful because they are being contrasted with findings from other cultures. Let us now examine some of these other cultures in greater detail by turning to the reports of anthropologists and other cross-cultural observers. The United States, as we shall see, is appreciably more competitive than many other cultures; in fact, some cultures appear to be entirely noncompetitive.

Consider first the case of primitive cultures, which many people (relying on caricatured images of growling cavemen) associate with fierce competition. As with ideas about the animal world, this perception is largely mistaken. Prehistoric people actually were remarkably cooperative, and in fact may have distinguished themselves from other primates precisely by virtue of the extent of their cooperativeness. A growing number of anthropologists are concluding that cooperation — not brain size or the use of tools, and certainly not aggressiveness — defined the first humans.[83] The distinguished biologist George Edgin Pugh wrote:

> Primitive human societies differ greatly from other primates in the *amount* of cooperation that is achieved. Within primitive human societies "sharing" is a way of life. . . . The sharing is not limited to food, but extends to all types of resources. The practical result is that scarce

---

*The use of "American" to refer to people who live in the United States may itself be regarded as ethnocentric since this is not the only country in this hemisphere. I reluctantly adopt this usage here only because "United States" does not have a convenient adjective.

resources are shared within the societies approximately in proportion to need.[84]

Through the medium of kinship, early humans developed cooperative arrangements that, according to Marshall Sahlins, were apparently mandated by virtue of the conditions of life. In his words, "The emerging human primate, in a life-and-death economic struggle with nature, could not afford the luxury of a social struggle. Co-operation, not competition, was essential. . . . Hobbes's famous fantasy of a war of 'all against all' in the natural state could not be further from the truth."[85] Substantiation for this conclusion is provided by extant hunter-gatherer societies, such as the Congo pygmies, Kalahari Bushmen, Australian Aborigines, and the Waoranis of the Amazon, all of which are overwhelmingly cooperative.[86]

The fact that some of these cultures still exist today invites a wider consideration of contemporary noncompetitive societies that cast our own competitiveness into sharp relief. It was Margaret Mead and her associates who first attended to this characteristic: *Cooperation and Competition Among Primitive Peoples* (1937) described several such cultures in some detail. These include:

THE ZUÑI INDIANS — "The orientations of all institutions, with little exception, to a basic principle of cooperative, nonindividualistic behavior is the pattern of Zuñi culture."[87] Possession of material goods is not seen as desirable; wealth circulates freely, and there is therefore no competition in the economic sphere. The major recreation *cum* religious ritual is a ceremonial four-mile footrace. Anyone can participate, the winner receives no special recognition, and his name is not even announced. In fact, someone who has consistently won is prevented from running.[88]

THE IROQUOIS INDIANS — "Beyond the degree of cooperation required to achieve the greatest efficiency in production, there was found, especially in agricultural activity, cooperation for the purpose of experiencing the pleasures of group work."[89]

THE BATHONGA — "Bathonga society is highly cooperative within the bounds of the village, and in all other social and economic relations it is essentially noncompetitive. . . . In economic organization, in technology, in social relations little range is given to any expression of competition."[90]

On the basis of a dozen cultural studies that comprise the book, Mead writes that the most basic conclusion which comes out of this research [is] that competitive and cooperative behavior on the part of individual members of a society is fundamentally conditioned by the total social emphasis of that society, that the goals for which individuals will work are culturally determined and are not the response of the organism to an external, culturally undefined situation.[91]

Cross-cultural research in this vein has continued and expanded in the half century since Mead's study was published. This research substantiates her conclusion by documenting significant differences in competitiveness among people of different cultures. Consider:

BLACKFOOT INDIAN children cooperated far more effectively than urban Canadian children in a series of experimental games, and this occurred whether they were being rewarded collectively or individually.[92]

ISRAELI KIBBUTZ children cooperated far more effectively than urban Israeli children, the latter being "unable to stop their irrational competition . . . even though they obviously realized . . . [this was] not paying off for any of them." What's more, the kibbutzniks spontaneously arranged to divide their prizes equally among the members.[93] In later experiments that replicated this result, "Kibbutz groups characteristically demonstrated a high degree of organization . . . in sharp contrast to the unrestrained and unorganized tug of war that was typical of the city groups."[94]

KIKUYU children from Kenya cooperated more effectively than American children at an experimental game.[95]

RURAL MEXICAN children were more cooperative than Mexican-Americans, who were in turn more cooperative than Anglo-Americans. The latter, as noted above, tended to compete even when the situation was arranged to reward cooperation and tended to take away another's toy for sheer spite twice as often as did the Mexican children.[96] Americans often missed the cooperative solution, "spontaneously declar[ing], 'This game is too hard,' or 'No one can win.' When asked after the experiment how they might have gotten some toys, competitive subjects most often responded, 'If I could play alone,' or 'If I could move more than once [not take turns moving].' "[97] Among the reasons proposed for this significant cultural disparity is the fact that "rural Mexican mothers tend to reinforce their children noncontingently, rewarding them whether they succeed or fail, whereas Anglo-American mothers tend to reinforce their children as a rigid function of the child's achievement."[98] The idea that children should be accepted and loved unconditionally — rather than in proportion to the number of others they have beaten at something — is a very peculiar idea to many Americans.

THE MIXTECANS OF JUXTLAHUACA, MEXICO, "regard envy and competitiveness as a minor crime."[99]

THE TANGU OF NEW GUINEA eschew competitive games, preferring one called *taketak* in which two teams spin tops. The objective of the game is to reach an exact draw.[100]

THE INUIT OF CANADA live with virtually no competitive structures. Their recreation, like their economic system, is cooperative.[101]

AUSTRALIAN ABORIGINES display a marked preference for "cooperative action," and one experiment found that they cooperated just as readily with members of other tribes as with their own tribe members.[102]

NORWEGIANS almost always responded in kind to cooperative behavior in an experimental game, whereas American subjects did so only about half the time.[103]

JAPANESE education is said to be far less competitive than ours. "The Japanese have always been inventive in devising ways of avoiding direct competition," Ruth Benedict reported in the mid-1940s. "Their elementary schools minimize it beyond what Americans would think possible."[104] As of 1980, this was still the case: "Teachers . . . try to create balanced groups composed of people with diverse abilities, and they encourage the students to help each other."[105] And from yet another source, in 1982: "Challenging problems are posed to entire classes, whose members are encouraged to talk to, and to help, one another and are allowed to make mistakes; at times, older children visit the classrooms and aid the younger ones."[106]

CHINESE people, despite becoming more serious about sports[107] and despite the recent introduction of a system encouraging academic competition, remain far more cooperative than Americans. Students say they prefer cooperative activities to competitive ones, and "peer group norms approving helpfulness and the simple enjoyment of social rather than isolated studying often led students to cooperate even if they had to give more help than they received."[108]

· · ·

These research summaries do not by any means constitute an exhaustive account of noncompetitive societies or of the discrepant levels of competitiveness across different cultures. But even this brief survey should suggest that competition is a matter of social structure rather than human nature. Competition may be an integral part of certain institutions in contemporary Western society, such as capitalism, but it is clearly not an unavoidable consequence of life itself.

The cross-cultural data allow for several generalizations. First, as must be obvious, "rural children in all cultures studied are more cooperative in conflict-of-interest situations that require mutual assistance,"[109] and we may tentatively propose that urban living is generally associated with — if not causally related to — structural as well as intentional competition. This, of course, does not mean that all rural societies will be noncompetitive or that all urban areas will be equally competitive.

Second, competitive societies tend also to hurry their children toward adulthood,[110] a feature of American society described and decried recently by several critics. Third, there is a remarkable correspondence between competitiveness in a society and the presence of clearly defined "have" and "have-not" groups.[111] This correlation between economic maldistribution and competition seems to fit with the findings of Mead et al. concerning the absence of possessiveness and hoarding behavior in cooperative cultures.

These studies also allow us to debunk several widely held assumptions about competition. First, there is no necessary relationship between competitiveness and achievement. That this is true on the individual level will be explored in detail in the next chapter. On the societal level, Roderic Gorney conducted a careful study of the research available on 58 cultures. He defined achievement as complex accomplishments in the arts, sciences, the law, and other fields, and found, to his surprise, that there was no significant relationship between achievement and competition.[112]

Second, competition is not a prerequisite for strong ego development, which is used by some psychologists as a shorthand expression for psychological health. "Strong ego development can occur in individualistic, competitive, or cooperative societies," according to Mead's findings.[113] In fact, competition's deleterious effect on self-esteem and health will be explored in chapter 5.

Finally, it is sometimes argued that cooperation is a luxury permitted in places or times of plenty; when resources are scarce, people are said to resort to competitive behavior. This is simply false. Mead and her colleagues found counterexamples of both types: competitive societies where there was an economy of abundance (e.g., the

Kwakiutl Indians) and cooperative societies where there was an economy of scarcity (e.g., the Bateiga of East Africa). It is the norms of the culture that determine its competitiveness, not the presence or absence of resources. As Mead put it, "It is not the actual supply of a desired good which decrees whether or not the members of a society will compete for it or cooperate and share it, but it is the way the structure of the society is built up that determines whether individual members shall cooperate or shall compete with one another."[114] In fact, Mead went further than this, suggesting at one point that the relative plenty in several societies was the *result* of their cooperative arrangements, not the cause.[115] Put differently, cooperation can be seen as an appropriate, rational response to scarcity since it is probably more effective at maximizing what one has. This is what Marshall Sahlins was getting at on page 35, and William O. Johnson put it even more bluntly: "Pioneers were not competitive people, they were a cooperative people. They wouldn't have survived otherwise."[116] To say that people naturally become competitive when there isn't enough to go around is not merely inaccurate, but a reflection of how easily we universalize our own cultural norms.

PSYCHOLOGICAL ARGUMENTS FOR INEVITABILITY

Anyone who accepts Freud's model of the personality and human development is likely to assume that competition is unavoidable. Even if Freud does not come out and say this explicitly, the implications of his thought are clear, so a few words about psychoanalytic theory are in order.[117]

In Freud's view, we begin life screaming for gratification, little more than a bundle of needs. This is how we leave life, too; maturity consists only in learning to put off that gratification and reconfigure some of the needs. We remain self-centered creatures in search of pleasure; the ego always is in the service of the id. Moreover, "men are not gentle creatures who want to be loved . . . they are, on the contrary, creatures among whose instinctual endowments is to be reckoned a powerful share of aggressiveness."[118] According to this view, if I appear to be concerned about cooperating with others, you may safely assume that I have either (1) cleverly figured out some way to use other people to my own ends and to make it look like cooperation, or (2) unconsciously transformed my feelings of hostility into their opposite so as to keep these feelings out of my awareness. Other people are means to my own (primarily sexual) satisfaction or else rivals to be bested. Any appearances to the contrary represent the desperate attempt of culture to tame our base instincts. But this attempt is finally futile because "instinctual passions are stronger than reasonable interests."[119] Life, as Hobbes had written three centuries before, is nasty, brutish, and short — but for Freud there is no Hobbesian body politic to rescue us from this condition.

Competition, in this view, is inevitable, of course. Its development is elaborated in the early parent-child relationship. A desire to win the parent's love can fuel endless competitive struggle; an internalization of the parent means that adults, with parents long dead, can still be driven to win for the same reason. Psychoanalysts also explicate competition (particularly among men) according to the Oedipal conflict: the opponent is always Daddy; the prize, Mommy. To evince some reluctance to compete cannot be based on a rational decision (ultimately, for the classical psychoanalyst, virtually nothing is). Rather, one is unconsciously anxious about the symbolic consequences of beating the father. In all, competition is natural and, like other drives, can be hidden or sublimated but never escaped. To attempt the latter is inadvisable, according to Anna Freud: "Inhibition of exhibitionism, of curiosity, of aggression, of competition, etc., produces the same crippling effect on the individual's personality whether they occur early or late in life."[120]

To attempt a refutation of this position is to take on the very heart of Freudian thought, which is well beyond the scope of this book. Much of this chapter, however, is responsive to these assumptions, and the interested reader is referred to the writings of the ego psychologists, the neo-Freudians (particularly Karen Horney), and the humanistic psychologists. Even among psychoanalytically inclined psychiatrists, in fact, one can find chinks in the armor of inevitability. One rather obscure British psychoanalyst, Ian Suttie, sees competition as a manifestation of the "search for the security and satisfaction of social integration (fellowship)" rather than as an autonomous instinct.[121] Following him, Roderic Gorney describes human development as a progression from "being preponderantly dependent on others for survival" to having "others predominantly depend on us." Throughout our lives, he argues, we are involved in cooperation.[122] To take another example, the psychiatrist Herbert Hendin talks about fathers who become involved with their sons "in a way that cement[s] them in competitive, anxiety-ridden situations, or under-mine[s] their ability to become independent. The competitive work situations that constitute the major bond between such fathers and sons serve to create models for the sons' future relations with men."[123] The clear implication here is that the Oedipal prototype for competi-tive interaction can be traced to particular styles of child-rearing that are avoidable. These, of course, are minority reports, but however unfortunate the implications of psychoanalysis may be regarding the question of inevitability, its framework can be useful in exploring the relationship between competition and psychological health (see chap-ter 5).

.   .   .

Another argument for inevitability, drawn from social psychology, concerns the phenomenon of social comparison. Our identities are a function of our social world; others define who we are. Therefore, it is proposed, we are always in the process of comparing ourselves with others — and our behaviors and products with those of the people around us. This process is said to be particularly critical during child-hood when our identities are quite literally being formed. It continues because social comparison tells us whether what we do is any good. The second step in this argument is that comparison implies competi-tion: if I am looking over at you, I naturally will want to be better than you.[124]

Because of its familiarity and apparent plausibility, this argument demands a response. In fact, the very simplicity that makes it ap-pealing also undermines its explanatory power. It is true that compar-ing what we do to what someone else does goes on all the time, but let us not assume that this is the only way to check how we are doing. As Rainer Martens wrote, "To evaluate one's abilities, it is necessary to make a comparison between at least two elements: your own perform-ance and some other standard . . . [that] can include another individ-ual, a group, one's own past performance, or some idealized perform-ance level."[125] Notice how the second element does not have to be another person. It is true that an "idealized performance level" origi-nally may have been derived from others' performances, but in practice neither of Martens's last two standards is experienced as competition.

It is not a fact of human nature that a person's sense of competence or identity has to be derived from social comparison. It is instead a matter of what kind of task is being performed at the moment and what kind of culture one lives in. The latter is especially important. Psychologist Albert Bandura observed that "in competitive, individualistic societies . . . where one person's success represents another person's failure, social comparison figures prominently in selfappraisal." In other societies, this is not necessarily the case.[126] Consider Jerome Kagan's illustrations:

> The seminal experiences of this era [the years just prior to puberty] are those that persuade youth that they can successfully gain the prizes they want. A father in a cornfield teaching his eight-year-old son how to plant maize finds it easy to create a situation that will accomplish this goal. It is more difficult when the child is with one teacher in a class of thirty children. From the child's perspective, the private evaluation of progress is based primarily on a comparison of one's performance with that of one's peers.[127]

Most of us have spent more time in a crowded classroom than in a quiet cornfield, so we assume that our own situation is an unavoidable part of growing up.

Even to the extent that one's esteem or sense of mastery initially is the result of comparing oneself with others, this may well be temporary — a developmental stage. While acknowledging that competition may well become the dominant basis of self-definition "in a highly competitive school system or neighborhood," Joseph Veroff adds: "with adequate social comparison about valued characteristics a person can relax about social comparison [and] . . . move back into considering his own autonomous capacities for mastery."[128] An adult with a reasonably healthy self-concept, in other words, does not need to continue asking ritualistically, "How'm I doin'?" or even to compare herself or himself with others. Interestingly, a number of psychologists have included autonomous self-evaluation in their definitions of psychological health.[129]

My intent up to this point has been to qualify the assumption that we all have to compare ourselves with others. The next step, then, will be to ask whether this comparison, when it does occur, necessitates competition. We can immediately see that the answer is no: I can compare my hobbies (or shoes or kitchen) with yours without feeling in the least that one is better than another. I may make the comparison with the intention of making sure I am not appreciably different from you; social comparison may be geared toward conformity. But even when this is not the case — and even when the comparison is suffused with judgment — it does not follow that I must feel competitive with you. The Bathonga of South Africa, we are told, compare their fishing catches, but "there is no indication that individuals strive to outdo one another."[130] Closer to home, I may compare my own writing with Shakespeare's (or, for that matter, with that of a contemporary) and sense my own relative inferiority. This could motivate me to improve or, specifically, to emulate features of his writing that I admire. Neither of these means that I feel the need to become better than he. If you and I run together for recreation, your greater speed or endurance may help to improve my own without my ever trying to beat you. As John Harvey puts it, "It is one thing to act from a desire to excel somebody else at something. It is quite another to act with a view to getting something done . . . and yet to be stimulated in the activity by the parallel or contrasted activity of others."[131]

To the proponent of competition who insists that differences in ability will always exist, then, we may reply that it is the significance invested in these differences and not the differences themselves that constitutes competition. The inability to observe discrepant abilities without turning the situation into a contest is a learned disposition. The degree of an individual's competitiveness can be expressed as a function of how *frequently* this happens and how *strongly* one feels the need to be better. But there is not a shred of evidence that this inclination is an unavoidable feature of human life.

.   .   .

Even if it is true that both structural and intentional competition are far from inevitable, their pervasiveness in our society is a concrete and formidable barrier to change. We cannot make this society noncompetitive by the end of the week, and this chapter should not be read as claiming such. At the same time, we should be on guard against the claim that competition is inherent in our culture. When it is contended that competition is destructive, some people will reply that there is nothing *we* can do about it, regardless of the existence of other noncompetitive cultures. This tack has been used to argue against the possibility of changing any number of objectionable features in a society. It is another version of the self-fulfilling prophecy we encountered, and — to return to the subject of this chapter's opening — it is a profoundly conservative posture in its consequences, if not in its intention.

Any example of people behaving noncompetitively should, strictly speaking, have been enough to refute the human nature argument. But we are dealing with people here rather than with mathematical proofs, so it has been necessary to show that a noncompetitive orientation — if not the deliberate practice of cooperation — is a serious possibility, a realistic alternative for our lives. That has been the point of this chapter. Now it is time to move from *can* to *should:* since competition is not necessary, we are free to consider whether it is desirable.

3

Is Competition More Productive?

THE REWARDS OF WORKING TOGETHER

> Competition, which is the instinct of selfishness, is another word for dissipation of energy, while combination is the secret of efficient production.
>
> — Edward Bellamy,
> *Looking Backward* (1888)

Leaf through a few popular articles about competition, engage a few people in conversation on the subject, and you will find a single conviction that appears as a refrain: Even minimal productivity, to say nothing of excellence, would disappear if we ceased competing. Competition brings out the best in us. To compete is to strive for goals, to learn competence, to reach for success. A noncompetitive society would represent, in Spiro Agnew's assorted metaphors, "a bland experience . . . a waveless sea of nonachievers . . . the psychological retreat of a person . . . into a cocoon of false security and self-satisfied mediocrity."[1]

Whether competition promotes "success" (however we choose to define that word) seems a rather straightforward question — one that could be resolved by the available evidence. Many people, however, do not look at this evidence because they do not see the question as an empirical one. The most common defense of competition turns out to rest on the assumption that success (or productiveness or goal attainment) *means* competition. Given this assumption, the assertion that no one would get anything done without competition doesn't require proof; it is self-evident. "The American mind in particular has been trained to equate success with victory, to equate doing well with beating someone," wrote Elliot Aronson.[2]

But success and competition are not at all the same thing. Put plainly, one can set and reach goals — or prove to one's own and others' satisfaction that one is competent — without ever competing. "Success in achieving a goal does not depend upon winning over others just as failing to achieve a goal does not mean losing to others."[3] A moment's reflection reveals this as an undeniable truth. I can succeed in knitting a scarf or writing a book without ever trying to make it better than yours. Better yet, I can work *with* you — say, to prepare a dinner or build a house. Many people take the absence of competition to mean that one must be wandering aimlessly, without any goals. But competing simply means that one is working toward a goal in such a way as to prevent others from reaching *their* goals. This is one approach to getting something done, but (happily) not the only one. Competition need never enter the picture in order for skills to be mastered and displayed, goals set and met.

Given that success and competition are *conceptually* distinct, how are they related in the real world? Does competition really make us more motivated to complete tasks? To do these tasks well? To learn better? Let us turn to the evidence on achievement and productivity and then speculate on the reasons behind what it reveals.

ACHIEVEMENT AND COMPETITION

The question posed by this chapter's title requires a point of reference: Is competition more productive than *what*? To ask this is to realize that it makes little sense to inquire whether competition has ever led anyone to be productive. It is far more useful to determine whether we are substantially more productive in competitive situations than in other situations — or, better yet, whether competition is sufficiently superior to other arrangements as to outweigh its costs. These other arrangements, as set out in chapter 1, are cooperation (working together so that my success is linked to yours) and independent effort (working alone so that my success doesn't affect yours). Some of the studies that are reviewed below contrast competition with one or the other, but a comparative picture of all three eventually emerges.

What we want to ask is this: *Do we perform better when we are trying to beat others than when we are working with them or alone?* It is necessary, of course, to specify the nature of the task, the measure of performance, the age and temperament of the subjects, the setting of the experiment, and a dozen other variables. But the evidence is so overwhelmingly clear and consistent that the answer to this question already can be reported: *almost never*. Superior performance not only does not *require* competition; it usually seems to require its absence.

This conclusion, to say nothing of the near unanimity of the data, will be astonishing to most readers — even those generally critical of competition. As the preceding chapter noted, we are carefully trained not only to compete but to believe that a competitive arrangement results in superior performance. This belief has practically attained the status of received truth in our society, so a consideration of the evidence could (or should, at any rate) have a profound impact on how our schools and workplaces are structured.

The great majority of studies cited in this chapter, as will quickly become apparent, have to do with education — or, more precisely, with learning tasks (anagrams, card games, problem solving, and so forth). Some are even set in the classroom and use standard curricular material. While subjects range in age from preschool to adult, most tend to be either undergraduates or in the elementary school range. Research measuring other kinds of performance is, unfortunately, in short supply, but what does exist along these lines supports the same conclusion.

Margaret M. Clifford assumed, as many of us would have, that a competitive game would help fifth-grade students to learn a set of vocabulary words. "However, contrary to prediction, neither performance nor retention was noticeably improved," she reported, and while the competition did seem to spark some interest, it did so mostly among the winners.[4] Morton Goldman and his associates discovered that undergraduates solved anagrams more effectively when they were cooperating rather than competing with each other.[5] Abaineh Workie found "cooperation significantly more productive than competition" for high school students working on a card game.[6] A well-known experiment that Morton Deutsch conducted with college students in 1948 turned up the same result, and, when he returned to the topic twenty-five years later, he was able to cite thirteen other studies that replicated his findings.[7]

A review of thirteen studies all showing that competition does not get results sounds impressive. But David and Roger Johnson and their colleagues published a far more ambitious meta-analysis (that is, review of others' findings) in 1981.[8] In what is surely the most conclusive survey of its kind, they reviewed 122 studies from 1924 to 1980 (only one of which overlaps with Deutsch's list, incidentally), including every North American study they could find that considered achievement or performance data in competitive, cooperative, and/or individualistic structures. The remarkable results: 65 studies found that cooperation promotes higher achievement than competition, 8 found the reverse, and 36 found no statistically significant difference. Cooperation promoted higher achievement than independent work in 108 studies, while 6 found the reverse, and 42 found no difference. The superiority of cooperation held for all subject areas and all age groups.[9]

A number of qualifications about these conclusions have been proposed, some of which appear to be valid. Cooperation is more effective when the group is smaller[10] and when the task is more complex (particularly if it involves sophisticated problem solving).[11] Cooperation's relative effectiveness depends on the degree to which subjects have to rely on each other in the means by which they accomplish a task. The more "means interdependent" the task, the more cooperation helps.[12] In some instances, it is claimed, competition may produce better results — but only if the task is simple (such as rote decoding or carrying objects) and not interdependent at all. Even this caveat is questionable, however; the Johnsons contend that, at worst, the margin of cooperation's superiority is reduced in certain tasks.

> Currently there is no type of task on which cooperative efforts are *less* effective than are competitive or individualistic efforts, and on most tasks (and especially the more important learning tasks such as concept attainment, verbal problem solving, categorization, spatial problem solving, retention and memory, motor, guessing-judging-predicting) cooperative efforts are more effective in promoting achievement.[13]

Some of the older studies, including Deutsch's, set up the cooperative condition so that the subjects were cooperating with others in their group but the groups were competing with each other. (This is similar to the arrangement in Japanese industry, which lately has attracted considerable attention in this country: employees within a given company work closely with each other and are encouraged to develop loyalty to the company, but the companies continue to compete with each other.) This cooperative/competitive arrangement led some scholars, reasonably enough, to ask whether the greater achievement levels in cooperative settings were not actually due to the intergroup competition. By now enough experimenters have controlled for this variable so that we can be quite certain the answer is no. Unequivocally, "performance benefits [from] cooperative conditions whether [they involve] additional intergroup competition or not," as Emmy Pepitone wrote in 1980.[14] This may be because "students in an intragroup cooperation/intergroup competition situation behave primarily as if the intergroup competition did not exist."[15]

In recent years, Deutsch and his associates have investigated not only the way tasks are set up but the way rewards are distributed. Among the possibilities are a winner-take-all system (which is what many contests amount to), a distribution proportional to accomplishment, and an equal distribution. Much as we tend to assume that competing boosts performance, so it is often taken for granted that the first two arrangements provide a crucial incentive for working hard: reserving a desirable reward for the winner is thought to promote excellence. A series of six experiments with Columbia University students, involving tasks that ranged from decoding Japanese poetry to estimating the number of jellybeans in a jar, was devised to test this assumption. The results: When tasks could be performed independently — that is, when there was low means interdependence — the system of distributing rewards had no effect on how good a job they did. There was absolutely no evidence to suggest that people work more productively when rewards are tied to performance than when everyone gets the same reward. But for those tasks where success depends on working together, there *was* a clear difference. A system of equal rewards, Deutsch discovered, "gives the best results and the competitive winner-take-all system gives the poorest results."[16]

Many of the studies I have been reviewing define achievement in a rather conventional, quantified way. Traditional examinations to measure what has been learned in a classroom, for example, are biased in favor of the competitive approach, and this may account for why some studies found no significant differences between competition and cooperation.[17] It is remarkable, then, that even with such measures, competition does not work well.

Once we move from such measures of achievement as speed of performance, number of problems solved, or amount of information recalled, though, and consider the *quality* of performance, we find that competition fares even worse. Some of the rather primitive experiments in the 1920s that found people work faster at a mechanical task when they are competing nevertheless discovered that the quality of work was poorer under competitive conditions.[18] More recent research confirms that "significantly more complex products were made in the cooperative condition than in the competitive condition"[19] and that "the discussion process in cooperative groups promotes the discovery and development of higher quality cognitive strategies for learning than does the individual reasoning found in competitive and individualistic learning situations."[20] Creative problem solving was similarly hampered by competition in a study of undergraduates.[21] A 1983 German study found that the competitiveness of fourth graders (as measured by a 15-item picture test) correlated negatively with school achievement.[22]

So far from making us more productive, then, a structure that pits us against one another tends to inhibit our performance. Children simply do not learn better when education is transformed into competitive struggle. To be sure, from the teacher's perspective it can be seductive to turn a lesson into a competitive game in order to attract and hold students' attention. But the real appeal of this strategy is that it makes teaching easier, not more effective; it circumvents rather than solves pedagogical problems. The fact that children seem to enjoy it says virtually nothing about how well it teaches them. And even the enjoyment may not be what it appears: the fact that a game is being substituted for the usual lesson — rather than the competitive nature of this game — could account for students' interest. Many teachers conclude that competition holds attention better even though they have never worked with cooperative alternatives. (Indeed, evidence reviewed in the last chapter shows that children tend to prefer cooperation once they have experienced it.)

Most of American education is highly individualistic, fueled by a competitive structure of evaluation. Sometimes competition (either individual or group) also finds its way into the curriculum itself. Given the unrelenting race for good grades,[23] this more explicit use of competition strikes the student as perfectly natural. On the other hand, cooperation of the kind described in all these studies is unfamiliar — no more than an abstraction, really — to many of us, including teachers. It is worth considering in more detail how a cooperative classroom actually works.

Cooperation means more than putting people into groups. It suggests, rather, group participation in a project where the result is the product of common effort, the goal is shared, and each member's success is linked with every other's. Practically, this means that ideas and materials, too, will be shared, labor sometimes will be divided, and everyone in the group will be rewarded for successful completion of the task. Aronson, for example, conceived the "jigsaw method" of learning: When the task is to learn about the life of a well-known person, each member of a group is given information about one period of the individual's life. Members of the group are thus dependent on each other in order to complete the assignment.[24] The brothers Johnson, by contrast, offered a straightforward assignment ("How many things can our group find that make a difference in how long [a] candle burns?") that involved less structured division of labor.[25] Elsewhere they suggest setting up groups of students who represent a range of abilities and instructing them to help one another. "When everyone in their group has mastered the solutions, they go look for another group to help until everyone in the class understands how to work the problems."[26]

Since "group performance in problem solving is superior to even the individual work of the most expert group members,"[27] it should not be surprising that students learn better when they cooperate. But the last technique — having students help one another — raises the question of whether students with lower ability are being helped at the expense of those with higher ability. Is this true? Knowledge, happily, is not a zero-sum product. Anyone who has taught or tutored knows that doing so not only reinforces one's own knowledge but often pulls one to a more sophisticated understanding of the material. The cliché about teachers' learning as much as their pupils is quite true, and the tutoring that takes place in a cooperative classroom actually benefits both the helper and the helped more than a competitive or independent study arrangement.

The evidence substantiates this view. As the Johnsons conclude:

> There can be little doubt that the low and medium ability students especially benefit from working collaboratively with peers from the full range of ability differences. There is also evidence that high ability students are better off academically when they collaborate with medium and low ability peers than when they work alone; at the worst . . . [they] are not hurt.[28]

Returning to the question in 1985, the Johnsons cited three studies that found gifted students are helped by such collaboration, one that found no difference, and none that found they were disadvantaged.[29] A study of 75 Midwestern second graders published that same year also reported that "high-, medium-, and low-achieving students all

academically benefited from participation in heterogeneous cooperative learning groups."[30] Moreover, earlier research discovered that
tutoring occurred *spontaneously* when the consequences for learning
were shared by the group — and that this "produced no long-term
complaints from the participants in this experiment." Once again,
"even the gifted [benefited,] possibly more than they would have
under individual consequences."[31] (The advantages of a cooperative
structure in education, incidentally, extend beyond mere performance; chapter 6 will consider the interpersonal consequences of cooperation and competition.)

Most of these studies assess performance in terms of learning, with
the schoolroom as the prototype if not the actual setting. But what of
the rest of the world? Don't competitive conditions — or personal
competitiveness — lead to better performance?

Research on productivity and competition in traditional work settings has been nowhere near as plentiful as the classroom data. The
findings, however, are remarkably consistent with those on learning.
One early study, which has become something of a classic in sociological investigation, was conducted by Peter Blau in 1954. Blau compared two groups of interviewers in an employment agency. In one,
there was fierce competition to fill job openings. The other group
worked cooperatively. Members of the first group, who were personally ambitious and extremely concerned about productivity, hoarded
job notifications rather than posting them so everyone could see
them, as they were supposed to do. This practice eventually was used
defensively and so became self-perpetuating. Members of the second
group, by contrast, told each other about vacancies. And it was this
second group that ended up filling significantly more jobs — the clear
index of performance.[32]

A quarter century later, Robert L. Helmreich of the University of
Texas and his colleagues decided to investigate the relationship between achievement, on the one hand, and such traits as the orientation toward work, mastery (preference for challenging tasks), and
competitiveness, on the other. A sample of 103 male Ph.D. scientists
were rated on these three factors based on a questionnaire. Achievement, meanwhile, was defined in terms of the number of times their
work was cited by colleagues. The result was that "the most citations
were obtained by those high on the Work and Mastery but low on the
Competitiveness scale."

This startled Helmreich, who did not expect that competitiveness would have a deleterious effect. Could the result be a fluke? He conducted another study, this one involving academic psychologists. The result was the same. He did two more studies, one involving male businessmen, measuring achievement by their salaries, and the other with 1300 male and female undergraduates, using grade point average as the attainment criterion. In both cases he again found a significant negative correlation between competitiveness and achievement.[33] Of the four studies, the one involving businessmen was particularly "exciting" to him because "the stereotype of the very successful businessman is of someone who is . . . highly competitive" — a stereotype called into serious question by these findings.[34] In fact, as he and his colleague Janet Spence later observed, the data "dramatically refute the contention that competitiveness is vital to a successful business career."[35]

But Helmreich did not stop there. As of 1985, he had conducted three more studies. The first compared the standardized achievement tests of fifth- and sixth-graders to their competitiveness. They were negatively related.[36] The second examined the relationship between performance of airline pilots and competitiveness. The relationship between the latter and superior performance was negative.[37] The third looked at airline reservation agents and again found a negative correlation between performance and competitiveness.[38] Seven different studies, then, with vastly different populations and measures of success, have all determined that intentional competition is associated with lower performance.

Helmreich's research is particularly important because it does not rely on a compound personality measure such as the "motive for success." Rather, it teases out competitiveness from the other components of this variable. Before this was done, researchers simply assumed that all of these components were associated with better performance. Now it appears that competitiveness in particular is not. Other researchers who have used a comparable methodology have found the same thing. In the German study of fourth graders mentioned earlier, just as in Helmreich's, competitive students did not get better grades. And psychologist Georgia Sassen, in the course of looking for differences between male and female students, also found a slight negative relationship between competitiveness and achievement.[39]

Consider the question of artistic creativity. The little research that has been done suggests that competition is just as unhelpful here as it is in promoting creative problem-solving. In one study, seven- to eleven-year-old girls were asked to make "silly" collages, some competing for prizes and some not. Seven artists then independently rated their works on each of 23 dimensions. The result: "Those children who competed for prizes made collages that were significantly less creative than those made by children in the control group." Children in the competitive condition produced works thought to be less spontaneous, less complex, and less varied.[40] In the long run, contests do not promote excellence among performing artists, either. Here is critic Will Crutchfield on the subject of piano competitions: "The emotional stamina to tough it out through round after round, as the competition winds on and the stakes rise, does not necessarily go along with the emotional sensitivity to make five minutes worth of truly remarkable Chopin."[41] In a win/lose framework, success comes to those whose temperaments are best suited for competition. This is not at all the same thing as artistic talent, and it may well pull in the opposite direction.

Across many fields, the assumption that competition promotes excellence has become increasingly doubtful. Consider journalism, a profession that, while no more competitive than many others, is worth exploring by virtue of its unusual visibility to outsiders. The frantic race for news generates terrific levels of anxiety (and the attendant psychological symptoms) on the part of journalists.[42] Can we at least point to better reporting as a result of this competition? Setting reporters against one another in a battle for space on the front page or the first block of a television news show probably *lowers* the quality of journalism in the long run, and so, too, does the contest among news organizations for subscriptions or ratings. The latter is more likely to take the form of sensationalism, arresting graphics, or promotional games. A thorough study of science news reporting, which included interviews with 27 leading science reporters, led Jay Winsten to conclude as follows:

> The most striking finding which emerged from the interviews is the dominant distorting influence of the "competitive force" in journalism. . . . Science reporters, based at preeminent publications, stated that competition for prominent display of their stories creates a strong motivation to distort their coverage.[43]

Having to compete for space creates an incentive not for accurate reporting but for "hyping" a story — that is, exaggerating its significance. This tendency, Winsten adds, is complemented by the competition for publicity among scientists, hospitals, and universities; the combination practically assures that reporting will be distorted.[44]

In any sort of journalism, the ordinary pressures of having to work on deadline are exacerbated by the pressure to get a story on the air seconds before the competition or to get a fact that another newspaper does not have. The result is that the public gets less information over the long run than they would have access to if the various news organizations worked together. Moreover, news stories are more likely to be inaccurate and even irresponsible as a result of competition. When a jet was hijacked by Shiite Moslems in 1985, one observer blamed the "distorted and excessive coverage of terrorist incidents" on "the highly competitive nature of network television."[45] A second critic independently came to the same conclusion, noting that "too many decisions are made on the basis of beating the competition rather than deciding how to act responsibly."[46] The structure of competitive journalism creates a situation in which a professional or ethical inclination to forgo coverage — or at least to pause in order to consider the implications of running a story (or to double-check the facts) — is invariably overridden by the fear that one's rival will get the scoop. Such competitive pressures ultimately benefit no one, least of all the public. Working against, rather than with, colleagues tends to be more destructive than productive. This corroborates the bulk of evidence on the topic — evidence that requires us to reconsider our assumptions about the usefulness of competition.

EXPLAINING COMPETITION'S FAILURE

How can we make sense of the failure of competition to produce superior performance? Most of the studies reviewed here offer at best a couple of sentences in the way of explanation for their findings. Other writers have addressed the problem, but no one has yet collected these conjectures and sorted them out. That will be the task of this section.

The simplest way to understand why competition generally does not promote excellence is to realize that *trying to do well and trying to beat others are two different things.* Here sits a child in class, waving his arm wildly to attract the teacher's attention, crying, "Oooh! Oooh! Pick me!" The child is finally recognized but then seems befuddled.

"Um, what was the question again?" he finally asks. His mind is on beating his classmates, not on the subject matter. The fact that there is a difference between the two goes a long way toward explaining why competition may actually make us less successful. At the beginning of this chapter, I argued that excellence and victory are conceptually distinct. Now I want to add that the two are *experienced* as different. One can attend either to the task at hand or to the enterprise of triumphing over someone else — and the latter often is at the expense of the former.

It is true, of course, that the relative quality of performance is what determines who wins in a competition, but this does not mean that competition makes for better performance. This is partly because those who believe they will lose may see little point in trying hard. The same is true for those who feel sure of winning.[47] But even where there is enough uncertainty involved to avoid these problems, the fact remains that attending to the quest for triumph, to victory as such, to who is ahead at the moment, actually distracts one from the pure focus on what one is doing. Helmreich proposes this as one explanation for his surprising discovery that competition is counterproductive in the real world: "Competitive individuals might . . . focus so heavily on outshining others and putting themselves forward that they lose track of the scientific issues and produce research that is more superficial and less sustained in direction."[48] And, more succinctly: "They may become so preoccupied with winning . . . that they become distracted from the task at hand."[49]

Let us see how this distinction plays itself out in different fields. I have already noted, in the case of piano competitions, that artistic excellence is not promoted by making performing artists compete. This is true for the same reason that anyone who wants to run for president may, *ipso facto*, be a bad choice for the job: those who enjoy — and possess the skills necessary for — a competitive campaign may not be the kind of people we want running the country. (It is theoretically possible for one person to be both a good leader and a good campaigner, but these two talents are quite different and would coincide only by accident.) We find the same phenomenon even in sports, as philosopher John McMurty explains:

> Actually, the pursuit of victory works to reduce the chance for excellence in the true performance of the sport. It tends to distract our attention from excellence of performance by rendering it subservient to emerging victorious. I suspect that our conventional mistake of pre-

suming the opposite — presuming that the contest-for-prize framework and excellence of performance are somehow related as a unique cause and effect — may be the deepest-lying prejudice of civilized thought.[50]

Consider a different sort of example: the case of competitive debate. This is an activity as consuming and, in its own way, as brutal as football. High school and college students spend their days and evenings preparing for tournaments in which they will debate a major issue of public policy. These tournaments require them to argue in support of a resolution in one round and then against it in the next. The practical emphasis in debate is on tying logical knots, sounding persuasive, and even speaking so quickly that an opponent cannot respond to all of one's arguments. The point is not to arrive at a fuller understanding of the question at hand or to form genuine convictions. Debaters develop considerable expertise as a result of their preparations, but this is only a means to victory. As for convictions, a premium is placed on not having any; believing in something could interfere with one's ability to win on both sides of the issue. This arrangement is usually defended on the grounds that it forces participants to see both points of view, but it does so in a way that promotes a kind of cynical relativism: no position is better than any other since any position can be successfully defended. When asked whether he personally supported a guaranteed annual income (which was that year's national high school topic), one debater of my acquaintance could answer only that this depended on which side he was on at the moment. A recent newspaper feature story carried the apt headline: "Young Albany Debaters Resolve Who's Best."[51] Regardless of the resolution under consideration, the exclusive focus of competitive debate is to determine who is the better debater.

Since the adversarial model on which our legal system is based works the same way, we might ask whether it truly serves the interests of justice or whether here, too, excellence and competition pull in different directions. Several legal scholars have begun to ask just this question, challenging one of the most sacrosanct institutions to have emerged from our commitment to competition. Here is Marvin E. Frankel:

> Employed by interested parties, the process often achieves truth only as a convenience, a byproduct, or an accidental approximation. The business of the advocate, simply stated, is to win if possible without violating the law. . . . [He or she] is not primarily crusading after truth, but seek-

ing to win . . . [and these two] are mutually incompatible for some considerable percentage of the attorneys trying cases at any given time.[52]

I. Nelson Rose, in a law review essay entitled "Litigator's Fallacy," takes the argument a step further: "It is a simple step for an individual to move from the belief in [the adversarial] system of justice to the belief that he has justice on his side. A litigator has to convince himself of the rightness of his client's case, how else can the gladiator go into battle?"[53] This invites unethical behavior — using any means in the client's behalf — and, in the long run, makes for an inefficient and unjust method of resolving disputes. One writer has ridiculed the underlying assumptions of the adversarial system, for example, "Mutual exaggeration is supposed to create a lack of exaggeration. Bitter partisanship in opposite directions is supposed to bring out the truth. Of course," he continues, "no rational human being would apply such a theory to his own affairs."[54]

Perhaps the tension between trying to do well and trying to win is most straightforward in the classroom. In his novel *A Separate Peace*, about competition between boarding school students, John Knowles contrasts two markedly different styles of learning:

> I wasn't really interested and excited by learning itself, the way Chet Douglass was. . . . But I began to see that Chet was weakened by the very genuineness of his interest in learning. He got carried away by things; for example, he was so fascinated by the tilting planes of solid geometry that he did almost as badly in trigonometry as I did myself. When we read *Candide* it opened up a new way of looking at the world to Chet, and he continued hungrily reading Voltaire, in French, while the class went on to other people. He was vulnerable there, because to me they were all pretty much alike — Voltaire and Moliere and the laws of motion and the Magna Carta and the Pathetic Fallacy and *Tess of the D'Urbervilles* — and I worked indiscriminately on all of them.[55]

Chet is "weakened" and "vulnerable" only from the perspective of a competitive individual, buttressed by a competitive system. While Chet, unconcerned with his grade point average, attends to what he is studying, the narrator is more concerned with strategy than with learning. His aim is to win, and this goal is necessarily achieved at the price of regarding the ideas he encounters as interchangeable. If this seems to describe many of the most "successful" products of our educational system, competition may have something to do with it.

Actually, it may well be that genuine education, which is decidedly not the consequence of our schooling, may not even be its chief purpose. The point of competition, suggests education critic George Leonard, is "not really to help students learn other subjects, but to teach competition itself."[56] David Campbell similarly observes that "the whole frantic, irrational scramble to beat others is essential for the kind of institution our schools are . . . [namely,] bargain-basement personnel screening agencies for business and government. . . . Winning and losing are what our schools are all about, not education."[57] Just as standardized testing chiefly prepares one to be a competent taker of standardized tests, so competition perpetuates itself — and often does so to the exclusion of the subject supposedly being taught.

Forcing children to compete is sometimes defended precisely on these grounds — that is, that early experience with competition will lead to more effective competition in later life. To some extent, this is true: one does learn strategies of competing by virtue of repeated exposure, just as one learns to regard other people as so many barriers to one's own success.[58] But the distinction between competition and the task at hand will be present in the future just as it is today, so competition will not be any more effective then than it is now. Moreover, many people's early unsuccessful experiences with competition will cause them to try to avoid competitive situations for the rest of their lives.

The idea that trying to do well and trying to do better than others may work at cross-purposes can be understood in the context of an issue addressed by motivational theorists. We do best at the tasks we enjoy. An outside or extrinsic motivator (money, grades, the trappings of competitive success) simply cannot take the place of an activity we find rewarding in itself. "While extrinsic motivation may affect performance," wrote Margaret Clifford, "performance is dependent upon learning, which in turn is primarily dependent upon intrinsic motivation." More specifically, "a significant performance-increase on a highly complex task will be dependent upon intrinsic motivation."[59] In fact, even people who are judged to be high in achievement motivation do not perform well unless extrinsic motivation has been minimized, as several studies have shown.[60]

Competition works just as any other extrinsic motivator does. As Edward Deci, one of the leading students of this topic, has written, "The reward for extrinsically motivated behavior is something that is separate from and follows the behavior. With competitive activities, the reward is typically 'winning' (that is, beating the other person or the other team), so the reward is actually extrinsic to the activity itself."[61] This has been corroborated by subjective reports: people who are more competitive regard themselves as being extrinsically motivated.[62] Like any other extrinsic motivator, competition cannot produce the kind of results that flow from enjoying the activity itself.

But this tells only half the story. As research by Deci and others has shown, the use of extrinsic motivators actually tends to *undermine* intrinsic motivation and thus adversely affect performance in the long run. The introduction of, say, monetary reward will edge out intrinsic satisfaction; once this reward is withdrawn, the activity may well cease even though no reward at all was necessary for its performance earlier. Money "may work to 'buy off' one's intrinsic motivation for an activity. And this decreased motivation appears (from the results of the field experiment) to be more than just a temporary phenomenon."[63] Extrinsic motivators, in other words, are not only ineffective but corrosive. They eat away at the kind of motivation that *does* produce results.

This effect has been shown specifically with competition. In a 1981 study, eighty undergraduates worked on a spatial relations puzzle. Some of them were asked to try to solve it more quickly than the persons sitting next to them, while others did not have to compete. The subjects then sat alone (but clandestinely observed) for a few minutes in a room that contained a similar puzzle. The time they voluntarily spent working on it, together with a self-report on how interested they had been in solving the puzzle, constituted the measure of intrinsic interest. As predicted, the students who had been competing were less intrinsically motivated than those who had originally worked on the puzzle in a noncompetitive environment. It was concluded that

> trying to beat another party is extrinsic in nature and tends to decrease people's intrinsic motivation for the target activity. It appears that when people are instructed to compete at an activity, they begin to see that activity as an instrument for winning rather than an activity which is mastery-oriented and rewarding in its own right. Thus, competition seems to work like many other extrinsic rewards in that, under certain circumstances, it tends to be perceived as controlling and tends to decrease intrinsic motivation.[64]

Competing not only distracts you from a task at a given moment; it also makes you less interested in that task over the long run, and this results in poorer performance. In an article about female athletes, Jenifer Levin cited two studies showing that "when one does compete, intrinsic motivation tends to dramatically decrease, especially for women."[65]

Again, this effect is especially salient in the classroom. The late John Holt put it well:

> We destroy the . . . love of learning in children, which is so strong when they are small, by encouraging and compelling them to work for petty and contemptible rewards — gold stars, or papers marked 100 and tacked to the wall, or A's on report cards, or honor rolls, or dean's lists, or Phi Beta Kappa keys — in short, for the ignoble satisfaction of feeling that they are better than someone else.[66]

This process is shameful for many reasons, but the one I want to stress here is the resultant decline in learning. Performance ultimately suffers from competition just as it suffers from the use of any extrinsic motivator.

One final observation: to the extent that an extrinsic motivator *can* have a positive effect, one of the most powerful motivators is not money or victory but a sense of accountability to other people. This is precisely what cooperation establishes: the knowledge that others are depending on you.[67] The only stake others have in your performance under a competitive arrangement is a desire to see you fail.

.   .   .

The distinction between trying to do well and trying to beat others is not the only explanation we can come up with for competition's failure. *Competition also precludes the more efficient use of resources that cooperation allows.* One of the clear implications of the research conducted by David and Roger Johnson is that people working cooperatively succeed because a group is greater than the sum of its parts. This is not necessarily true for all activities, of course; sometimes independent work is the best approach. But very often — more often than many of us assume — cooperation takes advantage of the skills of each member as well as the mysterious but undeniable process by which interaction seems to enhance individuals' abilities. Coordination of effort and division of labor are possible when people work with each other, as Deutsch saw.[68] Noncooperative approaches, by contrast, almost always involve duplication of effort, since someone working independently must spend time and skills on problems that already have been encountered and overcome by someone else. A technical hitch, for example, is more likely to be solved quickly and imaginatively if scientists (including scientists from different countries) pool their talents rather than compete against one another.

Here it is not competition that is peculiarly unproductive; any kind of individual work suffers from this drawback. But structural competition has the practical effect of making people suspicious of and hostile toward one another and thus of actively discouraging cooperation. (The evidence on competition and affiliation will be reviewed in detail in chapter 6.) This occurred to both Peter Blau and Robert Helmreich as they tried to make sense of their respective findings. Blau's competitive employment agency workers "in their eagerness to make many placements . . . often ignored their relationships with others"; their noncompetitive counterparts, meanwhile, enjoyed more "social cohesion [which] enhanced operating efficiency by facilitating co-operation."[69] Helmreich likewise proposed that "highly competitive individuals may alienate and threaten others who are in a position to assist and support them in their activities."[70]

The dynamics of cooperative effort make this arrangement far more efficient, while competitors hardly are predisposed to like and trust each other enough to benefit from it. Moreover, as the Johnsons point out, people who feel accepted by others also feel safe enough to explore problems more freely, take risks, play with possibilities, and "benefit from mistakes rather than [endure] a climate in which mistakes must be hidden in order to avoid ridicule."[71] None of these is likely to occur when a potential partner has been transformed into an opponent — which is, of course, what competition entails.

Beyond the greater efficiency of cooperation, it is also true that *competition's unpleasantness diminishes performance*. While many people apparently enjoy competitive games — a subject to which we will return in the next chapter — it would seem that most of us find competition distinctly unpleasant in most circumstances. Recall, for example, the data indicating a preference for cooperation in both recreation and learning on the part of preschoolers through undergraduates (see pp. 31–32). Largely because it is more fun, but also because it is more productive — thus setting an auspicious cycle in motion — cooperation induces people to perform better. In the classroom, it also "promote[s] more positive attitudes toward the subject area and the instruction experience,"[72] thereby promising more intrinsic motivation and continued superior work in the future.

The pattern that keeps appearing, in which competition not only fails to contribute to success but positively inhibits it, turns up again here. Not only is competition not enjoyable enough to elicit high achievement — it is a distinct cause of anxiety. Even if the tangible stakes (money, job, trophy, grades) are not always high when people compete, the psychological stakes invariably are. In any given competition, most people will lose. Anticipation of failure combined with — and fueled by — memory of previous failure is a recipe for agitation, nervousness, and similar emotional states that interfere with performance when they occur to any significant degree. Ruth Benedict describes Japanese adults who

> began to make mistakes and were far slower when a competitor was introduced. They did best when they were measuring their improvement against their own record, not when they were measuring themselves against others. . . . They felt the competition so keenly as an aggression that they turned their attention to their relation to the aggressor instead of concentrating on the job in hand.[73]

Of course this effect is far from uniform across all cultures or all individuals. It does, however, appear to be a widespread phenomenon even in a highly competitive society like ours, where one might have expected people to have become inured to the effect. In his study, Blau pointed to the reduction of anxiety in the cooperative group as another explanation for its higher productivity.[74] Other studies, too, have discovered higher levels of anxiety among subjects who compete, which is, in turn, correlated with inferior performance.[75] One line of research within behavioral psychology, in fact, regards competition as an aversive stimulus, rather like electric shock. To the extent that some people complete a task more rapidly in a competitive condition, then, it may be because they are attempting to end the competition as quickly as possible so as to escape from its unpleasantness.[76]

Those who defend competition typically do not deny that it produces anxiety; instead, they insist that anxiety motivates us to perform better. It is true that slight anxiety can be productively arousing. The "Yerkes-Dodson law," as it has come to be known, states that there is an optimum level of arousal for every task, and that this level is lower for tasks that are more complex and difficult. But it would seem that competition often produces inhibiting levels of anxiety. At best, the stressfulness of a competitive situation causes us to try to avoid failure. And trying to avoid failure is not at all the same thing as trying to succeed. On the contrary, as the well-known motivation theorist John Atkinson wrote, "The tendency to avoid failure . . . functions to oppose and dampen the tendency to undertake achievement-oriented activities."[77] The need to cut one's losses often results in reluctance to enter the competitive arena in the first place: deciding not to apply for the job or promotion,[78] staying away from competitive recreation, remaining silent in the classroom, and so on. The person trying to avoid failure who is forced to compete may, paradoxically, become so agitated as to bring on failure — and this can happen irrespective of the task's nature or difficulty. In any case, he or she certainly will not be in an ideal state for creative problem solving.

While this effect is very widespread, it will naturally be most pronounced among those who believe, rightly or wrongly, that they stand little chance of winning. Competition will lower achievement markedly for such individuals — which seriously affects the performance of the whole group (class, corporation, society). One way a competitive culture deals with those who find competition unpleasant, of course, is to accuse them of being "afraid of losing." This language typically is used for purposes of derogation rather than explanation. The people who use such language often imply that fear is the *only* reason competition is opposed. Michael Novak, for example, refers to "those who deplore (and secretly dread) the intense competitiveness of American life,"[79] while Christopher Lasch transforms criticism of competition into "distrust" and then asserts that this distrust "seems to originate in a fear that unconscious impulses and fantasies will overwhelm us if we allow them expression."[80]

This is really a fancy version of taunting one's playmates by calling them chicken. It impugns the courage of critics — and perhaps their manliness, too, if one reads between the lines. But it is also a clever rhetorical move: it counterposes those who can offer reasons for their advocacy of competition with those who oppose it sheerly because of their emotional state. Furthermore, those who refer to a "fear of losing" mean to imply that this is a shameful reason for avoiding competition or for allowing it to adversely affect one's performance. Many support a system that elicits such fear, saying, in effect, "*Let* the losers drop out if they can't take the pressure." Here I will not belabor the cruelty of this position — which is considerable in light of the number of people to whom it applies — nor attempt a psychological analysis of those who offer it. Instead, let me merely observe that the state in which many people find themselves during competition —

whatever we choose to call it — apparently reduces the quality of performance and goes a long way toward explaining the evidence offered in the last section that competition does not promote excellence.

PRODUCTIVITY:
BEYOND THE INDIVIDUAL'S PERSPECTIVE

The fact that we do not generally do our best in a competitive situation will strike some people as being beside the point. Here are two hungry individuals; there is one dinner. Here are ten unemployed laborers; there is one job. How can the individuals involved be expected to do anything but compete? Isn't competition the most productive response — indeed, the only rational one?

The answer, I will argue, is that it depends on the perspective we take and even on our definition of rationality itself. Calling our basic assumptions into question tends to make habitual solutions seem much less obvious. Consider the question of whether a person being shot at is morally permitted to shoot back. We can offer a definite opinion — or any opinion, for that matter — only if we have accepted at face value a hypothetical situation (condensed into one sentence) that freezes the action. When we watch the whole film, so to speak, other questions present themselves: Is the first person a marauder invading the second person's home? Are there less deadly means of self-protection? Will returning fire result in the deaths of many others?

The case of competition is analogous. Competing for a job or a plate of food is a reasonable choice only if we restrict our vision to the situation as it exists in a given instant — if we disregard causes, consequences, and context. Really, we should want to know why the desired object is in short supply, what might have prevented this situation from having developed in the first place, how a competitive response will affect the two individuals tomorrow (as well as what other consequences it will have), and so forth.

Let me propose two different shifts in perspective, one radical and the other moderate, both of which will have the effect of making competition seem far less necessary or productive. The first shift proceeds from a question that very few of us ever ask: Whose advantage is being considered? In the traditional Western picture — and specifically that of classical economic theory — the very idea of rational behavior pertains to the individual. Decisions are based on the costs and benefits to the single actor, and a society is construed as just a collection of such actors. An individual theoretically chooses to accept the burdens of belonging to a society if it is in his or her own personal interest to do so.

This point of view has become second nature to us in the Western world, but as with so many other values and behaviors, there is no evidence to show that it is an inevitable feature of human life. Even contemporary China and Japan — to say nothing of less industrialized societies — contain elements of a qualitatively different worldview in which the *group's* well-being is the standard by which decisions are made. The singular self is thought to be an illusion in certain cosmologies; the costs and benefits to any particular individual are seen as irrelevant in certain social systems. "But what do *I* get out of it?" — a question posed continually and unashamedly in the West — seems appallingly selfish or even difficult to understand in other parts of the world.

This collectivist or holistic perspective, incidentally, has at least as much claim to the title of "natural" as the individualist perspective to which we are wedded. The biologist V. C. Wynne-Edwards has proposed that evolution can more usefully be understood at the level of the group instead of at the level of individual organisms. Much animal behavior — including sacrifices and other acts that have been likened to altruism — makes sense when interpreted in terms of benefits to the whole group.[81]

When we compete, we do so out of a primary concern for our own welfare. If the welfare in question is instead that of a group of people, then cooperation follows naturally. Working together as a group would not be a strategy for maximizing individual gain but a logical consequence of thinking in terms of what benefits all of us. Will I lose in order that the group will gain? Sometimes such a tradeoff will occur, but it will not be seen as catastrophic. More to the point, this question would not even occur to someone whose worldview is different from our own. It would seem as odd as your feet asking whether the body as a whole benefits from jogging at their expense.

Shifting to a concern for the group's welfare, which constitutes a change of *goals*, involves a radically different way of looking at the world. But even if we keep our individualism intact, an inquiry into various *strategies* for satisfying ourselves suggests that competition still makes little sense. The practice of trying to beat others, which derives from the assumption that my success depends on your failure, is productive only in the short run. If we evaluate our success over the long haul — a relatively modest shift in perspective that continues to ignore the question of what is best for the group — working together often benefits us *as individuals*.

Consider Garrett Hardin's notion of the "tragedy of the commons." From the perspective of each cattle farmer with access to a public pasture, it is sensible to keep adding animals to his herd. But the same reasoning that makes this decision seem sensible to one individual will make it seem sensible to all individuals. Each will pursue his self-interest, the grass will be depleted, and everyone will lose.[82] (If the farmers competed to feed more of their own cattle, or to get there first, the process would simply be accelerated: the more competition, the faster everyone loses.) In order to see this, we must adopt the perspective of the group. But even if we adopt this perspective temporarily, with our ultimate purpose still being to benefit each individual, it becomes clear that cooperation is more productive.

There are countless other examples of how cooperation works better than the competitive or independent pursuit of private gain. To cite a few:

· The economist Fred Hirsch pointed out that each individual in a crowd is able to see better by standing on tiptoe, particularly when others are doing so. But everyone would do better if no one stood on tiptoe.[83]

· Each individual thinks it in her interest to rush for the exit when fire breaks out, but a cooperative escape protects everyone's interests and saves lives.

· Each hockey player is reluctant to wear a helmet when others are not doing so, since it restricts his vision. But a group decision to wear them benefits everyone by reducing the risk of serious injury.[84]

· Social change that will benefit all workers can take place only if collective action supersedes the quest for individual rewards. "The achievement of short-run material satisfaction often makes it irrational [from an individual perspective] to engage in more radical struggle, since that struggle is by definition against those institutions which provide one's current gain."[85] This is precisely why "divide and conquer," along with the practice of co-opting activists, is such an effective strategy for maintaining the status quo — and why the individualist worldview is a profoundly conservative doctrine: it inherently stifles change.

The most thoroughly documented example of how cooperation is a more effective means to personal gain — and how working at cross-purposes has the paradoxical effect of hurting everyone — comes from the Prisoner's Dilemma (PD) game that is so popular among psychologists (see footnote on page 29). Each of two players — you and another — simultaneously chooses to "cooperate" or "defect," and your decisions, taken together, determine the reward:

Both cooperate:	You cooperate; the other defects:
You: 3	You: 0
Other: 3	Other: 5
You defect; the other cooperates:	Both defect:
You: 5	You: 1
Other: 0	Other: 1

Here is the intriguing part: If the other person has defected, your losses will be cut if you defect, too. On the other hand, if the other person has cooperated, you can maximize your gain by defecting. From a strictly individual perspective, then, it seems rational to defect in either case. But seen as a unit, the two players do best when both cooperate. In the long run, *each* player does best when both cooperate. The game is somewhat contrived, of course, but its point is readily applicable to real life. Many of us pursue strategies that appear to be productive just so long as our standard remains what is in our own immediate best interest. When our perspective is widened we can see how this strategy is self-defeating to the community and, ultimately, even to ourselves.

Political scientist Robert Axelrod used the PD game to help determine whether individual nations would do better by cooperating or competing — a question firmly rooted in conventional Western individualism. He invited game theorists to submit computer programs with PD strategies; each program was then matched against all the others. The most successful entry (TIT FOR TAT) was the one that began by cooperating and then simply reciprocated the opponent's last move. A second tournament elicited more devious strategies, many of which included frequent defections, but TIT FOR TAT won again. Axelrod notes that this program "succeed[ed] by eliciting cooperation from others, not by defeating them," and he concludes that "cooperation based on reciprocity can get started in a predominantly noncooperative world, can thrive in a variegated environment, and can defend itself once fully established."[86] He stresses that people (or nations) are most apt to cooperate when they are relatively likely to have to deal with each other again in the future. (Other research with

PD demonstrates that players do better — that is, cooperate more consistently — when they are given the chance to talk with each other beforehand.)[87]

The first shift in perspective — from considering what benefits me to what benefits the group — entails seeing most of Western political science and economics as fundamentally misconceived. Adam Smith asserted that when each person endeavored to further his or her best interests, each person gained. To someone who has rejected an individualist ethic, this proposition rests on a faulty assumption — namely, the *a priori* belief that our analysis should be based on the solitary actor. The second, more moderate shift in perspective — which leaves our worldview similar to Smith's but offers a long-range view — leads us to conclude that the prime theorist of capitalism was simply wrong. Everyone does *not* benefit when we struggle against each other for private gain. It is a simple matter of examining the evidence. To distinguish between what is rational for the individual and what is rational for the group is finally misleading because the former is "*not* rational, period. It is damaging not just to the group, but to the individual."[88]

But even this modest conclusion seems radical in light of our current zero-sum mentality. Having thoroughly assimilated the attitude that the better I do, the worse you do (and vice versa), we are not open to mutually advantageous agreement or cooperation of any kind. The costs can be high. The nightmarish problems now facing Mexico City, for example, are explained by its mayor as follows: "With our attitude in the past and perhaps also in the present, we have disordered this city because we have put individual interests before the collective interest."[89] Similarly, although nuclear war benefits no one, some Americans take Soviet endorsement of any arms control agreement as sufficient reason to oppose it: if it's in their interest, it automatically must be against our interest. The enormous potential in mutual benefit (cooperative) strategies will not be tapped — or even understood — until we broaden our perspective beyond the narrow prejudice that we always do best by trying to beat others.

ECONOMIC COMPETITION

In considering the social features of productivity, this chapter already has broached the matter of economic competition. This is a subject almost impossible to avoid in the course of exploring the effects of competition in our culture — particularly inasmuch as our economic system may well be the prototype of competition from which other varieties derive.[90] Capitalism can be thought of as the heart of competitiveness in American society.

Interestingly, most critics of capitalism are concerned not so much with the competitive basis of the system as with the fact that this competition is, in practice, unfair. Surely this criticism is well earned: it is a curious race indeed in which one competitor must try to scramble up from poverty while another starts out with a huge trust fund. A multinational corporation, similarly, has the capital and the tax advantages that allow it to trounce — or simply acquire — a small competitor. Once a business becomes large enough (e.g., Chrysler, Lockheed, Continental Bank), it simply cannot be allowed to fail. The result is that most sectors of the economy are becoming ever more concentrated, with a handful of concerns controlling the lion's share of business. Other profound inequities exist in an economy whose competition is so grossly unfair — or, to use the euphemism of choice, "imperfect." More than half of the largest 250 corporations paid no taxes (or received rebates) in at least one of three years in the mid-1980s,[91] while forty to fifty million Americans live in poverty.[92]

Despite the enormous discrepancy between perfect competition and the actual state of our economic system, competition is still the stated ideal. Businesspeople and public officials use the term as an honorific, discussing ways in which they can make their companies and countries "more competitive" and never pausing to ask whether a competitive system really is the best possible arrangement. Even progressive thinkers have come to identify true competition as the (rarely realized) ideal and cooperation, manifested as collusion, price fixing, and so on, as the salient evil.

When critics see things this way, they do not mean to repudiate genuine cooperation; they are simply accepting (often unconsciously) the premises and vocabulary of corporate capitalism. Within this framework, the word *cooperation* signifies little more than violation of antitrust laws. But critics of our economic system have, I think, made a serious mistake in accepting competition as a theoretical good and directing their energies to the question of how best to attain it. This not only has a stultifying effect on the discussion of economic issues; it spills over into other realms. Competition becomes generally identified as desirable and alternatives are regarded with suspicion when they are regarded at all. We need to develop a critique that will question the productiveness of competition itself and not simply assume that we are going about it in the wrong way. The following discussion will take this tack, although it will not provide anything like a comprehensive critique. It will simply raise a few questions about the value of a competitive economic system.

. . .

Economics is the study of how commodities are produced, distributed, and consumed. Most economists see their job as finding the most efficient means of satisfying demand for these commodities. Competition is justified on the grounds of its putative efficiency and, further, its usefulness at stimulating growth. The first question one could ask — although in practice almost no one does — is whether economic growth is always desirable. Paul Wachtel, in his book *The Poverty of Affluence*, shows how such growth entails significant costs to our health and safety, makes our working lives unhappy (for all we might gain in quality of life as consumers, we lose as producers), fails to bring about greater equity, and actually represents a desperate and futile attempt to compensate for psychological and social deficiencies.[93]

But let us assume for the sake of the argument that producing more goods is a legitimate goal. Does a competitive system represent the best way to meet this goal? We have considerable reason to doubt that it does.

· Working to maximize individual gain by competing against others can be counterproductive in the long run, as the last section suggested.

· The evidence already reviewed from Robert Helmreich demonstrates that competitiveness does not make people more productive — even when productivity is measured by a businessman's earnings. Other data confirm that structural competition promotes achievement less well than cooperation in a variety of settings. The obvious question is why this should suddenly cease to be the case when we turn our attention to the economic system as a whole.

· At least one study has found that competitive behavior appears more frequently and more vigorously on the part of children with lower socioeconomic origins.[94] We should be cautious in interpreting this finding: it may be that competition is a socialized response to poverty, an attempt (however misguided) to improve one's condition. Alternatively, it may reflect the fact that competition appears to be particularly stressed in lower-income schools.[95] But such a finding, considered alongside Helmreich's, suggests that competition may just be counterproductive.

· Margaret Mead's cross-cultural studies led her to conclude that cooperation is more effective than competition at maximizing production. A more recent review of the research forced Roderic Gorney to acknowledge that achievement on the part of a society did not depend on its competitiveness (see p. 38).

The case for the desirability of economic competition is usually made as a result of assumptions about scarcity. Mead emphasizes that it is cultural norms and not objective scarcity that determine whether a society's economic system is competitive, but one could still argue that competition is the best arrangement for dealing with scarcity. The subject deserves attention.

By "scarcity," most of us mean that goods are in short supply: there isn't enough of something to go around. While there often is no clear-cut understanding of what constitutes "enough," the simple fact is that there is more than sufficient food to sustain everyone on the planet.[96] The same is true of land and renewable energy. The important question, then, is why the staples of life are so egregiously maldistributed — why, for example, the United States, with a little more than 5 percent of the world's population, uses something like 40 percent of the world's resources. What appears to be a problem of scarcity usually turns out, on closer inspection, to be a problem of distribution. But mainstream economists are notably unconcerned with distributional issues: they talk only about whether a given system is productive or efficient, and it is up to us to ask, "For *whom?*" A high gross national product tells us nothing about who has access to the goods; likewise, the absence of goods on the part of particular individuals or nations raises the question of whether someone else has a surfeit.

The point is this: if there is enough of the necessities to go around but they are not going around, the debate must shift to the impact of competition on matters of distribution. Can the inequities be blamed on competition itself? Even if not, the key question is whether more competition would rectify the situation. It is hard to imagine how it could. Whoever has more resources is far more likely to win a contest, thus giving her even more resources for the next contest, and so on until the opponent is utterly vanquished or someone steps in to stop the competition. Government regulations and income transfer mechanisms — which free-market apologists correctly identify as limitations on pure competition — are all that prevent inequities even more pronounced than those now in existence. To take another kind of evidence, Gorney demonstrated a significant correlation between competition in a culture and the presence of sharply delineated "have" and "have-not" groups (see p. 38). On whatever grounds competition might be defended, equity simply cannot be considered one of its benefits. Thus it would seem to be precisely the wrong strategy for dealing with the maldistribution of goods, which is perhaps the most critical economic reality to be addressed.

When economists talk about scarcity, however, they generally are not using the word to mean that goods are in short supply. Their technical use of the term refers instead to (1) the fact that choosing one commodity involves giving up the chance to have another, or (2) the presumed failure of people to be satisfied regardless of how much they have. Let us take these in turn.

The first usage defines a scarce good as one for which a consumer would give up something else. Scarcity, then, concerns the mutually exclusive relationship between commodities. This may be a useful way of looking at the world in some respects, but it tells us nothing about the absolute status of a given commodity. The model is set up so all finite goods will always be considered "scarce"; the availability of each is being evaluated vis-à-vis the others. By definition, no economic system can remedy this state of affairs, so competition is no more sensible a way to deal with scarcity than any other arrangement.

The second definition rests economic theory on a very questionable (but rarely questioned) assumption about "human nature" — namely, the belief that we will always want more of something than we had before or more than the next person has. Far more reasonable is the proposition that insatiability and competitiveness reflect cultural mores. As Wachtel saw, "Our obsession with growth is the expression of neither inexorable laws of human nature nor inexorable laws of economics. . . . It is a cultural and psychological phenomenon, reflecting our present way of organizing and giving meaning to our lives . . . [that] is now maladaptive."[97]

This position defines scarcity as a matter of psychological state (perception or desire) rather than objective fact. Some social critics have gone along with this approach but have shown that this state, which is often used to justify competition, actually is a *product* of competition. Specifically, it is argued, capitalism manufactures scarcity.[98] Capitalism's driving force is the quest for profits; its alleged success at satisfying human needs is merely a fortuitous by-product. This goal requires the continuous — indeed, constantly expanding — consumption of goods, and these goods will be purchased only if they are desired. The advertising industry exists to create this desire, to produce a continual dissatisfaction with what we currently have and to tell us of the fulfillment that purchasing yet another product will bring.* We must be "educated" as to the desirability of low-calorie TV dinners, cordless telephones, and this year's model of video recorders. The sociologist Philip Slater has written lucidly on this topic, and he is worth quoting at length:

> Scarcity is spurious. . . . It now exists only for the purpose of maintaining the system that depends upon it, and its artificiality becomes more palpable each day. . . . Inequality, originally a consequence of scarcity, is now a means of creating artificial scarcities. For in the old culture [the dominant disposition of American life], as we have seen, the manufacture of scarcity is the principal activity. Hostile comments of old-culture adherents toward new-culture forms ("people won't want to work if they can get things for nothing," "people won't want to get married if they can get it free") often reveal this preoccupation. Scarcity, the presumably undesired but unavoidable foundation for the whole old-culture edifice, has now become its most treasured and sacred value, and to maintain this value in the midst of plenty it has been necessary to establish invidiousness as the foremost criterion of worth. Old-culture Americans . . . find it difficult to enjoy anything they themselves have unless they can be sure that there are people to whom this pleasure is denied. . . . Since the society rests on scarcity assumptions, involvement in it has always meant competitive involvement.[99]

A competitive economic system offers itself as the best way to deal with scarcity (here defined as the inability of consumers to get enough) while quietly *promoting* scarcity. The result is the perpetuation of the system and, not incidentally, the encouragement of intentional competition. Capitalism works on the same principle as a glass company whose employees spend their nights breaking people's windows and their days boasting of the public service they provide.

---

*The cost of this advertising is, of course, passed through to the consumer, often accounting for a substantial proportion of the total purchase price — and offering yet another reason to doubt claims of competition's efficiency.

Manufactured scarcity, of course, is not limited to economic matters. Every contest that is staged (the most facts memorized, the fastest runner, the most beautiful) involves the creation of a desired and scarce status where none existed before. Social psychologist Emmy Pepitone emphasizes the artificiality of this status:

> There seem to be exceedingly few essential objects that are so unique that they can be possessed only by one person. In the state of nature, most objects come in a form that can be shared by a large number of people. . . . Uniqueness seems to be invented by humans, who invent activities deliberately designed to allow entry into the goal region to one individual only.[100]

This process can occur even without formal contests. Charles Derber, for example, has described at some length the competition for attention in a conversation. "While attention is not intrinsically 'scarce,' " he argues, "it tends to become so under . . . individualistic conditions of allocation and distribution."[101] To ask whom I listen to or care for the most is to turn attention or love into a finite commodity.

To return to economics, neither a specialized nor a commonsense definition of scarcity leads us to accept competition as the most rational or appropriate system. If we view scarcity as a function of expanding human desire, this situation is largely created by the very system recommended to us as its solution. If we view scarcity as a situation of objective insufficiency, then the real problem turns out to be one of distribution — something that competition is more likely to exacerbate than remedy. In any case, the assumption that a competitive economic system is productive presupposes that competition stimulates optimal performance — something we now know to be false.

. . .

If any benefits can still be claimed for economic competition, they must be weighed — as any economist should insist on principle — against the disadvantages. The psychological and interpersonal costs of competition, per se, will be discussed in later chapters, but there are some unique problems with competition in the economic sphere that should be sketched here. I have already suggested that competition may contribute to an inequitable distribution of resources. But there is also the matter of its failure with respect to the standards favored by economists: competition may be unsuccessful even on its own terms.

In 1940, Lawrence Frank listed some of the costs of economic competition. He included business failures, copious litigation, idle equipment, a reduction in quality, unsafe working conditions, and the need to regulate the private sector in order to keep all of these problems under control.[102] These problems were experienced most dramatically in the laissez-faire economy of the last century, which, according to economist John Culbertson, "performed badly, provoking general demands for reform and regulation. The country's 'production miracle' occurred in the Second World War, under the wartime economic controls."[103]

When regulation is cut back in order to bring more competition to the marketplace, we again witness the true consequences of this competition: its advantages often prove illusory or short-lived or selective. A few examples:

· The recent deregulation of the airline industry, has, it is true, led to lower fares on busy routes (e.g., New York to Los Angeles), but service to less heavily traveled cities is either much more expensive or no longer available.[104] Precisely the same thing happened when bus companies were able to compete without regulation: they "cut out less-profitable routes, and the cheap service that the young, the elderly and the poor have historically depended on [was] less available."[105]

· Increased competition for large depositors has led banks to offer high-interest accounts. But how do banks pay for this? They have either had to make riskier, high-interest loans or jack up fees and minimum requirements on small accounts, thus penalizing poorer people.

· Is it advantageous to have book publishers compete for the rights to publish a desirable manuscript? The author may receive extravagant sums, but this often means that there is less money for other authors (whose names cannot guarantee enormous sales); arguably, the reading public loses, too.

· States compete fiercely for business investment by lowering their taxes. The corporations benefit, but citizens lose critical services when the tax base declines.

Examples of this sort are limited only by the varieties of economic competition. I am intentionally calling attention to cases where it is competition itself — rather than unfair competition — that is involved. A fierce price war between two giant conglomerates often has the effect of driving small businesses out of the market, and even apologists of capitalism usually acknowledge this is not desirable. I would contend that this is the rule rather than the exception in our economic system — as rapid concentration in virtually all sectors demonstrates — and I would also argue (though I will not follow through here) that such unfairness inevitably develops as a result of competition itself.

This aside, competition is of questionable value. The watchword of classical economics, that competition keeps prices down, is far from obvious. When economists are presented with counterexamples, they sometimes respond by saying that the higher price (for, say, an airline ticket) is perfectly appropriate since this is its "natural" price. But in what sense is it natural? In that the market (i.e., a competitive system) decrees it. Since the value of the competitive system is precisely what is at issue, it begs the question to say that anything resulting from the system is *ipso facto* justified. We need to ask whether it is really true that competition is the most efficient arrangement across the board. A comprehensive investigation is beyond the scope of this book and my competence, but these few remarks may at least open this dogma to question.

Beyond the matter of prices, let us ask what effect competition has on quality. Even if the race for profits results in a higher speed of production and greater volume, this may well come at the expense of quality. Norman Lear, for example, insists that the dreadful mediocrity of television programming is a direct result of competition among the networks.[106] Earlier I noted that trying to be number one and trying to do a task well are two different things; here we may observe the relevance of this distinction to economics. "The aim of competition often becomes one of winning the market rather than producing a better product," argues Arthur W. Combs. "Competition seeks to prove superiority, even if it does not exist. It places the emphasis upon capturing the buyer rather than producing a better product."[107] It is exactly in this vein that Sinclair Lewis has Babbitt hear a confession from his friend in the roofing business: " 'You know, my business isn't distributing roofing — it's principally keeping my competitors from distributing roofing. Same with you. All we do is cut each other's throats and make the public pay for it!' "[108] Similar examples can be found in virtually any competitive sector.

Competition may reduce not only quality but safety. With airplanes, as with most products, "the best design from an economic standpoint is the worst thing for safety";[109] the more ferocious the competition among manufacturers, the less consideration we can expect that safety will receive. "While no manufacturer would build an unsafe aircraft intentionally," argues Frederick C. Thayer, "competitive pressures can affect judgments. . . . The race to 'keep up' may have introduced hidden dangers."[110] What is true of the shoddily assembled DC-10 is true of the dangerous drug that a pharmaceutical firm has marketed hastily in order to beat its rivals or of the wastes spewed out by a business that feared installing pollution control equipment would cause it to lose its competitive edge.

Let us not overlook, finally, the noneconomic costs of economic competition, which have been said to include a loss of community and sociability,[111] a heightening of selfishness,[112] and such other consequences as anxiety, hostility, obsessional thinking, and the suppression of individuality.[113] In all, we may conclude from this admittedly incomplete discussion that economic competition of any kind may be a more dubious proposition than is generally assumed. This, let me emphasize again, is not to suggest that criticism of *unfair* competition is misplaced or that all kinds of economic competition are equally harmful. (The typical competition among workers for jobs and the atypical competition among employers for workers are hardly equivalent, and neither are competition between a small family business and a giant corporation, on the one hand, and between two family businesses, on the other.)

Let me also acknowledge that this discussion, intended to raise questions about the fundamental bases of our current economic system, does not include a consideration of alternatives. It may well be that a centralized economy — even one based on group-interest rather than self-interest principles — cannot function without some kind of competition. But this should lead us to investigate decentralized possibilities — small-scale cooperatives, for example — rather than to shrug our shoulders and accept the inevitability of competition. There is good evidence that various cooperative models in the workplace are considerably more productive than competitive businesses.[114] This search for noncompetitive alternatives will be informed not only by this consideration of productiveness in the economic realm but by all the research reviewed in this chapter — research that challenges the myth of competition's contribution to achievement.

4

◁▷

Is Competition More Enjoyable?

ON SPORTS, PLAY, AND FUN

> That ain't no way to have fun, son.
> — Randy Newman

From the sober issues of individual achievement and economic productivity, we now turn, quite literally, to fun and games. Even if competition cannot be defended on the basis of its contribution to performance, proponents may insist that certain competitive encounters are enjoyable. Relatively few people profess to enjoy the frantic scramble for position, prestige, and profit that occurs in the workplace; the reference here is almost always to recreational pursuits. The defense of competition has shifted, so to speak, to the weekend.

Competitive games obviously are different from the competition we find in most other realms of our lives. "To live with the hope of immediate success and fear of immediate failure in an enterprise which has no significance beyond itself is a totally different thing from living permanently on the brink of that abyss into which competitive industry throws its failures," as John Harvey put it.[1] Still, the fact that competition is so unpleasant — often the source of considerable anxiety — in other contexts is worth keeping in mind as we ponder the question posed by this chapter's title. The pressure to be a winner on the playing field is not totally different from its counterpart in the office, so we are entitled to a measure of skepticism as we consider the prospect of competing for enjoyment. In any case, there is no denying that this country's most popular recreational activities are structured so that one individual or team must triumph over the other. Sports, in particular, are competitive by definition,* while, in practice, the extent of their competitiveness is such that George Leonard referred to our "overblown, institutionalized, codified worship of winning."[2]

Just as competition is the salient characteristic of sport, so is sport, in turn, a prominent feature of American life. The vernacular of football and baseball has leached into the language. We take for granted the astonishing fact that results of various competitive games automatically qualify as "news"; indeed, every daily newspaper and local television news program in the country reserves space or time to report on the results of these pastimes. Certain sporting events are among our most popular forms of entertainment, with the Super Bowl being watched in some forty million households each year. Sociologist Harry Edwards once set out, rather playfully, to determine "the relative impact of sports as opposed to politics." At the height of a hotly contested mayoral election in New York City, he stopped 150 passers-by and asked them, "Who is going to win?" Thirty-four people named one of the candidates and most of the rest said, "The Mets."[3] Even if the story is apocryphal, finally, it may be worth thinking seriously about the college administrator who once said he wanted a university that the football team could be proud of.

THE QUESTION OF PLAY

Except for the people who depend on them for their livelihood, sports, like all other forms of recreation, presumably exist for no other reason than to provide enjoyment. Thus we are led to ask whether competition truly represents the most enjoyable arrangement we can imagine in a recreational setting. Let us narrow the question by first considering the phenomenon of play, which might be thought of as enjoyment in its purest form. (The next section will address the larger question of whether we need to compete to have fun.) As I noted in chapter 2, one of the classic works on the subject, Johan Huizinga's *Homo Ludens,* goes so far as to suggest that play and competition are virtually synonymous.[4] Other students of play, such as Roger Caillois and Jean Piaget, have treated competition as a kind of play, if not its prototype. I want to challenge not only Huizinga's

---

*I follow common usage in taking *sports* to refer to certain competitive games that require vigorous physical activity. It follows, then, that *noncompetitive sports* is a contradiction in terms, but the extent of competition in a given sporting event is not fixed.

extreme position but even the weaker claim that competition and play are compatible. To do so, it makes sense to begin by defining play.

A review of the literature[5] discloses considerable overlap — which is not to say consensus — among previous efforts. Huizinga, who goes on to argue that play is the touchstone of civilization itself, offers a rather broad definition. He proposes that play is "a free activity standing quite consciously outside 'ordinary' life as being 'not serious,' but at the same time absorbing the player intensely and utterly . . . occurring within certain limits of space, time, and meaning, according to fixed rules."[6] The critical part of this definition, I think, is the reference to freedom. Play must be chosen voluntarily, and it is chosen because it is pleasing. Other activities are commended to us because of their utility, their instrumental worth. Play, by contrast, is intrinsically gratifying; it is an end in itself. We do not play in order to master a particular skill or to perform well, although these may be adventitious results. The master aphorist G. K. Chesterton perfectly captured the spirit of play when he said, "If a thing is worth doing at all, it is worth doing badly."[7] Results will not matter, in other words, if we love what we are doing for its own sake. (That this idea seems peculiar, if not unnerving, to us is evidence of how little room our worldview makes for play.) Play represents a "process orientation," a concern for what one is doing in itself, as opposed to a "product orientation," in which one's activity is justified by what it contributes to some other goal. Play, quite justifiably conceived as the opposite of work, has no goal other than itself.

This is not to say that play cannot turn out to be useful or cannot be encouraged for heuristic purposes. Adults, who are typically less process-oriented than children, often read serious business into children's play. It is seen as (1) an opportunity for the player to experiment with roles and cultural norms, develop the ego, and enhance a sense of personal competence;[8] (2) an opportunity for the player to work through unconscious fears;[9] (3) a diagnostic tool by which the psychotherapist can gain access to the child's inner life; and (4) a way to instill certain values in a child.[10] The player, though, does not engage in play for these purposes — or for any purpose except to have fun. As soon as play becomes product-oriented or otherwise extrinsically motivated, it ceases to be play.

Two final points need to be made about the nature of play. First, while we sometimes speak of play as relaxing, it tends not to be homeostatic (that is, motivated by a need to produce a state of rest or balance). On the contrary, the person at play delights in seeking out challenges and overcoming them.[11] Second, while all human behavior is in some sense rule-governed, and while we can and do play within specific structures, the tendency of play to be free suggests that it is also more or less spontaneous. Thus, rules, while not precisely inimical to play, may frustrate its purest expression. An activity might be said to approximate play in inverse proportion to the extent to which it is rule-bound.

·   ·   ·

Huizinga was probably not the first and certainly not the last to complain that "with the increasing systematization and regimentation of sport, something of the pure play-quality is inevitably lost. . . . The real play-spirit is threatened with extinction."[12] He wrote that in 1944, and books lamenting sport's fall from grace, as it were, are still being published regularly.[13] The diminution of playfulness is often high on the list of grievances. It is said that our leisure activities no longer give us a break from the alienating qualities of the work we do; instead, they have come to resemble that work.

The chief reason our recreation is like our work is that it has become more competitive. But sports, by definition, have always been competitive. By virtue of this fact, sports never really qualified as play in the first place. Although it is not generally acknowledged, most definitions of play do seem to exclude competitive activities. First, competition is always highly rule-governed. "If the participants do not mutually define themselves as opponents, rules are mostly irrelevant," writes Frank Winer.[14] (To be precise, they are not *always* irrelevant in the absence of competition. We will see shortly that noncompetitive games, too, can have rules. Still, rules tend to be more numerous and more rigid in competitive activities.) Second, competition often is motivated by a search for approval, which is an extrinsic motivator and thus irrelevant to play. Third, and most important, competition is goal-oriented striving *par excellence*. Novak is quite right to insist that "play is to be played exactly because it *isn't* serious; it frees us from seriousness."[15] Competition, though, is very serious indeed — unavoidably so. Consider the following passage from Joseph Heller's novel *Something Happened*, in which a school gym teacher is complaining to the narrator about the behavior of the latter's son:

> "I try to give him a will to win. He don't have one. . . . He passes the basketball deliberately — he does it deliberately, Mr. Slocum, I swear he does. Like a joke. He throws it away — to some kid on the other team

just to give him a chance to make some points or to surprise the kids on his own team. For a joke. That's some joke, isn't it? . . . When he's ahead in one of the relay races, do you know what he does? He starts laughing. He does that. And then slows down and waits for the other guys to catch up. Can you imagine? The other kids on his team don't like that. That's no way to run a race, Mr. Slocum. Would you say that's a way to run a race?"

"No." I shake my head and try to bury a smile. Good for you kid, I want to cheer out loud . . . for I can visualize my boy clearly far out in front in one of his relay races, laughing that deep, reverberating, unrestrained laugh that sometimes erupts from him, staggering with merriment as he toils to keep going and motioning liberally for the other kids in the race to catch up so they can all laugh together and run alongside each other as they continue their game (after all, it is only a game).[16]

Contrast the whimsical, mischievous, other-affirming, spur-of-the-moment delight depicted here with the grim, determined athletes who memorize plays and practice to the point of exhaustion in order to beat an opposing team. Clearly competition and play tug in two different directions. If you are trying to win, you are not engaged in true play. Several investigators have come to just this conclusion. M. J. Ellis, in his study of play, writes that "feelings of power, trophies, or money for the winners . . . are extrinsic to the process. To the degree that competition is sustained by extrinsic pressures, it is not play. . . . In this sense, competition and play are antithetical."[17] Similarly, Günther Lüschen remarks that the more sport is extrinsically rewarded, "the more it tends to be work; the less it tends to be play."[18] But we do not even need to point to the trophies and the money: The very experience of having beaten someone else is extrinsic to the process itself. The presence of this reward structure in competition disqualifies it as play.

Here, too, is sociologist Harry Edwards:

The bracketing off of play from the activities of daily life predisposes it to restriction within nonutilitarian bounds. Thus, none of the following actors could be considered as engaging in play: the office worker or executive who takes part in a badminton match [substitute "squash" or "handball"] in order to relax and take a break from the rigors of work; the professional participant in football; the high school and college football participants who see themselves as preparing for a college athletic grant-in-aid or for a professional career; persons who engage in such activities as card games with the goal of winning or gaining financially; or participants in checkers or chess.[19]

Edwards inexplicably stops short of making his generalization explicit: the point is that *any* activity whose goal is victory cannot be play. Another perspective is provided by psychologist Mihaly Csikszentmihalyi's study of the "flow" experience — a sensation of total, unselfconscious involvement that is associated with play. Csikszentmihalyi comments that if basketball "is not as flow-producing as composing music, for instance, that is at least partly because its competitive structure fails to isolate the activity from everyday life, making concentration and the loss of ego relatively more difficult."[20]

William A. Sadler, finally, notes that sports not only are not isolated from daily life (as play must be), but they actively train participants for that life as it is lived in our society.

> Athletes often are well aware that what they do is not play [he writes]. Their practice sessions are workouts; and to win the game they have to work harder. Sports are not experienced as activities outside the institutional pattern of the American way of life; they are integrally a part of it. . . . In other words, the old cliché is true: "Sports prepare one for life." The question which must be raised is: "what kind of life?" The answer in an American context is that they prepare us for a life of competition.[21]

Competitive recreation is anything but a time-out from goal-oriented activities. It has an internal goal, which is to win. And it has an external goal, which is to train its participants. Train them to do what? To accept a goal-oriented model. Sports is thus many steps removed from play.

The argument here is not merely academic. Even when they do not talk explicitly about play, apologists for sport like to argue that it offers a "time out" from the rest of life. No matter how brutal or authoritarian sports might be, we are supposed to see them as taking place in a social vacuum. This claim has the effect of excusing whatever takes place on a playing field. (While governor of California, Ronald Reagan reportedly advised a college football team that they could "feel a clean hatred for [their] opponent. It is a clean hatred since it's only symbolic in a jersey.")[22] It also has the effect of obscuring the close relationship between competitive recreation and the society that endorses it.

That relationship, as Sadler saw, is reciprocal. Sports not only reflect the prevailing mores of our society but perpetuate them. They function as socializing agents, teaching us the values of hierarchical power arrangements and encouraging us to accept the status quo. In a 1981 study of children's competitive soccer and hockey programs in New York and Connecticut, Gai Ingham Berlage was even more specific: "The structural organization of [these] programs resembles the structural organization of American corporations. . . . The values stressed in children's competitive sports are also similar to corporate values."[23] It is hardly a coincidence, then, that the most vigorous supporters of competitive sports — those who not only enjoy but explicitly defend them — are political conservatives (Michael Novak, Spiro Agnew, and William J. Bennett are among those quoted in these pages) or that interest in sports is highest in the more politically conservative regions of the country.[24]

Writing in the *Journal of Physical Education and Recreation,* George Sage observed that

> organized sport — from youth programs to the pros — has nothing at all to do with playfulness — fun, joy, self-satisfaction — but is, instead, a social agent for the deliberate socialization of people into the acceptance of . . . the prevailing social structure and their fate as workers within bureaucratic organizations. Contrary to the myths propounded by promoters, sports are instruments not for human expression, but of social stasis.[25]

Sport does not simply build character, in other words; it builds exactly the kind of character that is most useful for the social system. From the perspective of *our* social (and economic) system — which is to say, from the perspective of those who benefit from and direct it — it is useful to have people regard each other as rivals. Sports serve the purpose nicely, and athletes are quite deliberately led to accept the value and naturalness of an adversarial relationship in place of solidarity and collective effort. If he is in a team sport, the athlete comes to see cooperation only as a means to victory, to see hostility and even aggression as legitimate, to accept conformity and authoritarianism. Participation in sports amounts to a kind of apprenticeship for life in contemporary America, or, as David Riesman put it, "The road to the board room leads through the locker room."[26]

One of the least frequently noticed features of competition — and, specifically, of its product-orientation — is the emphasis on quantification.[27] In one sense, competition is obviously a process of ranking: who is best, second-best, and so forth. But the information necessary to this process is itself numerical. There are exceptions — one can usually determine who crosses the finish line first just by watching, for example — but competition usually is wedded to specific measures of how much weight, how many baskets, how much money, and so on.

Competition not only depends on attention to numbers — it shapes and reinforces that attention. By competing, we become increasingly reliant on quantification, adopting what one thinker calls a "prosaic mentality" in the course of reducing things to what can be counted and measured — a phenomenon that obviously extends well beyond the playing field.[28] Play, by contrast, is not concerned with quantifying because there is no performance to *be* quantified. Like the seven-year-old athlete who was asked how fast he had run and replied, "As fast as I could,"[29] the process-oriented individual gladly gives up precision — particularly precision in the service of determining who is best — in exchange for pure enjoyment. He who plays does not ask the score. In fact, there is no score to be kept.

Within the confines of a competitive game, finally, there exists a phenomenon that could be called "process competition." This is the in-the-moment experience of struggling for superiority that is sometimes seen as an end in itself rather than simply a step toward the final victory. Thus, college football coach Joe Paterno: "We strive to be Number One . . . But win or lose, it is the competition which gives us pleasure."[30] For enjoyment to derive wholly from the process of besting another person is more than a little disturbing, but it does more nearly qualify as play since it is a process. What we need to ask is whether it really is the essence of competitive recreation. After waxing rhapsodic over process competition, Stuart Walker writes: "The philosophy [athletes] hear announced is that the game's the thing, participation is what matters. But the questions they hear asked are, Who beat whom? Who got the medals? . . . The modern competitor feels that to be approved, admired, respected, he must win."[31] In fact, there is nothing especially modern about this phenomenon. The concern with who beat whom — the "product" of the event — is hardly an accidental feature of competition; it is not an afterthought that just receives too much attention these days. To structure an event as a competition is often to cause participants to struggle against each other in-the-moment, but it is first and foremost to designate a goal: victory. Process competition may exist as a pocket of play (though a rather ugly version thereof), but the overall effort is unavoidably product-oriented. It should come as no surprise, moreover, to find that this pocket will shrink: the last chapter considered the corrosive effect of extrinsic motivation upon intrinsic motivation. Any gratification from the game itself can be expected to diminish when an external reward (victory with its trappings) is introduced. And there is no competition without such reward. Overall, then, we must conclude that the pure pleasure of play excludes sports and all other competitive activities.

FUN WITHOUT COMPETITION

To have challenged the identification of competition with play is not to have proved that competitive recreation cannot be enjoyable. After all, various rule-governed, product-oriented activities do fill our leisure hours. In particular, the popularity of sports does not seem to depend on whether they qualify as play. Enthusiasts of such competitive recreation often specify — and commend to us — its unique advantages, so these qualities bear close examination. They are as follows:

EXERCISE: The player improves his or her overall fitness, strength, and coordination.

TEAMWORK: Team sports are said to promote a kind of group loyalty and *esprit de corps* that can come only from working toward a common end such as the defeat of the opposing team.

ZEST: Without competition, we are sometimes told, recreational activities would hold no interest for us. Even critic George Leonard concedes that competition, "like a little salt . . . adds zest to the game and to life itself."[32] Betty Lehan Harragan uses the identical metaphor: "The competitive impulse adds salt and pepper, the spices, to an otherwise bland and tasteless dish of aimless exercise. . . . Competition is what makes it all worthwhile."[33]

PUSHING ONESELF: In striving to win, the competitor is said to test his or her limits, to feel invigorated from the challenge, to experience a sense of sweaty accomplishment that is immensely gratifying.

STRATEGY: Against an opponent, one has to think on one's feet as well as move them. To anticipate and counter the other's moves is to overcome an obstacle, which can be a lot of fun.

TOTAL INVOLVEMENT: Sports aficionados frequently describe the complete experiential engagement that they enjoy, the sense of having transcended time. This theme is enthusiastically sounded in two books written as paeans to sports: *The Joy of Sports* by Michael Novak and *Winning: The Psychology of Competition* by Stuart Walker, a doctor whose free time is spent on competitive sailing. The same concept is described by several psychologists: Abraham Maslow's "peak experiences" involve just such an unselfconscious immersion, while Robert Jay Lifton calls this "experiential transcendence" and Mihaly Csikszentmihalyi, as we have already seen, refers to it as the "flow" experience.[34]

EXISTENTIAL AFFIRMATION: In sweeping, almost mystical language, several sports enthusiasts maintain that while competing one tastes perfection, asserts one's freedom, and triumphs over death. For Walker, the competitor "enters a world of challenge, risk, and uncertainty and for a few moments re-creates it in accordance with his own design."[35] For Novak, the winner wrestles with "being" and "nonbeing." "Each time one enters a contest, one's unseen antagonist is death. . . . [It is] the exercise of freedom . . . against the darkness." One becomes "more than self," "expressing the highest human cravings for perfection."[36] For Gary Warner, competition is "so valuable [because] . . . every life needs moments of exultation."[37] And for A. Bartlett Giamatti, former president of Yale University, winning has "a joy and discrete purity to it that cannot be replaced by anything else."[38]

THRILL OF VICTORY: Some people, finally, report that beating someone else is an intrinsically, irreducibly satisfying experience.

A careful analysis of these enjoyments reveals that none of them (except the last) actually requires competition. William Sadler put it well:

> We should not make the mistake of equating meeting a challenge with competition. There are many sports which can be exciting, can test the abilities and skills of individuals and groups, can bring harmony and happiness, can provide healthy exercise and an exhilarating change from the workaday world, can reunite persons with nature, can express . . . the highest human values, which do not require competition.[39]

Let us take each advantage in turn. First, physical fitness obviously does not require competition — or even any rule-governed game. As the recent popularity of aerobics and other noncompetitive approaches to exercise makes clear, one can get a fine workout without a win/lose structure. Second, the camaraderie that results from teamwork is precisely the benefit of cooperative activity, whose very essence is working together for a common goal. Intergroup competition — the creation of a common enemy, a We-versus-They dynamic — is not necessary for group feeling, as I will show in chapter 6. The distinguishing feature of team competition is that a given player works with and is encouraged to feel warmly toward only half of those present, so cooperative activities are twice as desirable if this is our criterion. (This comparison actually understates the case since it does not account for the suspicion of, contempt for, and even violence toward one's opponents that one finds in team sports.)

As for the claim that competition, like salt, provides zest, the metaphor may be more apt than its proponents intended. Salt contributes to hypertension and also becomes a substitute for the natural flavor of the food itself. Only when we come to depend on salt does food seem bland without it. Similarly, competitive games create something very like an addiction so that recreation without the possibility of victory becomes less exciting. "It is not only work that is poisoned by the philosophy of competition," wrote Bertrand Russell, "leisure is poisoned just as much. The kind of leisure which is quiet and restoring to the nerves comes to be felt boring."[40] Perhaps a better analogy is provided by the task of trying to interest a TV-dependent child in reading. Books quickly exhaust an attention span that has been attenuated by television. We might benefit from being weaned from what one critic called "the glass teat" just as we may eventually know greater pleasure from unsalted food and noncompetitive recreation.

The dependence on sports to provide a sense of accomplishment or to test one's wits is similarly misplaced. One can aim instead at an objective standard or attempt to exceed one's own previous record* — the latter being what some people mean by the unfortunate phrase "competing with oneself." Such noncompetitive striving can be very satisfying indeed, and cooperative games requiring skill and stamina similarly seem no less invigorating for the absence of a winner and a loser at the end. These games, as I will show shortly, often involve considerable strategy, proving that the obstacle to be overcome need not be another person. If large numbers of people defend competition because they want to be challenged, this cannot be surprising: it is the same confusion between achievement and competition that we

---

*The psychologically destructive elements of competition are not automatically eliminated by avoiding interaction. Any individual activity that can be quantified can also be turned into a compulsive effort to push oneself forward. This neurotic driven-ness is a sad enough spectacle in the workplace; it becomes that much worse when it spills over into recreational activities — such as running, swimming, or weightlifting — where the point is supposed to be enjoyment.

have encountered before, and it is understandable given the hegemony of competitive games in our culture. Within such a game, striving *is* striving for victory, so someone who knows only competitive games will come to equate the two.

The experiential engagement that includes transcending time does not require physical activity of any sort, let alone competitive activity in particular. Maslow and Lifton scarcely mention sports in their descriptions of the phenomenon, while Csikszentmihalyi, who does focus on recreation, not only includes dancing and rock-climbing, but specifically states that competitive sports are less conducive to the flow experience than noncompetitive activities. It may be possible to achieve this sensation in competition (including in battle), then, but one hardly needs to compete in order to experience it.

Precisely the same is true of the grander claims made to the effect that sports represents an existential triumph. Anyone oriented toward spirituality to the extent that playing football becomes a religious experience is likely to find many activities have a similar effect. Rebelling against death and flexing one's freedom, meanwhile, were central themes for Albert Camus, but his attention was directed toward love and creation, and toward rebellion against injustice, as the means for living these things. Camus's later works reflect a special emphasis on the need to work *with* others and affirm their humanity as part of our own expression; this principle is reflected in the writings of such religious existentialists as Martin Buber and Gabriel Marcel, both of whom probably would have been appalled to hear competition cited as an example of affirmation and transcendence.

This leaves only "thrill of victory": the base justification that it feels good to prove oneself better than someone else, to succeed by making another player or team fail. In practice, it is difficult to isolate this rationale from the others; the gratification thought to result from competition itself can in many cases be traced to a feature that actually does not require competition at all. Thus, it is difficult to know how widespread is the irreducible enjoyment of beating other people. To whatever extent it does exist, though, we cannot just assert that someone who claims that this does bring him pleasure is mistaken: "You only *think* it's fun." On the other hand, it is quite appropriate to explore the psychological dynamics of such enjoyment, and I will attempt this in the next chapter. For now let me simply say that the pure pleasure of competitive triumph is first cousin to the pleasure of punching someone in a state of manic excitement. Perhaps the best we can do in either case is to insist that because of both its psychological origins and its consequences to all parties concerned, this is a pleasure we should not nurture and encourage. Both as individuals and as members of a society, we would do better to take our enjoyments from more constructive (or at least less destructive) pursuits. The free-time activities we set up for ourselves and our children ought not to reflect and perpetuate our least admirable inclinations.

. . .

The constituents of enjoyment that are used to argue for recreational competition actually do not, for the most part, require competition at all. We do not need to try to beat other people in order to have a good time. Why, then, are competitive games so popular? The first response is that the extent of their popularity may not be so great as we imagine, at least if participation is our standard of measure. Some people, of course, avoid or drop out of sports because of disabilities, other interests, an aversion to exercise, and so forth. But a huge proportion dislike such activities precisely because they are competitive. "For many children competitive sports operate as a failure factory which not only effectively eliminates the 'bad ones' but also turns off many of the 'good ones,' " writes sports psychologist Terry Orlick. "In North America it is not uncommon to lose from 80 to 90 percent of our registered organized sports participants by 15 years of age."[41] Research in nonrecreational settings clearly shows that those who are not successful in initial competitions continue to perform poorly,[42] thereby setting up a vicious cycle. Other research suggests that these individuals drop out when given the chance.[43]

Many people who defend competition actually encourage this, invoking a "survival of the fittest" ethic. School athletic programs implicitly do likewise, concentrating resources where the very best athletes are. Expressions of indifference or even satisfaction when many participants drop out of a given activity are disturbing under any circumstances, but they seem particularly outrageous when it comes to recreation. What, after all, is the point of games if not to encourage widespread participation and enjoyment? This sort of attitude has become self-defeating, moreover, since many accomplished (or potentially excellent) athletes find the competitive pressure distasteful and onerous enough to bail out.

The situation has reached the point that dozens of magazine articles and popular books are published every year decrying the exces-

sive competitiveness of children's athletic programs, such as Little
League baseball. The spectacle of frantic, frothing parents humiliating their children in their quest for vicarious triumph is, of course,
appalling, and the cheating and violence that result will be explored
in a later chapter. For now, consider the simple fact that these experiences with competition are so unpleasant as to lead uncounted children to leave sports permanently.

Is this mass exodus a bad thing? Unlike most critics, I am not at all
sure that it is. In order to regret the fact that children are turned off
to sports, you must assume that competition *itself* is unobjectionable if
not delightful — and that potential athletes are alienated only because
they receive too large a dose. I propose instead that while ill effects
increase in direct proportion to the extent of competitiveness in an
activity, it is competition itself that is to blame (although its effect will
depend on an individual's temperament and specific experiences).
There is no threshold of competitiveness below which we could expect all children to enjoy sports. From this position, it follows that
disaffection with sports should not occasion regret on our part —
unless children generalize their reaction to all physical activity.

My point in showing that the competitive dimension of sports is
creating millions of future ex-jocks is not to argue that this is a
tragedy but only to show that the link between competition and fun is
largely spurious. Some people quit sports outright, while others may
continue participating from force of habit, out of an unrelenting need
to demonstrate their competence, or for any one of a number of other
reasons that have little to do with genuine enjoyment. For all the
emphasis on competitive recreation in our culture, then, its popularity is not what it first appears.

But what of those who *do* enjoy such activities? A cross-cultural
perspective is helpful here, reminding us that the members of some
societies not only cooperate in their work but also enjoy noncompetitive pastimes. The unavoidable implication is that we are socialized to
regard competition as an indispensable part of having a good time.
We have been raised to associate recreation with the win/lose model
that pervades our society, to assume that having fun means someone
has to wind up a loser. We enjoy what we have been brought up to
enjoy. A child in our culture knows without thinking how he is supposed to have fun with his friends: play a game whose structure
requires that not everyone can be successful. When he does not play,
he goes to watch other people play such games. This socialization is so

thorough that alternatives to competitive recreation are almost inconceivable to many of us. "How can it be a game if no one wins?" we ask, with genuine puzzlement — the same puzzlement occasioned by talk of cooperative education.

In resisting competitive recreation, most liberal-minded writers have implicitly or explicitly suggested that we should place less emphasis on winning. We can stop keeping score, for example, and try to shift our focus from winning to having fun. "Every young athlete should be judged *only on his own or her own*," sports psychologists Thomas Tutko and William Bruns urge. "They should not be measured in terms of how they do as compared to others."[44] This amounts to suggesting that we be less intentionally competitive even within a structurally competitive environment. Like most reformist approaches to systemic problems, this recommendation is likely to be limited in its effectiveness. Where we are unable or unwilling to abandon competitive games, minimizing the importance of who wins and who loses does indeed make sense. But the usefulness of this approach depends on the kind of game involved.

It is relatively easy to stop keeping score in golf, which consists of two or more people taking turns at independent pursuits and then comparing their success at the end. A more interdependent competitive activity, however, makes this far more difficult, if not impossible: "One simply cannot expect two tennis players to place their shots in such a position, provided they did possess the necessary skill, as to assist in the increased development of the opponent. This is simply not the *reason* for the sport as we know it today. The name of the game *is* win."[45] It is not merely that tennis is structured so that only one player can win in the end, but that in each instant of play success consists in hitting the ball so that one's opponent is unable to return it. All team sports, as well as most competitive indoor games (e.g., chess, poker), are more like tennis than like golf. In such cases, wellmeaning exhortations to be less competitive seem naive at best.

To say we find competition enjoyable because we are socialized to do so is not merely to say that we teach our children to *want* to win, but that we offer them games where the whole point is to win. The only real alternative is noncompetitive games, and children, as we saw earlier, generally prefer these games once they are exposed to them — an extraordinarily suggestive finding.

But how are such games played? All games involve achieving a goal despite the presence of an obstacle; in football, for example, the goal is to move a ball from one point to another, and the obstacle is the other team. In noncompetitive games, the obstacle is something intrinsic to the task itself rather than another person or persons. If coordinated effort is required to achieve the goal, then the game becomes not merely noncompetitive but positively cooperative. Such coordination invariably involves the presence of rules. While competitive activities are particularly dependent on rules — and inflexible rules, at that[46] — it is not the case that the only alternative to competition is the "Caucus-race" described in *Alice in Wonderland,* in which participants "began running when they liked, and left off when they liked."[47] While such an activity more closely approximates pure play, noncompetitive games are generally rule-governed. Thus, the presence of rules does not imply the presence of competition.[48]

Partly because they do have rules, noncompetitive games can be at least as challenging as their competitive counterparts. They are also a good deal of fun, and, like the Caucus-race, can have the happy result that " '*Everybody* has won and *all* must have prizes.' "[49] Consider musical chairs, an American classic for small children. In this game, a prototype of artificial scarcity, x players scramble for x − 1 chairs when the music stops. Each round eliminates one player and one chair until finally one triumphant winner emerges. All of the other players have lost — and have been sitting on the sidelines for varying lengths of time, excluded from play. Terry Orlick proposes instead that when a chair is removed after each round, the players should try to find room on the chairs that remain — a task that becomes more difficult and more fun as the game progresses. The final result is a group of giggling children crowded onto a single chair.

This is only one of hundreds of noncompetitive games that Orlick has invented or discovered, and they have been collected in *The Cooperative Sports and Games Book* (1978) and *The Second Cooperative Sports and Games Book* (1982). Another good collection is Jeffrey Sobel's *Everybody Wins: Non-competitive Games for Young Children* (1983). As early as 1950, Theodore F. Lentz and Ruth Cornelius published their own manual of cooperative games. Among them are Cooperative Chinese Checkers, the object of which is not to move one's marbles faster than the other player but to coordinate the two players' movements so that they reach their respective home sections simultaneously. In Cooperative Bowling, similarly, the purpose is to "knock down the ten pins in as many rounds as there are players" — a very challenging task indeed.[50] Other cooperative games require that each player make a specified contribution to the goal, that all the players attempt to reach a certain score (as in Cooperative Shuffleboard, which requires a modified court), or that all players work together against a time limit. Orlick also has defused the competitive element in more traditional games by manipulating the scoring procedures or constitution of teams. In "Bump and Scoot" volleyball, for example, a player who hits the ball over the net immediately moves to the other side. "The common objective [is] to make a complete change in teams with as few drops of the ball as possible."[51] A small family business in Ontario, Canada, called Family Pastimes manufactures about fifty indoor games for adults and children, including cooperative versions of chess, backgammon, go, Scrabble, and Monopoly. There may well be other such publications and products, but with a little ingenuity anyone can invent or reinvent many such games. Change the rules of Scrabble, for example, so that the two players try to obtain the highest possible combined score. Allow each to see the other's letters. The game is at least as challenging with this adaptation, given that one must be thinking about saving certain spaces on the board for one's partner and anticipating later developments from a joint perspective.

Note the significance of an "opponent" becoming a "partner." This is far more than a semantic transformation: the entire dynamic of the game shifts, and one's attitude toward the other player(s) changes with it. Even the friendliest game of tennis cannot help but be affected by the game's inherent structure, as described earlier. The two players are engaged in an activity that demands that each try to make the other fail. The good feeling that attends a cooperative game — the delight one is naturally led to take in another player's success — may cast in sharper relief the posture one routinely adopts toward other players in competitive games — perhaps without even being aware of it. Cooperative recreation can, in other words, allow us to experience retrospectively just why competition is less enjoyable — and less innocuous — than we may have otherwise assumed.

5

◁ ▷

Does Competition Build Character?

PSYCHOLOGICAL CONSIDERATIONS

A competitive culture endures by tearing people down.
— Jules Henry,
Culture Against Man

Let us pretend for a moment that the popular mythology about competition's being necessary for excellence is true — which is to say that all of the evidence reviewed in chapter 3 does not exist. Does this clinch the case for the desirability of competition? Not at all. The effect of competition on productivity tells us nothing about its effect on the competitors themselves. When we shift our attention from performance to people, we find more than enough reason to oppose competition.

The question of psychological impact, while generally ignored by empirical studies, is a matter that touches us far more deeply than productivity. Even people who have never questioned the shibboleths about the usefulness of competition will confess that the ways it affects them and the people around them can be profoundly disquieting. Given a real choice, most of us will try to avoid unusually competitive organizations or activities. More significantly, we will steer clear of unusually competitive people. When we say that someone is "one of the most competitive people around," we generally are not recommending that person as a friend. Such people, in fact, find themselves mistrusted if not simply avoided by others. When we become aware of our own competitiveness, we often become uncomfortable — a fact that is all the more remarkable in light of the professional rewards for acting this way. All told, the alleged benefits of competition do not keep most of us from reflecting on how "the rat race" of American life takes its psychological toll.

This chapter will explore that toll carefully. It will argue that the closer we look, the more damaging we find competition to be. Its effects are sometimes insidious, sometimes practically invisible, but almost always unhealthy. Before considering the consequences of competition, however, it might be wise to look into its causes. The two questions, as we shall see, are more closely related than they might seem.

WHY WE COMPETE

The reasons for trying to be successful at the price of other people's failure are numerous and multilayered. Sociologists and anthropologists explain this, as they do most things, in terms of cultural norms. These norms congeal into structural competition, and can become so entrenched that noncompetitive alternatives virtually disappear from the workplace, the schoolroom, and the playing field. This structural competition also shapes our attitudes and beliefs, thus encouraging intentional competition. Behavioral psychologists, meanwhile, are less concerned with norms than with the specific ways we are trained to be competitive. We are directly rewarded for displaying such behavior, and we also watch others being rewarded for it. As we saw in chapter 2, the combination makes for an effective learning program. In simple language, we act competitively because we are taught to do so, because everyone around us does so, because it never occurs to us not to do so, and because success in our culture seems to demand that we do so.

It does not deny the usefulness of these explanations to supplement them with the perspective of depth psychology, which is concerned with the unconscious roots of our behavior. Psychoanalysts have contributed incalculably to the way we think about ourselves, but one of their central contributions — whose relevance to competition will shortly become clear — is the idea that we may unconsciously turn a wish or fear into its opposite. This can happen in several ways. Unacceptable feelings of hostility (toward people we are expected to love, for example) may be transposed into exaggerated concern. A dangerous attraction may present itself as extreme aversion, as in the classic case of the latent homosexual who incessantly ridicules gays. Finally, powerful anxieties may be dealt with by exposing oneself continuously to that which is dreaded; thus, the person who is deeply fearful of being alone may avoid other people and make a fetish of privacy in an unconscious attempt to overcome the fear.*

Only when we understand these reversals can we grasp one of the most fascinating legacies of depth psychology: the insight that two apparently opposite kinds of behavior can be traced to the same underlying dynamic. If we are faced with someone who makes a fetish of privacy, we may come to see this as a manifestation of separation anxiety. But if we come across someone who hangs on to other people, even refusing to let go of destructive relationships, we may decide that this, too, can be understood in terms of separation anxiety. Very different — indeed, antithetical — personality patterns often converge once we peer beneath the surface.

This phenomenon is nowhere clearer than in the case of self-esteem. Mr. A is usually seen as conceited; he talks constantly about his talents and accomplishments. Ms. B, on the other hand, is almost paralyzed by her enduring conviction that she will fail at anything she tries. Both individuals, as almost everyone in this post-Freudian age will suspect, may have low self-esteem.

But now let us add Mr. C, most of whose waking hours are devoted to seducing women, and Ms. D, who acquires power over others by eliciting personal details about their lives while revealing nothing of herself. Then there is Mr. E, who schedules his day with inordinate precision and is upset by anything that does not go according to plan. Ms. F, by contrast, is always late for appointments, extremely forgetful, and unable to direct her own life. More than any other single formulation, lack of self-esteem can profitably be used to make sense of all these individuals. In fact, we could continue through the alphabet with other personality capsules without exhausting its explanatory utility.

As a concept, self-esteem is extremely useful for those trying to understand why people act as they do. As a reality, the importance of high self-esteem simply cannot be overstated. It might be thought of as the *sine qua non* of the healthy personality. It suggests a respect for and faith in ourselves that is not easily shaken, an abiding and deep-seated acceptance of our own worth. Ideally, self-esteem is not only

---

*Psychoanalysts usually refer to the first two phenomena as examples of a defense mechanism called "reaction formation," while the third is classified as "counterphobic" behavior.

high but unconditional; it does not depend on approval from others, and it does not crumble even when we do things that we later regret. It is a core, a foundation upon which a life is constructed.*

The absence of self-esteem, conversely, is at the root of a wide range of psychological disorders. Karen Horney, a theorist to whose work we will return, described all neurosis in terms of the absence of "basic confidence" in oneself.[1] Another neo-Freudian, Harry Stack Sullivan, wrote that "customarily low self-esteem makes it difficult indeed . . . to maintain good feeling toward another person."[2] In his major work, the humanistic psychologist Abraham Maslow similarly observed that "satisfaction of the self-esteem need leads to feelings of self-confidence, worth, strength, capability, and adequacy, of being useful and necessary. But thwarting these needs produces feelings of inferiority . . . [that] in turn give rise to either basic discouragement or else compensatory or neurotic trends."[3] Indeed, as one social psychologist recently concluded, "few psychologists would disagree that positive self-esteem is essential to emotional well-being"[4] or that negative self-esteem is integral to our understanding of many kinds of problems — from depression to narcissism, from severe character disorders to alienating patterns of dealing with other people. While we must always be on guard against reducing the complexity of human beings to a tidy theoretical framework, there is very little about our personalities that does not flow from how we feel about ourselves.

I have argued that our behaviors sometimes turn our true motivations inside out, and I have emphasized the crucial role of self-esteem in the personality. When we put them together, these two ideas allow us to understand competitiveness more fully. Specifically, I would offer the proposition that *we compete to overcome fundamental doubts about our capabilities and, finally, to compensate for low self-esteem.*†

---

*"Self-esteem" (which, unmodified, is sometimes a shorthand for unconditional or high self-esteem) does not imply that one cannot or will not accurately gauge one's limitations. In fact, those with high self-esteem are better able to achieve the perspective and sense of safety that permit such assessments. People who appear to think that they can do no wrong are more likely suffering from *deficient* self-esteem. Likewise, self-esteem is not at all inimical to growth; a fundamental trust in oneself is very different from what we call "self-satisfaction," which breeds stagnation.

†This proposition and the ones that follow are not hypotheses; they cannot be proved or disproved in the scientific sense. Rather, their persuasiveness will depend on the extent to which they capture our experiences and enhance our understanding of others and ourselves. For people who are particularly competitive, this line of thinking may ring true only after more careful introspection; we usually resist seeing our own behavior as unhealthy.

Let us consider the two components of this formulation in turn. First, competing at a given activity reflects insecurity with a particular facet of ourselves. We try to be the best lover (or have the most lovers) because we fear we are not really lovable. We want to have a more impressive job than others because we suspect our skills are actually deficient. Second, these specific capacities stand for a global sense of inadequacy — that is, low self-esteem. Lovableness or professional skills in these examples can be said to recapitulate the whole self. To say that we become invested in certain qualities is to say that they are placeholders for our very selves.

Sometimes, though, there are no such placeholders — no mediating qualities or skills. Some competitive desires (to earn more money, for instance, or be judged more attractive) can be understood immediately in terms of low self-esteem. This is even more evident with people whose competitiveness is not restricted to a particular activity — those who turn almost every interaction into a contest. Here we see most sharply how the need to be best at anything at all, which is to say at *everything*, actually represents an attempt to stave off a persistent and pronounced sense that one is fundamentally no good. The important point, though, whether or not there is some mediating quality involved, is that competitiveness eventually comes down to self-esteem.

Doing well, as we saw earlier, is different from doing better than others. This is nowhere clearer than in the case of their respective motivations. All of us enjoy the sense of accomplishment that comes from being particularly good at something. Sometimes it is convenient to assess that performance by comparing it to those of other people. But the individual who feels good about herself and is simply interested in doing well does not go out of her way to outperform others. She does not seek out relative judgments. She is content with a sense of personal satisfaction, sometimes buttressed, depending on the activity, by a consideration of absolute standards. (She can check out the number of questions she answered correctly or see how long it took her to run the mile.) The desire to be better than others feels quite different from this desire to do well. There is something inherently *compensatory* about it. One wants to outdo in order to make up for an impression, often dimly sensed, of personal inadequacy. Unlike the joy of flexing one's muscles or intelligence, which is sufficient unto itself, one wants to be stronger or smarter than others in order to convince oneself at some level that one is a good person. If competition has a voice, it is the defiant whine of the child: "Anything you can do, I can do better." A competitive society is a chorus of such voices. And the energy of such a society (to switch metaphors) is provided by a combination of "obsessional thinking, anxiety over personal inadequacy, and hostility requiring an outlet,"[5] according to Lawrence Frank.

It is not quite accurate to talk about "wanting" to beat others, however. Because one is responding to the push of self-doubt rather than the pull of accomplishment, competition is more a need than a desire. Maslow has distinguished between "B" (for Being) and "D" (for Deficit) motivations with respect to love and cognition. B-love, he said, is characterized by an almost aesthetic pleasure, an admiration for a specific person. D-love is experienced as an urgent need, a drive whose object is generic. We can think of psychological growth as the process of moving from D to B: only after our basic needs are met can we proceed to a higher level of loving and thinking and living.[6] Notwithstanding the finery in which it comes dressed, competitiveness is in reality a deficit-motivated trait. Being good at an activity is something we choose to do; outperforming others is experienced as something that we *have* to do. Our self-esteem is at stake.

The obvious way to verify that competition is more a need than a desire is to see what happens when a competitive person is deprived of a chance to compete. Or, since the need to compete is really the need to win, we can watch what happens when such an individual loses. The result is more reminiscent of depriving a hungry person of supper than of removing a choice dish from the gourmet. One extraordinarily competitive businesswoman, who was transferred to a noncompetitive work environment, described her situation to me recently as being like "suffering a slow death." This sort of reaction suggests that one's very self is on the line. Lending further credence to this is the fact that the original urge to compete may be experienced as a fear of *not* competing. "Whenever I enter a competition," said one marathon runner, "I'm fearful and apprehensive to try it. It's hard to go to the line. But I'm fearful and apprehensive not to try it."[7] To do something because the psychological consequences of not doing it are too painful is quite different from doing something because of the gratification it provides. When the opportunity to alleviate that pain is removed, we would expect a reaction of anxiety or panic or rage. Thus, the actual reactions of competitive people support the proposition that it is low self-esteem that motivates them. For many, competition feels like damage control. The point is not so much triumph as vindication, not so much winning as not losing. To lose is to have one's inadequacy exposed. It is dreadful confirmation of precisely what was feared in the first place. One struggles to win, to be better than everybody else, in a desperate, vain effort to convince oneself of one's value.

But how can competition be deficit-motivated if so many very competitive people are excellent at what they do? We sometimes need to be reminded that actual competence has little to do with self-esteem. No matter how many times they hear it, many talented or attractive people do not truly believe in their talent or attractiveness. Their quest to be noticed, rewarded, acknowledged is endless; it is like pouring liquid into a container with a hole in the bottom. This is because the source of the need lies not in the specific characteristic but in the underlying matter of low self-esteem. Recognition for some particular ability doesn't address the matter of overall worth. There is nothing surprising, therefore, about the fact that even some very capable individuals need to prove how much better they are than others.

If competitiveness is inherently compensatory, if it is an effort to prove oneself and stave off feelings of worthlessness, it follows that the healthier the individual (in the sense of having a more solid, unconditional sense of self-esteem), the less need there is to compete.* The implication, we might say, is that the real alternative to being number one is not being number two but being psychologically free enough to dispense with rankings altogether. Interestingly, two sports psychologists have found a number of excellent athletes with "immense character strengths who don't make it in sports. They seem to be so well put together emotionally that there is no neurotic tie to sport."[10] Since recreation almost always involves competition in our culture, those who are healthy enough not to need to compete may simply end up turning down these activities.

To all of this one might object that deficient self-esteem does not in

---

*The reverse of this proposition — that the less a person competes, the healthier he must be — does not follow, however. This is because competitiveness is not the only manifestation of low self-esteem. Many people, in fact, *avoid* competition because of their sense of inadequacy. In light of the psychological reversals spoken of earlier, this is not inconsistent with the fact that others embrace competition for the same reason. And thus it should not be surprising that children with low self-esteem in some circumstances showed the least competitive behavior[8] or viewed without pleasure the prospect of working at a competitive job.[9]

itself cause competition. This is quite true. Whereas many psychoana-lysts, including Freud himself, tend to inspect the individual in a vacuum, the neo-Freudians have emphasized that human develop-ment, intrapsychic conflicts, and everything else take place in a partic-ular environment. In order to do their job adequately, psychologists must be students not only of the individual or the family but of the culture as a whole. Thus we return to the sociological emphasis on norms and structures with which this section began. Each culture provides its own mechanisms for dealing with self-doubt. In our culture, which is wedded to the assumption that life is a zero-sum game, one of the chief mechanisms is competition. It is America's com-pensatory mechanism of choice. Low self-esteem, then, is a neces-sary but not sufficient cause of competition. The ingredients include an aching need to prove oneself *and* the approved mechanism for doing so at other people's expense. When we have both, we have millions of people who try to feel better by making the next person feel worse.

Many people insist that they compete because success in our culture demands that they do so. There is considerable truth to this, and, on one level, competing can be viewed as a deliberate strategy. But on another level, striving to outdo others is also the result of psychologi-cal needs, and it is in this respect that competing can be said to be unconsciously determined. In fact, these two levels are themselves causally related. The social norms that induce us to compete can shape our psychological state, as I will try to show in the next section. Just as it is important not to wave away structural forces by pretend-ing that the problem is unique to unhealthy individuals, so we must not completely reduce competition to these structural forces, ignoring its psychological basis. The average American does not talk in terms of "structural forces" or "sociohistorical determinants"; she says she competes because she fears being left behind if she doesn't. But this account, while grounded in an accurate reading of our society, is not exhaustive. The urge to become a winner can (and should) also be traced to underlying feelings of worthlessness.

I do not want to shy away from the incendiary implications of all of this. To suggest in effect that many of our heroes (entrepreneurs and athletes, movie stars and politicians) may be motivated by low self-esteem, to argue that our "state religion" is a sign of psychological ill-health — this will not sit well with many people. Yet most of these same people will agree there is something amiss with the fellow who cannot walk into a room without wondering whether he is the strongest or wealthiest, or his date is the prettiest, or his name is the best known. How is it that so many people accept the latter but resist the former?

The answer lies in the popular assumption that anything which is dangerous or unhealthy in excess is just fine in moderation. While we grow concerned, for example, about the person who can't function when a loved one leaves for even a short while, we find nothing wrong with wanting to spend *some* time with one's beloved. The problem is with the excess, and the extreme version of love (if it can still be called love) could be said to be qualitatively different from more moderate desire.

But is competition like love? In a society where most of us are somewhat competitive, we like to reassure ourselves by assuming that it is. Actually, though, "moderate" competitiveness and "excessive" competitiveness are only quantitatively, rather than qualitatively, different; their psychological causes are identical. A small handgun may be less noticeable or powerful than a bazooka, but the purpose of the two instruments is essentially the same. The hypercompetitive person may stand out in a crowd because of the urgency of his need to be the best, but the psychological forces at work are no different from those operating in people whose level of competitiveness is judged acceptable. He is just more extreme.

Imagine a society in which interrupting other people was encouraged — just as competing against other people is encouraged in our own. Suppose further that some people interrupted so frequently and so loudly that they never heard anyone but themselves. These people would likely be criticized and assumed to be neurotic for their need to interrupt in this fashion. Everyone else would be seen as engaging in "healthy" interruption. Leave aside the question of whether interrupting is an unwelcome behavior; we are not dealing here with consequences but only with motivation. What should be clear is that the need to overpower others in conversation once in a while is different only in degree from the need to overpower others in conversation all the time. The psychological source of this behavior does not change with its intensity or frequency. And the same is true of competition.

If we can use the word *unhealthy* to describe behavior that is deficit motivated or that arises from low self-esteem, then our startling conclusion must be that "healthy competition" is a contradiction in terms.

It is not the excess that is problematic in the relentlessly competitive individual; it is the need to compete in itself. The relentless competitor is simply more noticeable, and he affords us the luxury of condemning him while sparing ourselves. In reality he is but an exaggeration of ourselves. "What we see in neuroses," said Horney, "is only a magnified picture of what is often normal in a competitive culture."[11] It is rather like the person who unthinkingly cheats on his tax returns but becomes outraged over instances of "real" theft. The big-time thief is really just the ordinary tax cheat writ large. The technique is different, as is the number of zeroes, but the motivation is exactly the same.

To be sure, we should not pass lightly over the fact that some people are more desperate than others in their need to win. This desperation can be measured in terms of the felt intensity of the drive, the number of arenas in which it is experienced, the amount of pain associated with losing, and so forth. The extremely competitive individual often will project his own view of the world onto the situations he confronts, approaching virtually any environment as if it were objectively set up as a contest. Life is a constant struggle to stay on top, to be number one. Everything is seen in zero-sum terms, so that someone else's good fortune will occasion his anger or self-pity — as if there were only so much happiness to go around. Even when he is not personally involved, his first inclination will be to construe any situation or encounter he hears about in competitive terms. He assumes others are as competitive as he,[12] that rivalry is the way of the world, that his status is always on the line.[13] Now obviously not every person with a streak of competitiveness about him is in such dire straits. It makes sense to speak of a continuum: the greater the desperation, the lower the self-esteem, the worse the problem. The point, then, is not that anyone who is at all competitive is in urgent need of psychological help, but rather that significant differences in degree do not always make a difference in kind. The need to be better than others has the same essential psychological origin, regardless of its severity.

Finally, it should be noted that the need to win and the terror of losing are both exacerbated by the fact that most competitions are public events. It is not the simple fact of victory, the private knowledge of one's superiority, that is used to overcome doubts about oneself. It is the fact that this victory will be noticed. If competition's destination is reassurance about oneself, its vehicle is approval from others. Not just winning but the acceptance that is supposedly attendant on winning — this is the appeal of competition. In sports, acceptance may mean the approval of the coach, as former pro football player Dave Meggyesy writes:

> Although I played time and again with injuries, and told myself I was doing this because it was in the best tradition of the game, it was really to get approval from the coaches. . . . We moved in an Oedipal lockstep: the more approval they gave me, the more fanatically I played.[14]

The "Oedipal" reference here signifies, of course, that the coach functions as a parent surrogate. In her interviews with competitive swimmers, Jenifer Levin found that " 'love,' a 'family,' the approval of a significant paternal figure . . . came up time and time again when women spoke of the early motivation to compete."[15] The psychoanalytic equation runs something like this: winning = coach's approval = parent's acceptance = acceptance of self (self-esteem).

Often approval is sought from spectators, too, and this is not only true of athletic contests. Other kinds of competition offer the same sort of reinforcement. There are the officemates who quickly learn of one's promotion, the dinner companions who listen to one's games of one-upmanship, the other students who see the honor roll posted on the wall. Furthermore, as Stuart Walker observes, competitors seek to be admired and accepted by those they compete against. The competitor "returns to competition repeatedly, and seeks to perform well, partly in order to please them. He knows that all the world loves a winner, and believes that his competitors will love him when he wins."[16] Where there is no love, envy will do. Where approval is not forthcoming, it will simply be assumed. To be number one is, above all, to be noticed, whether by parent, coach, observer, or opponent. To be noticed is to be someone; to be a someone soothes a trembling self-esteem.

WINNING, LOSING, AND SELF-ESTEEM

A personality attribute could be considered healthy with regard to its effects even if it seemed unhealthy in light of its motivation. So we ask: Is competitiveness a psychologically constructive force? Does the act of competing strengthen the shaky self-esteem that gave rise to it?

Such an effect might take place for the simple reason that living up to the norms of one's culture is rewarding. When we do what is expected of us, we feel better about ourselves, and competitiveness is expected of us in this particular society. Where competition is *not* the norm, we would expect that this effect would not exist — and we would be right.[17] But even in a very competitive society, the cultural norm effect is overshadowed by the dynamics of competition itself. These dynamics, unhappily, have just the opposite result, undermining rather than bolstering self-esteem.

In her studies of children in the mid-1970s, educational psychologist Carole Ames decided to see how children act under competitive conditions. She found that competition can cause people to believe they are not the source of — or in control of — what happens to them.[18] Besides its disturbing implications for self-esteem, this "external locus" also inhibits performance, according to Ames. People who do not see themselves as directing their own actions tend to be lower achievers — yet another explanation for the data showing that competition does not lead to higher productivity.

Other researchers have approached this question by looking for personality attributes that are correlated with competitiveness. This does not prove a causal relation, of course; the other characteristics may even be the *reason* for competitiveness rather than a result of it. The evidence, however, is highly suggestive. In 1981, two psychologists studied more than 800 high school students to see what other characteristics described those who were competitive. "Students reporting positive attitudes toward competitive relationships with others," they discovered, "are unique by virtue of their greater dependence on evaluation- and performance-based assessments of personal worth."[19] Far from having unconditional self-esteem, the way the competitive subjects viewed themselves depended inordinately on how well they did at certain tasks and on what others thought of them.

The studies concerned with structural competition have typically used alternative arrangements — notably cooperation — as points of reference. The question then becomes: which is the better way to elicit the kinds of traits we think of as healthy — by having people compete or cooperate? In a competitive society like ours, it is common to assume that cooperation discourages a strong sense of self, that it has a whiff of dependence about it. In fact, just the opposite seems to be true. From a review of seventeen separate studies, David and Roger Johnson concluded that "cooperative learning situations, compared with competitive and individualistic situations, promote higher levels of self-esteem and healthier processes for deriving conclusions about one's self-worth."[20] "Cooperativeness," they have written elsewhere, is "positively related to numerous indexes of psychological health such as emotional maturity, well-adjusted social relations, strong personal identity, and basic trust in and optimism about other people."[21] And while competition promotes an external locus of control, cooperation promotes an internal locus of control.[22] Those who work with, rather than against, others feel more in control of their own lives.

Other researchers have found much the same thing. When Elliot Aronson tried out a model of cooperative learning in elementary schools, he found that participating students "developed greater self-esteem than children in traditional classrooms."[23] Another sociologist, Ruth Rubinstein, used a written measure of self-esteem with children between the ages of ten and fourteen who attended either a competitive or noncompetitive summer camp. Self-esteem levels did not change significantly in the former camp, but they increased for both boys and girls in the latter.[24] Morton Deutsch has found that self-esteem is "more negative under the competitive as compared with the cooperative grading system."[25] From his cross-cultural work with children, finally, Terry Orlick arrived at the conclusion that "experiences in human cooperation are the most essential ingredient for the development of psychological health."[26]

Whereas cooperation apparently contributes to high self-esteem, competition often seems to have the opposite effect. Why should this be? The first part of the question is easier to answer: Cooperation, which involves sharing skills, is, as we have already seen, a more productive arrangement. The greater success it yields helps each participant feel better about himself. Second, cooperation promotes greater interpersonal attraction, as we will see in the next chapter. People feel valuable and valued when their success is positively related to that of others (rather than negatively related, as in competition).

That cooperation is healthy, then, should not be surprising. By the same token, competition's effect on performance and interpersonal regard may tell us something about its unhappy psychological consequences. But we can go further than this. There are several very good reasons why trying to outperform other people fails to allay the very self-doubt that gave rise to this behavior.

The simplest explanation is that most competitors lose most of the time. By definition not everyone can win, and, in practice, few do. In a one-on-one contest, the odds are 50–50; more commonly, competition is structured to produce a single champion and many more losers. If we feel impelled to prove ourselves by triumphing over others, we will feel humiliated when they triumph over us. To lose — particularly in a public event — can be psychologically detrimental even for the healthiest among us. At best, some exceptional individuals might emerge without *damage* to their self-esteem, but it is difficult to see how losing can *enhance* it. No one in a culture as competitive as ours is unfamiliar with the experience of being flooded with shame and self-doubt upon losing some sort of contest. And when we add the phenomenon of anticipating loss to the occasions of actually losing, it becomes clear that the potential for humiliation, for being exposed as inadequate, is present in every competitive encounter.

The more importance that is placed on winning — in the society, in the particular situation, or by the individual — the more destructive losing will be. "The greater the investment," as Stuart Walker put it, "the greater will be the grief when we fail." When "emphasis is placed not upon what is accomplished but upon what is publicly recognized, not upon the demonstration of competence but upon winning," then the competitor eventually "comes to believe . . . that he is defective and deserves to fail."[27] Walker is describing the process of internalizing failure, of coming to equate losing with being a loser. It is a gradual process, but it is taking place at any given instant in our playing fields and classrooms, our offices, and even our homes.

As we might expect, this terrible process takes place more rapidly and decisively with those whose self-esteem is precarious to begin with. Self-doubt will predispose such people to expect failure, to be crushed by it when it comes, and even, as we will see later, to help bring it about. But competition does not kick only those who are already down. Ames found that even "high self-concept children tended to be more self-critical following failure in competitive than noncompetitive encounters."[28] For these high self-concept children, losing meant not only becoming very critical of themselves but also coming away with "inflated perceptions of the others' ability and deservingness." Over time, Ames speculates, this could "begin to undermine their own positive self-appraisal and contribute to a learned helplessness belief. Further, the differences in self–other perceptions may have negative implications for future social encounters."[29]

Frank Ryan, a sports psychologist, argues that the adverse effects of losing are particularly severe among those who are better competitors. Thus,

> following a failure in competition the poor competitor is usually relaxed, in good spirits, and even talkative. In contrast, the good competitor who has had a bad day is difficult to live with. He becomes temporarily a bitter, morose, and sometimes unpleasant person.[30]

Ryan, who is not a critic of competition, is concerned here only with what he takes to be temporary consequences. Bitterness and unpleasantness, he says, are indicators of a successful competitor, which is what we are strongly encouraged to become. Not low self-esteem but a winning record is what brings about these effects, he is contending.

The larger point is that anyone, regardless of self-esteem, can be shaken by loss. And apart from the actual number of times someone loses, losing is always possible and often anticipated. It is an inherent part of competition, and thus there is reason to think that competition is always psychologically damaging to some degree. But even this does not tell the whole story. Psychological health implies unconditionality — the conviction that one is a good person regardless of what happens. In competition, by contrast, one's self-esteem depends on the uncertain outcome of a contest, and this means that self-esteem is conditional. At best, one feels reassured and confirmed only sometimes. Since the idea is for self-esteem to exist without any strings attached, "sometimes" defeats the whole purpose.

Despite this conditionality, though, doesn't winning contribute to the high self-regard that is the undergirding of mental health? Can't it offset the ill effects of losing for the victor? Victory, after all, is the goal — both the structural objective of the competitive encounter and the psychological rationale for participating. And winning is a tonic: no one who has been awarded a prestigious prize or clinched a title or defeated a long-standing rival can deny the thrill of triumph.* De-

---

*That victory is the stuff of many dreams is clear from the popularity of mass culture entertainments that trade on it. A stock cinematic device, for example, consists in having a likable character come from behind in the final moments of a big game to win the trophy. The more obstacles he or she has had to overcome, the better. In the last few years, the same essential formula has been used for movies about basketball, karate, ice-skating, skiing, horseback riding, wrestling, boxing, football, baseball, dancing, and auto and bicycle racing. Of course, the vicarious thrill experienced in a movie theater is a pallid substitute for being a winner oneself, and the very demand for fictional triumphs bespeaks the inability of actual competition to satisfy our needs.

spite this excitement, however, winning fails to satisfy us in any significant way and thus cannot begin to compensate for the pain of losing. This is true, first, for structural reasons. Winning offers no genuine comfort because there is no competitive activity for which victory is permanent. Whether we are talking about chairman of the board, Super Bowl champions, or the perversely prized status of Most Heavily Armed Nation, to become number one is immediately to become the target for one's rivals. King of the Mountain is more than a child's game; it is the prototype for all competition. Subjectively, the status of being envied and targeted by others may be superficially gratifying, but it is also deeply unsettling. Objectively, the reality is that it is only a matter of time until one becomes a loser again. Even after winning the Super Bowl, writes George Leonard, Dallas Cowboys coach Tom Landry still wore his "mask of fear."

> The problem is this [he continues]: even after you've just won the Super Bowl — *especially* after you've just won the Super Bowl — *there's always next year.* If "Winning isn't everything. It's the only thing," then "the only thing" is nothing — emptiness, the nightmare of life without ultimate meaning.[31]

In some arenas, the problem isn't just having to win again next year but having to compete in a new population. The high school valedictorian finds her status counts for very little upon entering college; the contest (with the pressure) begins all over again. The writer competes against other writers for the opportunity to be published; then he must compete within his publishing house for attention and money so that his book will be adequately publicized and distributed; then he struggles for attention and sales, reviews and prizes. No sooner does the performing artist beat out others in an audition than she must begin the process again — perhaps at a higher level of prestige. Even a competition enthusiast like Harvey Ruben is forced to concede that "many strong competitors, upon reaching the summit of their aspirations . . . see their goals receding constantly the higher they climb on the social or economic scale. The discovery, ultimately, that 'making it' is often a hollow gain is one of the most traumatic events that the successful competitor can experience."[32]

The problem runs far deeper than these structural limitations, however. Apart from the objective absence of finality to competitive success, there is the psychological gulf between euphoria and fortification of self-esteem. One can get a powerful high from any number of substances and feel temporarily good about oneself and the world, but it would be difficult to argue that a snort of cocaine or a shot of whiskey can improve one's psychological health in any meaningful way. Winning similarly feels good but fails to address the underlying dynamics that gave rise to competitiveness in the first place. First, the focus in competition is on proving one's superiority to other people, and this, as we have seen, is not at all the same thing as establishing one's competence. In terms of both motivation and the skills involved, winning and succeeding are two different things. To beat any number of others is not a satisfying indicator of actual skill or accomplishment.

Second, and more important, even if one could demonstrate competence at a specific skill just by winning, this very specificity is limiting. One may be able to make oneself wealthier or more attractive than the next person, but no such particular quality gets to the heart of the matter. We want to be assured that we are fundamentally good, but goodness is difficult to pin down. The more desperate we are to believe in it, the more it seems to elude us. Thus we resort to reifying this goodness, externalizing it, literalizing it, trying to capture it in a specific quality. But being number one with respect to this quality can never satisfy the deeper, more global need for which it stands.

The proof for this argument lies in the ephemerality of victory's thrill. We may be giddy with delight for a time, but we soon come back to earth. In fact, those who compete on a regular basis report that both the intensity of the pleasure and its duration decline sharply over time — precisely as one develops a tolerance to a drug. After winning seven gold medals at the 1972 Olympics, Mark Spitz reported, "I became sick of myself. I never knew how far down someone could drop, especially after being up so high."[33] Even without such a pronounced mood shift, any competitor knows that the effects of winning are not lasting, and this alone tells us of its irrelevance to psychological health. Self-esteem is not a passing thrill.

But if we are not really reassured or satisfied even when we win, what do we do when the pleasure fades? We compete again. This answer is immediately obvious to us based on our experience but quite puzzling when we pause to consider the situation rationally. Instead of turning to other, more promising, means for meeting our needs, we return to the very approach that has failed us. Although boat racer Stuart Walker is, like Ruben, an enthusiast of competition, he accurately identifies this cycle:

> Winning doesn't satisfy us — we need to do it again, and again. The taste of success seems merely to whet the appetite for more. When we lose, the compulsion to seek future success is overpowering; the need to

get out on the course the following weekend is irresistible. We cannot quit when we are ahead, after we've won, and we certainly cannot quit when we're behind, after we've lost. We are addicted.[34]

The act of returning again and again to a strategy that fails does indeed suggest that something very like an addiction is at work here. One thinks of the compulsive gambler: he loses money and is driven to make it back in the next hand (or race or game); he wins money and, unsatisfied, tries to win still more.

Instead of contributing to our self-esteem, then, beating other people contributes only to the need to continue trying to beat other people. The consequence of competition and the cause of competition are reciprocally related, just as the consequence and cause of drinking salt water. When we talk about competition, we are talking about a vicious circle: the more we compete, the more we *need* to compete. "Feelings of competition cover the deeper feelings of insecurity. The competitive feelings then produce a new set of feelings of failure, lack of confidence, and inadequacy."[35] Which, in turn, begets further competitiveness.

This cannot be conveniently dismissed as the profile of a neurotic individual, as we shall see shortly; it is a description of how competition itself works. The strength of this cycle is not uniform for all people, however. We would expect that the intensity of the effect of competition would reflect the intensity of the original need to compete. This means that those whose self-esteem is lowest, whose psychological need is greatest, are those who will be most viciously hooked on competition. The effect is most powerful where the need is most pronounced. The other variable that affects the strength of the cycle is the importance placed on winning in the specific situation — and, in the long run, by the entire society. The more we reward being number one, the more we contribute to an addiction to competition. This is an addiction that takes hold despite competition's failure to contribute to our self-esteem — or, rather, precisely because of this failure. And since, as we have seen, both winning *and* losing have undesirable effects, it seems clear that the problem lies with competition itself.

DENYING THE DAMAGE

At the end of the Monty Python movie *The Life of Brian,* scores of people who have been nailed to crosses begin bobbing their heads and singing a cheerful ditty called, "Always Look on the Bright Side of Life." This irreverent sequence neatly satirizes a relentless, Candide-style optimism which should be quite familiar to us. One need not look very hard to find examples — often ludicrous, sometimes touching — of people trying to convince themselves that their suffering has a hidden purpose, that there is some underlying advantage to any terrible event that befalls them.

That there may be no reason for pain, no ultimate purpose to human life, no redeeming justification for loss — these recognitions can be too much to bear. And while less dramatic, self-defeating personality attributes and unpleasant situations can evoke the same frantic process of justification. Thus Karen Horney points out that people who are morbidly dependent and self-effacing may believe these characteristics mean they are loving and humble; those who are detached and alienated from others may congratulate themselves on their freedom. We see the same thing in the case of people who are competitive — or whose lives are immersed in a competitive environment. Competing drags us down, devastates us psychologically, poisons our relationships, interferes with our performance. But acknowledging these things would be painful and might force us to make radical changes in our lives, so instead we create and accept rationalizations for competition: It's part of "human nature." It's more productive. It builds character.

The last of these beliefs is the most remarkable. Empirical claims about inevitability or performance are relatively distant from ourselves, and an argument about them can be carried on in a wholly intellectual fashion. But the contention that competition is psychologically beneficial contradicts the intuitive knowledge that I believe most of us possess. Despite direct awareness of what competition does to people (to say nothing of the kind of analysis offered here), some individuals persist in claiming that its effects are constructive. This is a powerful example of how it is possible to adjust our beliefs so as to escape the threatening realization that we have been subjecting ourselves to something terrible, that we have internalized a corrosive personality attribute.

Also, this may be why "the traditional assumption that competitive sport builds character is still with us today in spite of overwhelming contrary evidence."[36] Apart from the absence of data to support it, the adage itself is exceedingly slippery. One sports sociologist reports that of all the writers he has encountered who repeat this assertion, not a single one actually defined the word *character,* let alone provided evidence for the claim. *Character* was "typically assumed to be understood as desirable and wholesome, or it was defined implicitly by association with such adjectives as 'clean-cut,' 'red-blooded,' 'upstanding,' 'desirable,' and so forth."[37] For Douglas MacArthur, competition is a "vital character builder" in the sense that it "make[s] . . . sons into men."[38] This definition, besides being irrelevant to half the human race, tells us nothing about which features of being a man are considered desirable.

In what may be the only explicit research of this claim, Ogilvie and Tutko could find "no empirical support for the tradition that sport builds character. Indeed, there is evidence that athletic competition limits growth in some areas." Among the problematic results they discovered were depression, extreme stress, and relatively shallow relationships. Ogilvie and Tutko also found, as mentioned before, that many players "with immense character strengths" avoid competitive sports. Finally, they discovered that those who do participate are not improved by competition; whatever strengths they have were theirs to begin with.[39]

Presumably related to the idea of "character" are such notions as self-confidence and well-being — as well as self-esteem. Popular magazines often contain articles asserting that competition promotes these things, and such unsubstantiated claims find a ready audience. Other proponents of competition take the more moderate view that while competition may well damage self-esteem, it does not *always* have this effect. Richard W. Eggerman, a philosopher, offers three such arguments, which will be considered in turn.

First, he proposes that competition may be harmful only to children, who "may be peculiarly liable to dangers of comparisons of relative worth in a way that adults are not."[40] It is true that much of the research on competition's psychological and performance-related effects has been conducted with children. However, this probably reflects the accessibility of children as research subjects and the special interest in children on the part of the investigators rather than an assumption that adults do not experience the same effects. Certainly, most theoretical studies of competition, including this one, are also concerned with its consequences for adults. Children may well be "peculiarly liable" to its dangers, as Eggerman suggests, because of their greater malleability. Indeed, a recent panel of sports medicine experts urged that children under the age of eight or ten "should not participate in organized, competitive sports . . . [because] they could impede children's psychological, sociological and motor skill development."[41] But this does not argue against the unfortunate consequences of competition at any age. The dynamics of self-esteem that make competition detrimental in our youth are not features that we outgrow. And research on the benefits of cooperation is "just as strong for adults as it is for students."[42]

Second, Eggerman contends that competition is damaging only for the insecure or neurotic competitor. The problem, in other words, rests with the individual and not with competition itself. This is the same assumption we encountered in the last chapter with critics who suggest that we can leave competitive games in place so long as players care less about who wins them. It is also similar to an assumption we will consider later — namely, that cheating and violence are aberrant behavior for which the wrongdoer alone, and not competition, per se, should be blamed. Now, clearly, structural competition will not elicit the same degree of intentional competition (and its attendant features) from everyone. But as should also be clear by now, even solid self-esteem does not confer talismanic protection from the effects of losing. Likewise, the vicious circle engendered by the hollowness of winning is not an event to which only neurotics are admitted — although the speed at which the circle turns may be a function of psychological health.

The hypothesis that the problem lies with (some) competitors and not with competition itself becomes increasingly less plausible each time we see the same essential pattern repeated with different people and in diverse arenas. It is like the psychoanalyst who one day realizes that the similarity of his patients' problems (e.g., dependency and self-punishment rituals in women) points to something beyond these individuals, to values woven into the institutional fabric of our society. In this case, we must recognize that the problem rests squarely with the structure of mutually exclusive goal attainment. We need not know anything about the individuals involved to see the destructive potential of a system that says only one of them can be successful. As Morris Rosenberg put it in his book *Society and the Adolescent Self-Image,* "Whenever a value is set forth which can only be attained by a few, the conditions are ripe for widespread feelings of personal inadequacy."[43]

Eggerman's last argument is that losing doesn't have to be experienced as failure. This is true, first, he says, because "only when one could reasonably have expected to win does losing mean failing."[44] He offers the case of someone who runs a major marathon faster than he has ever done before but is nevertheless beaten by a well-known athlete. Surely such a loss will not be construed as failure. This qualification is quite sound — and it has the unintended effect of proving that success and winning are two very different things (see chapter 3). It is true that there are some contests in which people take part without hope of winning. Losing is less likely to represent a crushing blow in cases of low intentional competition (that is, where one is not concerned about being number one). But the relevant question is what proportion of competitive encounters this describes. Most of us enter (or are involved, willy-nilly) in contests where winning is entertained as a distinct possibility — distinct enough so that losing hurts.

Eggerman goes on to assert that most competitors "usually do entertain fairly realistic impressions of what they are capable" and thus are cushioned from the pain of loss.[45] In the absence of hard data, this is a very dubious judgment indeed. But more important, it ignores the structural component of competition — the simple fact that losing *means* failure in a competitive context. It also ignores the fierce pressure to win and the stigma of losing that attend most contests. Only in extraordinary situations, such as a major marathon, for example, can one opt out of this context and assign another meaning to loss.

Consider a team of children that has just lost a game. Having been carefully instructed to be "good sports," they chant: "Two, four, six, eight, who do we appreciate?" — and then name the victorious team. But the chant is perfunctory and the kids are dispirited, resentful, sullen. As adults, we manage to camouflage our feelings more effectively when we congratulate the winner. But this is largely a matter of going through the motions of pretending that losing is not important. However generous our disposition or high our self-esteem, we can scarcely help but feel the brunt of a loss given the nature of competition itself and the powerful forces of a competitive society. Being a "good loser" is a matter of rearranging our face and affecting an attitude. In no way does this posture touch (or reflect) the actual ramifications of loss.

It is at best an exercise in self-deception to insist to ourselves and our children that losing should not matter. It is obvious to a six-year-old that it matters very much, because she has been told this repeatedly and in various ways. One cartoon has a Little League coach giving a pep talk to a small boy: "Okay, old buddy, get in there and play the game win or lose. But remember, nice guys finish last, there's no such word as chicken, and every time you lose you die a little." An article in a magazine for young women contains the boldface heading: "Don't worry about failure" — even though readers have been instructed just four sentences earlier that "the point of playing games is to learn that the object is to try to win."[46] Stuart Walker reverses himself within a single sentence: "Everyone makes mistakes ('he who makes the fewest wins')."[47]

These illustrations are unusually blatant, but the same sort of mixed messages are given and received constantly. For every proclamation along the lines of "It's how you play the game that counts" or "Making the effort is the important thing" or "*All* these kids out here today are winners," there are several powerful reminders that no one has the right to celebrate except number one. The simultaneous presence of these two levels of socialization throughout our culture has been observed for many years. "While paying respectful homage to cooperative ideals," wrote May and Doob in the 1930s, "we go right on with our competitive system."[48] In the 1950s, John R. Seeley's classic study of suburban life turned up the same phenomenon. In order to succeed, he said, the child "must compete but he must not *seem* competitive. The school deals with the dilemma by overtly 'promoting' cooperation . . . and by covertly 'tolerating' competition."[49] In the 1970s, yet another set of social scientists described our "rather schizophrenic condition" whereby "encouragement of cooperative behavior . . . [is] confined to moralistic maxims . . . [while] schools and other institutions in our society focus on developing competitive behaviors."[50]

Apart from the harms of competition, one could argue that this "double-bind"[51] represents a disorienting, destructive pattern in itself. The point here, though, is simply this: to argue that competitors cope well with failure is usually to mistake appearance for reality. The appearance of someone untroubled by loss probably reflects the "moralistic maxims" he has been taught. The other, far more substantial message he has absorbed concerns how important winning really is, how much it really does matter. In his panegyric to sports, Michael Novak writes:

> No use saying, "It's only a game." It doesn't feel like a game. The anguish and depression that seize one's psyche in defeat are far deeper than a mere comparative failure — deeper than recognition of the

opponent's superiority. . . . A game tests, somehow, one's entire life. It tests one's standing with fortune and the gods. Defeat is too like death.[52]

His florid language aside, Novak is simply describing the psychological destructiveness of losing, the threat to self-esteem. This is a threat that is only papered over with appearances of graceful defeat. It is a threat that is neither mitigated by the "realistic" perceptions of competitors nor magically outgrown when we reach adulthood. It is a threat intrinsic to the win/lose model that is then exacerbated by a culture which brutally dismisses whatever is not number one.

One final argument in behalf of competition needs to be examined. This is the position that while losing may indeed be construed as failure, this is not really a bad thing. On the contrary, some people tell us, failing keeps us from becoming "too big for our britches" and prepares children for the hard knocks of life. This argument is rarely propounded by psychologists and other serious students of human behavior, but it is widely heard nonetheless and so deserves a response.

It is surely valuable to learn that one cannot always be successful. One runs into obstacles both internal (a creative block, for instance) and external, and it is appropriate to realize that this is a fact of life. Infantile omnipotence fantasies are best laid to rest. However, some people go much further than this and romanticize failure so as to make it seem more bearable. This tendency represents the same need to convince oneself of the usefulness of pain that was discussed at the beginning of this section. Once this motivation is set aside, it becomes clear that the value of failing is very limited indeed. Most frustrations are psychologically redundant and often positively harmful.

The position that children, in particular, ought to compete in order to get used to losing is based on a largely discredited assumption of human development — namely, that depriving children is the best way to prepare them for the rude shocks of life. The hypothesis cannot be neatly confirmed or disconfirmed empirically, but its converse is actually far more plausible, not to mention more humane: it is unconditional *acceptance* in our early years that best allows us to deal with rejection; it is an initial sense of *security* that helps us to weather the problems we will later face. Again, it may be true that some limited acquaintance with failure is useful. But parents who systematically withhold approval or pleasures from their children or deny them the chance to experience success typically have unconscious reasons for doing so, such as shoring up their own doubtful self-esteem or trying to punish their parents for depriving *them*. These hidden agendas are then simply rationalized as being in the child's best interest. The idea that we are best prepared for unpleasant experiences by being exposed to unpleasant experiences at a tender age is about as sensible as the proposition that the best way to help someone survive exposure to carcinogenic substances is to expose him to as many carcinogens as possible in early life.

Even if we grant a limited usefulness to the experience of failure, furthermore, it is important to emphasize that this experience need not involve losing in competition. One can fall short of one's *own* expectations and develop all the appropriate virtues of tenacity and discipline. Competitive loss is a particularly noxious kind of failure, one that contains messages of relative inferiority and that typically exposes one to public judgment and shame. "Let it be granted that men should face mortal risks when they are seasoned to it and be schooled to self-reliance under stern adversity," writes John Harvey. "It may still be found possible to secure these ends without making men, so much as now, the enemies of their neighbours."[53] To say that failing has its value, then, is not at all to justify competition.

COMPETITION AND ANXIETY

Its effect on self-esteem, as serious as it is, does not exhaust the psychological consequences of competition. This section will consider the matter of insecurity and anxiety; the following section will touch on still other effects. Many are closely related to self-esteem, but they merit individual attention nonetheless.

A number of psychologists have proposed that optimal human functioning presupposes a sense of security about the world — a confidence that it is a safe place and one's needs will be met. One's trust in the "world out there" is closely related to one's trust in one-self: if I cannot depend on what is around me, I will lack the means to accept myself — and I may even come to blame myself for the world as I experience it.

That the process of competing can threaten our sense of security will be obvious to anyone who has ever competed. One of the reasons competition interferes with productivity, as we saw in chapter 3, is that it can be not only unpleasant but an occasion for severe anxiety. This effect has been noted in several research projects. One study found that pupils performing a motor-steadiness task became more anxious when they had to compete.[54] Another experiment, involving undergraduates, discovered that competitively structured discussion sections made students feel "distinctly more tense and anxious than they did in the cooperative sessions." This anxiety went hand in hand with a "greater incidence of self-oriented needs and . . . [a loss of] self-assurance" — underscoring again the link between security and self-esteem.[55] Other investigators, meanwhile, have observed that "athletics can be a continual source of anxiety, even for the most talented players."[56]

We can identify three reasons that competition leaves us insecure and anxious. The first and most obvious is apprehension about losing. Regardless of talent or psychological healthiness, the experience of having to prove oneself by outperforming someone else is invariably unsettling, to say the least. The constant possibility of being defeated simply is not conducive to feeling secure. When we do actually lose, this effect is compounded in subsequent competitive encounters. The process soon takes the form of a self-fulfilling prophecy: the fear of losing makes it more likely that this is just what will happen. Apart from its effect on performance, of course, anxiety is undesirable in its own right. It is one more unhappy legacy of the race to win.

The second reason for our anxiety concerns feelings of apprehension about *winning*. Now this seems most paradoxical given that the whole point of competition is to win. But if we think about it, we realize that it is not uncommon for capable competitors to trip themselves up just as it seems they are about to triumph. Consider the case of athletes who "choke" in the final round, a phenomenon that only recently has become the subject of scholarly interest.[57] The psychoanalytic tradition helps us to see that this pattern is neither random nor inexplicable. Rather, such people are recoiling from winning in a deliberate (if unconscious) way.

Why should they do this? Orthodox psychoanalysts believe that the prototype of all competition is the Oedipal contest with the same-sex parent, the prize being the opposite-sex parent. The little boy, Freud tells us, is deeply conflicted about this contest, since he believes punishment (specifically, castration) will result if he is successful. Winning Mommy's love — then, later, the act of winning itself — is terribly threatening because of this anticipated consequence. Unconsciously, the presumed wrath of the father may turn victory into a prospect as dreadful as defeat.

Like many others, I find this explanation both fanciful and reductive. As it happens, there are two other possibilities that also make use of unconscious processes but do not require us to assume that an early childhood event neatly accounts for one's adult behavior. The first is simply that competitors may feel guilty for making other people lose and thus either punish themselves for doing so in the past or take steps to avoid doing so in the present.

The second explanation is that competitors may fear that the people they beat will become hostile toward them. Karen Horney has written at length about this reason for fearing victory. "In many neurotics anxiety concerning the hostility of others is so enormous that they are afraid of success, even if they feel certain of attaining it," she says. While this can be conscious, the neurotic more often is "aware not of his fear but of the resulting inhibitions. When such a person plays tennis, for example, he may feel when he is close to victory that something holds him back and makes it impossible for him to win."[58] What holds him back is the fear that the person he beats will resent him for this and dislike him. The relationship between the two people may suffer and the winner will feel cast off, disconnected, unwanted. Others may admire his victory, but the more substantial kind of approval that is closer to nurturance and love may be withdrawn, and it is the latter kind of acceptance that matters more. The "neurotic person automatically assumes that others will feel just as much hurt and vindictive after a defeat as he does himself,"[59] says Horney. He therefore has a strong incentive to avoid winning.

Horney's analysis is incisive, marred only by her assumption that it applies exclusively to neurotic people. What she describes is in fact very widespread. Hostility and aggression in competitive situations may perhaps be most pronounced in, but hardly are confined to, neurotics. As the next chapter will argue, aggression is intrinsically connected to competition itself, and the fear that one's relationship with others will be changed for the worse by competing with them is, in truth, a very reasonable concern. Horney is referring to the neurotic tendency to project one's own characteristics onto someone else, but in the case of competition, the other person's hostility may be quite real. To expect the loser to be sore is hardly a symptom of ill health.

This anxiety based on interpersonal tension (or the anticipation of it) is not confined to neurotics, then. What is more, it does not manifest itself only as a fear of winning. It is the dynamic of competition itself that elicits anxious feelings, and, to this extent, interpersonal-based insecurity should be understood as a third, independent reason that competition engenders anxiety — alongside fear of losing and fear of winning. The psychoanalyst Rollo May, in his pioneering interdisciplinary study of anxiety, came to the conclusion that *competition is "the most pervasive occasion for anxiety" in our culture.*[60] Given the scope and rigor of May's work, such an unqualified declaration is very powerful; it is not merely a careless generalization or a rhetorical flourish. His assessment should give pause to the most enthusiastic defenders of competition. The reason for competition's generation of anxiety, May continues, lies not in the psychopathology of particular neurotic people but rather in the very nature of competitive individualism, which he takes to be one of the defining features of American society. This competitive philosophy "militates against the experience of community, and that lack of community is a centrally important factor in contempora[ry] anxiety."[61] When people are defined as rivals, it is difficult to build an overall sense of community or establish a genuine connection with a particular other. "Anxiety arises out of the interpersonal isolation and alienation from others that inheres in a pattern in which self-validation depends on triumphing over others."[62]

May then makes another point about this process: like so much else about competition, it works in a vicious circle. Not only does competing make us anxious by threatening our relations with others, but it sets up a scenario in which we try to solve this problem by returning to the very strategy that gave rise to it.

> The culturally accepted method of allaying anxiety is redoubling one's efforts to achieve success . . . [so] the anxious individual increases his competitive striving. But the more competitive, aggressive striving, the more isolation, hostility, and anxiety. This vicious circle may be graphed as follows: competitive individual striving → intrasocial hostility → isolation → anxiety → increased competitive striving. Thus the methods most generally used to dispel anxiety in such a constellation actually increase anxiety in the long run.[63]

In sum, the security that is so vital for healthy human development is precisely what competition inhibits. We are anxious about losing, conflicted about winning, and fearful about the effects of competition on our relationships with others — effects that can include hostility, resentment, and disapproval. Today there is no shortage of articles, books, and, most recently, workshops to help us with these insecurities. Any hesitations we might have about beating other people are seen as problems to be managed, not unlike overeating.

This makes perfect sense. In a hypercompetitive society, resistance to competing naturally is defined as a weakness (albeit a treatable one). In a nation bent on waging war, soldiers who seem reluctant to kill people similarly are candidates for psychotherapy so they can be returned to normal. The analogy really is not farfetched because compassion, too, can be construed as a weakness if it is experienced in a competitive situation. Here, for example, is Stuart Walker's reaction to the appearance of generosity during a competitive encounter: "Nowadays, whenever I hear myself say, 'Well, let's give him a break,' I pull up short and ask myself, 'Are you surrendering?' . . . Whether deliberate or accidental all forms of surrender represent regression — relinquishing the joy of self-demonstration for the solace of protection and passivity."[64] Coaches and sports psychologists alike teach athletes to conquer their fears of losing, to overcome their apprehensions about winning, even to equate helping behavior with "surrender." And after a while we do not need to be ridiculed and dismissed as a "quitter": we internalize the message and savagely attack ourselves for our anxiety and our reservations.

But is a reluctance to make other people lose (with the attendant guilt) — or, for that matter, an unwillingness to put victory before friendship — really something to be gotten over? I would contend it is more correctly viewed as an incipient sign of health. There is an important message in our recoiling from competition, just as there is in the coughing fit of a first-time cigarette smoker. Our task is to reflect on those anxieties, to weigh the values involved, instead of simply setting about the task of anesthetizing our sensibilities so that we can more efficiently triumph over others.

·   ·   ·

The link between anxiety and performance has been documented. I have also said that anxiety or insecurity is undesirable in itself. But there are other manifestations of this psychological state — behaviors and physiological effects — that bear some mention. May, for example, notes that "the high incidence of ulcer has often been related to the excessively competitive life in modern Western culture."[65] The psychiatrist Herbert Hendin, an expert on suicide, names "competitive pressures" as a prominent contributor to the alarming rise in suicide rates among young people.[66] Elsewhere, he suggests that drug abuse is another consequence of our culture's "voracious competitiveness."[67] These informal — though informed — observations tend to substantiate our own intuitions, but the hard data are still missing. It is difficult to isolate either structural or intentional competition as a variable, since competitive situations and people often are defined by other features that might also contribute to stress. In any case, I am not aware of any researchers who have attempted to test these hypotheses. One provocative exception is an experiment involving monkeys. Scientists in North Carolina have shown that "aggressive monkeys eating a high-fat diet developed more atherosclerosis (clogging of coronary arteries) than did submissive monkeys, but only if the monkeys lived under stressful social situations that encouraged competition."[68] More research on competition clearly is required, including longitudinal studies that test for the effects of switching to a competitive environment. The seriousness of the consequences and the strong likelihood of their relationship to competition unquestionably justifies such research projects.

FURTHER CONSEQUENCES OF COMPETITION

PRODUCT ORIENTATION: Play, it was argued in the last chapter, is activity for its own sake. It reflects a "process orientation" — an inclination to do something because of its intrinsic value. Such behavior is rare among adults in our society. We are product oriented. Our work is governed by the demands of the "bottom line" and often is justified as an onerous necessity of life. The time we spend in school similarly is construed as valuable only insofar as it contributes to later employment, with the pleas for relevance in our universities having evolved into a demand for marketable skills. Even leisure activities have come to resemble work: results are what matter.

When process has been supplanted by product in so many aspects of our lives, the same transformation must eventually occur with respect to the way we regard life itself. Who we are and what we are worth have come to be evaluated in terms of what we actually have produced or done, what tangible evidence of achievement can be adduced, what we have to show for ourselves. As soon as we illuminate this thinking, of course, its absurdity becomes clear. What is the point of all our frowning purposefulness? This shattering question — typically whispered in middle age when we can smell our mortality (and hastily dismissed as depression) — never gets a satisfactory answer. The pursuit of results is ultimately futile because there *is* no grand summation or coherent unity to our lives other than what we confer on them by the process of living. A bumper sticker that nicely satirizes the commodity fetishism which tends to accompany the product orientation reads: WHOEVER HAS THE MOST THINGS WHEN HE DIES, WINS. The economist John Maynard Keynes was similarly impatient with talk of "the long run." "In the long run," he is reported to have said, "we are all dead."

Competition is not the sole cause of the product orientation, but it is a mighty contributor to such thinking. The goal of competing is, by definition, to win. To enjoy aspects of the activity in its own right is beside the point. It can happen, but it is at best tangential. More typically, the process orientation is actively discouraged because it seems a distraction from the main purpose. The student who loves intellectual exploration will not want to rein in this impulse as the syllabus demands, and she will not have the highest grade-point average. The attorney who delights in the nuances of the law probably will not win as many cases as the one who cares only about the verdict and thinks in strategic terms. Competition is necessarily product oriented. And as more of our activities are directed toward winning, the process orientation becomes attenuated in our lives. Our eyes remain fixed on the scoreboard.

According to two social scientists, whose essays on sports were coincidentally published in the same year, this product orientation is associated with rigidity. "In competition," wrote William Sadler, "one's perspective is fixed on attaining a definite result. If this competitive posture were sustained, one's personality system would tend to become rigid."[69] The intrinsic rigidity of the goal orientation, not surprisingly, makes the individual rigid, as well. We might propose that the more competitive an individual is, the less spontaneous he is, the less receptive to surprise, the less flexible his cognitive process. Here is psychologist Dorcas Butt: "The character of the competitive athlete becomes increasingly undesirable as he develops an intense egocentric orientation with rigid psychological defenses and insensitivity. His obsession with his own winning status dominates his being."[70] Not all competitors are equally obsessed, of course, but competition it-self predisposes us — and not only athletes — to become invested in results to the exclusion of the process of working or playing or learning.

EITHER/OR THINKING: It is common to view a situation as if only two alternatives existed — the "black-and-white fallacy." America is either to be loved or left. I am either the most gifted and attractive person who ever lived or I am utterly worthless. Now we can respond to this thinking by pointing out that there are other alternatives (or a gray area in the middle, as the case may be) — treating it, in effect, as a lapse in logic. Or we can deal with such an all-or-nothing attitude psychodynamically, tracing the unconscious roots of perfectionism to the first years of life. But neither of these responses is quite sufficient. Dichotomous thinking is more than an error in logic. It is a real-life orientation, closely connected to how we deal with other people. And there is more going on than individual psychopathology: the social structures that shape our interactions also affect our assumptions about the alternatives that are open to us.

Specifically, dichotomous thinking is both conducive to and a conse-quence of competing. In a contest, there are only two possible results: you win or you lose. Those inclined to see the world in an either/or fashion will be attracted to competition, but, by the same token, com-petition will help to shape such an orientation. A recent study of more than three thousand women in careers found that "the vast majority . . . came to believe that there were only two possible outcomes to their actions. Either they would somehow manage to force themselves to run at top speed all day, every day, or they would lose so badly that they might as well not have entered the race to begin with. . . . There was nothing in between."[71] To slap a psychiatric label on these thousands (actually, millions) of people misses the point. More useful would be an investigation of how a competitive culture teaches us that the world is divided into winners and losers, and how we generalize this lesson and come to see everything in either/or terms.

The dichotomous worldview is a loaded one. When there are only two choices, typically one is seen as good and the other as bad. Every-thing we encounter can be neatly sorted out as rational or irrational, righteous or satanic, progressive or reactionary, reasonable or radical. A world that can be reduced to such simple antinomies is a much more manageable, comfortable world, one that does not ask us to grapple with tough moral questions. The price to be paid for this comfort is steep, however. To begin with, it is a distorted view of reality — akin to squashing the three-dimensional world into a two-dimensional flatland. Second, when dichotomous thinking is competitively generated, there is a tendency to be concerned almost compulsively about what is the best. People, including ourselves, are either number one or they are unworthy. This is not a terribly productive way of thinking about restaurant meals or computers, much less about human beings.

Finally, when we perform this kind of value-laden division, we normally place ourselves on the good side, and we want the good to triumph over the bad. A gulf opens up between "us" and "them," and this very division invites aggression — a topic to which I will return in the next chapter. This is what Anne Strick described in the context of our adversarial legal system: From seeing Right and Wrong as the only two possibilities,

> we claim righteousness for ourselves and require an "other," an opposite (religious, political, racial, national, sexual, name-it), a nonself who embodies evil. To that degree does blame become a basic behavior and revenge a solution. Such polarity not only implies superior-inferior; as it denies complementarity, it also invites battle. For superior tends to become pitted *against* inferior.[72]

The steps are short: from "either/or" to "good/bad" to "we/they" to "we against them." Structural competition is a significant contributor to this ominous progression.

CONFORMITY: Because the United States is both an exceedingly competitive and a highly individualistic society, and because competition here usually takes place at the individual (rather than the group) level, we often assume that competition promotes individualism. But the word *individualism* actually is associated with two very different philosophical movements. On the one hand, there is the individualism championed by such nineteenth-century Americans as Emerson and Thoreau and found in certain strands of twentieth-century existentialism: it has to do with genuine self-sufficiency, conscience, autonomy, and nonconformity. The concern here is with the freedom to think and act on one's own, the commitment to deeply held values, the courage to risk disapproval and worse from others.

On the other hand, there is the vulgar parody of this movement that one finds in contemporary pop psychology and parts of the human potential movement. This is the desperate attempt at self-reliance that bespeaks alienation from others — while, in turn, contributing to just this predicament. It is the blithe dismissal of relationship in "you do your thing and I'll do mine," the pathetic attempt to compensate for loneliness in "be your own best friend," the undisguised selfishness in "look out for number one." (It is not at all surprising, by the way, to find this egocentricity walking hand in hand with a uniquely American proclivity for instant intimacy. The latter is just a superficial chumminess that vainly attempts to compensate for the effects of an ugly individualism.) As political scientist Michael Parenti put it, our

> "individualism" is not to be mistaken for freedom to choose moral, political and cultural alternatives of one's own making. Each person is expected to operate "individually" but in more or less similar ways and similar directions. . . . "Individualism" in the United States refers to *privatization* and the absence of communal forms of production, consumption and recreation.[73]

It is with this latter kind of individualism that competition is compatible. A narrowly conceived self-interest is conducive to beating out others. It is a short step from looking out for number one to trying to *become* Number One. This version of individualism implies an alienation from others, and here, too, it is commensurate with competition. But competition does not promote the more substantial and authentic kind of individualism. On the contrary, it encourages rank conformity. Here is George Leonard: "A culture dedicated to creating standardized, specialized, predictable human components could find no better way of grinding them out than by making every possible aspect of life a matter of competition. 'Winning out' in this respect does not make rugged individualists. It shapes conformist robots."[74]

This is quite logical since one can speak of outdoing others only if one is doing the same thing they are. Apples are not better than oranges; one can make relative judgments only about like quantities. As Arthur Combs put it, "Competition can only work if people agree to seek the same goals and follow the same rules. Accordingly, as competitors strive to beat each other's records, they tend to become more alike. If total conformity is what we want in our society, worshiping competition is one effective way to get it."[75] Notice that this is not simply an empirical observation ("people tend to act alike when they compete") but an analysis of the nature of competition. Unique characteristics by definition cannot be ranked, and participation in the process of ranking demands essential conformity.

This is not to say that competition is the sole cause of conformity in American society. There are many other social, economic, and psychological forces at work that cannot be explored in this book. But competition at the very least tends to support and reinforce this process of standardization.

In chapter 3, I noted that competition dampens creativity. This is partly because the pressure to outdo someone else tends to make us conservative. We do not want to risk anything that could endanger our victory. Thus the music critic Will Crutchfield finds that piano competitions result in interpretations that are "all too similar to one another." In trying to win, performers concentrate on making no mistakes but "shy away . . . from the big technical risks, the truly astonishing effects."[76] Creativity is anticonformist at its core; it is nothing if not a process of idiosyncratic thinking and risk-taking. Competition inhibits this process.

The word *conformity* implies something more than acting like others, of course. To conform is to go along, to accept a situation as it is. Its opposite is not only individuality but the acts of questioning and rebelling. In this broader sense, too, competition seems to promote conformity. If winning is the goal, one naturally tries to avoid doing anything that could jeopardize it. It is true that skillful tennis-playing is all that matters on the tennis court; one can act like a petulant child and still win important tournaments. But in most arenas victory is at least partly subjective. Attitude toward authorities and general conduct do count in the kinds of competitions that take place in the office or the classroom. If I want to get the highest grades in class, I will not be likely to challenge the teacher's version of whatever topic is being covered. After a while, I may even cease to think critically altogether. "In order not to fail most students are willing to believe anything and [not to care] whether what they are told is true or false," writes Jules Henry.[77] If people tend to "go along to get along," there is even more incentive to go along when the goal is to be number one. In the office or factory where co-workers are rivals, beating out the next person for a promotion means pleasing the boss. Competition acts to extinguish the Promethean fire of rebellion.

The inclination to take risks is stifled by competition in other respects, too. Not only does the competitor try to play it safe within a given activity, but the matter of which activities she gets involved in will itself be affected by the need to win. It is common for people to try to "cut their losses" by abandoning activities and environments in which they are less likely to win. A student who is driven (structurally or intentionally) to have a superior grade-point average will avoid exploring subjects in which he may not succeed. A competitive sports enthusiast will stay with the games at which she is proficient. "Anything I couldn't be the best at, I didn't do," one writer confesses, adding ironically, "Vocational guidance counselors call this 'getting focused.' "[78] Again, the tendency to specialize and, more specifically, to play to one's strengths is not exclusively a function of competition. But competition exacerbates this tendency, with the result that the need to win (which is to say, the fear of losing) will result in narrowing our lives, failing to experience new challenges. Competition thus can have the effect of discouraging healthy risk-taking — precisely because, psychologically speaking, so much is at risk when we compete.

This phenomenon, too, shades into the matter of performance, since risk-taking is a prerequisite for many kinds of achievement. It is true that winning at some kinds of activities requires that competitors take risks. But the pressure to win generally has the opposite effect, and the quality of work suffers. When an artistic task is turned into a contest, children's products reveal significantly less spontaneity.[79] When television networks have to scramble frantically for ratings, they tend "not to innovate but to imitate, because innovation requires risk-taking, and risk-taking is antithetical to winning in the short-term."[80] (It is not a coincidence that the three major American commercial networks, operating within a competitive framework, produce virtually interchangeable programming, whereas the BBC channels in England, which do not have to compete, offer a real choice.)

Besides its effects on performance, a sterile kind of safety is also a good deal less fun than risking, exploring, daring, challenging. But here the point to be stressed is that competition affects the personality. Turning life into a series of contests turns us into cautious, obedient people. We do not sparkle as individuals *or* embrace collective action when we are in a race. We are less likely to take advantage of a new opportunity when we know that it sorts participants into winners and losers. In fact, the more one appreciates the values that stand in opposition to conformity, the more skeptical one will be of competition.

6

◁ ▷

Against Each Other:

INTERPERSONAL CONSIDERATIONS

> That trophy is the truth, the only truth. I told him to get
> mean, punish some people, put some fear into them, you
> have to hate to win, it takes hate to win. I didn't tell him
> to break anybody's ribs. . . . I told him there is no such
> thing as second place.
>
> — The Coach in Jason Miller's
> *That Championship Season*

POISONING OUR RELATIONSHIPS

The bug that is going around the office doesn't remain confined to
the office for long. Someone brings it home, and the whole family
comes down with it. The disease that starts in the workplace is carried
into living rooms and bedrooms.

The disease is competition. In a society that trains us to regard our
workmates as adversaries, we find no sanctuary in the private sphere.
"Industrial man, consciously or unconsciously, often considers not
only his business rivals as competitors but also his sex partners, siblings, neighbors, and peers of his group," wrote Walter Weisskopf
some thirty-five years ago.[1] Never mind the office; the race to win is
under way where you live.

The pursuit of a lover is a competitive game in which success is
called "scoring." Would-be suitors jockey for position to take the
prize, and they regard each other with suspicion or outright animos-
ity. A couple forms, and the two find their love frayed by the need of
each to outdo the other: Who has the bigger paycheck, the most
friends, the sharper wit? Who is giving more to the relationship, is
more skillful or selfless in bed, has sacrificed more to be with the
other? "It is quite sufficient for one partner to see life as a zero-sum

game . . . and one may rest assured that things will go all to hell," says Paul Watzlawick."[2] Let one lover be concerned with outdoing the other in some respect — any respect — and the relationship will be dragged down.

A child is born and with it two questions: Who will be the better parent and whom will the child prefer? "The ancient competition for the children between mother and father gains renewed vigor," said Jules Henry, "and the competitiveness in our culture from which the family is supposed to give shelter enters through the back door."[3] Another child arrives and is subtly encouraged to compete with the sibling to be Mommy's or Daddy's favorite. Affection becomes a scarce commodity, something one must obtain at the expense of someone else.

The parents socialize with other parents and trot out their children's accomplishments. Whose infant walked first, whose toddler came out with the most precious remark, whose teenager was admitted to the best college? The couples also compete to prove they have the best marriage, as Mary-Lou Weisman observes:

> It seems we are so essentially a capitalistic society that we can't even refrain from trying to sell one another our marriages, or at least we can't resist advertising them. We are after all a highly competitive society. We compete at work, at school, in sports and on television game shows. All of these are but pale imitations of the competitions that are played on Saturday nights on a field of hors d'oeuvres.[4]

The measure of our domestic untranquility is the number of articles in the women's magazines on the subject. *Seventeen* and *Glamour* and *Mademoiselle* tell of competitions with best friends and boyfriends; *Redbook* and *McCall's* warn of familial struggles. The headlines read "Can You Bear It When Your Best Friend Gets Ahead?" and "The Marriage Superbowl" and "How to Cope with 'Friendly' Competition." Even if we are not involved in the marketplace, these articles remind us, our personal lives are rife with rivalries. In an essay on the relationship between neurosis and American culture, Karen Horney summed up the situation:

> The character of all our human relationships is molded by a more or less outspoken competition. It is effective in the family between siblings, at school, in social relations (keeping up with the Joneses), and in love life. . . . The genuine erotic wish is often overshadowed or replaced by the merely competitive goal of being the most popular, having the most

dates, love letters, lovers, being seen with the most desirable man or woman. . . . Marriage partners, for example, may be living in an endless struggle for supremacy, with or without being aware of the nature or even of the existence of this combat.[5]

This state of affairs, Horney notes elsewhere, is all the more tragic since the same competitive forces in our society that generate anxiety, making our relationships so important as a coping mechanism, also undermine these very relationships.[6] In a competitive society, there is nowhere left to turn.

Competition acts not only to strain our existing relationships to the breaking point, but also to prevent them from developing in the first place. Camaraderie and companionship — to say nothing of genuine friendship and love — scarcely have a chance to take root when we are defined as competitors. In the workplace, one tries to remain on friendly terms with one's colleagues, but there is guardedness, a part of the self held in reserve; even when no rivalry exists at the moment, one never knows whom one will have to compete against next week. I was recently told that extended training seminars for computer programmers are sometimes set up as contests: one's ultimate status and salary are determined by how many programs one produces. The result, according to one reluctant participant, is that friendships are nipped in the bud because each person must try to outdo the others. Performing artists similarly find it hard to enjoy each other's company since they may audition for the same part or position. Says one actress: "I keep a distance from everybody because I know one day" — she snaps her fingers — "it's all going to be gone and you're going to be working against each other."

On the competitive playing field, the story is much the same. The occasional real friendship that develops is the exception that proves the rule. One article about professional tennis paraphrases an official as follows: "If it comes down to choosing between winning and maintaining a friendship . . . successful players sacrifice the friendship." He adds: "There's no place for sentiment. It's a matter of survival."[7] The win/lose structure inevitably affects the priorities and temperaments of the individual players, according to sports psychologists Bruce Ogilvie and Thomas Tutko. A personality profile administered to fifteen thousand athletes revealed "low interest in receiving support and concern from others, low need to take care of others, and low need for affiliation. Such a personality," the researchers conclude, "seems necessary to achieve victory over others."[8] Another study found that characteristics such as "kindness, sympathy, and unselfishness" are notably absent among *successful* athletes.[9] Psychotherapist Lillian Rubin describes how such a personality likely takes shape:

> To win for his team a boy beats his best friend . . . [so] winning means also losing something precious in the relationship with a friend. For it is not likely that the two will compete on the football field and have a close and loving relationship off it, not likely that they can put on a show of invincibility during the game and share their fears and vulnerabilities after it. Not very different, is it, from the world of work for which he is destined? . . . Not very good training, is it, for the kind of sharing of self and emotional support friendship requires?[10]

The assertion one sometimes hears to the effect that competition need not interfere with friendship assumes that our orientation toward someone can switch from supportive to rivalrous and back again as if we were changing television channels. It is simply unrealistic to think that the hostility engendered by and experienced during a contest will evaporate into thin air, leaving the relationship between the two individuals unaffected. I do not mean to say that no one has ever had a satisfying relationship with a competitor, but that competition inhibits such relationships, just as it corrodes the relationships we have already developed. This chapter is concerned with the reason this happens and the consequences it brings.

ANATOMY OF A RIVAL

Simply from knowing that competition damages self-esteem, we can predict that relationships will be in trouble. This seems to follow from Harry Stack Sullivan's comment in the last chapter to the effect that it is difficult for me to feel good about others when I don't feel good about myself. I feel my worth is in doubt — it is contingent on winning — so I am unable to extend myself to you. From her research with children, psychologist Carole Ames concluded that just such a connection between self-esteem and relationship exists: "The experience of failure in competitive settings that resulted in depressed beliefs in their own ability . . . is likely to affect negatively the child's own feelings of competence and self-worth and potentially interfere with future relationships with others."[11]

But the interpersonal consequences of competition do not depend solely on the psychology of the individual. Competition by its very nature damages relationship. Its nature, remember, is mutually exclusive goal attainment, which means that competitors' interests are inherently opposed. I succeed if you fail, and vice versa, so my objective is to do everything possible to trip you up. This attitude does not reflect a neurotic or sadistic orientation on my part. It is the heart of competition itself because competition decrees that both of us cannot succeed. This effect is easiest to see where we compete face to face, but even where the contest is indirect, such as the diffuse pursuit of a consumer's dollar in which market share is gained at the expense of anonymous competitors, I will regard others — and correctly so — as stumbling blocks on my path.

Under conditions of competition, "the failure of others has the same relative effect as one's own success,"[12] so the failure of others is devoutly to be wished. It is a small step from wanting someone else to fail at a particular task to wanting bad things in general for that person. I come to associate your disappointment with my pleasure, even when we are not in a zero-sum situation. It is another small step to adopting an adversarial posture all the time. One fails to distinguish between those others who are rivals and those who are not (at least for the moment). Put the two tendencies together and the pattern of behavior that emerges is one of treating virtually everyone as inimical to one's own goals and wishing them ill. "In a competitive culture," writes Henry, "anybody's success at anything is one's own defeat, even though one is completely uninvolved in the success."[13]

Earlier I referred to a study demonstrating that American children often choose to take away another child's toy despite the fact that they have nothing to gain from this. The experiment, with seven- to nine-year-olds, found that 78 percent of the Anglo-American children (who presumably had become well accustomed to competition) "took the other child's toy away for no other reason than to prevent the other child from having it." Mexican children, whose socialization had been less competitive, did so only half as often.[14]

Indiscriminate rivalrous behavior can be explained according to simple principles of learning theory. Baby Albert, the hapless subject of John B. Watson's classic 1920 experiment, was exposed to a loud noise every time he saw a white rat. He thereby learned to fear the rat — but also (though unexpectedly) to generalize this fear to everything furry. It is much the same for the rest of us: when we repeatedly encounter people under competitive conditions, we will spontaneously begin to regard *all* others as rivals and treat them accordingly.

Learning theory cannot capture the full import of this point, however. We need a model of human relationship — its potential richness and significance to our lives — against which to understand the effects of competition. The philosopher Martin Buber spent his life devising such a model. For him, the fulfillment of human life was relationship, the realm of the "interhuman." Buber described the wondrous possibility of treating another person not as an "it" but as a "Thou," not as a means but as an end, so that "each becomes aware of the other and is thus related to him in such a way that he does not regard and use him as his object, but as his partner in a living event."[15]

This possibility depends on my coming to understand our common humanity, which is to say, coming to see that your needs and feelings are analogous to my own. Now clearly I know myself as a center of experience, the one who perceives and acts in and reflects on a world. All of existentialist thought is a kind of rebellion against the intellectual systems and real-world practices that crush or deny my subjectivity by reducing me to a part of a crowd, a scientific datum, a pale approximation of some transcendent reality. What Buber adds to this assertion of my subjectivity is the necessity of affirming *your* subjectivity as well. You are not just a part of my world but the center of your own.

Some night while you are driving along a highway, try to imaginatively capture the reality of the other drivers. Each set of headlights represents a person who is, like you, on her way somewhere. In other situations, look deeply into someone's eyes and try to grasp the fact that this is a person who is not just being watched but is a watcher — just like you. If you succeed at reclaiming the subjectivity of the other, you will be unable to hurt him or even to dismiss him. You can dismiss an abstraction (a jock, some bureaucrat, that schizophrenic); you can mistreat an object (a "piece of ass," a terrorist). But as soon as you come upon *a human being,* you will be moved to share yourself with him, to care for him. It will be far more difficult to hurt his feelings or ignore him or simply analyze him. It will be almost impossible to kill him or cheer his death, which is why this sort of orientation can put armies out of business. Kafka once said that war is caused by a "monstrous lack of imagination"; it should be clear now that he meant the ability to imagine the subjectivity of others.

To say that you and I share a common humanity, however, is not to say that we are the same. On the contrary, I must encounter you as an other rather than as a mirror of myself or an object of my own experience. Empathy, in the sense of picturing myself in your situation, is not enough: The point is to see your situation from *your* perspective, which is not identical with mine. I must "imagine the real" — see the world as you do, experience your inner life. This, according to Buber, is "a bold swinging — demanding the most intensive stirring of one's being — into the life of the other."[16] When I both regard you as a subject and recognize your otherness, there is the making of human relationship at its fullest. All of us can strive to receive others this way, and in so doing we prepare the ground for genuine dialogue, a reciprocal sharing by which both participants are enriched.

The ideal of human relationship that Buber describes is, of course, only imperfectly realized. There are circumstances, both internal and external, that interfere with our coming to see another person as different from ourselves and as a subject. Our own needs can drown out the other's cry. The frantic pace of modern life can divert us from the other's humanity. But had we set out deliberately to sabotage relationship, we could hardly have done better than to arrange for people to have to compete against each other.

At this point, let me recall the distinction between pursuing a goal independently and pursuing it competitively. Obviously the former is not conducive to relationship since interaction is ruled out. My success and your success are totally separate, so I don't have to have anything to do with you. But competition entails a kind of perverse interdependence: our fates are linked in that I cannot succeed unless you fail. Thus I regard you merely as someone over whom to triumph. Because you are my rival, you are an "it" to me, an object, something I use for my own ends. This dynamic is found in virtually all exploitative relationships. All too commonly, for example, a busdriver is seen solely in terms of his function; he gets us from here to there. To the extent we perceive him this way — essentially as an appendage of the bus itself — we cannot enter into dialogue with him. But competition takes objectification a step further since I not only use you but try to defeat you. True, you regard me in the same way, and this creates a symmetry that is not present in, say, the boss's relationship to his worker. But it is a fearful symmetry. For competitors, the objectification is doubled; the prospects for relationship are twice buried.

The *reductio ad absurdum* of competition is war, and it is here that we find antagonists most thoroughly negating the humanity of others in order to be able to kill them. One fires on Krauts or gooks, not on people. But precisely the same process is in evidence in less deadly kinds of competition. Tennis players imagine "a faceless opponent,"

says one sports psychologist. Adds another: "The more you get involved with playing a personality, the worse you do."[17] A pro football
player writes:

> We were really fired up and felt we were going to annihilate "them." I
> particularly didn't want to see their faces, because the more anonymous
> they were the better it was for me — and I'm sure most of the other ball
> players felt the same way: they were a faceless enemy we had to meet."[18]

Depriving adversaries of personalities, of faces, of their subjectivity, is
a strategy we automatically adopt in order to win. Some people do this
more effectively than others, but the posture is demanded by the very
structure of competition. We may try to reassure ourselves with talk
about "friendly competition," but the fact remains that seeing another
person as a rival and seeing her as a "partner in a living event" are
fundamentally incompatible stances. It is difficult to imagine a more
telling indictment of an activity than the fact that it demands such
depersonalization.

There is some empirical confirmation of this phenomenon. A series
of ten studies conducted by David and Roger Johnson investigated
the effect of various learning environments on "perspective taking"
— that is, on "the ability to understand how a situation appears to
another person and how that person is reacting cognitively and emotionally to the situation." The studies show that "cooperative learning
experiences . . . promote greater cognitive and affective perspective
taking than do competitive or individualistic learning experiences."[19]
In one recent experiment, for example, undergraduates played at
managing businesses and had to negotiate with one another. Those
playing under competitive conditions were less able to take the other
company's perspective — which here was defined in terms of something as simple as understanding how many assets the other had.[20]

What is true of a competitive situation may well be true of a competitive individual. Mark Barnett and his associates asked first-grade
teachers to rate their students with respect to competitiveness. Then
the experimenters administered a well-tested measure of empathy in
which subjects were asked for their feelings after watching slides of
same-aged children who seemed happy, sad, angry, or fearful. The
result: "Children rated as highly competitive were found to have
lower empathy scores than children rated as relatively less competitive."[21]

Of course the absence of basic empathy precludes anything like the sort of relationship of which Buber spoke, but it has another, more easily observed, effect, as well: it means that one is less likely to help others. We are especially inclined to assist people when we can imaginatively experience what they are going through.[22] If empathy encourages altruism and competition depresses empathy, then we should find an inverse relationship between competition and altruism — and so we do. "There is considerable evidence to suggest that cooperative settings, when compared to competitive settings, promote more mutual liking, more sharing, and more helping behaviors," writes Carole Ames.[23] A 1968 study of nursery school boys found that those who were less generous in giving away candies also seemed more competitive while playing a racing game with dolls. Conversely, wrote the experimenters, "High generosity seems to be part of a pattern which involves less intense interpersonal competition."[24] Another pair of researchers confirmed this effect with fifth-grade boys several years later. After playing a bowling game and receiving some tokens, each child was permitted (in the experimenters' absence) to contribute some of them to a March of Dimes canister. Those who were told they had won gave away more than those who were told they had lost or tied. But those who had played noncompetitively contributed the most of all.[25] This finding is not very surprising, the experimenters note, since "charitable or helping behaviors . . . by definition are antithetical to competitive behaviors."[26]

The point here is not that competitive individuals never give money to charity. It is rather that competition ultimately discourages generosity. While we pay lip service to helping people in our culture, or write an occasional check to the United Way, our fundamental orientation toward others is trying to beat them. Because success seems to entail this, we subtly discourage our children from being too concerned about the welfare of others. "Parents generally want their children to be able to compete successfully — and how can they compete if they're altruists?" asks Maya Pines rhetorically.[27]

Now it may be possible to fall short of Buberian dialogue while still coexisting amicably. But competition's effects run far deeper than simply closing off an ideal; it tends to turn our relationships into something distinctly unpleasant. Here again is Karen Horney: "Competitiveness . . . creates easily aroused envy towards the stronger ones, contempt for the weaker, distrust towards everyone . . . so the satisfaction and reassurance which one can get out of human relations are limited and the individual becomes more or less emotionally isolated."[28] Let us take these three consequences — envy, contempt, and distrust — in turn.

To envy another person is to want what he has and to resent him for having it. As is usual for familiar (and disturbing) characteristics, we tend to assume that this is part of "human nature." But desire is largely a social creation, and so is the distribution of what is valued. Competition creates a prized status where none existed before (see page 75), thereby giving us something to desire. Then it insures that not everyone can get it. Finally, competition requires that those who obtain the reward can do so only by defeating everyone else. Both the objective and subjective conditions for envy are established, in other words: restricted access to something desired and a (quite accurate) belief that someone else has got it at one's own expense. Even if no social arrangement could do away with a taste for what others have, competition adds the sour flavor of resentment. It is the latter that spoils relationship. Indeed, Bertrand Russell once wrote, "There is, so far as I know, no way of dealing with envy except to make the lives of the envious happier and fuller, and to encourage in youth the idea of collective enterprises rather than competition."[29]

Contempt for others is induced by competition in two ways. First, envy for what the winners have (and bitterness at their having it) easily congeals into enmity. Jules Henry spoke of how we encourage this feeling in the classroom:

> Since all but the brightest children have the constant experience that others succeed at their expense, they cannot [help] but develop an inherent tendency to hate — to hate the success of others, to hate others who are successful, and to be determined to prevent it. Along with this, naturally, goes the hope that others will fail.[30]

The second kind of contempt, the sort that Horney had in mind, is directed at the losers. It derives from the effort of winners — and here we may specifically point to the economically privileged — to justify their success by maintaining that winning is their natural reward for *being* winners. This is not a tautology. Certain people are believed to enjoy the status of being winners in advance of actually winning. These winners are good people, not only capable but virtuous, and their victories are therefore always deserved. The corollary to this is that those who lose deserve their fate, too, and merit only contempt.

We usually do not spell out these assumptions, but they color our perception of winning and losing. They probably are the legacy of social Darwinism, which, as the historian Richard Hofstadter pointed out, "supplied [the competitive order] with a cosmic rationale. Competition was glorious. Just as survival was the result of strength, success was the reward of virtue."[31] George Orwell, reflecting on his school days, put it this way: "Virtue consisted in winning. . . . Life was hierarchical and whatever happened was right. There were the strong, who deserved to win and always did win, and there were the weak, who deserved to lose and always did lose, everlastingly."[32]

Despite the outrageous arrogance of this view, winners are sometimes successful in persuading losers of its validity. This has two consequences: (1) The losers' contempt for the winners is mixed with self-contempt, and (2) the losers will set about not to change the system (a move that would in any case be dismissed as "sour grapes") but only to become a winner next time. Thus there is no one to press for structural change. The contempt for losers, then, not only tears at the fabric of human relationship but functions as a powerfully conservative force.

Finally, there is the matter of distrust. Love, of course, is based on trust, but so, to a lesser extent, is our ability to function in any social system. Even if we are mere acquaintances, you and I expect certain things from, and are vulnerable to, each other. But set up a system where we must compete against each other, and a breeding ground for distrust has been established. Indeed, why *should* you trust me if I have every reason to want you to fail? Distrust spreads rapidly, too — first, because I am never sure that you might not become my rival even if you are not at present; second, because (as discussed earlier) we generalize what we learn to new environments; and, third, because a vicious circle is generated, in which I respond in kind to your attitude. Disclosing my self to others can be considered a key element of psychological health[33] and is, at any rate, an important part of relationship. But competition erodes the trust on which disclosure depends. Whatever I tell you about myself or do to help you will, in a zero-sum situation, be at my own expense. In a competitive culture, we come to look at each other through narrowed eyes.

When we compete, then, we objectify others, lose our ability to empathize, become less inclined to help. A chasm opens up between us, leaving us distrustful, envious, and contemptuous. The father of family therapy, Nathan Ackerman, saw the sad legacy of competition in the home. "The strife of competition reduces empathic sympathy, distorts communication, impairs the mutuality of support and sharing, and decreases the satisfaction of personal need."[34] All of this may well result in isolation, as Horney contended, which suggests the provocative hypothesis that competition is not only the result of hyper-individualism but its cause. The chief result of competition, though, as Ackerman observed and as should by now be clear, is strife. Competition of any kind is a sort of battle, a hostile encounter. The following section will investigate this closely.

AGGRESSION

What is the relationship between competition and aggression? On one level, the question makes little sense since the two are not really distinct phenomena that can be related: competition *is* a kind of aggression. In the preceding section, I tried to explore what it means to try to beat someone. The arrangement is by its very nature a struggle or (depending on how one uses the word) an aggressive enterprise. Thus Horney was able to write: "Hostility is inherent in every intense competition, since the victory of one of the competitors implies the defeat of the other."[35]

If there is a connection to be drawn, then, it is only between trying to defeat someone and trying to do him harm beyond what is necessary for victory. The mediator between these two actions presumably would be feelings of hostility — which invariably attend competition at some level. Morton Deutsch writes as follows:

> In a competitive relationship, one is predisposed to cathect the other negatively, to have a suspicious, hostile, exploitative attitude toward the other, to be psychologically closed to the other, to be aggressive and defensive toward the other, to seek advantage and superiority for self and disadvantage and inferiority for the other, to see the other as opposed to oneself and basically different, and so on. One is also predisposed to expect the other to have the same orientation.[36]

Indeed, hostility is practically indistinguishable from intentional competition, so an individual with this orientation will likely seek out competitive encounters. To this extent, the act of competition can be a consequence of hostility. But social scientists have been more concerned with the reverse proposition — the question of whether competition leads people to feel more hostile and, ultimately, to act more aggressive.

Once upon a time, theorists speculated that participation in or controlled exposure to competitive sports or other aggressive behavior would drain off one's reservoir of aggression. This came to be known as the "catharsis" theory, after Aristotle's notion that one can be purged of unpleasant emotions by watching tragic dramas. Freud and the ethologist Konrad Lorenz were two of the chief proponents of this view, and it is not a coincidence that both believed aggression was innate rather than learned and spontaneous rather than reactive: we naturally need to vent our aggressions, and it is best to do so where it can do little harm, such as by playing sports. The substitutive satisfaction of competition thus was said to reduce aggression.

There are few beliefs so widely held by the general public that have been so decisively refuted by the evidence. The catharsis theory by now has no leg to stand on, particularly with respect to the question of sports. Even Lorenz told an interviewer in 1974 that he had developed "strong doubts whether watching aggressive behavior even in the guise of sport has any cathartic effect at all."[37] And the well-known psychoanalyst Bruno Bettelheim conceded that "competitive or spectator sports . . . raise aggressive feelings of competition to the boiling point."[38]

Watching others be aggressive does not discharge our own aggressiveness. What seems to happen instead is straightforward modeling: We *learn* to be aggressive. Our restraints against aggression are lowered. Whatever explanation we devise for this effect, however, one study after another has failed to show any catharsis effect.

· Athletes were found to become *more* aggressive over the course of a season, as measured by personality tests. Another study found the same thing for high school football players.[39]

· Third graders who were frustrated by experimenters did not become any less aggressive when they engaged in aggressive play afterward. (On the other hand, those children who had the frustrating behavior explained to them became significantly less aggressive.)[40]

· Elementary-school-aged boys were more likely to shove or hit their peers if they had watched a boxing film.[41]

· A cross-cultural study revealed that "where we find warlike behavior we typically find combative sports and where war is relatively rare combative sports tend to be absent. This refutes the hypothesis that combative sports are alternatives to war as discharge channels of accumulated aggressive tension." If the catharsis theory were true, sports and war would be inversely related across cultures; in fact, they are directly related.[42]

Those social scientists who have reviewed or conducted the research on catharsis speak with one voice. "Innumerable studies of aggression in children have illustrated that attempts to reduce aggression through the use of aggressive and vigorous play therapy have the opposite effect. . . . Sports participation may heighten aggressive tendencies," says one.[43] "Engaging in aggressive sports or observing aggressive sports . . . typically lead[s] to *increased* rather than decreased aggression," says another.[44] "Participation in competitive, aggressive sports . . . may more rightfully be viewed as a disinhibition training that ultimately promotes violent reactions," says a third.[45] And from yet another source: "The balance of evidence . . . is that sports involvement may heighten arousal, produce instances of aggressive behaviors and their reward, and provide a context in which the emulation of such behaviors is condoned."[46]

Faced with such evidence, proponents of competition can no longer use catharsis to justify the aggressiveness of sports. Their last refuge is, as usual, the myth of "human nature." Michael Novak, for instance, asserts that "the human animal is a warlike animal" and that sports merely "dramatize conflict."[47] But whether or not we are unavoidably aggressive — and the data suggest that we are not — one cannot argue in good faith that sports merely dramatize conflict. The studies demonstrate that athletic competition not only fails to reduce aggression, as catharsis theory would predict, but actually encourages it. This is not really surprising given that sport represents a kind of circumscribed warfare — something pointed out not only by such critics as George Orwell, who called it "war minus the shooting,"[48] but also by generals: It was Wellington who said that the battle of Waterloo was "won on the playing fields of Harrow and Eton." It was Douglas MacArthur who said: "Upon the fields of friendly strife are sown the seeds that, upon other fields, on other days, will bear the fruits of victory." And it was Eisenhower who said that "the true mission of American sports is to prepare young people for war."[49] The point is not that athletes will rush to enlist, but that athletic competition both consists in and promotes warlike aggression.

There have been numerous anecdotal and experimental accounts of the relationship between violence and sports, but probably the most famous investigation was the series of studies conducted between 1949 and 1954 by Muzafer Sherif and his colleagues. In the so-called "Robbers' Cave" experiment (named after the area of Oklahoma where it took place), the researchers took a group of normal eleven- and twelve-year-old boys at a Boy Scout camp and divided them into two teams. These teams, the Rattlers and the Eagles, lived for three weeks in separate cabins and were pitted against each other in such competitive games as baseball, football, and tug-of-war — with prizes for the winning team. The hypothesis was that situations where one group could be successful only at the expense of the other (i.e., competition) would promote generalized hostility and aggressive acts. This is exactly what happened. The boys began taunting and insulting each other, in some cases turning against good friends who were now on the opposing team. They burned each other's banners, planned raids, threw food, and attacked each other after the games and at night. It is important to realize that there was no difference between the members of the two teams; they were in all respects homogeneous. Only the fact of structural competition can account for this hostility.[50]

The practice of dividing children into teams for a series of competitive encounters is still common in summer camps. These teams often are identified by colors, and the affair is aptly known as "Color War." It is a dreadful spectacle, a study in humiliation and rage, which I witnessed over several years as a camp counselor. Even very young children understand that the only thing that matters during the War is the relative standing of their team. Everything must be sacrificed for the Blues or Whites, and fervent loyalties develop as soon as the arbitrary team assignments are announced. Erstwhile friends on the other side are now met with a coldness that often erupts into nastiness. In the camp where I worked, the competition extended beyond sports: writing cheers and participating in a sort of quiz bowl insured that nonathletic youngsters, too, could use their skills in rivalrous fashion. (Indeed, one regularly finds hostility boiling up in chess matches, interscholastic debates, and any other sort of recreational competition one cares to mention. Athletes have no patent on aggression.)

Competition does not promote aggression merely on the part of participants. Fan violence is a frequent companion to sports, from high school students pelting the opposing team's bus with rocks to the death of three hundred soccer fans in a 1964 brawl in Peru. In 1971, sixty-six people died in similar fashion in Glasgow; in 1985, it was thirty-eight in Brussels. Looting and rioting regularly occur in U.S. cities following a hometown victory in the Super Bowl or World Series. After each such incident, pundits and political leaders scratch their heads and try to imagine what could have caused such "senseless" behavior. The Brussels riot, begun by Liverpool youths, produced hypotheses ranging from alcohol to the British character. The one cause that was not considered was the effect of competition it-self.[51] In any case, the frequency of such behavior on the part of fans again disproves the catharsis theory. "There are so many cases of spectators becoming violent as a result of an emotionally pitched game," says Terry Orlick, "that we have to wonder why the notion persists that the viewers will lessen their aggressive inclinations by seeing the game. Clearly someone forgot to tell these fans that watching highly competitive or aggressive sports is supposed to subdue their aggressive tendencies."[52]

.   .   .

It would be a mistake to confine a discussion of competitively inspired aggression to sports. Games, after all, are supposed to matter less than the rest of life; they are offered as something playful and fun. In other arenas, where competition is in deadly earnest, there may be fewer displays of brute violence but there is at least as much hostility. Joseph Wax's reflections on education are worth quoting at length:

> One must marvel at the intellectual quality of a teacher who can't understand why children assault one another in the hallway, playground, and city street, when in the classroom the highest accolades are reserved for those who have beaten their peers. In many subtle and some not so subtle ways, teachers demonstrate that what children learn means less than that they triumph over their classmates. Is this not assault? . . . Classroom defeat is only the pebble that creates widening ripples of hostility. It is self-perpetuating. It is reinforced by peer censure, parental disapproval, and loss of self-concept. If the classroom is a model, and if that classroom models competition, assault in the hallways should surprise no one.[53]

We are back to the inescapable fact of generalization: what we are taught is appropriate in one situation does not remain confined there. Competition spreads to other arenas, assumes other forms, and along with it — as part of a package deal — goes aggression. One interesting bit of evidence here relies on an empirical tool known as the F scale that was devised by the social theorist Theodor Adorno and his colleagues some years ago. People whose answers to certain questions led to their being classified as high on this scale were said to be aggressive as well as destructive, cynical, authoritarian in their thinking, and enamored of power and "toughness," among other things.[54] Harold Kelley and Anthony Stahelski, in an influential 1970 article based on Prisoner's Dilemma research, concluded that "persons low on the F scale and similar personality measures are like the cooperative persons identified in the present game research [while high scorers on the F scale] seem to correspond to the competitive type."[55]

I cite this correlational finding because it pertains to long-term personality patterns, something about which (at least with respect to competition) we have little data. As we have already seen, though, there is good evidence of a *causal* link between competition and aggression. Some have explained this evidence in terms of the theory that aggression results from frustration. Originally, the connection was proposed in just such simple terms;[56] today, the paradigm has been refined. Many theorists propose that competition generates a high level of *arousal*, meaning that we may not immediately become aggressive as a result, but that we are predisposed to respond in this way if we are then frustrated by something. Of course most of us encounter frustrations all the time, so the competition-aggression link remains fairly solid.

This theory neatly explains why losers become aggressive, but it raises the question of why winners (or fans of winning teams) do so as well. In an experiment with five- and six-year-olds, Janice Nelson and her associates found that "success as well as failure in competition produced consistent increases in aggression, as compared with the effects of noncompetitive play," although failure made the children more aggressive.[57] Another study, which first involved watching an adult be aggressive, discovered that the boys who won a subsequent competition were *more* aggressive than those who failed.[58] Such findings suggest two possibilities: (1) competition generates aggression as a result of something other than its capacity to frustrate participants, or (2) even winning is not enough to eradicate the frustrating elements of competition. The authors of the second study prefer the latter hypothesis: "Whether successful or not, competition is considered a frustrating experience because of the threat of defeat and the unpredictability of the outcome."[59] In any case, it is quite clear that the hostile encounter called competition — on the playing field and in other contexts, for both participants and spectators — leads us to become more aggressive.

RX: COOPERATION

Competition is the worst possible arrangement as far as relationship is concerned. There may be drawbacks to working or playing or learning independently, but at least this does not place us in the position of viewing each other as enemies. Happily, though, we do not have to settle for the lesser evil of isolation. There is a third approach — cooperation — which has a powerful positive effect on relationship. Chapter 3 showed that working together is more productive. Now I want to emphasize a somewhat less surprising but equally consequential finding: when we cooperate, we are inclined to like each other more.

Even in a mercilessly competitive society, there are pockets of cooperative activity — enough, at least, so that each of us knows what it is to work with others to paint a room, prepare a report, cook a meal. To remember such experiences is to know that cooperation encourages us to view our collaborators favorably; it is to understand how cooperation teaches us, more broadly, the value of relationship. Cooperation means that the success of each participant is linked to that of every other. This structure tends to lead to mutual assistance and support, which, in turn, predisposes cooperators to feel an affinity for one another. At the very least, cooperation offers an *opportunity* to interact positively (which independent effort does not and which competition actively discourages); at the most, it provides an irresistible *inducement* to do so.

There is by now an impressive pile of studies substantiating these conclusions, but their findings seem so predictable that I will review them only briefly. David and Roger Johnson conducted a precise statistical analysis of ninety-eight studies on this issue published between 1944 and 1982. Their collective finding:

> Cooperative experiences promote more positive relationships among individuals from different ethnic backgrounds, between handicapped and nonhandicapped individuals, and more homogeneous individuals than do [the alternative arrangements:] cooperation with intergroup competition, interpersonal competition, and individualistic experiences.[60]

As of 1985, the Johnsons themselves had conducted thirty-seven studies of interpersonal attraction under different learning arrangements. Thirty-five of them clearly showed that cooperation promoted greater attraction, while the results were mixed in the other two.[61]

"Interpersonal attraction" is a catchall phrase that stands for quite a number of positive effects. Among them:

· ENCOURAGEMENT GIVEN: Research by Brenda Bryant discovered that children who worked cooperatively "more actively encouraged and supported the self-enhancement of others than children from a competitive or individualistic learning environment."[62]

· ENCOURAGEMENT RECEIVED: Other studies have shown that students *perceive* such encouragement and support from their peers in a cooperative setup.[63]

· SENSITIVITY: Gillian King and Richard Sorrentino found more "sensitivity to the needs of others" displayed in cooperation; their experimental subjects also reported that cooperative situations were much more pleasant than competitive situations.[64]

· OTHER-ORIENTATION: Children can more readily move beyond a self-centered orientation and begin to take others into account once they are placed in a cooperative environment, reported Emmy Pepitone and her colleagues.[65]

· PERSPECTIVE-TAKING: Cooperation, as I noted earlier in this chapter, is by far the best way to promote perspective-taking. People tend to see things from the other person's point of view when they are working with, rather than against, each other.

· COMMUNICATION is improved through cooperation. Deutsch's classic experiment with undergraduates showed that when students worked cooperatively, "more ideas were verbalized, and members were more attentive to one another. . . . They had fewer difficulties in communicating with or understanding others." (With competition, Deutsch adds, communication tends to be "unreliable and impoverished.")[66]

· TRUST: Even when individuals have unequal power (as represented in an experimental game), they tend to trust each other in a cooperative structure. Trust is virtually absent under competition.[67]

Some of the most exciting research in this field concerns the effect of cooperation on students who are different from one another. It says quite a bit if any two people will come to like each other as a result of having cooperated on something. But it says far more if the same thing happens with people of different abilities or ethnic backgrounds. Research from the 1940s and 1950s suggested that "interaction within a cooperative context [was] a major determinant of whether cross-ethnic contact produced positive attitudes and relationships," and later work has confirmed this.[68] Simply bringing together children from different backgrounds does not produce harmony, as a chorus of bitter voices never tires of pointing out. But instead of simply indicting desegregation (or, worse, abandoning it), it seems more sensible to investigate what happens to students once they are in the same classroom. Whereas competition creates an atmosphere of hostility and does nothing to overcome differences, cooperation builds bridges. Its capacity for encouraging positive regard is no less potent when the cooperators are from different backgrounds, as the studies show quite clearly.[69] And this effect is not limited to class projects: once cooperative learning brings children together, they continue to enjoy spending time with each other. After the lessons are over, students in cooperative classrooms socialize more heterogeneously than those in competitive or independent learning situations.[70] In all, cooperation points the way to what child development researcher Urie Bronfenbrenner once called a "curriculum of caring."

Implicit in all of this is a truth that many people may find disconcerting. How we feel about other people is often put down, rather vaguely, to "chemistry" — not a subject for social science research, but a beguiling mystery to be wondered at by poets and songwriters. Even if we are willing to scrutinize patterns in our relationships, we tend to see them as a function of other people's behavior and personality. (We like people who are likable.) But the implication of what I have been reporting in this chapter is that our attitudes about others are largely dependent on the structure in which we interact. I do not mean to suggest that an individual's actions are irrelevant to how I regard her. Neither do I believe that science can (or should) eliminate all mystery from what happens between two people — or reduce the uniqueness of each relationship to generalizable laws. Still, there is no escaping the fact that the texture of our relationships depends to a significant degree on the context in which we come to know each other. I will look very different to someone for whom I am a rival than to someone for whom I am a partner. Of course, not all competitors will be lifelong enemies, just as not all cooperators will develop enduring friendships. But a predisposition toward hostility or attraction undeniably develops as a result of the structure under which we deal with one another. That is what the evidence — and, if we think about it, our own experience — demonstrates.

WE VS. THEY

The benefits of cooperation are so compelling that it seems even a competitive society must take notice. But how can such a society allow its members to taste the fruits of working together while still socializing them to keep the larger competitive framework? The answer is intragroup cooperation with intergroup competition. Work with *some* others, but do so in order to defeat everyone else. This is about as close as some of us ever get to genuine cooperation. I would argue that it represents a rather unsatisfying compromise — better than competition at every level but not as good as competition at no level. The conventional wisdom in a competitive culture, by contrast, is that intergroup competition heightens — or perhaps is even required for — cooperation within the group. Whatever is to be gained by cooperating depends on working to defeat a common enemy. Every "We" needs a "They."

Is this true? Recall that when studies found performance was enhanced by intragroup cooperation, people asked whether this effect actually relied on intergroup competition. The answer was unequivocally no (pp. 48–49). Such competition either was irrelevant to the cooperation-generated productivity or actually diminished it. The same seems to be true here. Intergroup competition is not necessary for intragroup cooperation to draw people together. Robert Dunn and Morton Goldman set out to test this question with college students in 1966. They found, first, that intergroup competition led subjects to view those from other groups negatively, and, second, that intergroup competition was not helpful in developing feelings of acceptance within each group. Such rivalry, they concluded, "may not only be unnecessary, but may do social harm through the intergroup tensions that it arouses."[71] The Johnsons, too, paid attention to this issue when they analyzed the results of scores of studies on interpersonal attraction. They found that subjects tended to like each other more where cooperation did *not* take place in the context of intergroup competition.[72] Finally, a 1985 study confirmed that

> intergroup cooperation promoted more positive cross-ethnic and cross-sex relationships than did intergroup competition. These results disconfirm the position that competition among groups leads to attraction among collaborators . . . and they provide some support for the position that the more pervasive the cooperation, the greater the interpersonal attraction.[73]

If these data seem surprising, it may be because we have confounded interpersonal attraction with group unity. The latter is associated with loyalty to the group as such, and often with uniformity among its members. Thus, the citizens of a nation will indeed wave their flags more vigorously when they have been persuaded that another nation poses a threat. This phenomenon is not at all what I have been discussing. Allegiance to a country or school or corporation does not necessarily promote sensitivity, trust, better perspective-taking, and so on among those in the group. Conversely, liking the individuals in my group does not mean I will reify and then glorify the group itself. Intergroup competition may be necessary for chauvinism, but not for relationship.

There is another reason that intergroup competition does not promote cooperation. Just as competition spreads from the workplace to the home, so it leaks from intergroup to intragroup level. This is partly the result of generalization of learning: it is not so easy to view some people as competitors, with all the attendant hostility, and then wipe away this orientation with respect to other people (those on the same team). The proof is in the furious competition for starting positions or higher salaries among athletes on the same team.[74]

This pervasive phenomenon does not mean that competition is an irrepressible part of human nature. It means that the most effective way to set up cooperation does not involve tacking on competition at another level. Far better is cooperation at both the intergroup and intragroup levels. When hostility mounted during the Robbers' Cave experiment, Sherif at first tried to unite the two teams by having them combine forces to beat a team from another camp. It didn't work.

> The short-term effects of this common enemy were to induce cooperation for "our camp" to beat theirs. However, when the common enemy was gone, the two rivals quickly retreated to their own in-groups, still unwilling to cooperate in other activities across group lines. Further, had we continued the "common enemy" approach, we would have ended by merely enlarging the scope of the generalized effects of win-lose competition that had already occurred within our camp. In effect, we would have had a bigger war.[75]

Sherif finally did end the vicious rivalry between Rattlers and Eagles by setting up "superordinate goals" for the boys to meet. These were tasks, such as pulling a truck up a hill or fixing the water supply system, in which the two groups had to cooperate — but without competing against anyone else.

Up until now, I have been arguing that intergroup competition is not necessary for cooperation; now I want to add that this arrangement is also positively undesirable. Consider the case of celebrating one's hometown. There is nothing offensive about the slogan "I Love New York" (except, perhaps, its dilution of the word "love"). This straightforward affirmation, however, is unusual today. Far more common is the defiant assertion that one's city is "Number One." As Michael Parenti has observed, "The lack of [a sense of] community does not prevent Americans from identifying with larger collective entities such as a school, a town or the nation. But even this identification is expressed in terms that are competitive with other schools, towns or nations."[76] And Frank Trippett, in a *Time* magazine essay that chucklingly approves of such competition, acknowledges that "local chauvinism habitually thrives on the disparagement of rival places or areas."[77] In a competitive culture, it is not sufficient to say that one is glad to live where one does; one must derogate all other towns and shout oneself hoarse about one's own town's being the best. Our usual reaction is, with Trippett, to dismiss such rivalry as harmless fun. This is also the prevailing view of sports and, for that matter, of any other competition that stops short of killing. But the sort of affirmation that is concerned with besting others, the sort of camaraderie that develops from working to beat another group — or from simply proclaiming the superiority of one's own — has an ugliness about it that I believe is intrinsically objectionable. Camaraderie is desirable, all things being equal. But all things are not equal when the feeling is derived from derogating an out-group. As to the defense that it is all in fun, I am reminded of the person who cruelly taunts someone and then remonstrates, "But I was only kidding!"

Beyond such principled objections are the practical problems. Sherif's fear of starting a "bigger war" is worth taking very seriously. The We vs. They structure and the attitude that accompanies it are, after all, at the heart of every war. It is one thing to feel hostile in a contest that pits one individual against another. It is something else again to stoke the aggressive fires that rage in *group* rivalries. One need not believe aggression is inevitable in human life to point out how horrible are the results of multiplying hatred by the number of people in a group. More: the whole of competitive fury, like that of cooperative creativity, is greater than the sum of its parts.

It is not readily apparent how we can end the awful legacy of nationalism — the tensions among countries that now threaten our very existence. But it is quite certain the answer does not lie in more rivalry — even the kind that is supposed to be "good-natured." After-dinner speakers urge us to rechannel our military competition into an effort to be number one in scientific or cultural endeavors. However uncontroversial this may sound at first hearing, it actually makes no more sense than the catharsis theory from which it borrows. Never mind that international scientific competition is likely to be far less productive than cooperation: the point here is that competition of any kind establishes an antagonism that contributes to, rather than deflects, feelings of hostility. The same is true for the Olympics, as George Orwell saw nearly forty years ago:

> Even if one didn't know from concrete examples . . . that international sporting contests lead to orgies of hatred, one could deduce it from general principles. . . . The whole thing is bound up with the rise of nationalism — that is, with the lunatic modern habit of identifying oneself with large power units and seeing everything in terms of competitive prestige. . . . I do not, of course, suggest that sport is one of the main causes of international rivalry; big-scale sport is itself, I think, merely another effect of the causes that have produced nationalism. Still, you do make things worse by sending forth a team . . . to do battle against some rival team, and allowing it to be felt on all sides that whichever nation is defeated will "lose face."[78]

Intergroup competition is too high a price to pay for intragroup cooperation, and it is fortunate that it does not have to be paid. Intergroup competition also is not the way to bring harmony and good fellowship to a brittle planet. Far more sensible is the premise that we should expand cooperation so as to include as many people as possible rather than restricting it to one's in-group. There are enough problems — enough superordinate goals — to occupy us indefinitely, and our work on them will have the felicitous consequence of binding us together if we join in solving them. Even if no individual can actively cooperate with everyone, he surely can approach others prepared to cooperate. Students can learn together in groups and then share their insights with other groups. Cities can work together on common problems rather than yelling about which is the best place to live or abasing themselves in a competition for corporate favors. Finally, we can heed Roderic Gorney's declaration that "Our ultimate safety depends only upon enlarging the circles of helpful cooperation one last step to encompass our largest units, the nations."[79]

CONSTRUCTIVE CONFLICT

To cooperate, as I have tried to show in earlier chapters, is not to sacrifice either an achievement orientation or a strong sense of self.

On the contrary, success will more likely be the result of working *with* other people, and the same might be said for healthy self-esteem. Here I would like to rescue cooperation from yet another misconception: it does not imply some idyllic state of harmony among participants. To the question "But how do you expect people to agree on everything?" we answer, "They won't — and that's why a cooperative framework for dealing with disagreement is so critical."

Conflict, per se, is not harmful. In fact, its absence suggests people who are frightened (to challenge a superior), resentful, or bereft of their rational faculties (as the total agreement among cult members demonstrates). Children know that disagreement exists; to force them to agree in a classroom is to ask them to deny reality and it is to deprive them of a real education. It is no coincidence that the word *challenge* means both to require someone to use her full range of abilities and to call something into question. Genuine learning does not smooth over or soothe. The same is true of effective problem solving: a rigid demand for agreement means that people will effectively be prevented from contributing their wisdom to a group effort.

What makes disagreement destructive is not the fact of conflict itself but the addition of competition. In a debate (as opposed to a discussion or dialogue), the point is to win rather than to reach the best solution or arrive at a compromise with which everyone is satisfied. Listen in at a board meeting or a dinner party and you can hear the difference between someone's participating in an exchange of ideas and someone's trying to score points. Both are examples of conflict, but only one involves competition. Morton Deutsch spelled out the distinction:

> A cooperative process leads to the defining of conflicting interests as a mutual problem to be solved by collaborative effort. It facilitates the recognition of the legitimacy of each other's interests and of the necessity of searching for a solution that is responsive to the needs of all. It tends to limit rather than expand the scope of conflicting interests. In contrast, a competitive process stimulates the view that the solution of conflict can only be one that is imposed by one side on the other . . . through superior force, deceptions, or cleverness. . . . The enhancement of one's own power and the minimization of the legitimacy of the other side's interests in the situation become objectives.[80]

When Deutsch refers to the use of "superior force" to resolve competitive conflict, he is not talking only about firepower. Tyranny of the majority usually takes place through voting. Trying to round up votes for one's position or candidate has more in common with coercion by force than it does with working cooperatively to achieve consensus. One of the reasons that conflict nested in competition can be ended only by some appeal to power is that competition interferes with communication. The difference between cooperation and competition is the difference between listening to each other's points of view and twisting each other's arms.

Cooperative conflict represents what Roger and David Johnson have called "friendly excursions into disequilibrium," and their classroom studies have made three things clear:

1. Students like it. In one study, arguing was less upsetting to fifth- and sixth-graders who participated in cooperative conflict than to those who had not.[81] In another, students were more enthused about cooperative conflict than about either independent learning or a "concurrence-seeking" model in which discussion was inhibited so as to minimize disagreement.[82] There was considerable dislike for debate in a third study, while not a single objection was raised against cooperative conflict.[83]

2. Students learn from it. Achievement tests revealed better comprehension under cooperative conflict than under concurrence seeking or independent learning.[84] A second study confirmed that this was true for high-, middle-, and low-ability subjects.[85]

3. It promotes interpersonal attraction. There were "greater feelings of peer academic support and personal acceptance" and "greater accuracy of perspective taking" in cooperative conflict than in concurrence seeking, debate, or independent learning situations.[86]

This last finding may be the most compelling. We feel better about each other when we air our differences than when we pretend everyone agrees. But such an airing must take place in the context of working with, rather than against, each other. Structural cooperation is not at all inimical to conflict. It simply allows conflict to work most productively by keeping out the poisonous hostilities of a win/lose arrangement.

7

The Logic of Playing Dirty

For nothing can seem foul to those that win.
— Shakespeare,
Henry IV, Part I, Act V, Scene 1

Even the most strident defender of the competitive spirit is willing to grant that one can go too far. Everyone shakes his head at "excessive" or "inappropriate" competition — and the "winning-at-all-costs" philosophy that fuels it. One manifestation of such excess is self-destructive behavior. There are those in business who wear themselves to a frazzle trying to get ahead, as if professional success could compensate them for having turned their private lives into a wasteland. There are those in school who think that subjecting themselves to a grim regimen of nicotine, caffeine, and no sleep is a small price to pay for another few points on the midterm exam. There are those in sports who devastate their bodies in search of a trophy, enduring hypothermia, hypoglycemia, and dehydration to the point of double vision and hallucinations. Never far behind this physical punishment is the psychological torment that waits to be unleashed on a loser.

Most people who speak of competitive abuses, though, are thinking of how we break the rules in order to win. In athletics, this may take the form of point-shaving, college recruiting scandals, performance drugs — all of which are quickly becoming as commonplace as six- and seven-figure salaries for sports stars. The playing field is also where we find "excessive" violence: immobilizing one's opponent by playing dirty, for example. The competitive pressures behind "winning ugly," as it is sometimes called, are hardly confined to the pros;

one need only attend a Little League game to witness a kind of institutionalized child abuse.

It would be a mistake, however, to restrict a discussion of cheating to athletics. A news dispatch from the 1985 meeting of the American Association for the Advancement of Science began as follows:

> Medical leaders and journal editors agreed today that highly competitive pressures in modern science were provoking cases of outright fraud and an even wider range of "white lies" and deceptions that they said were eroding the integrity of science. . . . Dr. Robert G. Petersdorf, vice chancellor for health sciences at the University of California at San Diego, said . . . the competition to win academic promotions and Federal research grants was causing an undetermined number of scientists to exaggerate or cheat in reporting research they had done.[1]

Consider also the wide range of unethical and sometimes illegal behaviors in political campaigns: smearing opponents, accepting and laundering illicit contributions, tapping phones, stealing documents, forging letters, and burying all of this under an avalanche of lies. (The point of Watergate, remember, was to win a contest.) Then there are the bribes and sabotage that have come to be seen as a routine part of doing business, the selective use of evidence and the hundred other dirty tricks that are common practice among lawyers, the way the truth is stretched for effect when journalists compete for space and recognition, the fact that premedical students sometimes ruin each other's experiments. Pick your field; if people are competing, many of them are going outside of the boundaries that have been established to delimit acceptable ways to win.

There are accepted and remarkably uniform ways of dealing with competitive abuses. Responding to rule-breakers is itself governed by rules. If you are a conservative, you will make sure that each wrongdoer is punished individually. The severity of the punishment will vary: When medical researcher John Darsee faked electrocardiogram data in 1981, he was stripped of his right to practice medicine in New York. When the Bank of Boston engaged in what was widely called a money-laundering scheme, it was fined the equivalent of about one day's after-tax profits.[2] Regardless of how stiff the penalty, the point is that each person who goes too far in an effort to beat out the competition is investigated and disciplined as if he were the only person who had ever done such a thing and as if he had acted out of sheer perversity.

Liberal, reform-minded people are less interested in punishing than in exhorting competitors to obey the rules and avoid getting carried away with the race to win. They are fond of unearthing an example of exceptional sportsmanship — a college coach who refuses to pay his athletes under the table, a tennis player who walks off the court arm in arm with her opponent — and they hold up this model to others. Competitors are told that the only thing that matters is how the game is played, that abuses can be eliminated if they would only "make more sportsmanlike gestures such as shaking hands or helping an opponent to his feet"[3] or "eliminate all authoritarian people from coaching"[4] or "replac[e] the term *opponent* with *associate*."[5] Thomas Tutko and William Bruns urge us: "Let's compete, let's play to win, but let's keep it all in perspective. . . . To learn to compete and face a challenge, to learn to accept victory and adjust to defeat, is quite different from a philosophy whereby one individual or team must emerge as a victor."[6] (Of course they fail to explain how it is possible to compete in such a way that one individual or team does not emerge as a victor.)

Underlying both approaches — isolating and punishing an individual who cheats and cautioning competitors about going overboard — is a single assumption. The assumption is that the ugly measures people use to get ahead represent a contamination of true competition. Thus, sports writer John Underwood says that cheating "defiles" competition,"[7] that violence has "perverted the good name of sport."[8] For William Bennett, now the U.S. Secretary of Education, violence is a "degradation of the game,"[9] while for Garrett Hardin, bloodiness is "only an accident of competition."[10] This is also the position of James Michener, who declared the problem "is not with competition per se but with the violence that excessive competition arouses."[11] The conservative's insistence that the fault lies with the individual competitors and the liberal's careful condemnation of *inappropriate* competition are really not so far apart. In both cases, competition itself is rescued from any blame. If we get rid of the troublemakers, if we don't go too far in our quest for victory, then there is nothing intrinsically wrong with the win/lose structure.

If you were an advocate of competition, this is precisely the tack you would take. No matter how frequently they seem to appear, you would argue that abusive, self-destructive, violent, or immoral behaviors are corruptions of *real* competition, which is in its essence as virtuous and healthy as these "exceptions" are nasty and neurotic. To argue in this way is also to enjoy an appreciable rhetorical advantage, since such a position appears pleasingly moderate: you are not saying *all* competition is bad, but merely that it should not be done to excess. What could be more reasonable?

This position coincides with the entrenched reluctance of Americans to consider structural explanations for problems. We prefer to hold individuals responsible for whatever happens or, at the most, to find a convenient proximate cause. Rarely are events understood in their historical or economic or social context. As one of many possible examples of this, consider how we respond when our children fail to learn. Typically we insist that they are not studying hard enough or else we put the problem down to poor teaching. What we do not do is acknowledge that a two-tiered educational system funnels most of the promising teachers and the privileged children to the private sector, virtually guaranteeing that students without the resources to follow will receive an inferior education. We do not ask why learning is defined in terms of a standardized test score, why obedience is valued above critical thinking — and we certainly do not look at the institutions in our country whose existence depends on a passive, acceptant public of precisely the sort that our schools manufacture.

The story is much the same when we confront poverty or crime or most other social ills.* As for psychological problems, we do not even recognize them to *be* social in nature; the trouble is framed as an "illness," purely an individual matter. This way of looking at the world has several consequences. It often results in blaming the victim, as many observers have pointed out. It leaves the foundations of our society undisturbed and even unexamined. And it all but assures that the problem itself will not go away.

In the case of competition, the root cause of abuses is the competitive structure itself. "Abuses," then, is really something of a misnomer since these actions do not represent the contamination of competition but rather its logical conclusion. In the last chapter, I argued that hostility is virtually built into an arrangement where someone else's fate is inversely related to your own. So it is that *a structural imperative to beat others invites the use of any means available.* "The aim of competi-

---

*We are moved to help a hungry individual but oblivious to how broad social policies have created hunger on a massive scale. In the face of considerable contrary evidence, we continue to believe that longer prison sentences will stop crime; we fail to consider how crime springs from structural barriers to the fulfillment of human needs.[12]

tion is to win and the temptation is to win at any cost," wrote Arthur Combs. "Although it begins with the laudable aim of encouraging production, competition quickly breaks down to a struggle to win at any price."[13] This process is part of the natural trajectory of competition itself. The only distinction that a competitor qua competitor knows is that between winning and losing; other distinctions, such as between moral and immoral, are foreign to the enterprise and must be, as it were, imported. They do not belong. The only goal that a competitor (again, qua competitor) has is victory; the only good is what contributes to this goal. If a new goal is introduced — particularly one that *interferes* with winning, such as staying within the guidelines of appropriate conduct — it is likely to be pushed aside. This does not mean that people who do so don't understand how to compete; on the contrary, they understand perfectly. Their behavior follows from the structure.

What this means is that we can no longer content ourselves with simply condemning cheaters or feeling sorry for self-destructive competitors. To do so is not only shortsighted but hypocritical: we set up a structure where the goal is victory and then blame people when they follow through. Pious admonitions about not getting carried away in competition, however well-meaning, are just exercises in self-deception. If we are serious about eliminating ugliness, we will have to eliminate the competitive structure that breeds the ugliness.

This perspective is radical and disturbing, but I think it fits the facts — that is, the frequency and pervasiveness of improper actions during competitive encounters — far better than the "contamination" view. Most people do not even keep the facts in view, failing to see the connections between campaign illegalities, scientific fraud, corporate trickery, and the use of steroids in college sports. Each appears in a different section of the newspaper, and it never dawns on us that there is a pattern. Once we acknowledge that these diverse shady activities all take place in the context of competition, we are more likely to see that the problem lies with the common denominator.

A few writers have identified competition itself as the problem. Anne Strick's critique of the American legal system, as we have already seen, questions the premise that justice is best served by an adversarial (i.e., competitive) model. She goes on to argue that this model is largely responsible for the abuses so common in the profession. "The Watergate lawyers were only doing what came naturally," Strick writes, because " 'enemies' is what our legal system is all about."

The need to beat the other side in the courtroom is the basis of "diversion, distortion, and direct deceit. . . . Where polarity shapes thinking and winning is the orthodoxy to which men chiefly adhere, deceit is absolutely justifiable."[14]

Günther Lüschen realized that the same is true on the playing field: "By and large the characteristic of a contest as a zero-sum game seems to explain why cheating should go on at all levels — even where the odds at stake are not high."[15] By definition, all competition is zero-sum (in the broad sense of mutually exclusive goal attainment), so the invitation to cheat is always present. George Orwell made the point even more strongly. "Serious sport has nothing to do with fair play," he wrote. "It is bound up with hatred, jealousy, boastfulness, disregard of all rules and sadistic pleasure in witnessing violence."[16]

Empirical research lends credence to this view. A sports psychologist found that

> both athletes and nonathletes used lower-level egocentric moral reasoning when thinking about dilemmas in sport than when addressing moral issues in other contexts. These and other findings suggest that moral norms which prescribe equal consideration of all people are often suspended during competition in favor of a more egocentric moral perspective.[17]

These findings also suggest that competition itself is responsible for the development of a lower moral standard. Indeed, another pair of researchers point to "evidence that regular sport participants become more committed to winning at any cost and less committed to values of fairness and justice as their competitive experience increases."[18] Ironically, Michael Novak, whom we already know to be a staunch defender of competition, agrees that sports naturally lead participants to try to win at any cost:

> The true practise of sport goes on, beneath the moralistic mythology of virtue and clean-living. Basketball without deception could not survive. Football without aggression, holding, slugging, and other violations — only a few of which the referees actually will censure — could not be played. Baseball without cunning, trickery, and pressing for advantage would scarcely be a contest. Our sports are lively with the sense of evil. . . . Sports provide an almost deliberate exercise in pushing the psyche to cheat and take advantage, to be ruthless, cruel, deceitful, vengeful, and aggressive.[19]

However appalling one might find Novak's cheerful endorsement of these attributes, he is accurately reporting that they form the basis of sport, that they issue from the contests' very nature. It remains only to emphasize once again that they are not confined to sports. They are to be found, albeit in different forms, in virtually any kind of competitive activity — and, for that matter, throughout a culture defined by a competitive worldview. Bertrand Russell put it well:

> The trouble does not lie simply with the individual, nor can a single individual prevent it in his own isolated case. The trouble arises from the generally received philosophy of life, according to which life is a contest, a competition, in which respect is to be accorded to the victor. This view leads to an undue cultivation of the will at the expense of the senses and the intellect.[20]

What, then, of sportsmanship and other calls to stay within certain guidelines? First, the notion is partly cosmetic; it offers a patina of respectability for the enterprise of making other people lose. The social pressures associated with the latter are far more powerful, and our sanctimonious noises about being a good sport allow us to condemn rule-breakers when it suits our purposes.[21] More important is the fact that sportsmanship is an artificial concept. It would not exist except for competition. Only within the framework of trying to win is it meaningful to talk about carrying this out in a graceful or virtuous fashion.* If we did not compete, we would not have to try to curb the effects of competition by invoking sportsmanship; we might well be working *with* other people in the first place.

Even viewed in this light, though, the question of sportsmanship reminds us that not every businessperson resorts to sleazy tactics to get ahead and not every football player tries to disable his opponent. There are plenty of factors that encourage or discourage the use of inappropriate techniques. One such factor is the level of the competitor's moral development. Not surprisingly, researchers have found that the maturity of an athlete's moral reasoning is inversely propor-

---

*There are many concepts that similarly depend on a social context for their very existence even though we take their ultimate reality for granted. The idea of theft, for instance, is literally without meaning in cultures where private property does not exist. There is no such thing as leisure unless work is experienced as alienating or unfulfilling. You cannot commit blasphemy unless you believe there is a God to be blasphemed.

tional to the number of aggressive acts he or she engages in or views as legitimate.[22] Other factors include the severity of the penalty, the likelihood that violators will be caught, and the perceived willingness of other participants to abide by the rules. The implication is that it is possible to try to counteract the natural consequence of the imperative to win and thus reduce the level of intentional competition. It is possible, but we Americans generally do not do so. On the contrary: The trouble with a hypercompetitive culture like ours is that we not only leave the mechanism intact but we create a network of reinforcements for winning at any cost. Cheating and the like can be said to be overdetermined — called forth by both the intrinsic structure of competition and the societal attitude toward it.

The latter has been remarked on more frequently than the former. In her analysis of lying, Sissela Bok writes:

> The very stress on individualism, on competition, on achieving material success which so marks our society also generates intense pressures to cut corners. To win an election, to increase one's income, to outsell competitors — such motives impel many to participate in forms of duplicity they might otherwise resist. The more widespread they judge these practices to be, the stronger will be the pressures to join, even compete, in deviousness.[23]

The last sentence is crucial: The pressure we feel to be number one creates a vicious circle as we expect others to play dirty and feel justified in breaking the rules ourselves — if not obligated to do so. If I play it straight, the next guy is just going to take advantage of me. To complain, as the lawbreaker often does, that honesty does not pay may be self-serving, but it is largely correct in a competitive society.

When we dismiss someone as a "loser" — one of our most scathing epithets — we are underscoring the importance of winning. It is not seen as important that we win with restraint or in accordance with ethical principles — just that we win. An athlete who plays dirty develops a reputation as someone to be reckoned with, someone impressive and fearsome; he is "bad" or "tough" in the admiring sense that children use these words. The concrete advantages of such a style also are clear: What's a 15-yard penalty if you can put the other team's receiver out for the game? No one gets kept on the team for being a good sport. The more substantial penalties are handed out for losing. Moreover, as Tutko and Bruns observe, "the American culture has built so much guilt into losing that the person who tries to make a healthy adjustment to it — like cracking jokes in the midst of a losing streak — is thought to be a lousy competitor, if not a little crazy."[24] Clearly it is better to be thought overzealous than a lousy competitor.

The pressure to win at all costs, again, is not limited to athletics. Unethical campaign practices are partly the result of our society's priorities, as sociologist Amitai Etzioni explained:

> Truth to be told, the Watergate gang is but an extreme manifestation of a much deeper and more encompassing American malaise, the emphasis on success and frequent disregard for the nature of the means it takes to achieve it. Not only high level administration officials, but many Americans as well, seem to have accepted the late football coach Vince Lombardi's motto, "Winning is not the most important thing, it's the *only* thing." Thus, the executives of ITT who sought to overthrow the government of Chile to protect their goodies, the Mafia [chieftains] who push heroin, the recording company executives who bribe their records onto the top-40 list, and the citizens who shrug off corruption in the local town hall as "that's the way the cookie crumbles," all share the same unwholesome attitude. True, the Watergate boys have broken all known American precedents in their violation of fair play, but they are unique chiefly in the magnitude of their crime — not in the basic orientation that underlies it.[25]

The tendency to shrug off political corruption as expected and unexceptional is not only distressing but very dangerous — rather like the refusal to differentiate among health hazards on the grounds that "everything is bad for you." The effect is that politicians know that the reaction to their improprieties, if discovered, probably will not outweigh the fruits of victory. By the same token, the lawyer who resorts to gutter tactics is well aware that his or her win/loss record is what really matters. Marvin Frankel put it this way: "In a system that so values winning and deplores losing, where lawyers are trained to fight for, not to judge their clients, where we learn as advocates not to 'know' inconvenient things, moral elegance is not to be expected."[26]

Such social pressures, I want to reiterate, merely reinforce the inherent qualities of competition. Our approval of winning at all costs is the secondary inducement to cheat; the primary inducement is the nature of competition itself. It is true that contests without cheating or violence can occur if we successfully introduce considerations that are external to the impetus to win. Such contests seem unobjectionable, however, precisely because the element of competition has been diluted. To point to a morally exemplary lawsuit or an examination where the honors system is respected is not to refute the basic point here. The less competitive a given activity, the less likelihood, all things being equal, of "abuses." This is consistent with the arguments offered in earlier chapters of this book: the higher the concentration of competition in any interaction, the less likely it is to be enjoyable and the more likely it is to be destructive to our self-esteem, our relationships, our standards of fairness.

8

◁ ▷

Women and Competition

I wish it could have been a tie.

— Amanda Bonner (Katharine Hepburn),
after defeating her husband in court
in *Adam's Rib*

Competitive cultures train their members to compete, but the training is not the same for everyone. It is affected by whether one lives downtown or in the country, whether one is born into wealth or poverty. Perhaps the single most important variable — one I have not yet mentioned — is gender. The lessons on when and how to compete, and on how to regard the whole enterprise of competition, are significantly different for boys and girls. Attitudes and behaviors remain different for men and women, with important consequences for the society as a whole.

The general rule is that American males are simply trained to win. The object, a boy soon gathers, is not to be liked but to be envied, not to reflect but to act, not to be part of a group but to distinguish himself from the others in that group. From her work with children, Carole Ames found that "the consequences of failing in competitive situations appear to have been more ego threatening for males than females."[1] Being number one is an imperative for boys, so a good deal is invested in whether one makes it.

There has been other research on sex differences. Eleanor Maccoby and Carol Jacklin reviewed a number of studies conducted in the late 1960s and early 1970s, concluding that "boys tend to be more competitive, but the behavior is evidently subject to situational and cultural variations to a considerable degree."[2] In 1979, two researchers surveyed the attitudes of more than twenty-four hundred students from grades two through twelve. At all ages, they discovered, boys were more enthusiastic about competition than girls and more likely to prefer it. Boys were also less enthusiastic about, and less likely to prefer, cooperation.[3]

Recent research has confirmed that this disparity does not disappear when we grow up[4] — which, of course, is hardly news to most of us. The male competitive orientation may manifest itself as blatantly as it did during childhood, as little boys wrestling after school grow into men who sabotage rivals for the vice presidency or vie for an attractive woman or explode in infantile fury on the squash court. Then again, the urge may be tempered, sublimated, rechanneled. Even when grown men eye each other on the street, says one writer, what flashes through their minds is:

> Can I take this guy, or not? . . . Maybe it isn't so physical. Questions like, "Am I smarter than this guy?" and "If we start talking about jobs, will mine sound more impressive?" are part of the same response. So is "Am I better looking (or thinner, or funnier)?" It's the competitive instinct reduced to its pettiest essence, but there it is. Boys are taught to win. If winning involves beating some other boy who wants to win just as badly, then you've got to take him or suffer the consequences.[5]

This observation appeared in the "About Men" column of the *New York Times Magazine,* a forum for male rumination. The very frequency with which competition appears as a theme in these essays is noteworthy. Here, for example, is a column written by one of the magazine's editors:

> Sports is where the boy child of our culture learns what's expected of him when he grows up: winning. Some of us may seem to outgrow any need to heave our middle-aged carcasses around a softball diamond or a tennis court, but we have an unconscious inner core where that painfully vivid childhood lesson is ever fresh. It emerges when we put down our kids, when we undercut our colleagues — and when we dream.[6]

It emerges also in the way men talk, often arguing even when there is no substantial disagreement, just for the chance to come out ahead. For men, the very act of speaking is often an opportunity to establish "who *really* is best, stronger, smarter, or, ultimately, more powerful."[7]

So much for men. The training they receive and the character structure it builds are depressingly straightforward. Competition appears in full-strength concentrate. On the other hand, some girls are raised to compete while others are not. Mixed messages are common, creating profoundly ambivalent feelings toward competition. Finally, attitudes about the desirability of competing for women are in flux today. The question for females is, in short, far more complex — more interesting intellectually, more urgent politically. This is why I have devoted a chapter to the subject of women and competition without a corresponding chapter about men.

One of the most influential ways of accounting for women's greater reluctance to compete was devised by Matina Horner in the 1960s. Psychologists who study motivation have long talked about "the motive to approach success" and "the motive to avoid failure," two constructs used to predict behavior and explain levels of accomplishment. In her doctoral dissertation at the University of Michigan, Horner proposed a new motive: "fear of success" (also known as "the motive to avoid success"). The idea was created to explain differences between the sexes: women are brought up to regard pursuit of achievement as unfeminine and thus to become anxious throughout life at the prospect of doing well. Presumably, then, they exhibit more fear of success. Horner tested this by asking undergraduates to write a story about a fictitious student (of the same sex as the subject) who was said to be "at the top of her (his) medical school class." She reported that two thirds of the women, as compared to only about 9 percent of the men, told stories that contained fear of success imagery. Since the basis of all projective testing is that such stories reflect the psychological state of the storyteller, the women here were understood to be saying that they hold themselves back because they are afraid of success.[8]

Horner's work received considerable attention, and the catch phrase "fear of success" quickly became part of the language. Unfortunately, it has not stood up well under careful scrutiny and further study. The concept's status as an enduring trait has been questioned, and Horner's technique for measuring it (on which the findings of differences between men and women depend) has seemed dubious to many scholars. "The projective measure of fear of success is ambiguous, has low reliability, and lacks predictive validity," as two psychologists put it.[9] What Horner scored as fear of success in the stories told by her subjects might have been affected by the testing situation or the occupation she used (medicine) or the sex of the person being written about rather than the sex of the subject. In any case, attempts to replicate her findings have rarely succeeded. Sex-based differences in fear of success imagery usually have been slight, and many studies have found no difference at all — or even more fear among men.[10] Part of the problem may be that the disparity Horner discovered was rooted not in underlying differences between the sexes but in social factors. As the latter have shifted, women's and men's attitudes toward success have converged.[11]

The real problem with Horner's "fear of success" construct, though — or at least the problem with how her data have been interpreted — is the tendency to confound success with competition. As I tried to show in chapter 3, these two are not at all the same thing; in fact, competitiveness can be an impediment to success. Horner quite explicitly stated that she "refer[s] to this disposition to become anxious in competitive achievement situations as the motive to avoid success."[12] Similarly, a later study that corroborated Horner's findings assumed that anyone disagreeing with such statements as "I am happy only when I am doing better than others" or "The rewards of a successful competition are greater than those received from cooperation" was exhibiting fear of success.[13] This raises the possibility that women are backing away from the prospect of having to beat other people, not from success itself.

Psychologist Georgia Sassen made just this point in a 1980 article, noting that when fear of success tests do not limit themselves to competitive success, there is no difference between the sexes.[14] Then she went a step further. At about the same time Robert Helmreich and his associates were taking the long overdue step of breaking down success into its constituent parts (or what are assumed to be its parts) — and discovering that the most competitive professionals are actually among the *least* successful (see pp. 52–53) — Sassen did something similar. She devised a way to measure how much someone's idea of success is based on competition, a scale she called the competitiveness-of-success concept (COSC). Sure enough, while there seemed to be no difference between the sexes on fear of success, per se, men's COSC was higher than women's. Sassen concluded that "the sex difference in earlier work on fear of success was actually a sex difference in how people define success for themselves. . . . Men define success competitively, as Horner [and] those who replicated Horner's research . . . did."[15]

So what happens when women are allowed to work at a task in a noncompetitive situation? Horner herself provided the answer: "In the absence of interpersonal competition and its aggressive overtones, whereby the tendency to avoid success is minimally, if at all, aroused, these women [who are high in fear of success] will perform efficiently."[16] Several years later, when Maccoby and Jacklin reviewed the literature on the subject, they found that: "Boys need to be challenged by appeals to ego or competitive motivations to bring their achievement up to the level of girls'. Boys' achievement motivation does appear to be more responsive to competitive arousal than girls', but this does not imply a generally higher level."[17]

Even those women who are said to fear success do just fine at noncompetitive tasks. This much is fact. But what of our values? What do we make of this state of affairs? Let's begin by acknowledging that the phrase "fear of success" is not merely imprecise but loaded. It suggests a deficiency, a problem to be remedied. There would seem to be something wrong with people who have such a fear, just as with those who are afraid of the dark. If we substitute a more neutral term such as "aversion to competition," we are then freer to ask whether this is really a bad thing. One of Horner's subjects spun a story which imagined the mythical medical student "no longer feels so certain that she really wants to be a doctor . . . [and] decides not to continue with her medical work but to continue with courses that she never allowed herself to take before but that have a deeper personal meaning for her." Another subject has the student saying, " 'To hell with the whole business' " and going into social work — "not hardly as glamorous, prestigious, or lucrative; but she is happy." These two excerpts are cited by Horner under the heading "Concern About One's Normality or Femininity" and are said to reveal fear of success.[18]

In light of the psychological and interpersonal destructiveness of competition (not to mention its unproductiveness), these comments ought to be seen instead as intimations of health, an altogether appropriate sense that one can and should step off the competitive treadmill. As Sassen puts it, Horner's subjects may be indicating

> a heightened perception of the "other side" of competitive success, that is, the great emotional costs at which success achieved through competition is often gained — an understanding which, while confused, indicates some underlying sense that something is rotten in the state in which success is defined as having better grades than everyone else.[19]

.   .   .

It is competition and not success that separates men and women. There are signs, however, that the gap between the sexes is narrowing even here — and not because men are coming to share a distaste for beating others. Over the last decade or two, a chorus of voices has been urging women to compete and to accept competitiveness as appropriate and even healthy. Magazine articles and books too numerous to list here sing the praises of winning. One sample, fairly representative of the genre, should suffice to convey the flavor. Entitled "The Thrill of Competition," it appeared in *Seventeen* magazine in 1982. "Don't get hung up — climb that ladder to success," it counsels teenage girls. Betty Lehan Harragan, author of a book called *Games Mother Never Taught You,* is quoted as follows: "It's true that some people would rather that you weren't competitive. These people may prefer to succeed themselves rather than see you get ahead." Thus warned that all critics of competition are cynical opportunists, readers presumably will be more receptive to the advice that they "start competing in high school and . . . get a strong foothold on the ladder to self-improvement."[20]

Similar exhortations aimed at grown women typically observe that a sexist culture has limited its endorsement of competition to men — and then go on to urge women to correct this imbalance by becoming as competitive as possible. This is the gist, for example, of a book called *The Femininity Game,* written by Thomas Boslooper and Marcia Hayes. In another article, a psychiatrist says this:

> We haven't integrated rivalry into the development of women. It's only been worked out for boys. I was at a swimming pool the other day, and two little boys were racing to the other end of the pool. When one of the boys lost, his father said, "Mikey, listen, this is why you lost: You didn't start off soon enough." But the mother said, "Listen, Michael, it's just a game." You see what I mean? I think a lot of women are still not comfortable with competition.[21]

Notice, first, that the mother's comment is assumed to reflect discomfort rather than principled opposition to competition or a simple sense of perspective about the importance of games. Second, the speaker not only assumes that this discomfort is problematic — something to be gotten over — but makes no effort to defend her assumption; it is so obvious as to require no support.

The pro-competition line has been winning adherents, changing the way both sexes think about women. Not only has it become the dominant viewpoint on the issue in the United States, but it has succeeded in reframing the controversy. There are now only two positions: either you agree that competition for women is desirable and long overdue or you are part of a patriarchal structure that believes only men have a right to be successful. This kind of rhetoric, combined with a legitimate impatience with sex-based discrimination, has led women to readjust not only their behavior but their cognitive and emotional response to the idea of competing.

Now it may be argued that women in competitive cultures have always competed — for men, for the status of being most attractive, and so on.[22] What is new is the sheer intensity of the competitive drive, the absence of shame or hesitation, the fact that women are now competing with men, and the shift to the public arena (notably, the marketplace). Consider some examples of the last. A recent advertisement for *Fortune* magazine, which bore the legend, "Every success story starts with a kid who hated to lose," featured a photograph of an unhappy little *girl* in a baseball uniform. Pro-competition magazines for businesswomen, like *Savvy* and *Working Woman,* are prospering. Women increasingly are "modeling themselves after the hard-driving men who have preceded them on the fast track . . . with single-mindedness that can disrupt families and friendships," according to an article that profiles investment banker Karen Valenstein.[23] (Valenstein is quoted as praising her mentor, who " 'taught me the words *gelt* and *shmuck.* I figured out for myself that if you don't have any you are one.' ")[24]

It may not be terribly important in itself, but fashion in the business world reflects this transformation. Women bought 24 million suits in 1984,[25] suggesting a style of dress that is conservative, asexual, "powerful," and that can even include shoulder pads. Clearly the idea is to look as much like a man as possible. Again, clothing is merely the outward manifestation of a rush to emulate male, competitive models of success. One writer remarks that "so many of the women I know are driven people, more afraid of failure than success, more afraid of complacency than of competition, more afraid of one another's successes than of the successes of the men in their lives."[26] The wistful preference for noncompetitive success — such as the sentiment in this chapter's epigraph — now tends to be mocked rather than taken seriously.

Precisely the same thing is happening in sports, and, again, it is difficult to find a single voice raised in dissent. "Whether they change reluctantly or enthusiastically," one observer reports, "women's athletic programs look more like men's athletic programs every year. . . . Excelling at the highest levels of competition is emerging as the first commandment of women's sports."[27] In March 1985, *Ms.* magazine featured a musclebound female body builder on its cover; several months later, editor Gloria Steinem interviewed another body builder — this one boasting a physique that seemed literally indistinguishable from that of a male body builder.

The presentation of women in cinema is another good index of the cultural conversion. Indisputably, females still appear as little more than window dressing in many contemporary movies — a sidekick to comfort the hero or cheer him on or be rescued by him, someone to be ogled or seduced. But to the extent there has been a departure from this sexist tradition, it has chiefly been to feature women in the same dismal roles that men have hitherto occupied. In 1968, *Funny Girl* depicted a love story in which Barbra Streisand as Fanny Brice clowned and swooned, allowing Omar Sharif to chuckle at her antics and indulge her girlish whims. She was a girl who won her man. Fifteen years later, in *Yentl,* Streisand played a girl who *became* a man. This is a literalization of what was beginning to happen in American film by the early 1980s. In *Flashdance* and *Heart Like a Wheel,* for example, women overcome considerable obstacles to win, enthusiastically embracing a competitive dream, no matter what the cost. They derive their fulfillment from triumphing over others, becoming, in effect, men with higher voices. In *Heart Like a Wheel,* the heroine's private life is in a shambles by the time she brings home the trophy as a victorious race car driver. Hearts don't win, so they have to be transformed into wheels. The story has been told a thousand times before, of course, only with men at the controls. We are supposed to cheer the woman who insists that it's her turn to drive.

In real life, the conversion to competitiveness can, at the risk of some oversimplification, be broken down into three stages. At the beginning, a woman resists the whole enterprise of competition. In the second stage, she competes, but with serious misgivings: "I had no choice," she might apologize to someone she has stepped on. Finally, her feelings and beliefs catch up to her behavior. She internalizes the competitive values, stops feeling conflicted about what she is doing, and rids herself of guilt. This last stage is precisely what women are urged to reach. Workshops and seminars, books and articles, therapy sessions and informal support groups, all encourage women to compete without reserve. Moreover, these exhortations often use language such as "Accept your own competitiveness!" in order to disguise the conversion as self-discovery.

There has always been opposition to this model, but it seems lately to have been drowned out by the pro-competition clamor until only a few lonely voices of protest are audible. I want to add my own in support of the dissident position. This perspective does not deny the reality of sexism; it asserts that becoming competitive is a spurious and unhelpful response to it. It resists the pseudofeminist posture — I think this blunt label is warranted — which seeks the liberation of women through the imitation of men. It does not object to androgyny in the name of *la différence* but instead to the particular male values, such as competition, that women are being encouraged to adopt. It rejects the implicit motto of pseudofeminism: If you can't join them, beat them.

A commitment to relationship, an other-regarding posture that places special emphasis on the connections between people, traditionally has been a signal feature of women's worldview. In the choice between competition and relationship — and it *is* a choice, as I tried to show in chapter 6 — women have affirmed the latter.[28] Carol Gilligan's 1982 book, *In a Different Voice,* represents one of the most lucid descriptions (and, if one reads between the lines, defenses) of this orientation. She calls it the "feminine voice," noting that it is predominantly found among women but is not necessarily beyond the reach of men. Let me offer three examples of how this concern with relationship plays itself out and how it usually has been regarded.

The first case is the central focus of Gilligan's book: moral development. Some theorists have pronounced women less sophisticated in their ethical thinking, by which they mean that women are less likely to resolve dilemmas in accordance with abstract notions of rights and duties. Women have tended to think in terms of the obligations that flow from a sensitivity to our interdependence. While girls approach moral problems by wondering how to avoid hurting people, boys more often see the whole enterprise as "sort of like a math problem with humans," in the words of one eleven-year-old subject.[29] Gilligan's point is that the allegedly universal standards of moral development, according to which women have been found wanting, are actually based on an implicitly male-oriented model. Rather than trying to conform to it, perhaps women and men alike should consider the value of an ethical orientation enunciated in the feminine voice. In Gilligan's words:

> When one begins with the study of women and derives developmental constructs from their lives, the outline of a moral conception different from that described by Freud, Piaget, or Kohlberg begins to emerge

and informs a different description of development. In this conception, the moral problem arises from conflicting responsibilities rather than from competing rights and requires for its resolution a mode of thinking that is contextual and narrative rather than formal and abstract. This conception of morality as concerned with the activity of care centers moral development around the understanding of responsibility and relationships, just as the conception of morality as fairness ties moral development to the understanding of rights and rules.[30]

To take a second example of these divergent approaches, Piaget was among several investigators who observed that when girls who are playing a game come to a disagreement about the rules, they often will start over or switch to another game. This has usually been interpreted as a failing — an indication that girls are not learning negotiation skills or are threatened by conflict. But the same reality can be understood in another way. Perhaps girls cherish their friendships and do not wish to risk them for the sake of continuing a game or learning legalistic skills. Perhaps the female priority system ranks relationship ahead of rules and perhaps this appears skewed only when viewed from a male point of reference.

Yet another arena in which we find these two differing orientations is conversation. Research by sociolinguists demonstrates that, in our culture at least, women and men tend to play different conversational roles. According to Charles Derber, men often acknowledge what someone else has said in a perfunctory way and then shift the conversation to talk about themselves. ("Huh, that's interesting, because yesterday you know what happened to me?") Women more often respond supportively, encouraging the other individual to continue. ("Really? And then what happened?")[31] Men are also more likely to interrupt outright — in one study of mixed-sex conversation, 96 percent of the interruptions were men breaking in on women[32] — whereas women tend to ask more questions and generally take responsibility for starting and maintaining conversations as well as putting other participants at ease.[33]

In response to these speech patterns, one could conceivably say that because women are being trampled in conversation, they should, in effect, give men a dose of their own medicine by competing more aggressively for attention and authority. (This prescription seems to follow naturally from one prominent researcher's characterization of women as "the 'shitworkers' of routine interaction.")[34] On the other hand, it is possible to agree that one should not allow oneself to be interrupted — or one's topic of conversation to be ignored — without suggesting that the answer is to try to beat men at their own game. One surely ought to be assertive enough in conversation to avoid being dismissed; likewise, women should not convey by their tone and conversational role that what they have to say is not important. But this need not lead them to begin interrupting or stop being supportive. As linguist Robin Lakoff, one of the pioneers of research in this field, put it:

> Although in many ways the typical feminine style doesn't get you what you want, nevertheless it's exceedingly valuable. It would be a pity if it were to vanish. The alternative, the male style, has so many bad aspects of its own that nobody is advised to acquire it. . . . Anything that allows the other person to have room is in itself a good thing, something that suggests cooperation. Questions tend to draw other people into the discourse and encourage them to make contributions.[35]

The female commitment to relationship, as it is manifested in moral reasoning and childhood play and conversation, is terribly important. The shift toward competition represents nothing less than an abandonment of this commitment, the attenuation of care. Perhaps it is unfair to hold women responsible for such a loss; the other half of the human race is even more alienated from the rewards of relatedness by virtue of its immersion in competition. Yet this is exactly the point. To be a bit melodramatic, it is more tragic to watch the process of corruption than to deplore the condition of those who are already corrupt. Put more hopefully, one makes a greater fuss about those who are still able to listen, those who are not yet beyond being recalled to their own values.

To reaffirm the value of relationship, I should emphasize, is not at all to glorify dependence. To cherish the part of our lives that involves connection with others hardly entails subjugating oneself to others' needs. Neither does it mean that one has sacrificed healthy self-directedness or autonomy. What Gilligan has styled "the feminine voice" is perfectly compatible with a secure sense of self. In any case, competition would be a poor strategy for reaching this goal. As I tried to show in chapter 5, competition is associated with neediness and an external locus of control. Those who talk or act as if becoming more competitive were a sign of growth may have simply confused competition with autonomy or relationship with dependence.

Those who would have women endorse competition may offer an

objection to this talk of relationship, as follows: Women may be associated with this orientation rather than with competition, but they cannot really be said to have "affirmed" it. The repudiation of relationship does not amount to giving up something that was freely chosen because women have had connectedness and the like thrust upon them. Competition, by the same token, was never refused by most women so much as withheld from them as an option. Women tend to be more *unable* to compete than unwilling; they shrink from rivalry. This suits the purposes of men, who have profited from the exclusion of women from the competitive arena.

There is truth in this account. Choice in the fullest sense has been in scarce supply for both sexes as regards competition. It might be said that while women *couldn't* compete, men have *had* to compete. In terms of political and economic power, these situations have not been symmetrical, I should add. The man's "predicament" has left him to run the show, to monopolize the public sphere. But any feminism that leaves it at that is a feminism that accepts a male set of priorities, that fails to question the infatuation with wealth and power, that accedes to the devaluation of relationship, that says "Me, too!" instead of "What a mess!"

It is pathetic and outrageous that women have had to wait, like Sleeping Beauty, to be awakened with a kiss. But it would be tragic indeed if, finally able to rouse themselves, they did so only to mimic the prince. This is why I call the cheerleaders of competition for women pseudofeminists: they are responding to sexism by appropriating the worst of male values, which represents a serious error in judgment if not a kind of betrayal. The fact that men have had a virtual monopoly on competitiveness does not, in itself, make it desirable. Men may resist new competitors in the marketplace, but they can grin with arrogant satisfaction knowing that women have decided to emulate them. Here is the classic Pyrrhic victory for women: opposing male oppression by becoming indistinguishable from a male oppressor.* Sure, says sociologist Barrie Thorne, "Women should be getting equal pay and having access to every occupation and being President and so on. But I wouldn't want to end with that because I think this society is structured in an ugly, competitive way. I think the challenge is to pursue that strategy as a right that we have but at the same time

---

*The slogan "Smash patriarchy!" is an extreme example of this. It is a perfect paradox, neatly refuting itself.

critique it and create alternative forms of community and human relations."[36]

For women to pump up their biceps or break into the club of hard-driving money grubbers on Wall Street is a peculiar and sad kind of liberation. For the feminine voice to slide down into a baritone that rasps about being number one is a poor excuse for deliverance. The fact that women's values have tended to clash with the demands of competitive, male-dominated institutions does not mean that the former ought to adjust to fit the latter.

> [It's not] that there is something wrong with women . . . [but] that there is something wrong with this definition of success and that there is something right with women's inability to accommodate this definition. . . . It no longer seems appropriate to rout out success anxiety and re-place it with acceptance of the masculine rules of the game. Rather, women now need to focus on affirming the structures and values they bring to the question of competition versus relationships and start re-constructing institutions according to what women know.[37]

The situation is analogous to something that baffles and dismays those committed to social change. Members of the underclass in America often seem less interested in ending a system of privilege than in becoming privileged themselves. They rarely challenge the basic script, preferring to concentrate only on the casting. The economic system that predicates wealth on poverty, power on powerlessness, is implicitly accepted even by those with the greatest incentive to challenge it. This is a tribute to the effectiveness of our society's ideological apparatus, which encourages debate on tiny questions in order to deflect attention from the big ones, and which (as I mentioned in the last chapter) perpetuates a myth of individual responsibility to the exclusion of attention on structural causes. However it works, though, it works. Now something similar is happening with women, who are buying into a competitive system rather than challenging it. "Buying into" is an apt phrase, in fact: The case of women and competition is not merely analogous to, but part of, the question of privilege. Pseudofeminism may celebrate competition in women's athletics or competition in the abstract, but it is primarily concerned with competition for money. The current call to become competitive cannot be differentiated from the acceptance (and thus the perpetuation) of our economic system. Pseudofeminism is, in its consequence if not in its intention, a conservative movement.

The three-stage socialization process I mentioned — from avoiding competition to competing guiltily to competing wholeheartedly — needs to be reversed. Women, along with any men who are not too far gone, ought to summon back their guilt. I realize this sounds strange to our ears, since we regard guilt (along with anything else that makes us feel bad) as something to be eliminated. But guilt can be appropriate if it is not irrational, if it directs our attention to something about ourselves that is genuinely problematic. The point here — as, indeed, with all healthy guilt — is not to trap us in an endless cycle of self-punishment but to provide the impetus to real change. The woman who hears a squawk from her conscience when she begins to see her friends as obstacles to her own triumph should not seek to silence that voice. Rather, she should question her actions — along with the win/lose structure that led her to feel bad.

The goal is not to be unable to compete, as some insist was the departure point for women. It is to arrive not at "cannot" but "will not." The ideal of psychotherapy is not to become a particular kind of person — a person similar to the therapist, for example — but to widen one's horizons, to be flexible and free enough to choose. Here, too, the objective is choice, and this requires psychological health as well as economic and political freedom (which includes an end to sex-based discrimination of all kinds). At such a point, I trust that women will choose to stop learning competition, that in its place they will truly affirm relationship. This time around, maybe the lesson will be cooperation and men will be the students.

9
◁▷

Beyond Competition:

THOUGHTS ON MAKING CHANGE

> The prevailing mode of competition in American cul-
> ture thus continues despite convincing evidence that it is
> damaging to physical, spiritual, emotional, and social
> health. And what is the reaction of members of the help-
> ing professions? Are we creative agents of social change
> or are we dispensers of Band-Aids to the injured and
> facilitators of adjustment to "the way things are"?
>
> — Vera J. Elleson,
> "Competition: A Cultural Imperative"

INTENTIONAL AND STRUCTURAL COMPETITION REVISITED

The cartoon animals children watch on Saturday morning TV continue to run even when there is no longer any ground under their feet
— at least until they look down. It is as if some combination of igno-
rance and momentum allows them to keep going. The same may be
said of competition. We persist in our furious efforts to be number
one, we continue to believe this is somehow in our best interests, and
we raise yet another generation to do the same. We do these things
despite the fact that

> cooperative, as compared to competitive, systems of distributing re-
> wards — when they differ — have more favorable effects on individual
> and group productivity, individual learning, social relations, self-
> esteem, task attitudes, and a sense of responsibility to other group
> members. This conclusion is consistent with the research results ob-
> tained by many other investigators in hundreds of studies. It is by now a
> well-established finding, even though it is counter to widely held
> ideologies about the relative benefits of competition.[1]

Despite this evidence, reviewed here by Morton Deutsch, we continue trying to succeed at the price of other people's failure. Often *we* are those "other people" who fail, but this scarcely diminishes our quest for victory or our belief that competition is good for us.

Changing this state of affairs is difficult because structural and intentional competition reinforce each other. How can we eliminate the competitive framework of our society so long as there still exists both a widespread belief that competition is desirable and a strong inclination to beat other people? On the other hand, how can we change these views so long as a structure remains in place that requires us to compete (and inclines us to bring our beliefs into line with our actions)? It is the same dilemma confronted a generation ago by civil rights activists: trying to end segregation by governmental fiat would run into resistance because of widespread racist attitudes — yet how could racism ever be overcome in a segregated society?

"Neither the individual's values nor those of the system are primary," Paul Wachtel has written; "each determines the other in continuous reciprocal interaction. People in a system with competitive values tend to become competitive, and in so doing they keep the system competitively oriented."[2] How can we break this vicious circle? By tackling both levels at once. "What works best is a multiple approach, confining itself neither solely to changing overt behavior nor to promoting insight alone, but rather attempting to weaken a number of links in the causal chain simultaneously. . . . Since our beliefs and values shape our institutions, and our institutions shape our beliefs and values, a multifaceted effort is required."[3] Alas, Wachtel does not offer much in the way of guidance as to how to undertake this multifaceted effort. That will be the task of this chapter.

.   .   .

I argued in chapter 5 that intentional competition could be understood in terms of self-esteem needs: we try to beat others in an effort to prove our own worth. Ultimately this strategy reveals itself as futile, since making our self-esteem contingent on winning means that it will always be in doubt. The more we compete, the more we *need* to compete.

Escaping this trap ultimately means finding more successful ways of securing our self-esteem: building an unconditional sense of trust in ourselves that will make it unnecessary to keep demonstrating our superiority. The better I feel about myself, the less I will need to make you lose. Carl Rogers emphasized that the experience of being accepted by others permits us to accept ourselves. Intuitively this seems more promising than trying to triumph over others. Given the unique dimensions of these issues for each person, however, I would not presume to offer a recipe for setting this complex process into motion. All I can reasonably do here is to call attention to the connection between intentional competition and self-esteem. Overcoming the former means in some respect concerning oneself with the latter.

Self-esteem is not an all-or-nothing affair, of course. Those who are least secure about themselves may require the most confirmation of their talents (and, ultimately, of their goodness). But all of us want to check how we are doing and reassure ourselves that we are competent. We are accustomed to doing so by ranking ourselves — to the point that where we stand (in relation to others) defines who we are. Because of this, a critic should have something with which to replace comparison if he is going to urge us to move beyond it. If we have come to be dependent on ranking for our very identities, we cannot very well expect to adjust instantly to its absence. Happily, as I pointed out in an earlier chapter, comparing oneself to others is not the only way to measure our progress. We can look instead to our own past performance or to some absolute standard to see how well we are doing. (Content with swimming a few more laps than I did last week, I will not feel compelled to find out how many laps the person in the next lane has completed.)*

If we are obliged to participate in structural competition, we can still work to reduce personal competitiveness. At the very least, we can shift to what I have called "process competition" by directing attention away from the results of an activity. If we are playing a competitive game, we ought not to keep score. If it will be obvious who wins, we should at least avoid awarding any prizes or making a fuss over the victor. By minimizing the significance of winning, we simultaneously soften the blow of losing. Whenever we take part in a contest, we can

---

*Two qualifications are in order here. First, even such noncompetitive measures as past performance are product-oriented. In many instances it may be desirable to stop checking our performance and pushing ourselves to produce more. We can stop counting laps and simply swim for as long as it gives us pleasure. Second, even the process of comparing our performance to others — which I have been suggesting is unnecessary — does not necessitate competition. We can see how well others are doing without needing to do better than they (see pp. 42–43).

try to nest it in fellowship: by making a special effort to fortify the bonds between competitors, the destructive effects of having to work against each other can be eased a bit. Friendly gestures to rivals will be reciprocated more often than one might imagine; our opponents probably feel as isolated and trapped by the structure as we do. At the very least, such pleasantness can moderate the hostility that is generated by competing for the same position or prize.

Trying to be number one in all situations may be rooted in self-esteem needs, but it can be driven by force of habit as well. We simply become accustomed to thinking along these lines. It may be fruitful to monitor one's own competitiveness as it makes itself felt in various situations — and then make a conscious effort to tame this impulse. ("Why did I just interrupt him again? I'm trying to prove to everyone that I'm cleverer than he is. What if I just sat back and listened to what he had to say?" "Why am I resolving to go on a diet again — just because a woman who's thinner than I walked into the room? There are always going to be women thinner than I! Big deal!") A directed awareness of our own competitiveness can help us to confront and transcend the reflexive urge to outdo everyone else.

All of these considerations are particularly relevant to raising or teaching children. A child's performance should never be compared with that of someone else (including a sibling, a classmate, or oneself as a child) in order to motivate her to do better. Affection and approval should not be made contingent on a child's performance. This means more than offering transparent consolations to a child who has lost. ("Oh. Well, as long as you did your best, honey.") It means being genuinely unconcerned with the results of competitive encounters in which she is involved, including victories. We should be particularly alert to the subtle and insidious ways in which we encourage our children to tie their feelings of self-worth to winning; so long as *we* need them to be the best in their class, they will get the message and require the same of themselves. The result, as we have seen, is not excellence but anxiety, self-doubt, hostility, and a decline in intrinsic motivation, among other things.

The psychological and interpersonal damage wrought by competition is so severe that we should also let children know of it in explicit terms. There are school programs to tell children about the abuse of drugs, including tobacco and alcohol. Why not do the same with regard to mutually exclusive goal attainment? Surely the evidence is clear enough and the stakes high enough. Granted that what we do is more important than what we say; above all, we should not set children against one another and we should not act in such a way as to present them with competitive role models. But it also may be helpful to teach them — adjusting the lesson to their level of development, of course — about the myths of competition and the respects in which cooperation offers a healthier alternative. After all, we currently train children to compete (as chapter 2 describes), so we would not be moving from value-free education to indoctrination, but from a lesson in favor of competition to one against it. Let us show our children both how and why to cooperate.

·   ·   ·

All of this concerns intentional competition, the inclination to be better than others, which is a matter of values and self-esteem. There is every reason to attend to both in an effort to become less competitive. Still, the effectiveness of such efforts is circumscribed by the structure of our economic system, our schooling, and our leisure activities. If these are set up so as to condition one person's success on another's failure, then a healthy noncompetitive attitude will seem peculiar and downright maladaptive. It will, in any event, be difficult to sustain.

When I began to think about competition, I saw structural and intentional competition as reciprocally related in a fashion so perfectly balanced that they caused each other to the same degree. Over time I have come to revise this position, finally realizing that the structural level is far more significant. It is possible to minimize the importance of winning and losing, but to do so requires one to swim against the current, to ignore what is demanded by the structure of the activity. It is possible to remain on friendly terms with competitors, but the fact that their interests are inversely related to one's own predisposes each side to view the other with hostility. It is possible to be a "good sport," but even this runs counter to the competitive imperative.

Let us consider a concrete illustration of how a structure can elicit particular behaviors. Philip Zimbardo and his colleagues at Stanford University conducted a novel experiment on the effects of imprisonment by choosing 21 male college students to take on the roles of guards and inmates in a very realistic "prison" created in the basement of the psychology building. The 21 subjects were selected from a group of 75 volunteers precisely on the basis of their normality: they were stable and scored in the middle range of a personality profile. Equally important, they were randomly assigned to the role of prisoner or guard. Almost immediately, the subjects began to take on the pathological characteristics of their respective roles. The guards delighted in devising arbitrary tasks and absurd rules for the inmates, demanding absolute obedience and forcing them to humiliate each other. The prisoners became passive and obedient, taking their frustration out on each other and otherwise assuming the role of victim. As the guards became more abusive, the prisoners became more helpless and dependent. The patterns became so pronounced that Zimbardo grew alarmed and ended what was to have been a two-week experiment after only six days.

Given the design of this experiment, what happened cannot be explained in terms of the individuals involved. The researchers, like the subjects, had been inclined to "focus on personality traits as internal dispositions for individuals to respond in particular ways," thus "underestimat[ing] the subtle power of situational forces to control and reshape their behavior." Most of us make the same error, Zimbardo contends, leading us to try to solve problems by "changing the people, by motivating them, isolating them . . . and so on." In fact, he concludes, "to change behavior we must discover the institutional supports which maintain the existing undesirable behavior and then design programs to alter these environments."[4]

This is nowhere more true than in the case of competition. We are constantly reinforced for wanting to be number one because this orientation is appropriate to the win/lose structure in which we keep finding ourselves. It is the fact of having to participate in contests that leads us to try to outdo others. And it is the fact of having to participate in contests that we are going to have to change if we want to move in healthier directions.

Nearly seventy years ago, John Harvey and his colleagues distinguished between "deliberate" and "involuntary" competition, which are roughly comparable to what I have been calling "intentional" and "structural," respectively. "In the whole moral environment provided by our civilisation, involuntary competition easily becomes deliberate," Harvey concluded. Among the personality traits that involuntary competition elicits, he says, is selfishness. "We would not set out to generate [this quality] deliberately, but we cannot escape from doing so incidentally and inadvertently so long as our commercial practice pits one against another, as now it does."[5]

William Sadler similarly insists that the structure determines how individuals look at the world:

> The value orientation which holds competition high is perpetuated as individuals participate in institutions which help to shape their perception of reality. There is, in other words, a convergence of social forces which fosters a common perception of the world so that it is viewed in competitive terms. Added to this institutional factor is the dissipation of forces that would inhibit competition.[6]

The evidence offered in chapters 5 and 6 substantiates this view. *Our psychological state and our relationships with others not only are correlated with the extent of our intentional competitiveness but are changed by a framework of structural competition.* Deutsch, to cite yet another study, found that "the psychological orientations of the subjects [including] their views of themselves and of the others in their group were considerably different as a function of the distributive system under which they worked."[7] Another sort of evidence is provided by Susan Shirk's account of how Chinese students, who were cooperatively inclined, began to stop helping each other when a competitive structure was imposed on them.[8] Closer to home, one need only watch what happens to courteous and cooperative drivers when they move to a city where an informal but powerful structure demands competitive behavior on the roads: in remarkably short order, individual personality patterns shift to accommodate the structure.[9]

The primacy of structural forces also can be demonstrated by showing that a *cooperative* framework changes behaviors and attitudes. After reviewing several strategies for lowering intentional competition, Terry Orlick wrote: "It may be more fruitful to introduce new games than to change old orientations. We may come closer to achieving our objectives if we simply let cooperative games do the shaping."[10] When values follow from the structure, moreover, they are generalized throughout an individual's life, as Paul Breer and Edwin Locke found:

> To the extent that a man is rewarded for putting the organization's goals first, harmonizing his own efforts with those of his colleagues, and making himself personally attractive to the people around him, he will develop situationally specific orientations in which co-operation, harmony, teamwork, etc. are seen as instrumental to success, intrinsically pleasurable, and morally desirable. From his job, such orientations can be expected to spill over to his family, community, and even society as a

whole. This, it will be recalled, is precisely the sort of thing we found in the laboratory.[11]

A final example of the effects of structural cooperation is provided by Robert Axelrod. In the course of discussing the Prisoner's Dilemma game (in which a cooperative strategy proves most effective), Axelrod cites a fascinating historical illustration. During World War I, army battalions that faced each other from their respective trenches often agreed not to shoot — a kind of "live and let live" understanding that emerged spontaneously. This mutual restraint was, of course, infuriating to the high commands of both sides, but soldiers had the temerity to persist in not killing each other. Obviously they had not been predisposed to work together, having been trained to hate each other; structural cooperation took root in spite of their attitudes. In fact, the new arrangement *changed* these attitudes. Axelrod cites an incident in which a shot was fired inadvertently one day, prompting a German to call out, "We are very sorry about that; we hope no one was hurt." This apparently genuine concern, Axelrod comments, "goes well beyond a merely instrumental effort to prevent retaliation. . . . The cooperative exchanges of mutual restraint actually changed the nature of the interaction. They tended to make the two sides care about each other's welfare."[12] Individual orientations, in other words, were affected by the structure.

HOW TO PREVENT SOCIAL CHANGE[13]

Making our society less competitive ultimately depends on reducing structural competition. Unfortunately, bringing about structural change of any kind requires overcoming enormous resistance. It is much easier to describe how change can be blocked than how it can be furthered. For those so inclined, then, here are five simple ways to perpetuate the status quo.

1. LIMIT YOUR VISION: The long-standing American tradition of ignoring the structural causes of social and individual problems was mentioned in chapter 7. By pretending, for example, that psychological disturbance has nothing to do with the societal forces that shape personality development, you can help see to it that those forces continue unabated. It follows that all intervention should be done at the individual level. It is fine to help, say, homeless people on a case-by-

case basis, but inquiring into the policy decisions and economic arrangements that have brought about their predicament would only serve to invite drastic changes — and this is what we want to avoid at all costs. Similarly, if we continue to treat each example of corporate wrongdoing (from illegal dumping of toxic wastes to bribing of public officials) as if it has occurred in a vacuum, then we can manage to preserve the system responsible for these acts.

2. ADAPT: The best way to keep the status quo intact is to make sure that individuals adjust themselves to serve its needs. Such adaptation once was enforced by crude, authoritarian methods of "re-education." Today this is hardly necessary. A wealth of advice is available on how to become successful — what to wear, how to negotiate, and so forth — and virtually all of it proceeds from the premise that you should adjust yourself to conditions as you find them. Adaptation is a critical part of the self-help model: you must succeed within the institutions and according to the rules that already exist. To do well is to fit in, and to fit in is to fortify the structures into which you are being fit.

3. THINK ABOUT YOURSELF: Implicit in any exhortations to succeed by "giving them what they want" is the suggestion that you should be totally preoccupied with your own well-being. The more you limit your concerns to yourself, the more you help to sustain the larger system. But this does not apply merely to material success. Even therapeutic and spiritual enterprises are useful for preserving the status quo because in encouraging you to attend to your own needs, they effectively direct attention away from social structures. Groom yourself and let the rest of the world go on its way — what better strategy is there for perpetuating existing structures? A few people may argue, it is true, that personal growth can be a route to social change. But most of the human potential movement will not require you to wrestle with this question, since social change is irrelevant to its goals and techniques.[14]

4. BE "REALISTIC": Fortunately, it is not necessary for you to defend the larger system. You can even nod in sympathetic agreement with someone who indicts it. But it is crucial that this nodding be accompanied by a shrug. Phrases such as "like it or not" and "that's just the way it is" should be employed liberally in order to emphasize that nothing can be done about the larger picture. Such protestations of powerlessness are actually very powerful, of course, since they make sure that things are left exactly as they are. Every person who is

encouraged to take such a stance is another person rescued from social activism.

Occasionally a critic will refuse to resign himself to the way things are or to believe that we are helpless to make change. Such an individual should immediately be labeled "idealistic." Do not be concerned about the vaguely complimentary connotations of having ideals. It will be understood that an idealist is someone who does not understand "the world as it is" ("world" = "our society"; "as it is" = "as it will always be"). This label efficiently calls attention to the critic's faulty understanding of reality or "human nature" and insures that he is not taken seriously. Those who are "pragmatic," by contrast, know that we must always work within the confines of what we are given. After all, if alternative models really were workable, we would already be using them.

Appeals to realism have the virtue of allowing you to avoid messy discussions about the value of a critic's position (and thus of the status quo). Why bother with such issues when you can dismiss his vision as "well-meaning but unworkable"? Challenging the rightness of what he is proposing will only slow him down; it is the appeal to practicality that produces the knockout. Call someone wrongheaded or even evil and a lengthy discussion may follow. Call him utopian or naive and there is nothing more to be said.[15] This method of dismissing models of change is uniquely effective since it sets up a self-fulfilling prophecy. If enough people insist that an alternative arrangement cannot work, they will be right. Its failure then can be cited as substantiation of one's original skepticism. No one uses this maneuver more skillfully than policymakers who are mistrustful of public institutions. Because of their conviction that governments can do nothing right, they divert funds from public schools and hospitals. When the inevitable crisis develops, they say, "You see?"

Appeals to realism can insure that institutions which threaten to promote social change (e.g., legislative bodies, universities, the media) do nothing but reflect the status quo. In the name of democracy, descriptive accuracy, and objective journalism, respectively, these institutions can be tamed and made into powerful instruments for perpetuating whatever is in place. Here, to take a tiny example, is *New York Times* education writer Fred Hechinger:

> Regrettably, the importance of the "message" has also invaded children's television. . . . [One] episode of "The Flintstones," a favorite children's cartoon, had a hotly contested baseball game end in a tie,

followed by celebrations of brotherly and sisterly love — hardly the real aim in any normal child's view of competitive games.[16]

This exemplary criticism should be studied carefully. Hechinger is demonstrating how to dismiss as inappropriate any scenario that does not conform to the existing values and structures of our society. To challenge our current practices is idealistic and, worse, contains a "message." To reinforce our current practices is realistic and contains no message. Most children's programs do not offend Hechinger because they display, and thereby shape, "normal" people — i.e., those who are intent on winning at any cost.

5. RATIONALIZE: It is easier for critics to oppose existing institutions when those who defend and profit from them are obviously opposed to social change. You can make it more difficult for these critics — and salve your own conscience at the same time — by claiming that your real reason for acting as you do is to "change the system from within." Like most people who talk this way, of course, you do not actually have to *make* change. On the contrary, even if this really were your goal, you would be permitted to work only for insignificant reforms that never come close to challenging the structures themselves. By becoming part of these structures, you can proceed to seek personal aggrandizement while at the same time contributing your talents to something you profess to find problematic. (A variation on this maneuver is to claim that you are going to do so for only a short time — as if it were a simple matter to leave the fast lane and get over to the exit ramp.) If you are audacious enough, you can even rationalize your participation as the *most effective* way to change the system. The more people who accept this reasoning and follow your example, the more secure is that system.

TOWARD A NONCOMPETITIVE SOCIETY

Whether employed deliberately or not, these mechanisms for frustrating change have been devastatingly effective. My point in reviewing them is to make it easier to anticipate and deal with such maneuvers. Having considered some of the issues that arise with respect to "generic" change, we can return to the specific case of competition. If competition is indeed unhelpful and destructive, and if attitudes and personal goals are shaped by the win/lose structure, then we need to set about the formidable task of undoing the arrangements that set us against one another — from parlor games to geopolitical conflict.

While working to dismantle existing structures, we should also be careful not to produce new occasions for competition. This means taking pains to avoid creating scarcity. Most scarcity is artificial, I have argued, because a prized status has been set up where none existed before. As parents and teachers and managers, we are constantly transforming situations into contests. In fact, the widespread assumption that "*someone's* got to lose" arises only because we keep making goal attainment mutually exclusive. Every time we make salespeople try to outdo one another, every time we display the best homework assignment in class on the bulletin board, every time we call out to our children, "Who can set the table fastest?" — we are contributing to the unnecessary and undesirable competitiveness that suffuses our culture. The real alternative to being Number One, as I have already noted, is not being Number Two; it is dispensing with rankings altogether. Starting immediately, we can stop contriving contests and we can urge our friends and colleagues and children's teachers to do likewise. At the very least, we can present the case against competition to them so they understand the implications of what they are doing.

All of this applies to the vast number of cases where scarcity is created. But even where scarcity seems to be real, we need to look at the bigger picture to determine whether certain assumptions or policy decisions (which can be re-evaluated) lie behind competition and give it the appearance of necessity. Consider a familiar example: When cars prowl the city streets in search of parking spaces, the shortage is not invented and the quest is clearly competitive. But the number of spaces to be had downtown was not decreed by God. It is the result of a decision that can be changed. The same is true for the availability and convenience of mass transit, which indirectly causes or eliminates the frustrating race for space. Instead of taking competition for granted, we ought to be asking what broader arrangements might be altered so as to present us with a structure that does not require winners and losers. Sometimes the search for these broader arrangements will lead us to the very foundations of our economic and political system.[17] This does not mean we ought to drop the matter and resign ourselves to competition. On the contrary: whatever we encounter, however large the stakes, is open to question and, perhaps, transformation.

There are quite a few thinkers whose work is useful in beginning to think about reducing structural competition. Terry Orlick offers noncompetitive games as a way of reconceptualizing recreation. "Why not create and play games that make us more cooperative, honest and considerate of others?" he asks.[18] David and Roger Johnson propose noncompetitive alternatives in the classroom as a way of improving education. Robert Paul Wolff sketches a plan for severing the ties between high school performance and college admissions, and again between college performance and graduate admissions.[19] Both moves would allow genuine learning to replace the awful competitive scramble that now preoccupies students. On the political scene, Benjamin Barber has argued persuasively that the adversarial and individualistic underpinnings of politics as we know it are actually inimical to democracy; in their place he proposes a consensus-based system that is similar to the cooperative resolution of conflict discussed in chapter 6.[20] With respect to global rivalry, Morton Deutsch, among others, emphasizes that "the old notion of 'national security' must be replaced by the new notion of 'mutual security.' "[21]

In each case, the revolt against competition is wedded to the affirmation of an alternative vision. This is a practical necessity, since we can hardly tear down one set of structures without offering something in its place. But the alternative also is the very reason for objecting to competition in the first place. It is because we value human relationship, among other things, that we found competing to be problematic. The motive for opposing competition and the arrangement to replace it are one and the same: cooperation.

Despite the productivity and sense of fulfillment that come from working together, we often act as if cooperation is something for which we must sit passively and wait, like a beautiful sunset. In fact, there is scarcely an arena of human life which cannot be transformed into a cooperative enterprise. I have hinted throughout this book at how this might be done, from leisure activities to workplace cooperatives, but I have not laid out anything like a comprehensive guide for coordinating our efforts. Having concentrated my efforts on a critique of competition, I leave that task to others, confident that there will be no shortage of suggestions once our energies are freed from planning and participating in competitive projects. Once the myths justifying competition are behind us, the prospects are good for changing the structures that perpetuate it.

.   .   .

So long as we remain a competitive society, however, it will be possible to insist that one has got to compete to survive. This argument is heard most often from those who actually have no inclination to stop competing and often from those who, as Bertrand Russell pointed out, are really invoking "survival" in order to justify their desire to beat others. But let us assume that this objection is offered not as a rationalization but as an expression of genuine discomfort, arising from the inability to reconcile one's own values with the competitive demands of our culture. What can we say in response?

There are no easy answers here. We should begin by reviewing the catalogue of competition's disadvantages. It may seem prudent to enter contests and devote ourselves to winning, but the many respects in which competition is destructive should be weighed against the need to join the race.

> To follow out the price we pay for this way of life into all the intricacies of social and personal life, the frustration and wastage of temperaments and abilities that do not and can not conform to this competitive stereotype, the inevitable failure of the many who try to conform and fail, more often from lack of aggressiveness rather than absence of ability, these are some of the inquiries that we should and probably will make as time goes on.[22]

Furthermore, the apparent necessity of competing is another of the self-fulfilling prophecies that we keep encountering. As each of us sighs and says he has no choice but to stay ahead of the next person, that next person feels compelled to do the same. You become part of the "they" to which someone else refers.

To take this perspective is to move beyond our customary individualistic frame of reference. Even if it seems appropriate for me to compete — overlooking for the moment the price I pay for doing so — I need to ask whether it is in our collective interest to keep competing. (That such a discrepancy can exist is, of course, the lesson of the Prisoner's Dilemma game described earlier.) If it is not, then we need not only to think but to act as a group. Replacing structural competition with cooperation requires collective action, and collective action requires education and organization. An individual tenant is at the mercy of her landlord, but if all the tenants in the building unite, they can demand their rights. The same is true of competition. An individual may in some respects lose out by refusing to take part in a mutually destructive struggle, but a group of people who work in an office or study at a college or send their children to a school can join forces. By helping others to see the terrible consequences of a system that predicates one person's success on another's failure, we can act together to change that system.

As with other features of the status quo, the stakes are highest here for those with the least power. People who have systematically been denied the opportunity to earn a decent wage, to lead a life with dignity, to make decisions about what affects them, may think it peculiar to be told that competition is destructive. After all, they might argue, "my only hope is to enter the race and try to win, to beat them at their own game." It is not a coincidence that this is precisely the response to oppression encouraged by those who hold the power. First, this strategy rarely works (even in conventional terms) because the deck is stacked: those who already are winners are in better shape to win succeeding contests. Edgar Z. Friedenberg put it this way:

> The classic device for legitimating the unequal distribution of rewards in a democratic society is, of course, competition in which the same rules are applied to all the contestants and the status system of the society is protected by the nature of the rules rather than by their inequitable application. The people in the society thus learn to divide themselves into winners and losers and to blame themselves for being among the losers if they are.[23]

Second, to participate in competition is to help perpetuate an arrangement that caused the problem in the first place. No one stands to benefit more from a noncompetitive society than those who have been cheated by a competitive society.

Transforming the nature of society, then, requires a collective effort and a long-term commitment. In the meantime, each of us has a series of choices to make. Once it becomes clear why competition ought to be avoided, we must re-examine our own lives to determine what concessions to the prevailing ethic, if any, we are prepared to make. These concessions should be made with a clear understanding of the costs — both personal and societal — that they entail. And they should strengthen our resolve to work at the same time to create healthy, productive, cooperative alternatives.

10

◁ ▷

Learning Together

I consider . . . the tendency toward a selfish individualism one of the strongest counts against our customary . . . sit-alone-at-your-own-desk procedure. . . .
Wholehearted purposeful activity in a social situation as
the typical unit of school procedure is the best guarantee
of the utilization of the child's native capacities now too
frequently wasted.

— William H. Kilpatrick, 1918

INTERVIEWER: What is it like to work in a group?
JUSTIN (age ten): You have four brains.

BACK TO SCHOOL

Every so often, parents and teachers and policymakers get swept up
in yet another earnest discussion about whether values should be
taught in the schools. Kids need them, someone will exclaim, bran-
dishing fresh evidence that today's young people routinely violate
standards of decent conduct. No, values ought to be taught at home,
comes the predictable reply. But the point is that they're *not* being
taught at home, the first speaker rejoins. Well, then, whose values
would we teach? another challenger wants to know.

Despite their differences, the speakers in this imaginary colloquy
share a profound naiveté. To argue about whether it is time for values
to be introduced into the classroom is like asking (to take Molière's
charming example) whether you ought to start speaking in prose: the
point is you have already been doing so, even if you never thought
of it that way. Teachers do not need to lecture children about stealing
in order to exude values. Their choice of stories, the order in which
they are taught, and the tone of voice in which a character is men-

tioned; the fact that children must raise their hands to speak or obtain permission to go to the bathroom or address one person in the room by his or her last name; the objects that decorate the walls and who decided they should be there; how students' work is evaluated (and for what purpose) — all these and many other aspects of life at school already vibrate with values whether we realize it or not. There is no question, then, of introducing values into a neutral environment, but only of critically examining existing values in light of others that could be there instead.

I have already argued that few values are more persistently promoted in American classrooms than the desirability of trying to beat other people. Sometimes this lesson is presented with all the subtlety of a fist in the face, as with the use of spelling bees,[1] grades on a curve (a version of artificial scarcity in which my chance of receiving an A is reduced by your getting one), awards assemblies, and other practices that redefine the majority of children as losers.

At other times, competition is promoted tacitly, perhaps even unwittingly, by pitting students against one another for the teacher's attention and approval. This may occur through the use of manipulative behavior management strategies — for example, a public announcement such as: "I like the way Joanne is sitting so nice and quiet." (A contest has been created for Nicest, Quietest Pupil, and everyone except Joanne has just lost.) Or it may follow from the conventional arrangement of asking a question of the whole class.

> The teacher asks the question, the students who think they know the answer raise their hands, and the teacher calls on one of them. We've all seen it many times: when one student is called on, the other students who have their hands up register their disappointment with a little "Oh." It's a structure that sets the kids against each other.[2]

Anyone who doubts that competition is the subtext of most whole-class question-and-answer sessions need only continue watching the faces of the children who were not recognized. Are they rooting for Jeremy, who now has the floor, to succeed? Hardly. They are hoping he says something stupid because this will present them with another opportunity to triumph. The teacher's face is scanned for signs of dissatisfaction with Jeremy's answer; once they find it, the children's hands shoot up again, fingers reaching anxiously for the fluorescent lights. Some students participate energetically in this scramble to be first with the right response, while others stare dully and look beaten (which, at some point, they have been). Our attention, however, is properly focused not on the temperament of the individual participants but on the structure that has turned learning into a contest.*

Alongside competition stands another value, stressed with equal vigor by educators: individualism. Between the American flag in the corner and that preprinted strip of impossibly proper cursive letters that stretches above the blackboard, there might as well be a sign that proclaims: I WANT TO SEE WHAT YOU CAN DO, NOT WHAT YOUR NEIGHBOR CAN DO. Children sit at separate desks, as if on their own private islands, instructed to keep their eyes on their own work. Helping is construed as cheating, since it goes without saying that one is evaluated only on the basis of one's solitary efforts. Quite a bit goes without saying, in fact, since even talking with one's classmates is usually regarded as inappropriate. The fact that each child is supposed to be responsible for his or her own assignments and behavior means that even when students are not led to see one another as obstacles to their own success, each is, at best, irrelevant to the other's learning.

The two standard classroom arrangements in the United States require children to work *against each other* or — as a result of the ostensibly progressive reform of a few decades ago known as individualized learning — *apart from each other*. Earlier (pp. 50–52), I indicated that some teachers are making use of an alternative to these two models, known as cooperative learning. My scant three paragraphs on this subject do not begin to do justice to the topic, however, with respect to the research supporting its use, the various models for implementing it, or the extent of its potential impact on education. Since writing that brief account in chapter 3, I have discovered a great deal more about cooperative learning and have become an enthusiastic and outspoken proponent of its use. Meanwhile, the movement itself has taken root in many schools around the country —

---

*Having a conversation with a large group of people does not in itself establish a competitive interaction. One way to avoid transforming a discussion into a contest is to ask deeper questions for which there are no clear-cut answers ("What would happen if there were no countries?" instead of "What's the capital of Italy?") or to encourage students to do some of the asking themselves. Where there are unambiguously right answers, formats other than whole-class discussions might be preferable. In any case, these conversations can always be conducted so that each participant's contribution is valued, an atmosphere of safety prevails in which students feel able to take risks, and verbal fluency and simple recall are not the only skills seen as worth having.

indeed, around the world. Cooperative learning (CL) is, in my judgment, one of the most promising alternatives to structural competition not just in the classroom but in any arena. If there is a single concrete image that represents the transcendence of mutually exclusive goal attainment, it is a picture of three or four children sitting around a table animatedly exchanging information and ideas.

BETWEEN STUDENT AND STUDENT

From Morton Deutsch comes the notion of promotive (or positive) interdependence: my success is facilitated by, or even dependent on, your success. The explicit application of this model to classroom learning in the U.S. began quite recently. David Johnson, a former student of Deutsch's,* and his brother Roger published the first major book on CL in 1975.[3] The 1970s also saw early work on a reward-driven model of team learning at Johns Hopkins University by David DeVries and his doctoral student, Robert Slavin, as well as the development of the Jigsaw approach by Elliot Aronson and the Group Investigation method by Shlomo and Yael Sharan in Israel. (From another perspective, though, students have been working together, although not necessarily cooperatively, for as long as there have been too few Bunsen burners to go around in science classrooms. In fact, the practice of having students learn from each other can be traced to the seventeenth century, and probably all the way back to Aristotle.)[4]

CL means working toward a common goal in the classroom — learning in pairs or small groups in the context of positive interdependence. This context implies that merely dividing a class into teams and announcing that students should work with their groupmates ("You four do this ditto together") is not sufficient for, much less equivalent to, cooperative learning. Because of this, teachers who have merely put children in groups and are unimpressed with the results have not yet given CL a chance to prove itself. Virtually everyone who has thought seriously about CL has, at one time or another, warned educators that it takes time and skill to foster positive interde-

---

*Deutsch, in turn, had studied with Kurt Lewin, whose work in the 1930s and 1940s was instrumental in developing a systematic theory of how people behave in groups. Lewin's influence passed, on the one hand, to Deutsch and then to the Johnsons, and, on the other, to a second well-known student, Leon Festinger, who, in turn, was mentor to Elliot Aronson, developer of the Jigsaw model of cooperative learning.

pendence successfully, particularly in light of the competitive and individualistic norms that students have internalized from other settings.

If CL is something more than casual groupwork, it is something less than altruism, or at least less than the narrow version of altruism that requires an individual to sacrifice his or her own interests.[5] In asking children to work together, we are not demanding that they ignore their own academic well-being in order to make sure that someone else understands the material. Positive interdependence means that when you succeed, I succeed, too; my interest in your learning is matched by your interest in mine.

No catalogue of misconceptions about CL would be complete without reference to the idea that working in groups is just a gimmick to perk up a classroom now and then, providing a break from serious instruction. ("Okay, kids, it's the third Friday of the month. Remember, that means today we work in teams!") While teachers doubtless will want to continue making some use of whole-class discussion[6] and individualized work, CL can — and, I would argue, ought to — become the standard or "default" classroom arrangement starting in kindergarten.

Finally, to echo my earlier remarks on constructive conflict (pp. 155–57), CL does not entail harmony or concurrence about controversial issues, even after a discussion has been concluded and an assignment completed. Teachers who properly want to avoid constructing adversarial encounters need not demand a premature consensus: "Your assignment is to come to an agreement about whether abortion should be legal." One likely result of such an instruction is that the student with the loudest voice, or the one holding the pencil, will write down whatever she wants, everyone else in the group will give in so as to be done with the whole business, and no one will learn anything. Conversely, teachers who properly want to preserve controversy need not set up a win/lose structure to do so. In a classroom whose members have come to feel part of a community and who have been helped to develop a range of social skills, disagreement can occur without debate, and conflict without competition.*

---

*It makes sense for teachers and students to create a cooperative context before tackling tasks that will provoke strong disagreement. Conflict should be introduced gradually, with care taken to ensure that students' social skills (and the bonds between students) can accommodate mildly opposing views before asking them to thrash out more incendiary issues.

Perhaps it is easier, then, to say what CL is not than to say what it is, at least beyond a one-sentence formula that is about as helpful as saying a poem is a careful arrangement of words. Yes, we can add that in classrooms where CL is used, teachers communicate the message "I want to see what you and your neighbor can do together." They are likely to ask students to turn first to a peer to check out an idea or request an explanation. They may evaluate some projects as group efforts, which is what they are. These teachers probably have arranged the room so that children are clustered around tables most of the day instead of being seated at separate desks. They recognize that "socializing" is not something relegated to recess and lunch, something that distracts from learning; rather, they know that learning emerges not only from what transpires between student and teacher, or between student and text, but also from what happens between student and student.

Beyond this, though, it is difficult to say with certainty what CL is, for the simple reason that it is strikingly different depending on which theorist, trainer, or teacher you ask. From a distance, the distinction between CL and traditional classroom arrangements is so pronounced that those who promote learning in pairs or groups seem distinguished principally by this commitment. But seen from up close, those who huddle together under this conceptual umbrella often differ from one another in the way they conceive of cooperation and, for that matter, learning itself.

THE EFFECTS OF COOPERATIVE LEARNING

Before exploring some of the different varieties of CL, I want to say why that discussion — and, for that matter, the whole movement — is so terribly important. Several versions of CL have been tested in literally hundreds of studies, and the results of that research should be much better known than they are at present. The gains realized from CL are so impressive and consistent that it is difficult to understand how any talk of school reform could omit the critical question of whether students should be learning alone or together.

SELF-ESTEEM: Consider first the issue of how a student feels about himself and his abilities. The evidence in chapter 5 might be summarized as follows: competition is to self-esteem as sugar is to teeth. Far from providing a lasting sense of confidence in oneself, a competitive environment leads one to ask "What have I done for me lately?" But CL does not merely avoid the abrasive effect of competition: at its best, it has a fortifying effect of its own.

Recent reports of CL's impact on self-esteem are remarkable. Positive outcomes were found in "eleven of the fifteen studies in which the effects of cooperative learning on self-esteem were studied," Robert Slavin wrote in 1990.[7] In a much larger review of the research comparing competitive and cooperative arrangements on self-esteem — a review that, for better or worse, lumped together studies of many different types and of varying quality — the Johnsons reported that a fair number failed to find any statistically significant difference between the two conditions. But of those studies that did turn up a significant difference, exactly one showed an advantage for competition while *eighty-one* showed an advantage for cooperation. This sort of consistency is, to put it mildly, very uncommon in the social sciences.[8]

On the other hand, it should not be concluded that CL is a magical cure for low self-esteem. First, children sometimes feel lousy about themselves because they are abused or humiliated at home or do not get enough to eat; these problems require changes far deeper and wider than bringing CL to the classroom.[9] Second, the research on self-esteem (from which conclusions about the effects of educational arrangements are drawn) leaves a great deal to be desired in terms of rigor. While many of us have gotten in the habit of casually tossing the term around, a global version of self-esteem (how you feel about yourself in general) is far less useful, scientifically speaking, than specific aspects of self-esteem (how positive you feel about your capacity to do math problems, for instance). Moreover, the tests used to measure self-esteem are often idiosyncratic and badly designed, which means that the result of one self-esteem experiment cannot meaningfully be compared to the result of another that used a different test.[10] Finally, even some of the better pencil-and-paper measures are intended to tap how one feels about oneself at the time the test is taken, and this tells us little about one's persistent, stable, underlying beliefs or feelings about oneself, assuming such things can be identified or measured at all.

Notwithstanding all of these (and other) limitations on the theory and practice of self-esteem, there is reason to believe that to whatever extent the time a child spends in school can make a difference in how she sees herself, CL is far more likely to promote a positive self-image than are conventional methods of instruction.[11] Learning in well-functioning groups provides an environment of social support and enhances the chances of academic success; these effects, in turn, help children to develop more confidence in themselves, more resilience in the face of failure, and more of a sense that their fate is (at least sometimes) in their own hands rather than at the mercy of external forces.

SOCIAL INTERACTION: No one is likely to be astonished by the fact that a structure of positive interdependence (your success equals my success) inclines us to look more favorably on the people with whom we are interacting than a structure of negative interdependence (your success equals my failure) (pp. 139, 149–51). The only question for those with an interest in education is whether reducing hostility, improving social skills, promoting an acceptance of people from different backgrounds and with different abilities, and coming to view others as potential collaborators (rather than as obstacles to one's own success) are judged to be sufficiently important goals to warrant the use of CL. To ask this question is, I think, to answer it. In fact, David Johnson has said that his work is motivated more by a desire to help children accept people who are different from themselves than by a desire to boost achievement.[12]

Once again, recent reviews of evidence confirm that CL leads children to view one another more favorably, increases the likelihood of cross-ethnic friendships, enhances acceptance of students with handicaps, and promotes perspective taking (that is, the capacity to imagine someone else's point of view).[13] Moreover, "cooperation seems to promote better relationships when intergroup competition is absent."[14] At a time when managers frequently complain that employees seem unable to get along with each other or work together effectively — and, indeed, "poor interpersonal skills represent the single biggest reason for failure" of the managers themselves, according to one study[15] — the fact that children learn social skills from CL seems to be a persuasive argument in itself for making American education less competitive and more cooperative.

ACHIEVEMENT: The most gratifying (and perhaps surprising) finding from CL research is the news that there is no trade-off between helping students to feel better about themselves and each other, on the one hand, and helping them to learn more effectively, on the other. Working together offers "bottom-line" benefits in terms of achievement just as surely as it enhances self-esteem and the quality of relationships. These benefits are enjoyed by students of all ages, in all subjects, and at all kinds of schools.

Anyone who finds personal testimonies compelling ought to seek out a teacher who has been using CL over a period of time and ask what the effect has been on students' comprehension, problem-solving strategies, creativity, or even simple recall of facts. The change can be literally difficult to believe. One teacher in New York told me that her students' academic performance improved so drastically after they began working in teams that her principal noticed the difference in her grade reports. Rather than asking what accounted for the children's higher achievement, however, he demanded to know why she had suddenly become an easier grader.

Research confirms the improvement, even on relatively superficial measures like standardized tests. Slavin picked sixty-eight achievement comparisons, making a point of excluding studies he thought were inferior and including a disproportionate number of his own. Of these, forty-nine (nearly three quarters of the total) found superior results from CL as opposed to standard classroom arrangements.[16]

At the other end of the continuum, methodologically speaking, the Johnsons reviewed every available study from 1898 to 1989 — some 369 in all — that examined task achievement in cooperative, competitive, or independent conditions. (Only some of these were conducted in classrooms.) In comparing the effects of cooperation and competition, no significant differences were found about one third of the time. When there *was* a difference that probably was not due to chance, cooperation produced better results than competition did in 87 percent of the comparisons. Cooperation produced better results than *individualized* task achievement in almost exactly the same proportion where there were significant differences.[17] Elsewhere, the Johnsons have observed:

> That working together to achieve a common goal produces higher achievement and greater productivity than does working alone is so well confirmed by so much research that it stands as one of the strongest principles of social and organizational psychology.[18]

This principle has been noticed even at the farthest reaches of higher education. A 1992 assessment of teaching and learning at Harvard University, based on interviews with 570 undergraduates, led to the central conclusion that intellectual growth was associated primarily with "interpersonal activities with faculty members, or with fellow students, built around substantive, academic work." The report urged the creation of study groups where they do not already exist and noted that many students avoided taking science classes not because of the heavy workload but because of the competition for grades.[19]

Chapter 3 offers a few reasons to explain why competition in general proves less successful than cooperation.* Here I would like to summarize and supplement those accounts, widening the focus of our inquiry to ask how it is that CL is so effective at helping children to learn. Some of these reasons are negative: *CL works because it avoids having children compete,* thus avoiding a number of counterproductive effects.

1. ANXIETY: Competition promotes anxiety of a kind and level that interferes with performance.

2. EXTRINSIC STATUS: Like other extrinsic motivators (that is, artificial incentives outside the task itself) such as money, grades, certificates, extra dessert, and gold stars, competition leads children to complete a task as quickly as possible, which means they avoid taking risks and exploring ideas in the way that is necessary for creative problem solving and deep learning. Competition and other extrinsic motivators tend to reduce interest in, and ultimately impede performance on, many kinds of tasks.[20]

3. ATTRIBUTIONS: Whether they win or lose, children typically attribute the results of a competitive encounter to luck or fixed ability. The result is a diminished sense of empowerment and responsibility for their learning.[21]

4. PREDICTABILITY: If the chance to win a contest is the chief reason students have been given for learning something, most of them have figured out in September who is likely to come out on top. The presumptive winner therefore has been given no reason to do anything more than is necessary to defeat everyone else. More important, all the likely losers have been given no rationale for bothering with the subject matter at all.[22]

The remainder of the reasons are positive: *CL works because of benefits that cooperation itself offers,* namely:

---

*I should emphasize that it is not necessary to arrive at the position I have taken in this book, that competition is inherently destructive and counterproductive, in order to recognize the merit of cooperative learning.

5. EMOTIONAL BENEFITS: CL's positive effect on self-esteem and relationships with peers tends to translate into a positive effect on achievement. Our experience in the workplace bears this out: people who feel good about both themselves and their colleagues are more likely, all things being equal, to do a better job. Self-esteem, relationships, and performance are integrally related so that enhancing any one variable can positively affect either of the others.

6. ELIMINATION OF NERD STIGMA: A student in the conventional classroom who gives evidence of being too interested in the lesson is liable to be on the receiving end of any number of unlovely labels that have replaced "teacher's pet." But CL helps to create a new set of norms. "When students are working together toward a common goal, academic work becomes an activity valued by peers."[23] CL, in other words, makes it cool to learn, and this increases the probability that effective learning will indeed take place.

7. INTEREST IN THE SUBJECT: Not only is it more fun to be part of an effective and supportive group than to work against, or apart from, others, but CL also leads students to become more enthusiastic about what they are learning. (This is surely an independent benefit: beyond how children score on today's test, we want them to become hooked on playing with words and numbers and ideas.) The Johnsons cite twenty-two studies to support the claim that CL promotes "more positive attitudes toward the subject area being studied and the instructional experience."[24] One of their favorite stories concerns a teacher who advised them to warn other participants in their training sessions against using CL just before lunch. Puzzled, they asked why. The teacher explained that each class in her school was supposed to arrive in the cafeteria at a different, precisely assigned time in order to prevent long lines from developing. When her students were working in groups, though, it was difficult to drag them away from what they were doing. She would tell them it was time to stop for lunch, and they would protest: "Wait! Wait! We're almost finished!"*

---

*This reluctance to leave could also, in theory, be explained by the sort of food that awaited them. However, other reports corroborate the excitement that students demonstrate for their work when engaged in CL, groaning when the bell rings and displaying other signs of being engrossed that many teachers thought they would never live long enough to witness. CL sometimes makes learning so engaging, according to one researcher and trainer, that students may "be prepared to remain in the classroom and continue working on learning tasks rather than taking a recess and going out to play."[25]

By contrast, students in most American classrooms are eager to be free of them. They count the minutes until the end of the period, the days left before the weekend, the weeks they must endure until the next vacation. Perhaps this is because they hear their parents articulating similar sentiments about their work by thanking God for Friday. But maybe students genuinely find life at school to be a collection of tedious tasks and humiliating evaluations from which any reasonable person would want to escape. John Goodlad's mammoth study of more than a thousand representative classrooms across the country confirmed that "the kinds of classroom practices found most often were well liked by relatively small percentages of students"; the older the child, the less satisfaction was expressed.[26]

Of course, everyone is aware that most kids do not care for most aspects of school. Everyone is also aware that too many students are graduated without the intellectual skills or knowledge that we expect the schools to have provided; indeed, it has become a popular entertainment of late to describe how much students do not know. But rarely do we connect these two pieces of data. If children seem unhappy about going to school, we typically attribute this to the fact that kids just are wont to complain, that they don't like anything — or at least anything good for them. Then we insist that they had better get used to things that aren't any fun. (The premise here seems to be that the chief purpose of school is not to get children excited about learning but to get them acclimated to doing mind-numbing chores.)

It is also possible, however, to conclude that the problem may just lie with what happens in school rather than with some character flaw in the individual child. The extent of "on-task" behavior in a classroom, by the same token, may tell us something about the teacher as well as about the students. When a teacher complains that children are off task, our first response should be to ask "What is the task?" (In the long run, though, individual teachers probably are not to blame, given that decisions about what children must learn and how they must learn it are frequently made by administrators, school board members, parents, politicians, and faculty members at schools of education.) Moreover, the sharp line drawn between enjoying the process, on the one hand, and buckling down to learn how to spell, on the other, may reflect a philosophy of self-denial — or, more accurately, other-denial — that yields the worst of both worlds, since it often produces neither enjoyment nor effective results.

Goodlad ticks off what students are asked to do: passively listen to teachers' ceaseless talking (in his survey, the average teacher "out-talked the entire class of students by a ratio of about three to one"), submit to close and constant monitoring, work separately and silently on textbooks and worksheets, and so on.

> How would I react as an adult to these ways of the classroom? I would become restless. I would groan audibly over still another seatwork assignment. My mind would wander off soon after the beginning of a lecture. It would be necessary for me to put my mind in some kind of "hold" position. This is what students do.[27]

More to the point, students come to find boring[28] and detestable not only the place called school but the subjects taught there and activities such as reading and solving problems. This is why CL, by virtue of making learning (and what is being learned) more enjoyable, can also make learning more successful.*

8. INTELLECTUAL INTERACTION: Most important, CL succeeds because "none of us is as smart as all of us."[29] A well-functioning group — and, of course, not all groups function well — can be more successful, particularly on open-ended, challenging tasks, than any member of the group could be on his own. Ten-year-old Jason, quoted at the beginning of this chapter, captured the phenomenon as succinctly as any researcher has. The whole of the group truly becomes more productive than the sum of its parts.

Cognitive and social psychologists have tried to figure out just what it is about groups that accounts for the heightened quality of performance.[30] At the most basic level, everyone benefits from the sharing of talents and skills and resources, a process that is either discouraged or prohibited outright in noncooperative classrooms. When the different members of a group work separately to collect information and think through a problem, then reconvene to exchange the results, each individual has access to everyone else's labors.

When one student catches on to something quickly and helps her

---

*A couple of important qualifications are needed here. First, CL is not absolutely *necessary* for helping students to become more excited about school; enthusiasm can and does describe some noncooperative classrooms, too. Second, CL is not *sufficient* for changing attitudes about school. It does not in itself respond adequately to the fact that so many children view school as a series of unpleasant tasks, sweetened only by the chance to see their friends. As I will argue later, using team learning to more effectively cram the same pointless and disconnected bits of information into children's heads, or relying on the same carrot-and-stick approach to instruction (except this time with groups), will not transform the experience of learning in the way that CL has the potential to do. In fact, a student's view of CL may itself be contaminated by its continued association with an otherwise stagnant system of pedagogy.

teammate to understand, both tutor and tutee benefit. This, as No-reen Webb discovered in a series of studies, happens consistently, provided that the first student does not just announce the solution but explains how she got it and justifies her conviction that it is cor-rect.[31] As a group of British researchers put it, "Tutors may gain a deeper understanding of the material learned by virtue of having to teach it, and 'learning how to learn' strategies may spill over into learning contexts other than the immediate learning task."[32] Re-searchers also have found that simply telling a student that he will be asked to teach someone else what he is about to read (as opposed to reading it in order to perform well on a test) leads to higher interest in the material and greater conceptual understanding of the subject matter.[33]

Beyond explicit tutoring, when people work in groups there is a tendency for one person's idea to evoke another idea from someone else. The second idea emerges as a reaction to the first and might not have occurred at all if its creator had been working on her own. In one study, fifth- and sixth-graders were given batteries, bulbs, and wire and asked to make a variety of different circuits so that the bulbs would light up. The students working in groups found the task more engaging, seemed to get less frustrated, and, by building on one an-other's ideas, created both more circuits and more unusual kinds of circuits than their classmates who worked individually.[34]

This phenomenon applies not only to ideas about the topic being studied but also to ideas about how to examine the topic (meta-level or second-order ideas). Group work leads to "more frequent discov-ery and development of . . . higher quality cognitive reasoning strate-gies." First-graders, for example, were more likely to figure out the abstract categories to which words belonged (in order to memorize these words more effectively) when they worked together.[35]

Finally, CL not only permits conflict, as I mentioned above, but actually relies on it to some extent for its success. The process of finding that someone else thought a story's character had a motivation very different from the one you had inferred, or that another person assumed that dinosaurs became extinct for a reason that never dawned on you, nudges you to think through the problem in a new way, to take account of this brand-new perspective and try to recon-cile it with your own.[36]

Notice that none of this analysis supports the idea that children should — or, with CL, *do* — become interchangeable members of a collective, relinquishing their selves to some amorphous blob of a group. It is competition that creates conformity (pp. 128–31); cooperation thrives on the diversity of its participants and the distinct contributions made by each. I do think teachers ought to make time for students to pursue independent work, too, but the more compelling point is that cooperative interaction may simply be the most powerful way to help each child find his own voice, make his own discoveries, devise his own connections to ideas and texts. "Talking is not merely a way of conveying existing ideas to others; it is also a way by which we explore ideas, clarify them and make them our own."[37]

All of this impressive empirical evidence supporting cooperative learning — and, for that matter, the reliance on empirical evidence in general — needs to be placed firmly in perspective. Some researchers construct an imaginary brick wall, with those who respect the findings of science on one side and those who are in thrall to ideology on the other. But this dichotomy, which has its roots in a philosophy called positivism, confuses science with truth itself. It errs by overlooking the fact that all research, like all educational practice, is saturated in values, like it or not. But more than this, it suggests that there is something disgraceful about having and defending values; this is why many scientists label them "biases" or "ideologies" and treat them like last week's seafood dinner.

Having just finished reviewing the data that bear on the use of cooperative learning, I am obviously not arguing that it doesn't matter what the research turns up. It does matter, and it is with considerable relief that I can report that CL makes good sense when judged according to pragmatic and widely shared criteria. But the fact that I am relieved suggests that I am already drawn to CL because of other, deeper values that I hold. Frankly, it took me a few years to acknowledge this, to confess that I am not indifferent to how the evidence turns out (even though I hope I am able to assess it fairly).

Cooperative learning is worth defending even apart from its quantifiable consequences. Ideally, as Canadian educator Judy Clarke reminds us, the idea of interdependence is grounded in

> the belief in every person's worth. This belief frames people in relationships of positive interconnectedness and therefore reflects an ethical orientation to life. . . . Without this moral foundation, co-operative learning may simply appear to teachers as a set of techniques . . . to "master" and file in one's repertoire.[38]

Without this moral foundation, CL likewise may appear to researchers as simply one arrangement among many to be evaluated dispassionately, much as one might test different thicknesses of glass for the classroom windows.

I believe there is something intrinsically preferable about having children work with each other as opposed to against or apart from each other. I am glad that I can reassure parents and teachers that it is a sensible arrangement from any number of perspectives, but I stand with Robert Bellah and his colleagues when they remark that

> learning is never the result of the efforts of isolated, competitive individuals alone. . . . The evident weakness in American schools has much to do with the weakening of their community context. . . . Education can never merely be for the sake of individual self-enhancement. It pulls us into the common world or it fails altogether.[39]

Arguably, it *has* failed altogether. But while there is no shortage of critics willing to charge American education with failure, they often miss the point about what has gone wrong and why. The problem is not so much that students cannot find Turkey on a map but that they do not find themselves part of a community of learners; they do not find themselves, moreover, in a place where each person's worth is affirmed. The fact that cooperative learning can alter these sad realities is worth at least as much as anything the studies might tell us about achievement gains and the like.

THE PRACTICE OF COOPERATION

Cooperative learning takes many forms. It is present in a classroom where students edit each other's essays or help each other to develop and practice vocabulary or multiplication skills. It may mean finding an ad hoc partner with whom to have a quick exchange of ideas about evolution before resuming a whole-class discussion. Or it may mean that each student belongs to a permanent team of four that meets daily to make sense of current events.

A cooperative lesson plan may come from the teacher's notebook or it may be devised by the class. Perhaps the students find that their parents' talk about politics has made them curious to learn more about political systems in other countries, which they proceed to do with their teammates. Or maybe a student's announcement that her garage is now home to a litter of tiny, mewling kittens leads to an impromptu lesson on the subject, with children meeting in groups to read stories about cats, describe how a house looks from a cat's point of view, research specific scientific questions that they want answered (How are cats both similar to and different from lions? When do cats fight with each other? Do cats dream?) and then present their findings to the rest of the class.

All these examples share the premise that learning is an active and an interactive process. To that extent, it is decidedly not a silent process. This is one very practical reason that it is difficult for individual teachers to decide on their own to switch to CL; if the whole school has not made the change, the teacher in the next room may not understand the noise level. Furthermore, the Johnsons have proposed, only half in jest, that principals wander through the halls of their schools, listening at each classroom door. Whenever they hear nothing, they ought to make a point of asking the teacher, "Why isn't any learning going on in here?" As delicious as this reversal of customary practice may be, some trainers go even further, urging teachers to make sure their voices do not rise above and overpower the voices of students.

The latter idea, which suggests a pedagogical approach that would startle even some theorists and practitioners of CL, offers a useful point of departure for discussing different ways children might work together. Some of these issues are quite specific while others get right to the heart of a philosophy of learning; some are widely accepted among those who promote or use CL while others are controversial. The point here is to stimulate thought about the dimensions of cooperative learning, not to offer a comprehensive guide for implementing it.

ASSIGNING STUDENTS TO GROUPS: The size of CL groups will vary depending on the age of the students, their skill and experience working in teams, the type of assignment, and the time available. As a general rule, it is more challenging to integrate more people. As many as six students may be able to exchange information, but fewer — certainly no more than four — will be better able to produce a common product. Many tasks, particularly when attempted by younger children, can best be done in pairs.[40]

More complicated is the question of how to assign students to groups. Each of the most common methods has benefits and problems.

1. Letting students sort themselves offers a strong vote of confidence in their capacity to make decisions, but the temptation will be powerful for them to work with people they already know and like rather than learning to cooperate with those who are new to them. Moreover, some students will feel left out by a self-selection process, and the last thing teachers want is to introduce a competition for the most popular students, reminiscent of what happens when children choose up sides for team sports. One way around this, especially appropriate for open-ended cooperative assignments, is to let children form groups on the basis of the questions they are interested in exploring.

2. Teachers who construct groups may do so with an eye to making sure that each group includes students of different ethnic backgrounds and both genders. The advantages of CL that depend on working with those who are different are maximized when the groups are structured to be heterogeneous in this way.

3. Students with different levels of skill can be placed together deliberately, at least for some tasks, so that effective helping takes place. (One researcher finds that mixing students from two distinct ability levels works better than combining those of high, medium, and low ability in a single group.)[41]

4. Finally, students can be placed randomly in groups[42] to avoid the contrived quality of assignments for heterogeneity. To make sure that each student has the chance to work with a variety of others, groups should probably be shuffled more frequently if assignments are random. Since students can belong to more than one group at a time, some assignments can last longer than others: they may belong to one team only for the duration of a short assignment, for example, and to another, more permanent, multipurpose "base" team for as long as a year.[43] In any event, it is probably not a good idea for students to be able to switch groups just because they are having trouble resolving problems or getting along with their teammates. Such difficulties should be seen as learning opportunities — a chance to figure out (with the teacher's guidance) how to untangle conflicts; students should not be encouraged to assume that it is possible to bail out at the first sign of trouble.

TEACHING SOCIAL SKILLS: When students do not seem to be working together effectively, some educators are inclined to blame them for not being cooperative — or to give up on CL as unworkable. Others, though, reason that children may have been presented with a task that requires more subtle interpersonal skills than are currently in their repertoires. Many champions of CL emphasize that teachers must pay explicit attention to the phenomenon of working together — what it means and how it can be improved. The Johnsons, for example, emphasize that "collaborative skills are directly taught in classrooms where teachers are serious about using cooperative learning" — not only because these skills are a prerequisite for realizing academic gains but also because they are valuable in their own right.[44]

One teacher who recalled her frustration when she first tried to introduce CL to a class of sixth-graders concluded:

> We must not . . . make the mistake of expecting that cooperative group behavior and thinking for oneself will occur in the absence of classroom instruction and practice aimed at these specific goals. . . . We can't *order* it to work; we have to *make* it work. We have to teach children the skills of working thoughtfully and responsibly together. . . . I have heard teachers give it up after a single attempt. . . . But these very same teachers would *never* say, "These children cannot read by themselves," and thereafter remove any opportunity for them to learn to read.[45]

Social skills such as learning to listen carefully, to make eye contact, and to criticize someone's ideas without being insulting can be taught just as reading can be taught. Each lesson, in fact, can be introduced by laying out an academic goal (mastering the future tense in Spanish) and a social goal (helping everyone in the group to feel included). But I would offer two caveats to this approach. First, students of every age should have a role in deciding which social skills they could benefit from working on. It is important to let the specific needs of a given class determine how these issues are addressed rather than running through a packaged set of topics (If it's Tuesday, it must be time to work on listening skills). Second, as I will argue below, in the long run we need to move beyond a focus on teaching discrete skills to individuals in favor of creating a caring classroom community as the context for all lessons.

PROCESSING: A concern with *how* we learn, not only *what* we learn, requires attention after each lesson as well as before. A certain block of time — which, again, will vary with the age of the students and their experience with CL — should be set aside following the completion of a unit for each group to talk about how successful they have been at working together. They can be asked to consider whether everyone contributed to the final project or one person did most of the work, whether someone dominated the discussion, whether everyone felt free to present ideas, whether tasks were divided effectively. They can evaluate the process and, just as important, reflect on how it might be improved the next time they work together.[46] If they decide they have done well, the team members should have the opportunity to celebrate their success, taking pleasure in what they have done and how they have done it.

INDIVIDUAL ACCOUNTABILITY: Many adults react skeptically to the idea of CL because their memory of doing group projects in school is that they ended up being stuck with most of the work while their teammates loafed. (Two social scientists have observed with evident amusement that *everyone* seems to remember having been the one who had to carry the load; it is always "the others" who did nothing.)[47] To be sure, if one person in the group writes the whole report or works most of the problems, the benefits of CL will not be realized. The question, then, is how to ensure individual accountability.

Let us set aside the larger issue of how teachers can best find out, under any learning structure, what children have understood and what they need help with. Instead, let us consider how teachers can make sure that every group member is participating in the CL process. The simplest method is to give everyone a test on all the material or to choose someone from each team randomly to explain what his group came up with and how they came up with it.

The problem with this solution is that it assumes "accountable for learning" means accountable to an external authority.[48] It is taken for granted that the best — indeed, in many educators' minds, the *only* — way to make sure that children apply themselves to a task is, in effect, to threaten them with a poor grade or public humiliation if they do not pull their weight. These assumptions, in turn, reflect a set of beliefs about the nature of learning and human motivation that show up even more starkly in considering the basic issue of how to get students to work together.

POSITIVE INTERDEPENDENCE: We want members of a team to turn to one another for help, to exchange ideas, to feel a measure of group unity. One way to make this happen is to provide tasks that require students to work together toward a common goal. (By contrast, giving children individualized assignments and sitting them at a table with an admonition to help each other does not provide a group objective.)

Another way to draw students together is to give a team only one copy of a story or assignment sheet and only one pencil.

These methods are not particularly objectionable, as far as they go. Two other approaches, however, seem to me more problematic, even though they are widely used by CL teachers. The first is to assign a different role to each member of a group, so that one student writes down all the ideas generated, another checks to make sure that everyone is participating and keeping up, someone else offers words of encouragement, and so on. While there are times this might be useful — such as when CL is still new to students — roles may quickly come to be experienced as confining. Spontaneous, cooperative interaction in the process of engaging with ideas is likely to be frustrated by a child's coming to perceive herself principally as the recorder or checker, a perception facilitated by teachers who have children wear badges to remind them of their responsibility. In truth, a student's primary responsibility is simply to learn in concert with others; anything that could eclipse that process ought to be used with extreme caution. In a study of thirty-three classrooms using CL, researchers at the University of Missouri observed that

> in many cases, the designation of students as leaders, recorders, or materials managers seemed artificial. Students tended to switch roles when necessary and, unless the teacher reminded them, often abandoned roles altogether. Further, teachers often spent as much time reminding students of their roles as they did teaching a concept.[49]

The last method of creating positive interdependence is to use grades, certificates, gold stars, or other extrinsic rewards to induce students to work together. Thus, a team may earn a prize for a specified level of performance on a quiz, or part of one student's grade may be based on the improvement of someone else in the group. Models of CL can be divided into three categories with respect to this issue.

1. Some — notably the "student team learning" methods developed by Robert Slavin and his colleagues — are fundamentally and explicitly driven by the use of extrinsic motivators. For Slavin, the very idea of a "group goal" means "working to earn certificates or other recognition, to receive a few minutes extra of recess, or to earn bonus points on their grades."[50]

2. Other approaches seem to reflect some ambivalence about the

use of rewards, accepting them for promoting interdependence or boosting motivation, on the one hand, but expressing reservations, or at least not insisting on their use, on the other. The Johnsons endorse the strategic use of grades to ensure effective teamwork, calling this "one of the ways in which students are given the message, 'We sink or swim together.' " This, however, follows by a few pages their suggestion that extrinsic motivators "should probably be removed as soon as the intrinsic motivation inherent in cooperative learning groups becomes apparent."[51]

3. Finally, some models explicitly repudiate (or at least pointedly avoid) the use of extrinsic incentives on the grounds that they are manipulative, destructive, unnecessary, or all three. Included in this category are the Group Investigation method devised by Shlomo Sharan and his associates,[52] the version of CL used in programs implemented by the Developmental Studies Center in California,[53] various models that grow out of a "constructivist" model of learning (see below) such as the collaborative learning approach favored in English-speaking countries other than the United States,[54] the work of Nancy Schniedewind and Mara Sapon-Shevin,[55] and my own writings.[56]

As I have already mentioned, a substantial amount of research in social psychology has established that when students see themselves as performing a task in order to receive a reward, their interest in that task is likely to decline, as is the quality of their performance over the long haul (particularly, but not exclusively, when creativity is required). Recall that one of the chief reasons that competition tends to be counterproductive is precisely its status as an extrinsic motivator; to use other such motivators for groups would seem ill advised, to say the least.

But let us put aside for a moment the relatively straightforward empirical question of what long-term consequences the use of classroom incentives brings about. The belief that incentives are *necessary* to promote interdependence and therefore learning* — apart from relying on some very questionable assumptions[57] — reveals a rum-

---

*We should not overlook the corresponding belief that implied threats are necessary to ensure individual accountability. The impact of my earlier remarks is that even teachers who abhor the use of extrinsic motivators (preferring to foster interdependence in less artificial ways) may be sneaking them in the back door by leaning on tests and mandatory recitations to make students "accountable" for learning.

bling under the surface of discussions about CL. It is here that a great crevice between opposing approaches to learning itself is laid bare. Because CL has such potential to transform education and society — the power to let a new generation experience firsthand the possibility of achieving one's goals with others instead of against them — this division is worth exploring carefully.

On one side are those whose philosophy of learning is indistinguishable from that of mainstream U.S. educators except for the fact that traditional techniques and theories are applied at the level of the group instead of the individual. For them, cooperation is really a package of isolatable behaviors that are taught through the use of reinforcements. CL is a set of strategies that the teacher implements in prescribed ways[58] to improve children's performance on whatever curriculum is already being taught. (The curriculum often amounts to a collection of information bits that are transmitted by way of primers, basal readers, and worksheets; the effectiveness of that transmission is then assessed by way of standardized tests.) It is taken for granted in this view, once the layers of assumption are peeled back, that human beings are inclined to learn and to care about each other only when they are given extrinsic incentives for doing so. These beliefs and practices are separable, of course, but for convenience I refer to this whole constellation as the behaviorist position.

On the other side are those who see CL as part of a broader movement in education that represents a profound shift in how we construe and promote learning. Here children are seen not as passive receptacles for facts but as beings who actively struggle to make sense of themselves and the world around them. This they do, in large part, by talking to others. Group discussion is not a "bull session" during which students react to what they have already learned; this is where much of the learning occurs.

The teacher's role is to stimulate a child's curiosity, to facilitate the process of playing with ideas and constructing meaning, and to aid in the development of intellectual and social skills. The goal is to get the student to develop an intrinsic, enduring commitment to this process (and to working successfully with others), to take responsibility for her learning and her behavior. For this reason, children are *given* far more responsibility, separately and as a class, for making decisions and solving problems than is the case in most U.S. schools. I refer to this approach as the constructivist position.

The basic distinction I am drawing has been around for decades, but rarely is it brought to bear on the question of CL. It is not the only schema that can be used to distinguish various models in the field of cooperative learning, but it is a division of monumental importance. The fact is that some CL proponents differ from one another with respect to fundamental ideas about the purpose of schools.

Anyone who evaluates the behaviorist view must immediately concede that a sufficiently attractive reinforcement can get students to do almost anything in the short term. (This concept fascinates children, judging by the tendency to entertain themselves by speculating on how much they would have to be paid to perform various unappetizing feats.) What we care about, though, is the effect on motivation in the long term, once reinforcements are no longer present. Consider just one of many studies that speak to this issue: preschoolers who were praised or promised movie tickets for drinking an unfamiliar beverage did indeed drink more of it than those who expected nothing. But a week later, when the latter group liked the beverage just as much as, if not more than, they had earlier, the children who had been rewarded for drinking it no longer wanted to touch the stuff.[59]

Similarly, when children see schoolwork as a way, individually *or* collectively, to snag a good grade, avert a bad grade, receive a certificate, earn a popcorn party, win a contest,* or secure the approval of a teacher or parent, they have been given no reason to continue learning (or cooperating) when these rewards are no longer available. In fact, the continuous presentation of rewards to students helps to explain the very absence of interest in learning that is then cited as the reason teachers have no choice but to use rewards. Much like competing in order to feel good about oneself (see p. 266, *n32*), offering students extrinsic motivators to get them interested in a task is like giving them salt water to quench their thirst.

THE THREE C'S OF COOPERATION

Someone who accepts the premises of behaviorism would argue that CL, like anything else, is dependent for its success on extrinsic motiva-

---

*Sadly, some models of CL require groups of students to compete against each other. Like team sports, the central message this conveys is that the reason to work together in a group is to defeat another group; triumphing over a common enemy is established as the ultimate goal.[60] This not only sends children conflicting messages, but takes away with one hand everything that the other has given by making CL available.

tors. Speaking from within the constructivist tradition, I want to indicate, by way of response, how CL can work effectively in the absence of these incentives. I will focus on three interlocking domains to which we must attend in order to maximize the benefits of CL — or, for that matter, any learning environment. Let us call them control, curriculum, and community.

CONTROL: Adults who are routinely told exactly what they have to do at work and how they have to do it are likely to become victims of what is known as burnout, a vivid metaphor that suggests an extinguished candle or a dark bulb. Some become actively resentful while others just go through the motions of working in order to pick up their paychecks. Teachers, who know this syndrome well, do not always seem to realize that students are subject to it, too. Conversely, when students (or other people) feel a sense of control over what they are engaged in, they are more likely to find it engaging. Autonomy, then, is not simply an alternative to extrinsic motivators: it is far more effective than any such inducement could be at producing interest in learning, cooperative or otherwise. After all, it is the absence of felt control that, on some accounts, explains why rewards cause intrinsic interest to evaporate in the first place.

Teachers need to do more than minimize the use and salience of extrinsic motivators; they should affirmatively help students to become responsible for their own learning and relationships. When children were allowed to pick their own materials in one study, they produced more creative art projects than did those who used exactly the same materials, but had them handed to them.[61] A child who can make (teacher-guided) choices about what happens in his or her classroom is a child who will be less likely to require artificial inducements to learn and more likely to get hooked on learning.

One model of CL that takes the idea of autonomy seriously is Group Investigation. Here, students form inquiry groups based on what they want to know about a given topic and then make decisions together about how they will divide up the labor and conduct their investigation. Each group collects information and analyzes it, then prepares and shares a final report or innovative presentation that reflects what has been learned. Finally, each group contributes to the evaluation process, perhaps making up the questions on their unit that will be included in a classwide test, if there is to be one. The point is to "incorporate the evaluation into the learning process."[62]

At both the elementary and secondary levels, this model has been associated with a higher level of academic achievement (along with other advantages) precisely because "it gives students more control over their learning."[63] Elsewhere, Shlomo Sharan, its cocreator, has described CL itself as exemplifying the best of the constructivist tradition:

> Cooperative learning . . . gives students an active role in deciding about, planning, directing and controlling the content and pace of their learning activities. It changes the students' role from recipients of information to seekers, analyzers and synthesizers of information. It transforms pupils from listeners into talkers and doers, from powerless pawns into participant citizens empowered to influence decisions about what they must do in school.[64]

This is, to be precise, a description of what CL can be and should be, but not, alas, what it always is.

CURRICULUM: Many books have been filled with prescriptions for improving the curriculum used in various subjects at various age levels. I would therefore make only three points. First, when children are given assignments that stir their natural curiosity and are neither so difficult as to be anxiety producing nor so easy as to be boring, they generally do not require extrinsic motivators in order to approach them.[65] (The corollary to this principle is that if students are required to fill in the missing words in an endless series of unrelated sentences or memorize the kings and queens of England, they may *have* to be bribed to do so.)

Second, a meaningful curriculum is a necessary and perhaps even sufficient way to draw children into CL without the use of rewards. "If the task is challenging and interesting, and if students are sufficiently prepared for skills in group process, students will experience the process of groupwork itself as highly rewarding," according to Stanford University's Elizabeth Cohen.[66]

Third, if we do *not* address curricular issues in the context of CL, we may doom it to failure — or, put differently, we may doom it to success according to the wholly inadequate educational standards we have increasingly come to accept. Apart from the use of rewards, one of the most telling questions that anyone considering the use of CL can ask is what children are learning in their groups. Some models are advertised as being adaptable to any curriculum.[67] The soothing message here is not only that CL will work regardless of what is being taught, but that educators need not reflect on how challenging or valuable their material may be because students will benefit from learning whatever is presented as long as they do it in groups. Sapon-Shevin has wryly referred to this approach as the "Hamburger Helper" model of cooperative learning.[68]

If CL is not to become a technique for dressing up ground beef — and if schools are not to become outlets of a McInformation chain, as it were — teachers will need to provide groups with stimulating, personally relevant material that pushes them to engage together in higher-order thinking. Even the partisans of some extrinsically based models of CL concede that these methods are most appropriate for dealing with problems that have one right answer.[69] The question, then, is whether we resign ourselves to the continued reliance on such tasks or instead use the potential heuristic power of CL as an opportunity to find things more worthy of our children's (and teachers') time.

> Using cooperative techniques to have students cover the same boring, inconsequential, or biased material or to have them "get through" worksheets with more efficiency doesn't demonstrate the approach's full potential for changing what goes on in schools.[70]

Likewise, the potential of CL is lost if it is geared toward improving scores on standardized tests — or promoted and sold on that basis. The worshipful regard for these tests — and if this were not discouraging enough, the proposal to have schools *compete* to see who can get more students to blacken the correct bubbles with their No. 2 pencils — comes chiefly from people who are uninformed about pedagogical or motivational issues. Most educators, by contrast, know that these measures fail to capture what is meaningful about learning and have the effect of pressuring teachers to "teach to the tests," forgoing potentially innovative lessons in order to prepare children for exams. Anyone who wanted to destroy what is left of rich, creative teaching — or children's love of learning — could do no better than to increase our reliance on standardized tests.[71]

Of course, all educators ought to insist on a curriculum of quality and attempt to resist and reverse the diminution of schooling. But those who are associated with a reform as exciting as CL have a special responsibility to provide content worthy of the method.

COMMUNITY: The assumption that students will work together only on the basis of self-interest and, specifically, only in the hope of receiving a reward for doing so — the assumption, that is, that no classroom environment could possibly develop norms leading naturally to cooperation — betrays a profoundly cynical view of "human nature." Happily, it is a view that enjoys very little empirical support. Given the right circumstances, caring for others is no less natural than caring for oneself.[72]

A classroom that emphasizes and promotes the value of community — that has, in fact, been transformed *into* a caring community — allows positive interdependence to take hold. CL can thus become successful without promising each student extra points for helping someone else. This is one of the guiding premises of the Child Development Project in San Ramon, California, a comprehensive, long-term elementary school program that has achieved significant success in helping children to become more caring and responsible.[73] Drawing in part from the work of that project, I have elsewhere sketched an approach that all teachers can use to promote a sense of community, the idea being to provide an environment that does not offer incentives for helping or sharing but encourages children to ask "What kind of classroom do we want to have?"[74]

Once again, an exploration of this topic takes us beyond its role as an alternative to the use of extrinsic motivators in CL. In this case, it propels us clear beyond cooperative learning (at least in the way the concept is usually understood) and into the realm of what we might call the cooperative classroom. Anyone who needs to be convinced to make such a shift should consider the predicament of the teacher who confessed that "she caught herself yelling at a group of students, 'Stop helping each other; we're not doing cooperative learning now!' "[75]

I am arguing that cooperation must come to be seen as a fundamental orientation toward other people rather than a set of techniques that are hauled out for specific lessons. This means working to change the feel of the classroom itself. As one second-grade teacher (affiliated with the Child Development Project) put it:

> You can't just teach Cooperative Learning as a separate subject that you just do for thirty minutes a day and then just treat the children differently the rest of the time. The whole atmosphere of the classroom from the time the kids get to school until the time they go home is based on the idea that you expect them to get along, help each other, be cooperative, [follow] all the same guidelines in everything they do.[76]

Notice that this does not mean instituting a circumscribed program of CL and passively waiting for its benefits to seep out and improve the dynamics of other interactions and activities. It means teachers must broaden their vision, rethinking the entire learning experience and working with students to fashion that experience into something that is cooperative inside and out.

Too much of American education consists of teachers spewing out facts and requiring students to spew them back; if the latter is done correctly, the transaction is pronounced successful. This goes on in elementary school ("Europe is a what, boys and girls? That's right, a continent. Very good."), and it goes on in college as instructors reward polysyllabic conformity by playing a game that might be called Guess What's on My Legal Pad.* The research and values that support the use of CL can be understood as an invitation to change all this, not to abandon the teaching of basic skills but to distinguish necessary skills from trivia and to embed those skills in the more substantive process of meaningful thinking.

There is good reason to think that CL can be enormously successful without falling back on what are, in effect, bribes for cooperating — so long as students are provided with a measure of control over their learning, a meaningful curriculum, and the opportunity to create a palpable sense of community in the classroom.

Research from at least three CL programs has shown that extrinsic motivators simply are not necessary to produce academic achievement. First, as I noted earlier, the Group Investigation approach has achieved consistent advantages in terms of the quality of learning. Second, the Child Development Project found that children in its program classrooms did significantly better than a carefully matched group of comparison students on an essay exam measuring higher-order reading comprehension, while suffering no disadvantage on standardized tests.[78]

The third and most recent example comes from a second-grade mathematics program based on constructivist principles and small-

---

*One observer argues that this attenuated model of learning in higher education helps to explain why CL has rarely taken root in the college classroom. "The traditional role of the university professor as an expert who initiates novices into disciplinary ways of knowing and thinking is itself an impediment to creating genuinely cooperative learning environments," according to Steven A. Gelb, who teaches at the University of San Diego. The other impediments he mentions are the fact that many students *expect* to defer to authority rather than learning cooperatively, and the extraordinarily competitive milieu in which faculty members work, with cooperation construed as a hindrance to professional success.[77]

group work and characterized by "a complete absence of extrinsic motivation or external reward systems, including praise." In place of textbook assignments, students were encouraged to take an active role in figuring out and discussing problems that occurred in concrete situations. Compared to their peers who had been in traditional classrooms, these children developed more sophisticated higher-level reasoning skills without falling behind on basic computational tasks.[79]

To the extent that attention is paid to the issues of control, curriculum, and community, CL can flourish and, further, can be part of a radical transformation of American schooling. To the extent that these things are absent, education itself, not only CL, is in trouble.

THE PROSPECTS FOR COOPERATION

To what extent has CL made an impact on how our children are actually taught? The answer one gives will depend on when one takes a reading (the assessment that follows, written in 1992, may soon become dated) and where one happens to live (CL's popularity in California may lead residents to assume that children everywhere are now cooperating). It also may reflect one's feelings about the desirability of CL: partisans, carried away by their enthusiasm, sometimes exaggerate the influence of the movement, while opponents, seeking to alarm the populace, may do the same thing.[80]

By now, many — perhaps most — U.S. teachers have at least heard the phrase "cooperative learning." Tens of thousands have been formally trained in one version or another. CL has its own magazine, which is intended for researchers as well as classroom teachers.* Articles on the subject show up with some regularity in other education journals and magazines, and several bibliographies have been compiled, listing some of the hundreds of books and articles published to date.[81] In March 1992, the newsletter of a major American education organization declared that "unlike some other innovations in education, cooperative learning has not been a flash in the pan. After years of attention, it remains a hot topic among educators."[82]

Cooperative Learning magazine, the successor to the newsletter of the International Association for the Study of Cooperation in Education (IASCE), is published quarterly. For information, write to Box 1582, Santa Cruz, CA 95061.

Various mainstream organizations have come to recognize CL's potential for enhancing the quality of learning.* The American Association for the Advancement of Science released a report in 1989 declaring that "the collaborative nature of scientific and technological work should be strongly reinforced by frequent group activity in the classroom."[84] That same year, the National Council of Teachers of Mathematics also affirmed the value of small-group work.[85] (Some universities are beginning to use a collaborative approach for teaching higher-level mathematics.)[86] The National Council of Teachers of English has published an anthology on the subject and urged that secondary teachers offer "multiple opportunities for students to work together."[87] In Britain, meanwhile, "Her Majesty's Inspectorate (HMI) have been actively promoting group work in schools in the belief that it increases children's motivation, develops responsibility and initiative, and creates a context for effective learning."[88]

The growing popularity of CL, however, is cause for concern among those who recognize its potential to reshape the educational landscape. Any development that is sufficiently well known and well regarded may begin to take on the contours of a fad, which, in turn, means that it will be treated as a fad rather than with the necessary seriousness. In practical terms, this means that principals and superintendents, trying to keep up with pedagogical fashion, may hire consultants who offer to provide brief (and therefore seductively inexpensive) training sessions for their faculties: "Give me your teachers for two days of in-service and I'll show them how to do cooperative learning." Some trainers even claim to be able to give teachers sufficient skills to become trainers themselves.

One of the central theses of this chapter is that CL at its best requires a significant reconceptualization of what learning involves and how the people who spend the day together in a classroom relate to one another. Any attempt to implement CL will therefore raise a host of problems and questions, and many of them will not even occur to teachers until they have had the chance to work with the new arrangement for a time. The fact is that the process of making this kind of change must be done over a period of years, with frequent observation and coaching as well as continuous, structured peer sup-

---

*Some educators are also realizing that CL is the logical alternative to the practice known as tracking, that is, separating children by putative ability.[83]

port.[89]* (Moreover, it must be done in a way that is respectful of teachers' experiences and concerns. Even good ideas should not, and ultimately cannot, be forced down unwilling throats. In fact, we might even go so far as to say that policymakers, trainers, and administrators cannot change what goes on in classrooms. All they can do is invite *teachers* to change what goes on in classrooms.)

One writer has estimated that only 5 to 10 percent of participants in a CL workshop will continue to use the cooperative approach over time if ongoing coaching and support are absent.[91] If teachers receive quick-and-dirty training sessions, if the trainer is long gone by the time difficulties start to present themselves, many educators will discard CL as "unworkable" or "unrealistic" and settle back to wait for next year's fad. To this extent, there is cause for worry among those who discern its long-term potential about CL's short-term popularity.

On the other hand, the extent of that popularity should not be overstated. If it is not quite accurate to call it a drop in the bucket of national educational practice, cooperative learning is still not much more than a puddle. Walk into a random American classroom and you will still probably find those contests for attention and grades, that structurally enforced cruelty described more than three decades ago by Jules Henry (see p. 26), and rows of children at separate desks, each one facing the back of someone else's head. Flip through the pages of debate about education reform and you will see scant attention to the question of how one student's learning is related to another's.

Clearly, we have a very long way to go. The distance seems even greater, though, in light of the fact that some teachers who have been introduced to CL react much as a body does to the implantation of foreign tissue. The extent of this rejection is difficult to gauge, but

---

*Peer support, in fact, is an essential ingredient in the creation of effective schools. The higher self-esteem, more positive relationships, and enhanced performance that attend cooperation among students also attend cooperation among teachers. Conversely, "if teachers spend five to seven hours a day advocating a competitive, individualistic approach — telling students, 'Do your own work. . . . Try to be better [than your neighbor],' those are the values the teachers are going to have in their relationships with colleagues and their administrators."[90] Complicating matters further is the fear of making oneself vulnerable by seeking help from a colleague about a problem in the classroom. But the administrator who wants to create a cooperative school must do more than exhort teachers to exchange ideas; carefully designed structures and adequate time must be provided for collaboration.

one observer wrote that "despite the academic vogue of cooperative learning and efforts at dissemination made by its proponents, it remains an instructional strategy seldom used in a systematic manner over the course of a school year or more."[92] It is difficult to verify this pessimistic assessment, but no one seeking to promote the use of CL should minimize the challenge involved in doing so successfully.

The reasons for that challenge are multiple.[93] They include inadequate training in, and support for, the practice of CL and widespread misunderstanding about what CL does and does not involve. But some obstacles to the effective adoption of cooperation run deeper and would likely cause problems even if the training were perfection itself.

Specifically, we can identify four primary aspects of CL that may be unsettling to many educators. The first is that it challenges our cultural commitment to the value of competition; the second is that it challenges our cultural commitment to the value of individualism. I have already had my say on both of these issues.

The third attitudinal barrier is that CL demands attention to social goals. Teachers can scarcely avoid noticing that children sometimes seem indifferent to suffering, unable to resolve conflicts fairly, and likely either to try to get their needs met by coercing others or, conversely, to be victimized by coercion. But even those who recognize that the time spent together in the classroom *could* be used to attend to these problems may believe that this focus would be inappropriate because their charge is limited to providing instruction in the traditional academic subjects.

Whatever the reason, Goodlad's study — probably the most comprehensive survey of American schools ever made — found that with respect to goals such as "developing productive and satisfying relations with others based on respect, trust, cooperation, and caring," what goes on in the classroom at best contributes nothing and often actually impedes the promotion of such values.[94]

Even when attention is given to the development of children's social skills and prosocial orientation, this enterprise is "frequently viewed through an instrumental prism of how [these skills] affect academic achievement rather than as schooling goals with inherent legitimacy," according to educational researcher Yisrael Rich.[95] The models of CL that call for explicit instruction in social skills, especially those that recommend taking time to create a caring classroom community,

would presumably be resisted by teachers who are concerned to help
children become good learners but not necessarily good people. As
Rich observes,

> If cooperative learning is perceived by teachers as primarily promoting
> pupils' personal or social goals, we would not expect very many teachers
> to voluntarily participate. And if they are required to participate in the
> workshop, few of them will arrive at the decision to adopt the new
> method, assuming they are allowed some choice in the matter, no matter
> how well the workshop is conducted. And if they are required to adopt
> the new method, even fewer will implement it with a reasonable degree
> of fidelity.[96]

The final factor that may serve as an obstacle to the widespread
use of CL is that having children work in groups (at least in a way
consistent with the constructivist approach to learning) reduces a
teacher's control over the classroom and the predictability of what
happens each day. Someone — it might have been me — once said
that the traditional model of teaching amounts to a rehearsed solo
performance by the instructor (with students relegated to the role of
audience), whereas CL not only offers instruments to everyone in the
room but invites a jazz improvisation. The analogy has its limits, but
it captures two features of CL: its demand that the teacher guide
students in helping each other to learn (rather than being the only
source of ideas and information in the room)[97] and its introduction of
uncertainty in place of a predictable progression through a prepared
lesson plan. Some teachers have not bargained for either of these
changes.

There is a certain pleasure to be taken from the role of king or
queen, even if one's subjects are very short. To the extent that the
process of schooling has been predicated on compelling students to
follow directions, to absorb information and regurgitate it on com-
mand, to work silently on whatever task is presented, the profession
may have attracted some people who thrive on autocracy. I regularly
meet teachers who shine with generosity of spirit and an instinct for
what children need to grow. But others, let us frankly admit, are
disinclined to embrace an approach that gives students an active role
in their own learning and has them look to each other for help. With
CL the teacher has allies throughout the room — a scenario exciting
and refreshing to some educators but highly disconcerting to those
who, like trial attorneys during cross examination, never ask a question to which they do not already know the answer.[98]

One way around this barrier, of course, is simply to dilute CL until it is not so different from the present arrangement. When the nature of the interchange among group members is highly circumscribed — more than the students' age or the subject matter would seem to require — we might suspect that the teacher has compromised the process of cooperation more to maintain control than to maximize the heuristic value of the experience. Some trainers are water carriers, so to speak, for this dilution.

Interestingly, the versions of CL that seek to dictate to students each component of cooperation — thereby reducing their sense of autonomy as fellow meaning-creators and idea-explorers — are likely to be so structured and systematized that teachers, too, are deprived of authority. So-called teacher-proof curricula, we ought to have realized by now, are not only disrespectful but chimerical: they are the perpetual-motion machines of education. Cookbook approaches to CL similarly attempt to specify in advance what cannot be specified in advance, to reduce learning to a series of discrete steps that renders the process sterile and excludes both teachers and students from the real work (and joy) of what happens in the classroom.

CL is not simply the status quo except in groups. At its best, it is an entirely different way of approaching the act of learning. Sharan warns that if we reduce the potentially liberating principles of CL to

a set of prepackaged procedures for managing the movements of warm bodies in the classroom . . . to get them to study, with just a little less boredom, the same material that would bore them more if it were studied in some other way . . . [then CL] will soon be discarded as another fraud, as will so many other packaged methods now loudly touted in the educational marketplace.[99]

In fact, the lack of predictability that CL can engender is not a necessary evil; it is a requirement for learning. Neither CL nor education in general should allow itself to get too comfortable. A century and a half ago, Kierkegaard, observing that most public figures pride themselves on figuring out how to make people's lives easier in one way or the other, set for himself "out of love for mankind" the task of "creat[ing] difficulties everywhere."[100] In a sense, and with compassion, this is the teacher's task: to "design instructional activities that are likely to be problematic for children"[101] and to guard against relaxing when things are going too smoothly. "Deeper learning would look somewhat 'messier' than what I am seeing in most of our [cooperative] classrooms" is how Eric Schaps, the director of the Child Development Project, once put it.[102]

The prospects for CL to sweep the country, and for the country to stay swept, depend to some extent on the willingness of parents to demand that their children — that all children — be permitted the benefits of working together. Many parents, looking back on their own years in school, may recall a superlative teacher here, a few satisfying friendships there, an occasional moment of excitement when a connection was made or an idea understood. But the background to these pleasant memories may be something much like what Goodlad and Henry and scores of other observers have documented: isolation, humiliation, self-doubt, rivalry, pointless tasks, boredom. All of us for whom this account rings true have a choice to make. We can set our jaws and harden our hearts, muttering, "Hey, if it was good enough for me . . ." — thereby dooming another generation to the same fate. Or we can ask, "What can be done to make sure our children get better than we got?" Even to ask this question presupposes that we have recognized — and this may come as an epiphany — that, just as a game does not have to be a contest, so the stultifying aspects of our education are not inevitable features of going to school.

Is cooperative learning out of step with our society's values? Some proponents deny this heatedly, pointing out that even a culture or an economic system as steeped in competition as our own requires cooperation to be successful. To some extent this is true, but we might as well admit that CL does challenge the beliefs and practices that set people against one another. Some curriculum guides augment this challenge by making cooperation and competition explicit topics for study,[103] but the very fact of learning by working together presents children with another model, a different experience, a sense of perspective on the competition they otherwise might have taken for granted. Cooperative learning should not stand or fall depending on how well it serves our society's institutions. Rather, our institutions should stand or fall depending on how well they serve the sort of values represented by cooperative learning.

AFTERWORD

In the fall of 1982, a couple of years after considering and rejecting the possibility of writing my graduate thesis on the topic of competition, I found myself irresistibly drawn back to the issue. The research project on which I embarked, at first without much thought to whether it could result in a publishable book, eventually came to dominate my life. Now, a decade after scribbling my first notes on what it means to compete, I want to take a few minutes to look back — and especially to consider what has happened in the six years since *No Contest* went to press.

Specifically, I'd like to try to answer the questions I'm often asked when I speak on the topic: How have people reacted to the book and its thesis? Is our culture becoming more or less competitive? What new research has been published on the topic? (Now that I think about it, I cannot remember anyone actually asking the last question, but that is certainly not going to prevent me from answering it.)

The first thing that happened was that I received invitations to appear on more than one hundred TV and radio programs, including *Donahue*, to say nothing of interviews for newspaper and magazine articles. On *Donahue*, I was asked such questions as, "Well, if you're against competition, isn't that just because you're a loser?" (I invite you to consider how *you* would deal with this question in eight seconds on national television.) I realized pretty quickly that all this attention signified not that the book's reasoning was seen as cogent but rather that its position was seen as outrageously controversial. It was not that I had offered a meaty argument so much as that I had turned our most sacred cow into hamburger.

Today I am sometimes described as the country's leading critic of competition, but of course there is not much competition for that title. I have been invited to lecture at some organizations whose relentless pursuit of competitive advantage — they might as well have a bust of Vince Lombardi on display in the lobby — leads me to wonder whether my name is being circulated by an organization called Rent-a-Gadfly.

The reaction to my remarks on competition usually sorts itself into three categories. First, there are the people who nod continuously as I speak, as if to say "Yes! I've had these thoughts for fifteen years, but I've been embarrassed to say them out loud!" To my surprise, quite a few people react this way, but since attendance at most of my lectures is voluntary, these people, like those who take the trouble to write to me, probably do not constitute a representative sample of the American public. Nevertheless, I am always delighted to connect with kindred spirits and, if I can, to offer them further analysis and evidence with which they can work to replace competition with cooperation.

At the other end of the spectrum are those who accuse me of being either a Communist or a wimp.* In person, these people sit with their arms tightly folded, scowling or smirking, convinced that anyone who thinks competition is undesirable and unnecessary must live on Neptune. If they bother to stay for the question period, their comments usually begin with: "What you say is very nice in *theory*, but . . ." I enjoy talking to these people, too, in part because, like them, I am a skeptic. (Where we differ is that I would prefer to see skepticism directed at the status quo rather than employed in its service.) Perhaps I can plant a seed, I figure; even those who dismiss my critique may find that something has sprouted the next time they see a person's spirit crushed, or performance obviously impaired, by a win/lose structure.

Between these two categories sit the listeners (or readers) who are strongly inclined to resist the news that competition is counterproductive but find themselves unable to wish it away. Even though these people are gravely troubled by the implications of my argument, they are willing to question the conventional wisdom. One woman came up to me after a lecture, frowning, and confessed, "Now I'm really disoriented." This made my day.

One very specific response to the case against competition may also be worth mentioning here. I am regularly informed that we would be doing children a disservice by minimizing competition since they need to be prepared for the rivalry they will encounter when they grow up. My response is that we need to work on two tracks at once: preparing children for what they will find in our society, and prepar-

---

*These epithets tend to be mutually exclusive. If both could be applied to the same person, I suppose someone might raise serious questions about the Pentagon's budget.

ing them, if need be, to *change* what they find. To concentrate only on the latter, keeping our eye fixed on a distant goal, may make life difficult for children in the short term. But to concentrate only on the former ensures that *their* children will encounter the same destructive institutions and backward values.

Beyond this, however, the fact is that students in our society already are well acquainted with competition. Even if some experience with trying to triumph over others were useful, children have more than they could ever need. Imagine a school that studiously avoids competition, in the classroom or on the playing field, from kindergarten through twelfth grade. We may be confident that not a single graduate of this school, on entering college or the work force, would suddenly exclaim, "Whoa! What's all this about 'competition'?" Our best efforts to promote cooperation notwithstanding, children in this country are all too familiar with win/lose activities.

What students need is not more of the same but experience with alternative arrangements so that they can achieve a sense of perspective about the competition that proliferates in our culture. While a case can be made that students would benefit from a curricular unit in which they explicitly consider the effects of competition, talking about it is quite different from being immersed in it. (By way of analogy, consider the distinction between teaching schoolchildren *about* religion and indoctrinating them to *be* religious.) Moreover, there is no reason to imagine that having children participate in competitive activities week after week after week could provide any incremental benefit. The rationale for doing so, if made explicit, would look something like a sign I once saw tacked to a wall in a sixth-grade classroom: THE BEATINGS WILL CONTINUE UNTIL MORALE IMPROVES.

While I have continued to write and speak on competition, I have also been following three other lines of inquiry growing out of that work. First, I have been drawn to the field of education and, specifically, to the use of cooperative learning as an alternative to competition. The practice of having students work together in pairs or small groups was already attracting attention before *No Contest* was published. The research literature and practical record of success connected with this approach have mushroomed since then. I have discussed the topic in chapter 10, which is new to this edition.

Second, the question of whether competition is just part of "human nature" (chapter 2) led me to look at that concept more carefully, and specifically to ask whether selfishness, aggression, and other of our less noble attributes are really more natural than generosity, caring, and empathy. The result of that investigation was published in 1990 as *The Brighter Side of Human Nature: Altruism and Empathy in Everyday Life,* and it, in turn, has led me to try to devise strategies for promoting "prosocial" behaviors and attitudes in children.

Finally, the study of competition has opened up a broader issue, namely, the consequences of using other extrinsic motivators (discussed briefly on pp. 59–61). If any assumption drives our culture more powerfully than the faith that competition is valuable, it is the belief that all problems can be solved if only we find a big enough carrot to dangle in front of people. My next book (also to be published by Houghton Mifflin) will consider the unhappy consequences of manipulating people with rewards — at work, at school, and at home.

Is competition on the upswing today or has its day come and gone? I have seen no polls or studies seeking to measure the pervasiveness of competition in American life, much less any longitudinal data attempting to identify trends. I am more than a little suspicious of sweeping, facile pronouncements of epochal transformations currently under way, and, frankly, I don't even know what would count as evidence for the beginning of a significant change regarding something like competition.

I will say that I am heartened by the move toward cooperative learning in many schools and, to some extent, by the growing interest in real teamwork and "quality" among some managers. I am discouraged, however, by the fact that *competitiveness* has become more of a buzzword among politicians, businesspeople, and educators than it was even half a dozen years ago.

I am heartened by recent news reports about a school in Indiana where every willing student can be part of an athletic team or the cheerleading squad or the choir. Its "no-cut" policy in extracurricular activities has resulted in huge increases in participation and far fewer problems than some had anticipated.[1] I am discouraged by recent news reports about elaborate "Little Miss" beauty contests for three-to six-year-old girls[2] and pressure-filled interscholastic academic contests that reduce learning to a matter of preparing for victory at a quiz show.[3]

I am heartened when I see dissidents starting to raise questions about the value of competition in publications as diverse as a psycho-analytic journal (1986)[4] and magazines for guitar players (1989),[5] music teachers (1990),[6] and photographers (1992).[7] I am discouraged by the fact that most of the popular press, notably magazines intended for women, continues to treat competition as inevitable, desirable, amusing, or all three. Not every such article is as egregious as one recent quiz for teenage girls ("Compete, Don't Retreat!"), bursting with cheerful exclamation points, which awards more points to readers who know enough to put their desire to win ahead of their loyalty to friends.[8] In magazines for parents, articles often advise against putting too much pressure on children to win. Such cautions, however, are accompanied by a de rigueur concession that, "of course," competition in moderation is appropriate and productive.*

I am appalled when I read that forty-nine teenagers from one school district have been hospitalized for depression, suicide attempts, or substance abuse, all apparently connected to the stress caused by academic competition. (The school administrators responded by citing the "failure to teach adolescents coping skills." If, by way of comparison, a factory's polluting smokestacks had sent nearby residents to the hospital, presumably the factory manager would not have the audacity to attribute the problem to a failure to buy respirators.)[9] I am horrified when I read that some of the people who were killed when a plane crashed and burned on a runway in Los Angeles might have lived were it not for two men standing in front of the exit door, competing over who would get out first.[10] It is hard to take any consolation in such tragedy save for the faint hope that some people may begin to understand that competition by its very nature is a problem.

The unwillingness to acknowledge this is, I am convinced, the chief obstacle to freeing ourselves from the quicksand. People proudly tell me stories of someone they know who didn't care whether he lost, or of some competitive game in which participants were exhorted not to place too much importance on the outcome. These are steps in the right direction, and I am pleased to hear about them. But they do nothing to challenge the underlying structure of mutually exclusive

---

*My complaint here is not that so few writers on the subject take the same position I do, but that so few apparently have even bothered to question the shibboleth that competition is troubling only when done to excess. This assumption is stated as an obvious truth: everyone knows children need to be set against one another *sometimes*.

goal attainment, which is the ultimate cause of the problems detailed in the preceding 237 pages. This is often difficult to grasp in a culture that can imagine change only at the level of individual attitudes and behaviors. If next week we Americans suddenly began to recognize the destructive consequences of competition, books would start to appear in the stores with titles like "Ten Steps to a Less Competitive You."

That competition itself may be the problem is rarely considered, least of all in the context of what goes on in the workplace.[11] Nevertheless, research over the last few years continues to remind us of the importance of structural factors. In one study, people led to expect that they were going to be working cooperatively with strangers responded empathically when those strangers received a reward or punishment. But those who thought they would be competing against the others responded *counterempathically* — that is, smiling at their discomfort and grimacing at their good fortune.[12] Another study showed how people put into a situation of team competition tended to reject friendly overtures from people on the other side and came to view the members of that group as an undifferentiated They.[13]

In chapter 7, I argued that cheating and other problems result at least as much from competition itself as from the moral failings of the individual. Several recent comments by people in different fields illustrate the naiveté of condemning ugly behavior while taking no steps to challenge the basic win/lose framework.

• In sports, a safety for the New York Giants points out that he and other football players are

> expected and required to be good sportsmen when we are engaged in an endeavor that is hostile and aggressive . . . to go from being gentlemanly and following the rules of society to people who play violently and aggressively for two or three hours on Sunday. . . . It's not easy to do, especially when people across the line of scrimmage are literally the enemy.[14]

• In politics, a campaign consultant shrugs off the widespread indignation at negative advertisements, observing that

> a political campaign, like a trial in a court of law, has but one objective — to win. Staying within the confines of the truth, a candidate or consultant will use every available legal means to attain that objective. If you don't play by the rules of the game, your opposition will.[15]

• In business, the director of an organization called the Ethics Resource Center says we are kidding ourselves if we think the corporate world is going to be changed by putting business students through ethics courses:

> As long as you have a business culture that puts people in impossible situations — "your division has to grow 7 percent in the next year or else we're going to be No. 2 in the field and if we are, you're going to be job-hunting " — you're going to have people shipping inferior goods, juggling the books, bribing when they have to, trampling workers beneath them and generally conducting themselves in the time-honored tradition: Results, and only results, count.[16]

• In education, seventy-three students at the Massachusetts Institute of Technology were disciplined for "cheating," mostly for working in small groups to write computer programs together for fear of being unable to keep up with the class otherwise. "Many feel that the required work is clearly impossible to do by straightforward [i.e., solitary] means," according to the faculty member who chairs MIT's Committee on Discipline.[17]

Each of these examples invites us to shift our gaze from maladjusted individuals to a maladaptive system. The problem is that it is easy to suspend an athlete whose aggression slips over the edge of "acceptability," to condemn the creators of nasty political ads, to jail greedy Wall Street lawbreakers, or to punish students who work collaboratively. It is not so easy to undertake social change of the sort that must follow an admission that something is wrong with competition per se.

The growing clamor to make hospitals, schools, industries, and now even government more "competitive" raises once again the question of whether this goal has anything to do with reaching excellence, or whether we have simply blurred the two ideas, overlooking what should be an obvious fact — that beating others and doing quality work are two completely different concepts. Whether the first *leads* to the second is a legitimate question, but the answer, contrary to conventional wisdom, is that it almost always does not. The trouble with our schools, for example, is that they are much *too* competitive, which helps to explain why so little learning is taking place.[18]

A similar dynamic is now at work in the field of health care, where many institutions are being pressured for the first time to become "competitive." More hospitals and clinics are being run by for-profit corporations; many institutions, forced to battle for "customers," seem to value a skilled director of marketing more highly than a skilled caregiver. As in any other economic sector, the race for profits translates into pressure to reduce costs, and the easiest way to do it here is to cut back on services to unprofitable patients, that is, those who are more sick than rich.

This is exactly what insurance companies are doing under the banner of "competitiveness": denying coverage to those who need it most. In many cases, there is not even any greater efficiency to show for the greater inequity. "Among providers, competition has led to a stunning round of spending on facilities and equipment in an attempt to lure patients from other providers — and never mind if the new facilities are [unnecessary]."[19] The result: hospital costs are actually *higher* in areas where there is more competition for patients.[20]

There are few pockets of the U.S. economy in which competition between firms is introduced for the first time. When people talk about increasing the competition in a given sector, they often mean abandoning government regulation in order to more nearly approximate a laissez-faire or "pure" market. Recent developments of this kind, such as in the airline industry, serve only to increase one's skepticism about the value of competition.[21]

But the data with which I am more familiar concern the effects of competition within a given workplace. Add to the research cited in chapter 3 a bushel of new studies that Dean Tjosvold of Simon Fraser University in British Columbia conducted at utility companies, manufacturing plants, engineering firms, and many other kinds of organizations. Over and over again, Tjosvold has found that "cooperation makes a work force motivated," whereas "serious competition undermines coordination."[22] (Interestingly, one study from Georgia State University discovered that competition reduces the quality of one's performance, even if one happens to be a rhesus monkey!)[23]

Meanwhile, the management guru celebrated from Detroit to Tokyo, W. Edwards Deming, has declared that the practice of having employees compete against each other is

> unfair [and] destructive. We cannot afford this nonsense any longer. . . . [We need to] work together on common problems [, but] annual rating of performance, incentive pay, [or] bonuses cannot live with teamwork. . . . What takes the joy out of learning . . . [or out of] anything? Trying to be number one.[24]

What *does* lead to excellence, then? This depends on what field and task we are talking about, but generally we find that people do terrific work when (1) they are inspired, challenged, and excited by what they are doing, and (2) they receive social support and are able to exchange ideas and collaborate effectively with others.* The data show that competition makes both less likely.

The dissolution of the Soviet Union has led a lot of Americans to construct the following syllogism: since (a) our economic system is based on competition, (b) their system collapsed, and (c) we were rivals, this must mean that (d) competition works. It would take considerably more space than I have been allotted here to offer a serious challenge to this rather dubious bit of deduction. Suffice it to say that the very adversarial nature of the relationship between the two countries — competition writ large, in other words — has had a great deal to do with trouble experienced on both sides of the old iron curtain. Of course, many factors played a part in sinking communism, but if we are looking for a simple explanation, we would do well to focus not on the absence of competition but on the absence of the Soviet citizen's commitment to his or her work, chiefly due to the lack of personal autonomy and genuine democracy in that country. Then we might consider that the very same factors are present in this country.[25]†

Another unsettling event, although it is already fading from our memories, was the stock market crash of October 1987. Many analysts attributed that event to the "failure of international cooperation" — specifically, a struggle involving German interest rates and U.S. currency, and ultimately affecting the economic condition of many countries.[26] The nations of the world seem to become more inter-

---

*Thus, for example, we might question the assumption that the United States was able to put a man on the moon as soon as it did by virtue of being in a race with the USSR. Rather than inspiring excellence, the fact of being in a contest meant that each country was struggling with problems that the other country had already solved. Competition in general is distinguished by just such redundancy; it is inherently wasteful, since each rival cannot benefit from what the other knows. (Of course, the space-race example overlooks the question of whether putting someone on the moon was worth the enormous expense in the first place. That, not coincidentally, is exactly the kind of question that people almost never ask when they are in a race.)

†The absence of both genuine cooperation and autonomy is captured in a single corporate phrase: being a "team player." In context, this exhortation is very much like urging elementary school students to "cooperate." The desired behavior has nothing to do with self-directed teamwork and everything to do with obedient conformity.

dependent with each passing week; in the face of this fact, competition seems a mutually ruinous proposition. This is why it is dismaying that so few voices are raised against such competition,[27] leaving U.S. politicians across the ideological spectrum to assume that the only question is *how* we can beat the Japanese (the enemy *du jour*), as opposed to whether triumph is preferable to cooperation — or even possible in any meaningful sense.

The lessons to be drawn from what happened to the USSR, why the market crashed, and how the United States should deal with other nations are, for the most part, matters for argument and speculation. But hard research continues to accumulate on specific questions related to the effects of small-scale competition.

I cited a 1982 study, for instance, in which children who were competing to make the best collage did less creative work than those who were not in a contest (p. 54). Five years later, the same researcher described how she found the identical effect with adults, including corporate executives and managers, who were working on the kind of problems used to measure creativity: those who were competing to devise better solutions than anyone else were less likely to solve them correctly than were those who did not compete at all.[28]

I also described a 1981 study in which participating in a contest made adults less interested in the task on which they had been working (p. 60). Five years later, *this* finding was replicated with children: fifth- and sixth-graders were less likely to continue playing a balancing game if they had been competing earlier to keep themselves balanced longer than others.[29] Moreover, a book from two of the country's leading theorists of human motivation concluded that, compared to other ways of rewarding people, competition is the "most controlling (and thus most undermining of intrinsic motivation)."[30]

Speaking of balancing acts, I am reminded of the difficulty of persuading some people to question the value of competition once it dawns on them that the logical conclusion of this process may affect their tennis game. Since I am not on a nationwide crusade for the abolition of tennis — the race to win in the classroom, the workplace, and the home being far more destructive, as I see it — I have faced the very practical question of how to handle the inexplicably powerful attachment many Americans have formed to the idea that recreation must be structured so as to produce winners and losers. I have addressed groups of educators or managers who express a willingness to consider transforming what they do on the job every day but whose faces darken when I hint that competition does not suddenly become benign if it takes place on the weekend.

Some people respond by insisting that they play for fun and don't really care who wins. I have not met many people for whom this is actually true — people who walk away from a victory and from a loss with exactly the same emotional state. But let us assume it happens. This delightful nonchalance about results offers an opportunity to take one small step away from the playing-field-as-battlefield model by resolving not to keep score. This suggestion, however, furrows brows. No score? The game will become boring! And so it may. But what have we here if not a powerful indictment of an activity so intrinsically tedious that we manage to stick with it only by relying on the artifice of quantifying our triumph over someone else?

If it is performance we seek — and I must confess to the heretical opinion that our lives would not be miserably impoverished in the absence of new records being set at the Olympics — then let us listen to what consulting sports psychologists tell their clients. Stop thinking about winning! these experts counsel: focus on the quality of your own performance.

At least one study has found that people are more likely to drop out of sports if they are motivated by victory rather than mastery.[31] Moreover, a survey of more than 1,200 teenage athletes discovered that of all the factors thought to promote enjoyment of sports, winning "had the weakest relationship with Sport Enjoyment . . . and was not significantly predictive for the total sample, either gender, or any of the age groups."[32] And from yet another source we hear this: "When there is less focus on winning or losing and more focus on playing well in a competitive situation, there will be less detrimental effects of competition on intrinsic motivation."[33] This, however, is not just a sly tip to help athletes win. It is a fact that raises questions about the value of competing at all, in sports or anywhere else. It is further confirmation that doing well and beating others are, structurally as well as intentionally, altogether different enterprises.

An essay in *Sports Illustrated* tentatively questioned some of the common wisdom about competition a few years ago.[34] An article in *Psychology Today* reviewed evidence that domestic violence increases whenever football games are televised.[35] But the most satisfying news is not really new at all: cooperative games for children and adults are still available, offering fun without a struggle for triumph.*

I want to close by telling you about a few books and articles, most of them published since 1985, that I have found enormously useful. If you have read this far, you, too, may want to take a look at them. Bibliographic particulars can be found in the newly expanded reference section.

For parents who view sibling rivalry as something to be solved rather than accepted as a Fact of Life, I recommend *Siblings Without Rivalry*, an accessible and practical collection of advice by Adele Faber and Elaine Mazlish.

Readers who want further substantiation for the argument made in chapter 2 to the effect that competition is not really the dominant theme of the natural world might have a look at *The New Biology* by Robert Augros and George Stanciu.

For anyone interested in the problems inherent to an adversarial legal system, *Partisan Justice* by Marvin E. Frankel complements Anne Strick's *Injustice for All*, which I have already mentioned, as does Thomas L. Shaffer's article "The Unique, Novel, and Unsound Adversary Ethic." For a fresh perspective on the corresponding view in philosophy (and other disciplines) — namely, that reason itself demands an adversarial challenge to ideas — see Janice Moulton's article "A Paradigm of Philosophy: The Adversary Method."

Readers hungry for a thorough analysis of education in the United States, backed by solid research on children's developing conceptions of ability and achievement, should not miss John Nicholls's splendid book, *The Competitive Ethos and Democratic Education*. The emphasis we place on how well children are performing compared to their peers winds up undermining learning, Nicholls argues, and while fair competition may be better than unfair, "competition cannot be fair if competing with others itself produces inequalities in the motivation necessary to develop skills."

---

*In chapter 4, I mentioned noncompetitive outdoor games collected by Terry Orlick and indoor games devised by a small Canadian company. I neglected, however, to include the address of the latter. Request a catalogue from Family Pastimes, R.R. 4, Perth, Ontario, Canada K7H 3C6. Also try Animal Town at P.O. Box 485, Healdsburg, California 95448 (800-445-8642). I have not been promised any free games in exchange for these endorsements, although I would not return any that happened to arrive.

To understand the problems with competition is, for many of us, to begin a search for concrete alternatives. I have already mentioned some resources for noncompetitive recreation and cooperative learning. But I should not overlook the large number of successful cooperative food stores, electric utilities, banks, insurance companies, and other businesses owned by consumers or workers. Co-op America (2100 M St. NW, Suite 403, Washington, DC 20037), which publishes a quarterly magazine, is one good place to look for more information about cooperatives; another is a book called the *Cooperative/Credit Union Dictionary and Reference* (available in paperback for $17 from the Cooperative Alumni Association, 250 Rainbow Lane, Richmond, Kentucky 40475).

Finally, for those interested in the possibility of not only working, learning, or playing together, but actually of *living* cooperatively, there are more than 300 "intentional communities" in North America composed of people who share any of a variety of interests. The *Directory of Intentional Communities: A Guide to Cooperative Living* offers a descriptive list of these communities as well as a collection of essays exploring what it means to be part of one. (It is available for $18 from Sandhill Farm, Route 1, Box 155, Rutledge, Missouri 63563.)

I hope that in another five or six years I have a great many more publications and programs to recommend to you, signifying that a critical view of competition is becoming less and less a fringe position. But let's not wait for this to happen by itself. Let's work together so our workplaces and classrooms, our playing fields and families, begin to provide opportunities for us to succeed together instead of at each other's expense.

NOTES

═══════════════◁▷═══════════════

CHAPTER 1

1. Walker Percy, "Questions They Never Asked Me," p. 178. Percy used the analogy to elucidate the difficulty of thinking about the nature of language.
2. Elliot Aronson, *The Social Animal*, pp. 153–54.
3. Paul Wachtel, *The Poverty of Affluence*, p. 284. In fact, religion itself is a competitive enterprise in this country. "Denominations have traditionally vied with each other for numbers, wealth, power, and status; and they increasingly are in competition with secular interest groups," writes William A. Sadler, Jr. ("Competition Out of Bounds," p. 167). See also chapter 6 of Peter Berger's *The Sacred Canopy*.
4. Anne Strick, *Injustice for All*, p. 114. Here is Strick's historical analysis: "Losers, predominantly, settled our nation: younger sons with neither purse nor title; refugees from religious and political persecutions, from slums and ghettos, from hopelessness, from debtor's prisons and famines. With each new wave of immigrants, new Losers came. But they were Losers come here to win. And win they did: not merely, for many, opportunity and wealth; but a continent from its rightful owners. Those who won, however, did so essentially in struggle *against* wilderness and fellow man. Winning was the American dream and ultimate blessedness; losing the nightmare and unforgivable sin" (p. 112).
5. Sadler, p. 168.
6. Bernard Holland, "The Well-Tempered Tenor," p. 28.
7. Apparently Lombardi himself regretted the comment, which seemed to take on a life of its own. "I wish to hell I'd never said the damned thing," he was said to have remarked shortly before his death. "I meant having a goal. . . . I sure as hell didn't mean for people to crush human values and morality" (James A. Michener, *Sports in America*, p. 432).
8. The first figure is from *U.S. Statistical Abstract* for 1985. The second is from "Survey of Consumer Finances, 1983" in the September 1984 issue of *Federal Reserve Bulletin*.
9. Morton Deutsch, the social psychologist who pioneered research in this field, defined competition as a situation of "contrient interdependence," which means that "participants are so linked together that there is a negative correlation between their goal attainments" (*The Resolution of Conflict*, p. 20). Back in 1937, Mark A. May and Leonard Doob defined it as a situation in which two or more individuals worked toward an end that could not be achieved by all of them (*Cooperation and Competition*, p. 6). Leonard Berkowitz's definition was along the same lines: "Two or more units, either individuals or groups, engaged in

pursuing the same rewards, with these rewards so defined that if they are attained by one unit, there are fewer rewards for the other units in the situation" (*Aggression: A Social Psychological Analysis*, p. 178).

10. Karen Horney, *The Neurotic Personality of Our Time*, p. 160.
11. Robert N. Bellah et al., *Habits of the Heart*, p. 198.
12. Bertrand Russell, *The Conquest of Happiness*, p. 45.

CHAPTER 2

1. For a good discussion of the Burt phenomenon, including speculation as to why so many have been so eager to accept his conclusions, see R. C. Lewontin et al., *Not in Our Genes*, chapter 5.
2. An outstanding and wide-ranging critique of biological determinism is contained in *Not in Our Genes*, by R. C. Lewontin, a highly respected evolutionary geneticist; Steven Rose, a neurobiologist; and Leon J. Kamin, a psychologist. They explore such issues as schizophrenia, gender-based differences, and intelligence, concluding, "The only sensible thing to say about human nature is that it is 'in' that nature to construct its own history" (p. 14). Stephen Jay Gould also put it well: "Why imagine that specific genes for aggression, dominance, or spite have any importance when we know that the brain's enormous flexibility permits us to be aggressive or peaceful, dominant or submissive, spiteful or generous? Violence, sexism, and general nastiness *are* biological since they represent one subset of a possible range of behaviors. But peacefulness, equality, and kindness are just as biological — and we may see their influence increase if we can create social structures that permit them to flourish" ("Biological Potential vs. Biological Determinism," p. 349). Also see Gould's essay, "The Nonscience of Human Nature."
3. Richard Dawkins, *The Selfish Gene*, p. ix.
4. Konrad Lorenz, of course, attempted to do just this. Some of the best critical essays on his work and that of such other naturalists as Robert Ardrey are contained in *Man and Aggression*, edited by Ashley Montagu. Aggression, naturally, is of special interest to us here because of its relationship to competition (see chapter 6).
5. This is usually formulated by ethical theorists as "ought implies can," and was articulated by Immanuel Kant: "Duty demands nothing of us which we cannot do. . . . When the moral law commands that we *ought* to be better men, it follows inevitably that we must *be able* to be better men" (*Religion Within the Limits of Reason Alone*, pp. 43, 46).
6. Leslie H. Farber, "Merchandising Depression," p. 64.
7. See, for example, "The Grand Inquisitor" chapter of Dostoyevsky's *Brothers Karamazov*, Erich Fromm's *Escape from Freedom*, and almost anything by Sören Kierkegaard or Jean-Paul Sartre.
8. Roger Caillois, *Man, Play and Games*, p. 55.
9. John Harvey et al., *Competition: A Study in Human Motive*, p. 12.
10. James S. Coleman, *The Adolescent Society*, p. 318; his emphasis.
11. Harvey Ruben, *Competing*, p. ix.
12. Ibid., p. 22.
13. Ibid., p. 20.
14. Ibid., p. 39; his emphasis.

15. The tendency to construe apparently friendly acts as hostile has been found to be one of the signal differences between normal and disturbed populations (Harold L. Raush, "Interaction Sequences," p. 498).
16. Harold J. Vanderzwaag, *Toward a Philosophy of Sport*, p. 127.
17. Mary Ann O'Roark, " 'Competition' Isn't a Dirty Word," p. 66.
18. Garrett Hardin, *Promethean Ethics: Living with Death, Competition, and Triage*, p. 36.
19. There are certain areas of thought from whose contributions we are sometimes asked to *infer* the conclusion that competition is inevitable. These include the study of other species, which is the subject of the next section; and two currents within psychology — psychoanalysis and social comparison theory — which are addressed in the last section of this chapter. I am not aware of any serious arguments for competition's inevitability explicitly offered from within these fields, however.
20. David W. and Roger T. Johnson, "Instructional Goal Structure: Cooperative, Competitive, or Individualistic" (hereafter "Structure"), p. 218.
21. Ashley Montagu cited in Johnson and Johnson, "Cooperation in Learning: Ignored But Powerful," p. 1. Psychiatrist Roderic Gorney agrees: "Any objective appraisal of modern man will disclose that in the overwhelming preponderance of human interactions cooperation *completely overshadows* competition" (*Human Agenda*, pp. 101–2; his emphasis). See also Arthur W. Combs, *Myths in Education*, pp. 15–17.
22. "Aggression, anxiety, guilt, and self-centered motives and behavior have been so much the cloth of theory and research that questions of a 'softer' side of young human beings seem almost unscientific" (Marian Radke Yarrow et al., "Learning Concern for Others," p. 240).
23. For example, see H. L. Rheingold and D. F. Hay, "Prosocial Behavior of the Very Young"; Marian Radke Yarrow and Carolyn Zahn Waxler, "The Emergence and Functions of Prosocial Behaviors in Young Children"; Yarrow et al., "Learning Concern"; James H. Bryan, "Prosocial Behavior"; Maya Pines, "Good Samaritans at Age Two?"; and my own "That Loving Feeling — When Does It Begin?" Yarrow and Waxler write as follows: "The capabilities for compassion, for various kinds of reaching out to others in a giving sense are viable and effective responses early in life. . . . Very young children were often finely discriminative and responsive to others' need states" (pp. 78–79).
24. Rheingold and Hay, p. 101. On the other hand, Roderic Gorney claims that the view "that human beings are predisposed to be not individualistic and competitive but social and cooperative . . . [is] endorsed by the majority of students of human social biology and evolution" (*Human Agenda*, p. 140). Also see Martin L. Hoffman, "Is Altruism Part of Human Nature?"
25. Richard Hofstadter, *Social Darwinism in American Thought*, p. 204.
26. Stephen Jay Gould, personal communication, 1984.
27. Charles Darwin, *The Origin of Species*, Chapter III, p. 62. Thus, Patrick Bateson writes that "the restriction of differential survival to mean simply conflict is an obvious abuse of Darwin's thinking" ("Cooperation and Competition," p. 55).
28. George Gaylord Simpson, *The Meaning of Evolution*, p. 222. Similarly, Ashley Montagu writes: "Natural selection . . . has been rather more

operative in terms of co-operation than it has been in terms of what is
generally understood by competition. . . . Natural selection through
'competition' may secure the immediate survival of certain types of
'competitors,' but the survivors would not long survive if they did not
co-operate" (*Darwin, Competition and Cooperation*, pp. 70, 72).

29. Petr Kropotkin, *Mutual Aid*, pp. 74–75; emphasis in original.

30. A revised version of W. C. Allee's *The Social Life of Animals*.

31. Montagu lists some fifty books and articles in *Darwin*, pp. 35–37.

32. Marvin Bates, *The Nature of Natural History*, quoted in Montagu, ibid.,
p. 58. William Patten's better known *The Grand Strategy of Evolution* summarized it as follows: "There is but one creative process common to all
phases of evolution, inorganic, organic, mental, and social. That process is best described by the term cooperation, or mutual service" (p. 33).
See also Roderic Gorney's *Human Agenda*, esp. pp. 100–101, and Lewis
Thomas's *The Lives of a Cell*. Even on the genetic level, Patrick Bateson
points out that "the perpetuation of each gene depends on the characteristics of the gene team" ("Cooperation and Competition," p. 55). The
relative importance of competition in ecological theory is being questioned, too (see, for example, Stephen Doig, "Ecology May Never Be
the Same After Daniel Simberloff," p. 17).

33. W. C. Allee, *Cooperation Among Animals*, p. 16. He continues: "[The
roots of] an unconscious kind of mutualism . . . are deep and well
established and its expression grows to be so spontaneous and normal
that we are likely to overlook or forget it" (p. 176).

34. Richard Dawkins and Garrett Hardin are examples.

35. A similar fallacy resides in sociobiologists' arguments about altruism,
which term is likewise used in two senses. See Gunther Stent, "You Can
Take the Ethics Out of Altruism But You Can't Take the Altruism Out
of Ethics." Marshall Sahlins, in *The Use and Abuse of Biology*, and Anthony Flew, in "From Is to Ought," make essentially the same point
about confusing two levels of meaning with respect to terms like "law of
nature" and "natural selection."

36. John A. Wiens, "Competition or Peaceful Coexistence?" p. 34.

37. For example, Sahlins, Montagu, and Gorney. Also, Elliot Aronson
suspects that "Kropotkin's work . . . has been largely ignored, perhaps because it did not fit in with the temper of the times or with the
needs of those who were profiting from the industrial revolution"
(p. 153). And Richard Hofstadter: "American society saw its own image
in the tooth-and-claw version of natural selection, and . . . dominant
groups were therefore able to dramatize this vision of competition as a
thing good in itself. Ruthless business rivalry and unprincipled politics
seemed to be justified by the survival philosophy" (p. 201).

38. Quoted in Lewontin et al., p. 309, fn. 30. The sociobiologists continue
to make vigorous use of this gambit. Slavery, love, and a good many
more human institutions are said to be found in other species. Consider, for example, this excerpt from Edward O. Wilson's *On Human
Nature:* "The species that have evolved long-term bonds are also, by and
large, the ones that rely on elaborate courtship rituals. It is consistent
with this trend that most of the pleasures of human sex constitute
primary reinforcers to facilitate bonding. Love and sex do indeed go

together" (pp. 146–47). Notice what he has done here: After describing a phenomenon called "bonding," he suddenly substitutes the word "love." Now he can proceed as if he had actually demonstrated that human love is identical to the bonding common to all animals.

39. Montagu, *Darwin*, p. 72.

40. Mark A. May, "A Research Note on Cooperative and Competitive Behavior," p. 888.

41. May and Doob cited in Emmy A. Pepitone, *Children in Cooperation and Competition: Toward a Developmental Social Psychology*, p. 14.

42. Deutsch, *Resolution of Conflict*, p. 89.

43. Thomas Tutko and William Bruns, *Winning Is Everything and Other American Myths*, p. 53.

44. David Riesman, "Football in America: A Study in Culture Diffusion," p. 252.

45. Aronson, pp. 153, 206.

46. Jules Henry, *Culture Against Man*, pp. 295–96.

47. Susan Schiffer Stautberg, "The Rat Race Isn't for Tots." See also a *New York Times* article by Michael deCourcy Hinds: " 'There is as much pressure to get [children] into kindergarten as there will be to get them into law school' " ("Private Schools: The First Steps"). "Young professionals want the best: the best job, the best BMW, the best baby," writes James Traub. "They know they have to compete for it" ("Goodbye, Dr. Spock," p. 61).

48. Deutsch, "Education and Distributive Justice," p. 394. He continues: "If educational measurement is not mainly in the form of a contest, why are students often asked to reveal their knowledge and skills in carefully regulated test situations designed to be as uniform as possible in time, atmosphere, and conditions for all students? . . . A strange thing, this artificially induced scarcity of rewards: Its effects are probably quite opposite to its ostensible purpose, discouraging rather than encouraging the growth of educational merit" (ibid.).

49. See Joan I. Roberts, *Scene of the Battle: Group Behavior in the Urban Classrooms*, p. 184.

50. Peter L. and Brigitte Berger, *Sociology: A Biographical Approach*, p. 189. Terry Orlick similarly notes that children "are *taught* that winning is what counts, since they certainly do not begin feeling this way. Initially the child plays for fun, for the sheer enjoyment of the game, for stimulation and positive interaction with others. Winning is unimportant, irrelevant; fun is extremely important" (*Winning Through Cooperation*, p. 133).

51. Jean Piaget, *The Moral Judgment of the Child*, p. 37.

52. The work of New Zealanders N. B. and T. D. Graves is reported in Pepitone, p. 59. Nancy Chodorow also points to studies that have found less competitiveness among children raised in "more collective child-rearing situations (the kibbutzim, China, Cuba)" (*The Reproduction of Mothering: Psychoanalysis and the Sociology of Gender*, p. 217).

53. Ruben, *Competing*, pp. 66–67.

54. Deutsch, *Resolution of Conflict*, pp. 30–31; see also p. 365.

55. Robert Axelrod, *The Evolution of Cooperation*, p. 28.

56. Harold H. Kelley and Anthony J. Stahelski, "Social Interaction Basis of

Cooperators' and Competitors' Beliefs About Others." See also Alexander Mintz, "Non-adaptive Group Behavior." Morton Deutsch similarly found that "it is easier to move from cooperation to competition than in the other direction" (*Distributive Justice*, p. 271).

57. Ibid. "Of course the competitive person has experienced cooperative relationships and situations. But the . . . behavior is attributed to the situation rather than to the persons" (p. 89).

58. For example, Robyn M. Dawes et al., "Behavior, Communication, and Assumptions About Other People's Behavior in a Commons Dilemma Situation"; and Lawrence A. Messé and John M. Sivacek, "Predictions of Others' Responses in a Mixed-Motive Game: Self-Justification or False Consensus?"

59. Gerald Sagotsky et al., "Learning to Cooperate."

60. Linden L. Nelson and Spencer Kagan, "Competition: The Star-Spangled Scramble," p. 56. The study involved sixty pairs of ten-year-olds. There was no delay between presentation of the two games, as in Sagotsky's study.

61. Nina B. Korsh, "Effects of Preaching, Practice, and Helpful Evaluations on Third Graders' Collaborative Work."

62. Harold B. Weingold and Ronald L. Webster, "Effects of Punishment on a Cooperative Behavior in Children."

63. Aronson, pp. 206–10.

64. Morton Deutsch and Robert M. Krauss, "The Effect of Threat Upon Interpersonal Bargaining."

65. David N. Campbell, "On Being Number One: Competition in Education," p. 145.

66. Orlick, *Winning Through Cooperation*, pp. 179–80. The study was blind — that is, those recording the incidences of spontaneous cooperative behavior did not know in advance which group had been playing the cooperative games.

67. Ibid., p. 177.

68. David W. Johnson and Brenda Bryant, "Cooperation and Competition in the Classroom," p. 177.

69. Johnson and Johnson, "Motivational Processes in Cooperative, Competitive, and Individualistic Learning Situations" (hereafter "Processes") p. 31. Other studies have found that (1) sixth grade students believe cooperative grading is fairer than the traditional system of rewarding on the basis of individual achievement (Johnson and Johnson, "The Socialization and Achievement Crisis," pp. 151–52); and (2) of four proposed ways to distribute rewards, college students who worked at various tasks in an experimental setting had the most negative reaction to a "winner-take-all" system. Once they worked cooperatively, in fact, many students came to prefer a system of distributing rewards equally among the participants (Deutsch, *Distributive Justice*, pp. 157–59).

70. This is just what Emmy Pepitone and her colleagues discovered, p. 245.

71. Donald Bruce Haines and W. J. McKeachie, "Cooperative Versus Competitive Discussion Methods in Teaching Introductory Psychology," pp. 389–90.

72. Piaget himself (in *Moral Judgment of the Child*) is quite clear that intellec-

tual maturity can be defined in terms of the ability to cooperate — the child moves from egocentric to social activity — but I believe he confuses matters by blurring cooperation and competition. Interdependence is surely involved in both, as Deutsch explained, but Piaget, like many other theorists of play, does not acknowledge the possibility of cooperative activity that is devoid of competitive structure.

73. See, for example, Carolyn W. Sherif, "The Social Context of Competition," p. 22.

74. Nelson and Kagan (p. 54) point this out, as does Charles G. McClintock ("Development of Social Motives in Anglo-American and Mexican-American Children").

75. See note 23 above.

76. Cited in Rheingold and Hay, p. 99.

77. Orlick, *Winning Through Cooperation*, p. 176.

78. Millard C. Madsen, "Developmental and Cross-Cultural Differences in the Cooperative and Competitive Behavior of Young Children," p. 369.

79. Sagotsky et al., p. 1041.

80. Beatrice B. and John W. M. Whiting, *Children of Six Cultures*, p. 64. The mean proportional score for the other five cultures was 9.2; for the American town, it was 5.5.

81. Jeanne Humphrey Block, "Conceptions of Sex Role: Some Cross-Cultural and Longitudinal Perspectives."

82. Spencer Kagan and Millard C. Madsen, "Experimental Analyses of Cooperation and Competition of Anglo-American and Mexican Children" (hereafter "Experimental Analyses"), pp. 57, 53.

83. Boyce Rensberger, "What Made Humans Human?"

84. George Edgin Pugh, *The Biological Origin of Human Values*, p. 267.

85. Marshall D. Sahlins, "The Origin of Society," pp. 80, 82.

86. See, for example, David Pilbeam, "An Idea We Could Live Without: The Naked Ape," esp. pp. 118–20. James Yost's work with the Waorani hunters is described in the NOVA program "Nomads of the Rainforest": "The boys share the use of the blowgun. Competition is completely foreign to them. Spontaneous cooperation is the only way they know" (p. 6).

87. Irving Goldman, "The Zuñi Indians of New Mexico," pp. 344–45.

88. Ibid., p. 338.

89. B. H. Quain, "The Iroquois," p. 256.

90. Irving Goldman, "The Bathonga of South Africa" (hereafter "Bathonga"), p. 380.

91. Margaret Mead, *Cooperation and Competition Among Primitive Peoples*, p. 16.

92. Anthony G. Miller and Ron Thomas, "Cooperation and Competition Among Blackfoot Indian and Urban Canadian Children." The study involved ninety-six children, about eight years old.

93. Ariella Shapira and Millard C. Madsen, "Cooperative and Competitive Behavior of Kibbutz and Urban Children in Israel." The study involved eighty children, about eight years old.

94. Shapira and Madsen, "Between- and Within-Group Cooperation and Competition Among Kibbutz and Nonkibbutz Children." The study involved 320 children, ages eight to eleven.

95. Robert L. and Ruth H. Munroe, "Cooperation and Competition Among East African and American Children."

96. Kagan and Madsen, "Experimental Analyses." The study involved 160 children, ages seven to nine and ten to eleven.

97. Kagan and Madsen, "Cooperation and Competition of Mexican, Mexican-American, and Anglo-American Children of Two Ages Under Four Instructional Sets" (hereafter "Four Instructional Sets").

98. Nelson and Kagan, "Competition," p. 91.

99. Kimball and Romaine Romney, *The Mixtecans of Juxtlahuaca, Mexico,* p. 21.

100. George B. Leonard, "Winning Isn't Everything. It's Nothing," p. 45.

101. Orlick, *Winning Through Cooperation,* pp. 41–54, 223–35.

102. Elizabeth A. Sommerlad and W. P. Bellingham, "Cooperation-Competition: A Comparison of Australian, European, and Aboriginal School Children."

103. Gerald Marwell and David R. Schmitt, *Cooperation: An Experimental Analysis,* pp. 170–72.

104. Ruth Benedict, *The Chrysanthemum and the Sword,* pp. 154–55.

105. William K. Cummings, *Education and Equality in Japan,* p. 127.

106. Jack and Elizabeth Easley, *Math Can Be Natural: Kitamaeno Priorities Introduced to American Teachers,* paraphrased in Howard Gardner, *Frames of Mind,* p. 380. This, of course, is not to endorse all facets of Japanese pedagogy any more than the preceding expressed a blanket approval of the other cultures. At least one observer reports that Japanese schools tend to discourage questioning, autonomy, and individuation (Edward B. Fiske, "Japan's Schools Stress Group and Discourage Individuality"). Cooperative learning, however, can surely coexist with these goals.

107. Julian Baum, "Friendship No Longer Ranks Ahead of Winning for Chinese Olympians." Terry Orlick, however, offers a very different account of Chinese athletes and their fans — one that suggests winning is far less important to them than to their American counterparts (*Winning Through Cooperation,* pp. 69–77).

108. Susan L. Shirk, *Competitive Comrades,* p. 162.

109. Nelson and Kagan, "Competition," p. 90.

110. Margaret Mead, p. 495.

111. Gorney, *Human Agenda,* pp. 159–60.

112. Gorney, "Cultural Determinants of Achievement, Aggression, and Psychological Distress."

113. Margaret Mead, p. 511.

114. Ibid., pp. 481–82.

115. Ibid., p. 463.

116. William O. Johnson, "From Here to 2000," p. 443.

117. Two psychoanalysts who have applied themselves to sports psychology are Arnold R. Beisser, in *The Madness in Sports* (particularly the chapter entitled "The Problem of Winning"), and Robert A. Moore, in *Sports and Mental Health.*

118. Sigmund Freud, *Civilization and Its Discontents,* p. 58.

119. Ibid., p. 59.

120. Anna Freud, *Normality and Pathology in Childhood,* p. 150.

121. Ian Suttie, *The Origins of Love and Hate,* p. 20 and *passim.* This is a reference to the interdependent character of competitive interaction — which is also implicit in Piaget's formulation.

122. Gorney, *Human Agenda,* p. 472.

123. Herbert Hendin, *The Age of Sensation,* p. 97.

124. As with psychoanalysts, social psychologists generally do not explicitly argue in this manner that competition is unavoidable; social comparison theory instead is used by others to support their belief that this is the case. The theory itself was derived indirectly from the thought of George Herbert Mead (see especially *Mind, Self, and Society)* and articulated most clearly by Leon Festinger in his classic article, "A Theory of Social Comparison Processes."

125. Rainer Martens, "Competition: In Need of a Theory," p. 13.

126. Albert Bandura, *Social Learning Theory,* p. 132.

127. Jerome Kagan, *The Nature of the Child,* p. 273.

128. Joseph Veroff, "Social Comparison and the Development of Achievement Motivation," p. 55.

129. Carl Rogers, for example, writes that healthy development is characterized by the individual's coming to feel that the "locus of evaluation lies within himself" *(On Becoming a Person,* p. 119).

130. Irving Goldman, "Bathonga," p. 360.

131. Harvey et al., pp. 176–77.

CHAPTER 3

1. Spiro Agnew, "In Defense of Sport," pp. 257–58. One does not have to look very hard to find similar sentiments in other quarters. Sociologist Harry Edwards, for example, quotes a high school principal as saying, "If we had a country of individuals who didn't value competitiveness, we would have chaos, anarchy, and zero productivity" *(Sociology of Sport,* p. 119).

2. Aronson, p. 152.

3. Johnson and Johnson, "Structure," p. 218. John Harvey similarly notes: "The defeat of the unsuccessful has nothing to do with the real value of success" (p. 14).

4. Margaret M. Clifford, "Effect of Competition as a Motivational Technique in the Classroom" (1972).

5. Morton Goldman et al., "Intergroup and Intragroup Competition and Cooperation" (1977).

6. Abaineh Workie, "The Relative Productivity of Cooperation and Competition" (1974).

7. Deutsch, *Resolution of Conflict.*

8. The Johnson brothers are probably this country's most prolific contributors to the study of competition and cooperation in the classroom. Both educators and social psychologists at the University of Minnesota, they have published, at last count, about 100 books and articles on the subject — most of them within the last decade. Besides conducting and reviewing research, they serve as consultants to other educators, demonstrating cooperative teaching strategies.

9. David W. Johnson et al., "Effects of Cooperative, Competitive, and Individualistic Goal Structures on Achievement: A Meta-Analysis" (hereafter "Meta-Analysis").

10. Ibid., p. 53.

11. Ibid., p. 54; Bryant J. Cratty, *Social Psychology in Athletics*, p. 76; Johnson and Johnson, "Structure," p. 220.

12. Morton Goldman et al.; David R. Schmitt, "Performance Under Cooperation or Competition," pp. 660–62. However, Dorcas Butt rightly notes that "there are very few situations in life in which people are not interdependent" (*Psychology of Sport*, p. 41n.).

13. Johnson and Johnson, "The Socialization and Achievement Crisis: Are Cooperative Learning Experiences the Solution?" (hereafter "Crisis"), p. 146.

14. Pepitone, p. 30.

15. Johnson and Johnson, *Learning Together and Alone* (hereafter *Learning*), p. 191. A few years later, the Johnsons went further, suggesting that "cooperation without intergroup competition [may promote] higher achievement and productivity than cooperation with intergroup competition," based on their meta-analysis ("Meta-Analysis," p. 57).

16. Deutsch, *Distributive Justice*, p. 163. The research and its findings are described in detail in his chapter 10: "Experimental Studies of the Effects of Different Systems of Distributive Justice."

17. See Johnson and Johnson, "Structure," pp. 220–21.

18. For example, see Irving C. Whittemore's 1924 paper, "The Influence of Competition on Performance: An Experimental Study," p. 245.

19. Pepitone, p. 234. This study involved almost 1000 children, ages five to eleven.

20. Johnson and Johnson, "Crisis," p. 146.

21. John C. Adams, Jr., "Effects of Competition and Open Receptivity on Creative Productivity," pp. 16–17.

22. H.-J. Lerch and M. Rubensal, "Eine Analyse des Zusammenhangs zwischen Schulleistungen und dem Wetteifermotiv."

23. Deutsch has written a provocative essay on the effects of grading in American schools. He argues that grades (1) do not assess actual accomplishment so much as turn education into a contest in which students "are measured primarily in comparison with one another"; (2) do not intrinsically motivate students better than a cooperative system; (3) actually serve the purposes of setting students against one another, thereby inhibiting collective action, and socializing them to accept and succeed in a competitive, capitalist culture; and (4) ignore social contexts in mistakenly assuming that the individual can and should be evaluated independently. His conclusion: "If the competitive grading system in our schools — a less corrupted version of a competitive merit system than the one that characterizes our larger society — does not foster a social environment that is conducive to individual well-being and effective social cooperation, why would one expect that such values would be fostered in a society that is dominated by a competitive, meritocratic ideology? If the competitive-hierarchical atmosphere is not good for our children, is it good for us?" (Deutsch, "Education and Distributive Justice.")

24. Aronson, pp. 206–10.
25. Johnson and Johnson, *Learning*, pp. 79–80. The whole of this book provides teachers — particularly at the elementary school level — with useful suggestions for implementing a cooperative curriculum.
26. Johnson and Johnson, "Crisis," p. 122.
27. Johnson and Johnson, "Structure," p. 226.
28. Johnson and Johnson, "Crisis," p. 149. In fact, even the widely held assumption that "students learn more or better in homogeneous groups . . . is simply not true." A review of hundreds of studies fails to support this assumption even with respect to higher-level students (Jeannie Oakes, *Keeping Track: How Schools Structure Inequality*, p. 7).
29. Johnson and Johnson, "The Internal Dynamics of Cooperative Learning Groups," p. 105.
30. Stuart Yager et al., "Oral Discussion, Group-to-Individual Transfer, and Achievement in Cooperative Learning Groups," p. 65.
31. John S. Wodarski et al., "Individual Consequences Versus Different Shared Consequences Contingent on the Performance of Low-Achieving Group Members" (1973), pp. 288–89.
32. Peter M. Blau, "Cooperation and Competition in a Bureaucracy."
33. Robert L. Helmreich et al., "Making It in Academic Psychology: Demographic and Personality Correlates of Attainment," pp. 897, 902.
34. Helmreich et al., "Achievement Motivation and Scientific Attainment," p. 224.
35. Janet T. Spence and Robert L. Helmreich, "Achievement-related Motives and Behavior" (hereafter "Achievement-related"), p. 53.
36. Ibid., p. 52.
37. Helmreich, "Pilot Selection and Training."
38. Helmreich et al., "The Honeymoon Effect in Job Performance."
39. Georgia Sassen, "Sex Role Orientation, Sex Differences, and Concept of Success," pp. 38–39. The study involved twenty-eight undergraduates. Competitiveness was measured by a "Competitiveness of Success-Concept" test that she devised.
40. Teresa M. Amabile, "Children's Artistic Creativity," p. 576. There was high interjudge reliability (.77) with respect to the seven artists.
41. Will Crutchfield, "The Ills of Piano Competitions." Béla Bartók once said, "Competitions are for horses, not artists" (cited in Carl Battaglia, "Piano Competitions: Talent Hunt or Sport?" p. 31).
42. Sandra McElwaine writes: "If competition is one of the passwords in Washington, nowhere is it more keenly felt than in the media. News is big business in the capital, and for the thousands of reporters covering the Government it is a constant hustle to find a different angle. The pervasive rivalry that results can produce depression, anxiety and insecurity, leading many to seek psychiatric aid" ("On the Couch in the Capital," p. 63).
43. Jay Winsten, "Science and the Media: The Boundaries of Truth," p. 8.
44. "The result has been a spiraling competition, sometimes characterized by exaggerated claims, in which 'science by press conference' has begun to replace the traditional mode of scientific discourse" (ibid., pp. 14–15).

45. Stephen Klaidman, "TV's Collusive Role." Klaidman is senior research fellow at Georgetown University's Kennedy Institute of Ethics.

46. The comments of Fred Friendly, former head of CBS News and now journalism professor emeritus at Columbia University, are paraphrased by Adam Pertman in his article, "Media Observers Say News Coverage Is Pressuring U.S. to Act."

47. Johnson and Johnson, "Processes," p. 22.

48. Helmreich et al., "Making It in Academic Psychology," p. 907.

49. Spence and Helmreich, "Achievement-related," p. 55.

50. John McMurty is quoted by William O. Johnson, "From Here to 2000," p. 446. Robert N. Singer and Richard F. Gerson wrote as follows: "If the athlete is being evaluated only on the basis of whether or not a rival has been beaten, little information is really provided relating to the level of excellence achieved in performance" ("Athletic Competition for Children," p. 253). Frank Winer similarly distinguishes between trying to improve one's skill and trying to win ("The Elderly Jock and How He Got That Way" [hereafter "Elderly Jock"], p. 193).

51. Lisa Belkin, "Young Albany Debaters Resolve Who's Best."

52. Marvin E. Frankel, "The Search for Truth," pp. 1037, 1039.

53. I. Nelson Rose, "Litigator's Fallacy," pp. 92–93.

54. Thurman Arnold is quoted in Anne Strick, *Injustice for All*, p. 109. Strick's book offers a comprehensive indictment of the adversarial model, demonstrating that the problems frequently attributed to our legal system are "due less to any venality or inadequacy of the legal professionals than to the intrinsic nature of the adversary ethic itself" (p. 16). She urges that "consensus through cooperative exploration . . . replace the concept of truth through battle" (p. 217), whereas Rose recommends the more modest change of "shifting the emphasis in the Canons of Ethics from lawyers as zealous advocates of their individual client's interests to lawyers as well-considered representatives of the interests of the public" (p. 95).

55. John Knowles, *A Separate Peace*, p. 46.

56. George B. Leonard, *Education and Ecstasy*, p. 129.

57. David N. Campbell, "On Being Number One," pp. 145–46. Morton Deutsch also observes that "through the repeated and pervasive experience of competitive struggle for scarce goods in the classroom, students are socialized into believing that this is not only the just way but also . . . natural and inevitable" ("Education and Distributive Justice," p. 394).

58. "The idea is essentially, 'Make my kid suffer now so he gets used to it. Teach him to claw his way to the top by any means necessary. Teach him to hate those who win and himself when he loses and despise those who don't make it' " (Campbell, p. 144).

59. Clifford, pp. 134–35.

60. See, for example, Matina Horner, "Performance of Men in Noncompetitive and Interpersonal Competitive Achievement-Oriented Situations."

61. Edward L. Deci et al., "When Trying to Win: Competition and Intrinsic Motivation," p. 79. It is true that very competitive people may be said to have internalized the motivator. Structural competition then becomes fully intentional — a matter of temperament. With such people, the problems with extrinsic motivators may not be the best explanation for

achievement differentials. For most of us, though, the appeal of the activity itself and the reward of being better than someone else remain very different.

62. Johnson and Johnson, "Processes," p. 16.

63. Edward L. Deci, "Effects of Externally Mediated Rewards on Intrinsic Motivation," p. 114. Elsewhere he recommends that "one who is interested in developing and enhancing intrinsic motivation in children, employees, students, etc., should not concentrate on external-control systems such as monetary rewards, which are linked directly to performance, but, rather, he should concentrate on structuring situations that are intrinsically interesting and then be interpersonally supportive and rewarding toward the persons in the situation" ("Intrinsic Motivation, Extrinsic Reinforcement, and Inequity," pp. 119–20).

64. Deci et al., pp. 82–83.

65. Jenifer Levin, "When Winning Takes All," p. 94. Other writers who have addressed the detrimental effects of extrinsic motivators on athletic activities include Wayne Halliwell, "Intrinsic Motivation in Sport"; and Singer and Gerson, pp. 255–57.

66. John Holt, *How Children Fail*, p. 274.

67. See, for example, Johnson and Johnson, "Processes," p. 6.

68. Deutsch, *Resolution of Conflict*, p. 26 and *passim*.

69. Blau, pp. 533–34.

70. Spence and Helmreich, pp. 54–55. Elsewhere, Helmreich writes: "The competitive individual may find it harder to establish effective collaborative relationships with both peers and students and may thus be robbed of intellectual stimulation" (Helmreich, "Making It in Academic Psychology," p. 907).

71. Johnson and Johnson, "Structure," p. 1228.

72. Johnson and Johnson, "Crisis," p. 151. Seven studies are cited in support of this conclusion.

73. Benedict, pp. 153–54.

74. Blau, p. 534.

75. For example, Donald Bruce Haines and W. J. McKeachie, p. 390: "The contribution made by competition to tensions already existing in the student is so great that undesirable consequences may follow. The present research demonstrated that students in competitive discussion situations became more anxious, displayed a greater incidence of self-oriented needs, and found themselves losing self-assurance. Further, they were less able to perform effectively in recitation." See also Johnson and Johnson, "Structure," pp. 227–28.

76. For example, see Michele K. Steigleder et al., "Drivelike Motivational Properties of Competitive Behavior" — a contribution to the "accumulating body of literature" taking this position.

77. J. W. Atkinson, "The Mainsprings of Achievement-Oriented Activity," p. 16. See also Atkinson's *An Introduction to Motivation*, esp. pp. 244–46. The "attempt to avoid failure . . . takes many forms but [it] does not lead to real learning," writes C. H. Patterson (*Humanistic Education*, p. 86).

78. Henry A. Davidson supplies one example, in which an unusually competitive procedure for selecting office-holders of an unnamed organization discouraged the most talented individuals from running. "Many members were quite willing to offer themselves. But these were the

ones who had nothing to lose, since they had no outstanding prestige in the first place. What it amounted to was this: the competitive climate favored the inferior and not, as you might expect, the superior members" ("Competition, the Cradle of Anxiety," pp. 165–66).

79. Michael Novak, *The Joy of Sports*, p. 158.

80. Christopher Lasch, *The Culture of Narcissism*, p. 194.

81. Wynne-Edwards proposed the idea of group selection in his 1962 book, *Animal Dispersion in Relation to Social Behaviour*, in which he argued that individual animals sometimes reduce their birth rate in order to benefit the species as a whole. The group vs. individual selection controversy is far from settled among evolutionary biologists.

82. "As a rational being, each herdsman seeks to maximize his gain . . . [and] the only sensible course for him is to add another animal to his herd. And another; and another . . . But this is the conclusion reached by each and every rational herdsman sharing a commons. Therein is the tragedy" (Garrett Hardin, "The Tragedy of the Commons," p. 1244). Hardin uses the example to argue for mandatory birth control; my point is that the tragedy inheres in our shortsighted individualism.

83. Fred Hirsch, *Social Limits to Growth*, p. 5.

84. The example is Thomas Schelling's, and it is cited by Robert H. Frank in *Choosing the Right Pond: Human Behavior and the Quest for Status*, p. 133.

85. Joshua Cohen and Joel Rogers, *On Democracy*, p. 57. Cohen and Rogers note that "the structure in which [workers] find themselves yields less than optimal social results from their isolated but economically rational decisions" (ibid.). This illuminates a key division among those who work for social change. Is the "social result" the ultimate goal? This would suggest a subjugation of the individual to the collective, not unlike the radically different worldview discussed above. Or is the collective action merely a means for individual betterment? This would be closer to the second shift I have been discussing, using cooperation as a tactic but retaining the individualism of the liberal tradition.

86. Axelrod, pp. 189–90, 100.

87. See, for example, Robyn M. Dawes et al., "Behavior, Communication, and Assumptions About Other People's Behavior in a Commons Dilemma Situation."

88. Douglas Hofstadter, "Irrationality Is the Square Root of All Evil," p. 758.

89. Mayor Ramon Aguirre Velazquez is quoted in Richard J. Meislin, "Mexico City Gets Too Big a Million Times a Year," p. E26.

90. Horney argues this in *Neurotic Personality*, p. 160. Of course one can qualify such a position by observing, with Paul Wachtel, that "in the United States, the anticommunal forces of the competitive market place are reinforced, rather than checked, by prevalent cultural values" (p. 168). Institutions such as sports and schooling affect and are affected by economic competition.

91. A study by Citizens for Tax Justice was cited by James Reston, "Politics and Taxes," p. E21.

92. This estimate is offered and defended by Michael Harrington in *The New American Poverty*, p. 88.

93. Paul Wachtel, *passim.* See also E. F. Schumacher, *Small Is Beautiful: Economics as if People Mattered.*
94. John P. McKee and Florence B. Leader, "The Relationship of Socio-Economic Status and Aggression to the Competitive Behavior of Preschool Children."
95. Roberts, p. 184.
96. "Measured globally there is enough food for everyone now . . . [and] less than 60 percent of the world's cultivable land is now being cropped" (Frances Moore Lappé and Joseph Collins, *Food First*, pp. 13–14).
97. Wachtel, p. 58.
98. One of the best discussions of the creation of needs is contained in Herbert Marcuse, *One-Dimensional Man*, chapter 1.
99. Philip Slater, *The Pursuit of Loneliness*, pp. 103, 106–7, 110.
100. Pepitone, pp. 295–96.
101. Charles Derber, *The Pursuit of Attention: Power and Individualism in Everyday Life*, p. 16, n.17.
102. Lawrence K. Frank, "The Cost of Competition," pp. 314–16.
103. John M. Culbertson, *Competition, Constructive and Destructive*, p. 3. He continues: "The most effective economies have not been those with the least government regulation and guidance, but those with skillful, realistic, problem-solving regulation" (pp. 3–4).
104. See, for example, Robert Lindsey, "Airline Deregulation Stranding Some Towns," pp. A1, B19.
105. Fred Pillsbury, "Bus Industry Slips Into a Lower Gear," p. A1. Also see William Serrin, "How Deregulation Allowed Greyhound to Win Concessions from Strikers," p. A22.
106. Norman Lear, "Bottom Linemanship," p. E23.
107. Arthur W. Combs, "The Myth of Competition," p. 268.
108. Sinclair Lewis, *Babbitt*, p. 55.
109. Lawrence Gonzales, "Airline Safety: A Special Report," p. 210.
110. Frederick C. Thayer, "Can Competition Hurt?" p. A17. Paul Wachtel agrees: "It is in the very nature of a system in which one must constantly look over one's shoulder at the competition that corners will be cut — in design, in information to the public, and in morals" (p. 58). Also see John J. Nance's recent book *Blind Trust* for evidence of the safety hazards that have resulted from deregulation of the airline industry.
111. Wachtel, pp. 68–71 and *passim.*
112. Harvey et al., p. 95.
113. Lawrence K. Frank, pp. 318–23. The last consequence — the suppression of individuality — is not as paradoxical as it may appear. I will return to this issue later.
114. For a review of the productivity gains enjoyed by cooperatives, see Appendix I in John Simmons and William Mares's *Working Together.* Also see Morton Deutsch's review of the literature in his chapter "Suppose We Took Egalitarianism Seriously?" in *Distributive Justice.*

CHAPTER 4

1. Harvey et al., p. 13.
2. George Leonard, *The Ultimate Athlete*, p. 128.

3. Edwards, p. 4.
4. Johan Huizinga, *Homo Ludens:* "The ways in which men compete for superiority are as various as the prizes at stake. . . . But in whatever shape it comes, it is always play" (p. 105). And again: ". . . competition implies play" (p. 133).
5. M. J. Ellis's *Why People Play* offers a reasonably good review of selected definitions and theories of play — definitions and theories being difficult to disentangle — although the review is colored by his strong behaviorist bias.
6. Huizinga, pp. 13, 203.
7. Chesterton is quoted by Huizinga, p. 197, n.2.
8. George Herbert Mead saw play as a chance for the child to try on various adult roles (esp. pp. 150, 364–65). See also Mihaly Csikszent-mihalyi's bibliographic review ("Play and Intrinsic Rewards," p. 42).
9. "The child must somehow distance himself from the content of his unconscious and see it as something external to him, to gain any sort of mastery over it. In normal play, objects such as dolls and toy animals are used to embody various aspects of the child's personality which are too complex, unacceptable, and contradictory for him to handle" (Bruno Bettelheim, *The Uses of Enchantment,* p. 55).
10. Orlick, for instance, suggests that we help children play in such a way that they will learn to be honest and cooperative (*Winning Through Cooperation,* pp. 138–39). It might be noted that such inculcation of values takes place, willy-nilly, whenever we guide — or react to — our children's play. It is just that we are accustomed to sexist roles, competitive interactions, and so forth, so we are less likely to notice the ways in which most play (as well as stories and films) quietly perpetuates these values.
11. Whether humans are primarily motivated to reduce tension, as psychoanalysts and behaviorists alike maintain, is actually a controversial question in personality theory. Among those who argue that we evince a "resistance to equilibrium" is Gordon Allport (see, for example, his *Becoming*).
12. Huizinga, pp. 197, 199.
13. See Michael Novak, *The Joy of Sports* (1976), or John Underwood, *Spoiled Sport* (1985), for example.
14. Winer, p. 194.
15. Novak, p. 218.
16. Joseph Heller, *Something Happened,* pp. 221–24.
17. Ellis, p. 140.
18. Günther Lüschen, "The Interdependence of Sport and Culture," p. 127.
19. Edwards, pp. 47–48.
20. Mihaly Csikszentmihalyi, *Beyond Boredom and Anxiety,* p. 182.
21. Sadler, p. 169.
22. Reagan is quoted by Brenda Jo Bredemeier and David L. Shields, "Values and Violence in Sports Today," p. 23.
23. Gai Ingham Berlage, "Are Children's Competitive Team Sports Socializing Agents for Corporate America?" pp. 313–14, 331.
24. "Sport is a primary vehicle through which youth are socialized to accept

and internalize American values," wrote D. Stanley Eitzen. "Thus, sport is viewed as the darling of the conservatives and the culprit of radicals" (*Sport and Contemporary Society*, p. 90). Gerald Ford could be added to the list of conservative defenders of competition. "Broadly speaking," he wrote while president, "outside of a national character and an educated society, there are few things more important to a country's growth and well-being than competitive athletics" ("In Defense of the Competitive Urge," p. 17). The mention of regional differences in sport appreciation is based on Gallup Poll results, cited in Edwards, p. 92.

25. George H. Sage, "American Values and Sport: Formation of a Bureaucratic Personality," pp. 42, 44.

26. Riesman cited in Tutko and Bruns, p. 42.

27. Arnold V. Talentino has discussed this issue in "The Sports Record Mania: An Aspect of Alienation."

28. George W. Morgan, *The Human Predicament*, esp. pp. 82–93. Alongside the prosaic man's predilection for quantification, according to Morgan, is his inability to tolerate ambiguity or uniqueness, his fascination with technique, and his need to classify (and, finally, to control) whatever he experiences. The poet e.e. cummings was characteristically more blunt: "Nothing measurable matters a good goddam."

29. Cited in Tutko and Bruns, p. 206.

30. Ibid., p. 205.

31. Stuart H. Walker, *Winning*, p. 58.

32. Leonard, p. 47. "But," he continues, "when the seasoning is mistaken for substance, only sickness can follow" (ibid.).

33. Betty Lehan Harragan, *Games Mother Never Taught You*, p. 78.

34. This idea represents an important part of each psychologist's thought and is consequently discussed in many of their respective works. See, for example, Maslow's *Religion, Values, and Peak-Experiences*; Lifton's *The Life of the Self*, pp. 33–34; and Csikszentmihalyi's "Play and Intrinsic Rewards."

35. Walker, p. 3.

36. Novak, pp. 47–49, 222–31.

37. Gary Warner, *Competition*, p. 30.

38. Giamatti is quoted by John Underwood, "A Game Plan for America," p. 67. In *Toward a Philosophy of Sport*, Harold J. Vanderzwaag tried to develop an explicitly existentialist justification for sports, but he based this on the mistaken view that existentialism is a philosophy of individualism and the present moment. (Regarding this confusion, see my essay, "Existentialism Here and Now," esp. pp. 381–88.)

39. Sadler, pp. 173–74. Whether we can reasonably speak of *sports* achieving these goals without competition is questionable, given our nomenclature. For "sports" in his quotation, read: "types of recreation" or "ways to have fun."

40. Russell, *Conquest of Happiness*, p. 55.

41. Orlick, *Winning Through Cooperation*, pp. 131, 129–30.

42. Johnson and Johnson, "Structure," p. 224.

43. Schmitt, p. 672.

44. Tutko and Bruns, p. 202; emphasis in original. This is the thrust of the authors' entire last chapter, "Alternate [*sic*] Models and Approaches."

45. Howard S. Slusher, *Man, Sport and Existence,* p. 148.
46. This view is shared by Theodore F. Lentz and Ruth Cornelius ("All Together: A Manual of Cooperative Games," p. 12).
47. Lewis Carroll, *Alice's Adventures in Wonderland,* p. 33.
48. The examples that follow in the text substantiate this. Rivka R. Eifermann's study of some 14,000 Israeli children decisively refutes the belief of Piaget and others that "rules and competition necessarily go together." She points to the existence of "cooperative rule-governed games" as well as "individual games governed by rules" (pp. 276, 278). Interestingly, Eifermann's exhaustive study also found, "contrary to Piaget's explicit statement . . . and, indeed, to what is probably a rather general assumption, [that] there is a relative *decline* in participation" in competitive, rule-governed games as children grow older, after reaching a peak in fourth grade (ibid., pp. 279–80). In his review of Eifermann's work, M. J. Ellis explains that "the uncertainty inherent in traversing from response to outcome is motivating in itself, and sustains much of the behavior of older children. They do not need explicit rules and competitions to govern their play behavior" (p. 69).
49. Carroll, p. 33.
50. Lentz and Cornelius, p. 4.
51. Orlick, *The Cooperative Sports and Games Book,* p. 52.

CHAPTER 5

1. Horney, *Neurosis and Human Growth,* p. 86 and *passim.*
2. Harry Stack Sullivan, *The Interpersonal Theory of Psychiatry,* p. 351. That high self-esteem is a prerequisite for, rather than mutually exclusive with, healthy relationships is worth emphasizing. The adage that one cannot love others without first loving oneself is largely true, but this in no way diminishes the importance of loving others. One of the most popular books on the subject in recent years is Nathaniel Branden's *The Psychology of Self-Esteem,* which is grounded in Ayn Rand's glorification of selfishness. Her crude pop-philosophy, with all its reactionary political implications, is hardly a necessary counterpart to an emphasis on self-esteem. Erich Fromm, in fact, has shown how self-esteem and selfishness are actually opposites (see *Man for Himself,* pp. 124–45). Sociologist Samuel Oliner is now in the process of studying altruistic behavior during World War II. Provisional findings confirm that "a strong sense of self-worth and security [is] the psychological base from which people [can] reach out to help others" (Daniel Goleman, "Great Altruists: Science Ponders Soul of Goodness").
3. Abraham Maslow, *Motivation and Personality,* p. 45. The other leading figure in humanistic psychology, Carl Rogers, has throughout his work stressed the importance of unconditional self-esteem, correlating this with psychological health and describing how its development requires unconditional acceptance by others (see, for example, "A Theory of Personality").
4. Miles Hewstone, *Attribution Theory: Social and Functional Extensions,* p. 17. Marie Jahoda similarly notes that "the most common proposal in

the mental health literature is that [the individual] should *accept* himself." Such self-acceptance typically implies "a global benevolent view of the whole self, a positive feeling that pervades and integrates all other aspects of the self-concept" (*Current Concepts of Positive Mental Health*, pp. 28–29).

5. Lawrence K. Frank, p. 322.

6. Maslow, *Toward a Psychology of Being*, chapter 3; *The Farther Reaches of Human Nature*, chapters 9 and 20.

7. Hal Gabriel is quoted in Susan Orlean, "Taking It to the Limit," p. 45.

8. See John J. Vance and Bert O. Richmond, "Cooperative and Competitive Behavior as a Function of Self-Esteem"; and Marianne W. DeVoe, "Cooperation as a Function of Self-Concept, Sex and Race."

9. See Morris Rosenberg, *Society and the Adolescent Self-Image*, p. 227.

10. Bruce C. Ogilvie and Thomas A. Tutko, "Sport: If You Want to Build Character, Try Something Else," p. 63.

11. Horney, *Neurotic Personality*, p. 173. Thus, "In the general competitive struggle that takes place in our culture even the normal person is likely to show . . . destructive impulses involved in the neurotic striving for power, prestige and possession" (p. 167).

12. See p. 30.

13. For the theologian C. S. Lewis, this sort of competitiveness is closely related to the sin of pride: "Pride is *essentially* competitive — is competitive by its very nature — while the other vices are competitive only, so to speak, by accident. Pride gets no pleasure out of having something, only out of having more of it than the next man. . . . Once the element of competition has gone, pride has gone" (*Mere Christianity*, p. 95).

14. Dave Meggyesy, *Out of Their League*, pp. 79, 12.

15. Levin, p. 93.

16. Walker, p. 193.

17. This is, in fact, just what Spencer Kagan and George P. Knight found. See their "Cooperation-Competition and Self-Esteem: A Case of Cultural Relativism."

18. Carole Ames, "Children's Achievement Attributions and Self-Reinforcement: Effects of Self-Concept and Competitive Reward Structure" (hereafter "Achievement"), p. 353. The "locus of control" paradigm, still very popular in social psychology, was originated by Julian Rotter.

19. Ardyth A. Norem-Hebeisen and D. W. Johnson, "The Relationship Between Cooperative, Competitive, and Individualistic Attitudes and Differentiated Aspects of Self-Esteem," p. 420.

20. Johnson, Johnson, and Geoffrey Maruyama, "Interdependence and Interpersonal Attraction Among Heterogeneous and Homogeneous Individuals," p. 35.

21. Johnson and Johnson, "Crisis," p. 140. Among the studies they cite is the one by Norem-Hebeisen and Johnson mentioned above. That study found a sharp contrast between the dependency and conditional self-esteem of competitive students, on the one hand, and the "greater personal expressiveness (basic acceptance) and . . . high sense of general well-being" of cooperative students, on the other (p. 420).

22. Johnson, Johnson, and Linda Scott, "The Effects of Cooperative and Individualized Instruction on Student Attitudes and Achievement,"

p. 212. This study did not include a competitive arrangement; the comparison is with independent learning. Other research corroborates the view that independent learning is the worst of the three alternatives with respect to psychological health.

23. Aronson, p. 210.
24. Ruth P. Rubinstein, "Changes in Self-Esteem and Anxiety in Competitive and Noncompetitive Camps."
25. Deutsch, "Distributive Justice," p. 399.
26. Orlick, *Winning Through Cooperation*, p. 121.
27. Walker, pp. 111, 250. Walker is talking about competitive athletics, but the psychoanalyst Rollo May came to the same conclusion regarding competition in the marketplace: "Any failure in the competitive struggle is a threat to the quasi-esteem for one's self. . . . This obviously leads to powerful feelings of helplessness and inferiority" (*The Meaning of Anxiety*, p. 196).
28. Ames, "Achievement," p. 350.
29. Ibid., p. 353.
30. Frank Ryan, *Sports and Psychology*, p. 205.
31. Leonard, p. 46; emphasis in original.
32. Ruben, p. 147. Other students of competition have sounded the same theme. Writes Lawrence Frank: "Competition denies any status that can be considered terminal, hence the competitors, while always setting goals for themselves, are forced to a continual rejection of those goals when attained, in favor of a more remote goal" (p. 320). And sports psychologists Tutko and Bruns put the matter starkly: "No matter at what level we compete and in whatever sport [or other activity, we might add], when we attain a goal we simply move it up another notch, hunting for a perfection that is always just out of reach. Winning, in fact, is like drinking salt water; it will never quench your thirst. It is an insatiable greed. There are never enough victories. . . . Freud would have clearly defined our behavior as a repetition compulsion because there is no moment where the winner can feel, 'I've made it' " (pp. 2–3).
33. Mark Spitz is quoted in Walker, p. 38.
34. Walker, p. 37.
35. Luise Eichenbaum and Susie Orbach, *Understanding Women: A Feminist Psychoanalytic Approach*, p. 142.
36. Butt, p. 54.
37. Edwards, p. 103.
38. Douglas MacArthur is quoted in Moore, p. 73.
39. Ogilvie and Tutko, pp. 61, 63.
40. Richard W. Eggerman, "Competition as a Mixed Good," p. 48. His piece was intended as a rebuttal to my article, "Why Competition?"
41. *New York Times* story: "Team Play Drawback for Young."
42. Johnson and Johnson, "Structuring Conflict in Science Classrooms," p. 12.
43. Rosenberg, p. 281.
44. Eggerman, p. 49.
45. Ibid., p. 50.
46. Ellen Sherberg, "The Thrill of Competition," in *Seventeen*.
47. Walker, p. 110.

48. May and Doob are quoted in Pepitone, p. 16.

49. John R. Seeley et al., *Crestwood Heights: A Study of the Culture of Suburban Life*, pp. 229–30.

50. Vance and Richmond, p. 225.

51. Gregory Bateson and his associates coined the term "double-bind" to refer to the phenomenon of giving two mutually exclusive messages so that the recipient cannot carry out both (see Bateson et al., "Toward a Theory of Schizophrenia").

52. Novak, p. 47. Psychoanalyst Willard Gaylin agrees: "In games the competition may be playful, but the agony is real and the anger is there" (*The Rage Within*, p. 35).

53. Harvey et al., pp. 74–75.

54. The study by G. M. Vaught and S. F. Newman, entitled "The Effect of Anxiety on Motor Steadiness in Competitive and Non-Competitive Conditions," is cited by Johnson and Bryant, p. 173.

55. Haines and McKeachie, pp. 389–90.

56. Tutko and Bruns, p. 79.

57. See, for example, Roy F. Baumeister, "Choking Under Pressure: Self-Consciousness and Paradoxical Effects of Incentives on Skillful Performance." The author argues as follows: "Competition is arousing; arousal heightens self-consciousness; and self-consciousness disrupts performance of some tasks" (p. 610).

58. Horney, *Neurotic Personality*, p. 182.

59. Ibid., p. 167.

60. Rollo May, p. 173.

61. Ibid., p. 191.

62. Ibid., p. 233.

63. Ibid., pp. 233–34.

64. Walker, p. 235.

65. Rollo May, pp. 87–88.

66. Herbert Hendin, *Suicide in America*, p. 30.

67. Hendin, *Age of Sensation*, pp. 167–70.

68. Jane E. Brody, "Heart Attacks: Turmoil Beneath the Calm," p. C5.

69. Sadler, p. 172.

70. Butt, p. 41.

71. Srully Blotnick, *Otherwise Engaged: The Private Lives of Successful Career Women*, pp. 108–9.

72. Strick, pp. 83–84.

73. Michael Parenti, *Democracy for the Few*, p. 37.

74. Leonard, "Winning Isn't Everything. It's Nothing," p. 46. Also see Leonard's remarks on this subject in his *Education and Ecstasy*, pp. 82, 121. Parenti, too, goes on to observe that in our conformist version of individualism, "Everyone competes against everyone else but for the same goals and with the same values in mind" (p. 37).

75. Combs, *Myths in Education*, p. 19. Lawrence Frank makes essentially the same point about economic competition: "The usual defense of 'rugged individualism' is that competitive striving stimulates initiative and individuality. But it is evident that competition, by forcing each competitor to engage in activities that are prescribed by the other competitors and are stereotyped by the rules of the legal-economic game, actually sup-

presses individuality; the individual cannot vary or depart except in terms of intensity and magnitude, or lack of scruples, since competition means striving to defeat or outdo others *in a narrowly restricted pattern of activity*" (p. 318; emphasis in original).

76. Crutchfield, "Ills of Piano Competitions."
77. Henry, p. 297.
78. Elin Schoen, "Competition: Can You Bear It When Your Friends Get Ahead?" p. 210.
79. Amabile, p. 577.
80. Lear, "Bottom Linemanship."

CHAPTER 6

1. Walter A. Weisskopf, "Industrial Institutions and Personality Structure," p. 4. "The arguments of economic theory that competition is economically beneficial will not eliminate the fact that the individualistic, competitive, value-attitude system leads to aggressive interpersonal relations . . . [thus neglecting] the need for primary, warm, close, affectionate, personal interrelations," he says (p. 3).
2. Paul Watzlawick, *The Situation Is Hopeless, But Not Serious*, p. 120.
3. Henry, p. 135.
4. Mary-Lou Weisman, "Jousting for 'Best Marriage' on a Field of Hors d'Oeuvres."
5. Horney, "Culture and Neurosis," p. 161.
6. See Horney, *Neurotic Personality*, p. 175.
7. Elizabeth Stark, "Women's Tennis: Friends vs. Foes." The official is Ted Tinling, director of international liaison for the Virginia Slims world tennis championship. Sports psychologist Frank Ryan also sees a sharp polarity: "The poor competitor prefers or may absolutely need an atmosphere of friendliness. . . . When the good competitor offers 'help,' it is probably a form of gamesmanship, but the poor competitor's efforts seem to represent a genuine attempt to create a friendly atmosphere" (*Sports and Psychology*, p. 205).
8. Ogilvie and Tutko, pp. 61–62.
9. Walter Kroll and Kay H. Petersen, "Study of Values Test and Collegiate Football Teams," p. 446. The study paired members of six teams from similar schools in order to contrast responses from members of undefeated teams with those of teams at the bottom of their conference. For some reason, the researchers had expected that winners would score higher than losers on the "social variable"; instead, their results suggest that doing well in athletic competition comes at the expense of positive relationships.
10. Lillian B. Rubin, *Just Friends: The Role of Friendship in Our Lives*, pp. 81–82.
11. Ames, "Achievement," p. 353.
12. Rollo May, p. 173. Jeffrey Sobel adds: "In a competitive game, a player reaches the objective — winning — only if the other player or players fail . . . and the winner can't help but enjoy everyone else's loss" (*Everybody Wins*, pp. 1–2).
13. Henry, p. 153.

14. Kagan and Madsen, "Four Instructional Sets," p. 53.

15. Martin Buber, *The Knowledge of Man*, p. 74.

16. Ibid., p. 81.

17. Sports psychologists Julie Anthony and James Loehr, respectively, are quoted in Stark, "Women's Tennis."

18. Meggyesy, p. 28. Sports can lead participants to regard "an opponent [as] a player, not a person," write Bredemeier and Shields. "This objectification of opponents reduces an athlete's sense of personal responsibility for competitors" (p. 29).

19. Johnson and Johnson, "Crisis," pp. 136–37. Eight studies are cited here, and the authors conducted at least two more after this article was published. Some of the research contrasted cooperation with competition and some with independent learning, but a clear picture emerges from the research taken as a whole.

20. Dean Tjosvold et al., "Influence Strategy, Perspective-Taking, and Relationships Between High- and Low-Power Individuals in Cooperative and Competitive Contexts."

21. Mark Barnett et al., "Relationship Between Competitiveness and Empathy in 6- and 7-Year-Olds," p. 222.

22. On the relationship between empathy and altruism, see, among many other sources, Martin L. Hoffman, "Is Altruism Part of Human Nature?" (especially pp. 130–32), and Jim Fultz et al., "Social Evaluation and the Empathy-Altruism Hypothesis."

23. Ames, "Competitive Versus Cooperative Reward Structures," pp. 284–85.

24. Eldred Rutherford and Paul Mussen, "Generosity in Nursery School Boys."

25. Mark Barnett and James Bryan, "Effects of Competition with Outcome Feedback on Children's Helping Behavior."

26. Ibid., p. 838.

27. Pines, p. 73.

28. Horney, "Culture and Neurosis," p. 161.

29. Bertrand Russell, *Why I Am Not a Christian*, p. 82.

30. Henry, p. 296.

31. Richard Hofstadter, p. 57.

32. George Orwell, "Such, Such Were the Joys," p. 36. Tutko and Bruns make the same point: "All too often, the message that comes through to those who lose or who fail to reach the top is that obviously they didn't work hard enough and that they're not as worthwhile as the winners. Our tendency is to excuse the shortcomings of a winner — to gloss over his human frailties. But when a person starts to lose, we begin to question his character. Winners and losers are actually seen as good and bad people" (p. 7).

33. The late psychologist Sidney Jourard was the most vigorous proponent of the view that self-disclosure both contributes to and reflects psychological health. See his *Disclosing Man to Himself* and *The Transparent Self*.

34. Nathan W. Ackerman, *The Psychodynamics of Family Life*, p. 114.

35. Horney, *Neurotic Personality*, p. 164. Family therapist Salvador Minuchin has argued that "Violence is inherent in the idea that one must be superior" (*Family Kaleidoscope*, p. 191).

36. Deutsch, *Distributive Justice*, p. 85. In 1964, Theodore Caplow offered a

similar observation: "In virtually all competitive situations, some degree of hostility develops between the competitors as soon as they are aware of each other's existence" (*Principles of Organization*, p. 318).

37. Richard I. Evans, "A Conversation with Konrad Lorenz," p. 93.

38. Bettelheim, "Violence: A Neglected Mode of Behavior," p. 194. Bettelheim continues: "It is peculiar to our culture that, in encouraging an extremely competitive spirit, we stress those aggressive emotions that power competition although aggression itself is tabooed" (ibid.).

39. These two studies are cited by Michael B. Quanty in "Aggression Catharsis: Experimental Investigations and Implications," pp. 117–18.

40. Shahbaz Khan Mallick and Boyd R. McCandless, "A Study of Catharsis of Aggression."

41. Study conducted by Larry Leith and Terry Orlick, reported in Orlick's *Winning Through Cooperation*, p. 92.

42. Richard G. Sipes, "War, Sports and Aggression: An Empirical Test of Two Rival Theories," p. 71. Several studies have since replicated Sipes's finding. Sipes also investigated the relationship between military activity and the popularity of combative sports (football and hunting) within a single society (the United States) over time. He found that participation in these sports rose during wartime (ibid., pp. 78–79). Another cross-cultural study, while not concerned with sports, is also suggestive. If catharsis theory is true, wars should themselves offer an outlet for aggression. It follows that they should lower homicide rates. In fact, this massive study of 110 nations found that those with "the most fatal experiences in war were precisely those most likely to show homicide increases" (Dane Archer and Rosemary Gartner, "Violent Acts and Violent Times: A Comparative Approach to Postwar Homicide Rates," p. 956).

43. Cratty, p. 164.

44. Quanty, p. 119.

45. Dolf Zillmann et al., "The Enjoyment of Watching Sport Contests," p. 299. Also see Leonard Berkowitz's review of the literature: "Experimental Investigations of Hostility Catharsis."

46. George Gaskell and Robert Pearton, "Aggression and Sport," p. 276.

47. Novak, p. 213. To the argument that competition often humiliates participants, he has a ready reply: "Living with humiliation is part of not being equal to everyone" (p. 228). Novak also expresses regret that women are largely excluded from combative team sports and proposes that an activity "involving pushes and shoves" be set up for females (pp. 201–4).

48. George Orwell, "The Sporting Spirit," p. 153.

49. Wellington's remark is one of the most frequently cited aphorisms on the subject. MacArthur is quoted in Paul Hoch's *Rip Off the Big Game*, p. 70, among other places. Eisenhower is quoted in Warner's *Competition*, p. 171.

50. Muzafer Sherif et al., *Intergroup Conflict and Cooperation: The Robbers' Cave Experiment.*

51. See my brief essay, "Soccer Riot: Competition Is the Villain."

52. Orlick, *Winning Through Cooperation*, p. 92.

53. Joseph Wax, "Competition: Educational Incongruity," p. 197.

54. Theodor W. Adorno et al., *The Authoritarian Personality*, pp. 224 ff.
55. Kelley and Stahelski, "Social Interaction Basis of Cooperators' and Competitors' Beliefs About Others," p. 83.
56. The classic statement of the simple frustration/aggression hypothesis can be found in the 1939 book *Frustration and Aggression*, by John Dollard et al.
57. Janice D. Nelson et al., "Children's Aggression Following Competition and Exposure to an Aggressive Model," p. 1095.
58. Pauline R. Christy et al., "Effects of Competition-Induced Frustration on Two Classes of Modeled Behavior."
59. Ibid., p. 105.
60. Johnson, Johnson, and Maruyama, p. 23.
61. Johnson and Johnson, "The Internal Dynamics of Cooperative Learning Groups," pp. 112–13.
62. Brenda Bryant, "The Effects of the Interpersonal Context of Evaluation on Self- and Other-Enhancement Behavior," pp. 890–91.
63. The Johnsons cite 32 studies to substantiate this, as of June 1984 ("Processes," p. 10).
64. Gillian A. King and Richard M. Sorrentino, "Psychological Dimensions of Goal-Oriented Interpersonal Situations," p. 159.
65. Pepitone et al., p. 209.
66. Deutsch, *Resolution of Conflict*, pp. 26, 353. The Johnsons cite eight other studies that confirm superior communication under cooperation ("Structure," p. 229).
67. Tjosvold et al., p. 199. Also see Deutsch, *Resolution of Conflict*, p. 24.
68. Johnson, Johnson, and Maruyama, p. 7.
69. See the Johnsons' review of research in ibid., as well as their own studies: "The Effects of Cooperative and Individualized Instruction on Student Attitudes and Achievement" (1978) and "Cross-Ethnic Relationships: The Impact of Intergroup Cooperation and Intergroup Competition" (1984). When Elliot Aronson used his cooperative "jigsaw" classroom technique, he, too, found that children "grew to like each other better" and that this effect "crossed ethnic and racial boundaries" (p. 210).
70. "The positive cross-ethnic and cross-sex relationships built within cooperative learning groups do generalize to and are sustained in voluntary, self-initiated interaction in non-structured classroom, school, and home settings" (Douglas Warring et al., "Impact of Different Types of Cooperative Learning on Cross-Ethnic and Cross-Sex Relationships," p. 58).
71. Robert E. Dunn and Morton Goldman, "Competition and Noncompetition in Relationship to Satisfaction and Feelings Toward Own-group and Nongroup Members," pp. 310–11.
72. Johnson, Johnson, and Maruyama: "The comparison between cooperation with and without intergroup competition favors cooperation without intergroup competition by an effect size of .88 (indicating that the average liking among subjects in the cooperation without condition is equivalent to the liking at the 81st percentile in the cooperation with intergroup competition condition)" (p. 22).
73. Warring et al., p. 58.

74. Intragroup rivalry of this sort can also be explained in terms of the underlying framework of economic competition. It is here, too, that Paul Hoch looks to explain the aggressiveness of sports: "In a militarized society, gladiatorial combat brings in profits at the box office. . . . Professional athletes are encouraged to maim one another, not only by the macho-minded sportswriters and fans cheering them on from the side lines, but by the knowledge that if they're not tough enough there are literally thousands of minor league and college players around to take their jobs. It's the old reserve army of labor breathing down their necks" (pp. 27–28).

75. Carolyn W. Sherif, p. 34.

76. Parenti, p. 38.

77. Frank Trippett, "Local Chauvinism: Long May It Rave."

78. Orwell, "The Sporting Spirit," pp. 152, 154–55.

79. Gorney, *The Human Agenda*, p. 8.

80. Deutsch, *Distributive Justice*, pp. 255–56, 265.

81. Johnson, Johnson, and Scott, "Effects of Cooperative and Individualized Instruction on Student Attitudes and Achievement," p. 212.

82. Roger Johnson et al., "The Effects of Controversy, Concurrence Seeking, and Individualistic Learning on Achievement and Attitude Change" (hereafter "Achievement"), pp. 203–4.

83. Johnson, Johnson, and Margaret Tiffany, "Structuring Academic Conflicts Between Majority and Minority Students: Hindrance or Help to Integration?" (hereafter "Structuring"), p. 69.

84. Roger Johnson et al., "Achievement," p. 203.

85. Karl Smith, Johnson, and Johnson, "Can Conflict Be Constructive? Controversy Versus Concurrence Seeking in Learning Groups," p. 660. Conflict in a cooperative setting "leads to higher quality decision making and problem solving" and "promotes higher mastery and retention of the material," the authors conclude (ibid., pp. 652, 660).

86. Ibid., p. 661; Johnson, Johnson, and Tiffany, "Structuring," p. 70.

CHAPTER 7

1. Philip M. Boffey, "Rise in Science Fraud Is Seen; Need to Win Cited as a Cause."

2. Mark Green and John F. Berry, "Corporate Crime II," p. 732.

3. Irving Goldaber, head of the Center for the Study of Crowd and Spectator Behavior, quoted in Jack C. Horn, "Fan Violence: Fighting the Injustice of It All," p. 31.

4. William Beausay, sports psychologist, quoted in Gary Warner, *Competition*, p. 179.

5. Irving Simon, "A Humanistic Approach to Sports," p. 25.

6. Tutko and Bruns, pp. xiii, 47.

7. Underwood, "A Game Plan for America," p. 70.

8. Underwood, *Spoiled Sport*, p. 83.

9. William J. Bennett, "In Defense of Sports," p. 69.

10. Hardin, *Promethean Ethics*, p. 38.

11. Michener, *Sports in America*, p. 427.

12. A detailed and trenchant analysis of crime, which decisively refutes the assumption that incarceration solves the problem, can be found in Elliott Currie's recent book, *Confronting Crime.*

13. Combs, *Myths in Education,* p. 167.

14. Strick, pp. 57, 97, 117. Similarly, Jane Mansbridge observed: "It was not just paranoia that made former President Nixon compile an 'enemies list'; it was the spirit of adversary democracy" (*Beyond Adversary Democracy,* p. 301).

15. Lüschen, "Cheating in Sport," p. 71.

16. Orwell, "Sporting Spirit," p. 153.

17. Bredemeier and Shields, p. 25.

18. Johnson and Johnson, "Processes," p. 27.

19. Novak, pp. 311–12.

20. Russell, *Conquest of Happiness,* pp. 53–54.

21. "Any individual who has been around football for any period of time knows that 'elbows fly' on the first play from scrimmage. This is when each man tells his opponent 'who is boss.' Yet let a player get 'caught' for punching and everyone exhibits great shock.... Overtly we give the impression that the morality of sport is identical to the morality of the choir. It seems it is high time we either change the nature of sport (which is highly unlikely), or stop the hypocrisy and *admit* to ourselves the existing ethic. To condone, covertly, and punish, overtly, is not my idea of authenticity" (Slusher, p. 167).

22. This finding emerged from studies with three different populations, ranging in age from elementary school to college, and with two different tests of moral development. See Bredemeier and Shields, p. 29.

23. Sissela Bok, *Lying,* p. 258.

24. Tutko and Bruns, p. 84. Recall Stuart Walker's equation of generosity during a competitive encounter with "surrendering" (see p. 124).

25. Amitai Etzioni, "After Watergate — What?" p. 7.

26. Frankel, "Search for Truth," p. 1051.

CHAPTER 8

1. Ames, p. 353.

2. Eleanor Maccoby and Carol Jacklin, *The Psychology of Sex Differences,* p. 249.

3. Andrew Ahlgren and David W. Johnson, "Sex Differences in Cooperative and Competitive Attitudes from the Second Through the Twelfth Grades."

4. For example, a series of studies using the Work and Family Orientation Questionnaire developed by Robert Helmreich and Janet Spence has found that men score significantly higher than women on the competitiveness scale (see Spence and Helmreich, "Achievement-related," p. 45).

5. Bruce Mays, "In Fighting Trim," p. 28.

6. Robert W. Stock, "Daring to Greatness," p. 142.

7. The reflections of Mark Fasteau are summarized by Jack W. Sattel in "Men, Inexpressiveness, and Power," p. 122.

8. Matina Horner's unpublished doctoral dissertation from 1968 is entitled "Sex Differences in Achievement Motivation and Performance in Competitive and Noncompetitive Situations." She later summarized her work in several places. See, for example, her chapter "The Measurement and Behavioral Implications of Fear of Success in Women."

9. Miron Zuckerman and Ladd Wheeler, "To Dispel Fantasies About the Fantasy-based Measure of Fear of Success," p. 943.

10. Zuckerman and Wheeler (1975) conclude that "Horner's suggestion that success avoidance is more frequent among females than among males has not been supported" (ibid., p. 935). David Tresemer's meta-analysis of more than 100 studies (1976) led to the same finding ("The Cumulative Record of Research on 'Fear of Success' "). A recent Japanese study (1982) again turned up no significant sex difference (Hirotsugu Yamauchi, "Sex Differences in Motive to Avoid Success on Competitive or Cooperative Action").

11. "The fantasy material elicited from women by the story-telling technique has relatively little relationship to a gender-differentiating personality characteristic but instead largely reflects the respondents' perceptions of society's current sex-role attitudes and their expectations about the consequences of role conformity or violation under the particular circumstances described in the verbal cue. With greater societal acceptance of women's educational and vocational aspirations, sex differences in fear-of-success studies appear to be evaporating" (Spence and Helmreich, "Achievement-related," p. 37).

12. Horner, "Femininity and Successful Achievement," p. 54.

13. The study, by Miron Zuckerman and S. N. Alison, is cited by Georgia Sassen in "Success Anxiety in Women: A Constructivist Interpretation of Its Source and Its Significance," p. 16.

14. Sassen, ibid.

15. Sassen, "Sex Role Orientation, Sex Differences and Concept of Success," pp. 56–57.

16. Horner, "Femininity and Successful Achievement," p. 67.

17. Maccoby and Jacklin, *Psychology of Sex Differences,* p. 351.

18. Horner, "Femininity and Successful Achievement," p. 61.

19. Sassen, "Success Anxiety in Women," p. 15.

20. Sherberg, "Thrill of Competition."

21. Psychiatrist Carlotta Miles is quoted by Judy Bachrach in "Rivalry in the Sisterhood," p. 58.

22. Susan Brownmiller describes such traditional kinds of competition among women in her book *Femininity.*

23. Jane Gross, "Against the Odds: A Woman's Ascent on Wall Street," p. 18.

24. Ibid., p. 21. "I'm not in this to be a nice guy; I'm too profit-oriented," Valenstein adds (p. 68).

25. Sandra Salmans, "Women Dressing to Succeed Think Twice About the Suit," p. A1.

26. Anne Taylor Fleming, "Women and the Spoils of Success," p. 30.

27. Anita Diamant, "The Women's Sports Revolution," pp. 21, 20.

28. In *The Reproduction of Mothering: Psychoanalysis and the Sociology of Gender,* Nancy Chodorow offers a persuasive account of how women come to

incline toward relationship. Her theory, which concerns early-life experiences and specifically addresses the question of which parent bears the responsibility for caring for infants, has influenced Carol Gilligan and Georgia Sassen, among others.

29. Carol Gilligan, *In a Different Voice*, p. 26.
30. Ibid., p. 19.
31. Derber, chapter 2.
32. Don Zimmerman and Candace West, "Sex Roles, Interruptions, and Silences in Conversation."
33. Pamela Fishman, "Interaction: The Work Women Do."
34. Ibid., p. 405.
35. Robin Lakoff, personal communication, 1984.
36. Barrie Thorne, personal communication, 1984.
37. Sassen, "Success Anxiety in Women," pp. 21–22. Gilligan similarly writes that "the observation that women's embeddedness in lives of relationship, their orientation to interdependence, their subordination of achievement to care, and their conflicts over competitive success leave them personally at risk in mid-life seems more a commentary on the society than a problem in women's development" (pp. 170–71).

CHAPTER 9

1. Deutsch, *Distributive Justice*, p. 196.
2. Wachtel, p. 144.
3. Ibid., p. 174.
4. Philip G. Zimbardo et al., "The Psychology of Imprisonment: Privation, Power, and Pathology." The quotations are taken from pp. 282–85. Zimbardo cites a similar study, conducted by N. J. Orlando, in which personnel from a psychiatric hospital who agreed to play the role of mental patients for a weekend soon displayed the behaviors found among such patients: fighting, pacing, uncontrollable weeping, and so on (p. 284).
5. Harvey et al., pp. 23, 95.
6. Sadler, p. 168.
7. Deutsch, *Distributive Justice*, p. 154.
8. Shirk, *Competitive Comrades*, esp. pp. 161–62.
9. Boston, which by some measures is the most dangerous U.S. city in which to drive, offers a good case study. See my article "Stop!" for an analysis of these issues.
10. Orlick, *Winning Through Cooperation*, pp. 155–56.
11. Paul E. Breer and Edwin C. Locke, *Task Experience as a Source of Attitudes*, p. 271.
12. Axelrod, chapter 4. The quotations are from p. 85.
13. The style of presentation in this section was suggested by Jay Haley's essay, "The Art of Being a Failure as a Therapist."
14. For a very provocative essay on the implicit conservatism of humanistic psychology, see chapter 3 of Russell Jacoby's *Social Amnesia*. "One helps oneself because collective help is inadmissible; in rejecting the realm of social and political praxis, individual helplessness is redoubled and

soothes itself through self-help, hobbies, and how-to manuals. . . . The reality of violence and destruction, of psychically and physically damaged people, is not merely glossed over, but buried beneath the lingo of self, meaning, authenticity, personality" (pp. 51, 57). Jacoby is much less persuasive when he extends his indictment to take in the neo-Freudians and, for that matter, every variety of psychology except for orthodox psychoanalysis.

15. On the subject of realists and utopians, the philosopher Hazel Barnes has written, "We should not be afraid of the Utopian in our thinking, for it is only belief in the possibility of what has not yet been attained which makes progress even conceivable. A willingness to rethink all of our aims and to throw the whole system into question will prevent our painting the walls when we ought to be getting rid of the termites and strengthening the foundations" (*An Existentialist Ethics*, p. 306). C. Wright Mills addressed the same issue: "What *is* 'practical' and what *is* 'utopian'? Does not utopian mean merely: whatever acknowledges other values as relevant and possibly even as sovereign? But in truth, are not those who in the name of realism act like crackpots, are they not the utopians? Are we not now in a situation in which the only practical, realistic down-to-earth thinking and acting is just what these crackpot realists call 'utopian'?" (*Power, Politics, and People*, p. 402). Erich Fromm, Jonathan Schell, and Paul Wachtel have all expressed similar sentiments.

16. Fred M. Hechinger, "Experts Call a Child's Play Too Serious to Be Left to Adults," p. C4.

17. In his account of how we compete in conversation, Charles Derber remarks that "the allocation of attention inevitably mirrors the basic structure of the society in which it evolves; it can thus assume a new form only if fundamental social change occurs. . . . Where norms of self-interest govern economic behavior, face-to-face social behavior is invariably egoistic and competitive" (p. 88). Paul Hoch similarly observes that sports mirror the larger society (p. 10), while Robert Paul Wolff argues that "only a social revolution of the most far-reaching sort" will allow schooling to be noncompetitive (*The Ideal of the University*, p. 68).

18. Orlick, *Winning Through Cooperation*, p. 138.

19. Wolff, especially pp. 143, 149.

20. Benjamin Barber, *Strong Democracy*. Also see Jane J. Mansbridge's discussion of these issues in *Beyond Adversary Democracy*.

21. Deutsch, *Distributive Justice*, p. 281.

22. Lawrence K. Frank, p. 322.

23. Edgar Z. Friedenberg, *R. D. Laing*, p. 96.

CHAPTER 10

1. For a cogent discussion of how competitive classroom games are both unnecessary and destructive — followed by suggestions for the kinds of games that might replace them — see Mara Sapon-Shevin, "Cooperative Instructional Games: Alternatives to the Spelling Bee." One of Sapon-Shevin's major points is that the anger and hurt feelings that so

often attend these games do not reflect failings of the individual children but follow from the competitive structure of the games themselves.

2. Spencer Kagan quoted in Ron Brandt, "On Cooperative Learning: A Conversation with Spencer Kagan," p. 8. Elsewhere, Kagan has observed that teachers who make public the achievement of their students set up the conditions for competition even if that is not their intent. This would include posting either tests and papers that have been graded or charts with names and scores (Kagan et al., "Classroom Structural Bias," p. 279). We might add to this list the repugnant practice of announcing each student's score on a test or paper as it is handed back.

3. The third edition of that book, *Learning Together and Alone*, was published in 1991.

4. Lilya Wagner, *Peer Teaching: Historical Perspectives*. Also see Shlomo Sharan, "The Group Investigation Approach to Cooperative Learning," p. 30.

5. For a discussion of the difference between cooperation and altruism, see my article "Cooperation: What It Means and Doesn't Mean."

6. Shlomo Sharan, however, has argued forcefully that "whole-class instruction should be retired as the primary mode of teaching, and, at best, should occupy a fraction of the time it presently occupies in the instructional repertoire of teachers." Eschewing the qualifiers that typically mute the impact of recommendations offered in academic essays, Sharan declares that whole-class teaching "often generates . . . social distance between peers in the classroom and between those from different ethnic groups in particular, insidious social comparison processes, more tightly knit cliques in classrooms, and many more students at the lower levels of achievement. . . . The fact is that cooperative learning can be implemented only to the extent that traditional whole-class teaching is supplanted, not just altered!" ("Cooperative Learning," p. 298).

7. Robert Slavin, *Cooperative Learning*, p. 44.

8. David W. Johnson and Roger T. Johnson, *Cooperation and Competition*, p. 158. These numbers reflect measures of overall self-esteem. Of the studies that found a difference on measures of task or academic self-esteem in particular, twenty-three favored cooperation and one favored competition. Of the studies that compared cooperative and *individualistic* arrangements on overall self-esteem, thirty-nine found an advantage for the former and three for the latter.

9. "If we want to enhance self-esteem, we must first check to see whether the social environment is safe for the individual. A debilitating environment is likely to squash fledgling self-confidence no matter how much we exhort the individual to persist. . . . Moreover, suggesting that self-esteem can be preserved by developing 'coping skills' endorses the status quo" (James A. Beane, "Sorting Out the Self-Esteem Controversy," p. 27). Also see a thoughtful essay by Ellen Herman, "Toward a Politics of Self-Esteem?"

10. The work of Ruth C. Wylie is especially useful for understanding the

peculiar characteristics and weaknesses of some of the many instruments used to measure self-esteem.

11. For an account of "the role education itself has played in causing students to fail" (p. xiii) and to feel like failures, see William Glasser, *Schools Without Failure*.

12. Johnson, quoted in my article "It's Hard to Get Left Out of a Pair," p. 54.

13. Johnson and Johnson, *Cooperation and Competition*, chap. 7; Slavin, *Cooperative Learning*, chap. 3.

14. Johnson and Johnson, *Cooperation and Competition*, p. 122.

15. Carol Hymowitz, "Five Main Reasons Why Managers Fail."

16. Slavin, *Cooperative Learning*, chap. 2.

17. Johnson and Johnson, *Cooperation and Competition*, pp. 40–41. Those studies in which the subjects cooperated within their groups but the groups competed against each other found less of a benefit than those in which there was no intergroup competition. In seven studies that directly compared cooperation with and without intergroup competition, no differences were found. The Johnsons' conclusion is that having groups compete against each other "does *not* enhance achievement and may decrease it" (p. 46). (For a fuller discussion of the achievement effects of competition, see chapters 3 and 4 of their book.)

18. Johnson and Johnson, *Learning Together and Alone*, p. 40.

19. Richard J. Light, *The Harvard Assessment Seminars*, pp. 6, 21, 64–65. The science courses that students rated highest and lowest in overall quality had almost identical work loads. What distinguished the lowest-rated courses was more intense competition for grades.

20. For more on the destructive effects of extrinsic motivators than the brief remarks on pp. 59–61, see my article "Group Grade Grubbing versus Cooperative *Learning*." Three indispensable books on the topic are *The Hidden Costs of Rewards* (edited by Mark R. Lepper and David Greene), *Intrinsic Motivation and Self-Determination in Human Behavior* (by Edward L. Deci and Richard M. Ryan), and *The Competitive Ethos and Democratic Education* (by John G. Nicholls).

21. See especially the work of Carole Ames and her colleagues listed in the reference section, some of which I described in earlier chapters.

22. This dynamic was noticed by a researcher as early as 1932: "Generally, the usual classroom incentives call forth a response for maximum exertion only from the few very able pupils, while the majority of the pupils, knowing that their chances for excelling are limited, fail to be motivated to do their very best" (Joseph Zubin, *Some Effects of Incentives*, p. 50).

23. R. E. Slavin, "Cooperative Learning and the Cooperative School," p. 9.

24. David W. Johnson and Roger T. Johnson, "Motivational Processes in Cooperative, Competitive, and Individualistic Learning Situations," p. 272. Slavin, by contrast, reports mixed results from questionnaires that ask children whether they like class during CL sessions (*Cooperative Learning*, pp. 48–49). He suggests that this may be due in part to some

of the surveys having tapped students' general feelings about school rather than their relative preference for different classroom approaches. Here is another explanation for his ambiguous findings: the version of CL that Slavin uses (and tends to rely on in his research reports) depends on rewards to foster interdependence. We might expect, based on the documented consequences of using extrinsic motivators, that the enthusiasm generated by CL would be canceled out by the reduced interest in tasks for which a goody is offered. If this is true, then models of CL that do not reward children to get them to work together would be expected to produce much more enthusiasm than other approaches.

25. Sharan, "Cooperative Learning," p. 288.
26. John I. Goodlad, *A Place Called School,* pp. 232, 233.
27. Ibid., pp. 229, 233.
28. "The subject of student boredom in school in general, and under varying instructional conditions in particular, has yet to be studied systematically. It is almost as if this topic was purposefully shunned by educational researchers!" (Sharan, "Cooperative Learning," p. 287).
29. David W. Johnson, Roger T. Johnson, and Edythe Johnson Holubec, *Circles of Learning,* p. 65.
30. In addition to the sources cited below, see the discussions of this question in Bonnie K. Nastasi and Douglas H. Clements, "Research on Cooperative Learning," pp. 117–20, 124–26; Sharan, "Cooperative Learning," pp. 289–91; and Noreen M. Webb, "Peer Interaction and Learning in Small Groups."
31. See Noreen M. Webb, "Student Interaction and Learning in Small Groups," "Peer Interaction and Learning in Small Groups," and virtually any of her other articles and chapters for further findings regarding the conditions that must be present for peer teaching to benefit the giver and recipient of help.
32. Hugh C. Foot et al., "Theoretical Issues in Peer Tutoring," p. 72. Tutoring can also enhance the self-esteem, social skills, and motivation of the tutor.
33. Carl A. Benware and Edward L. Deci, "Quality of Learning with an Active Versus Passive Motivational Set."
34. Gerald W. Foster and John E. Penick, "Creativity in a Cooperative Group Setting."
35. Johnson and Johnson, *Cooperation and Competition,* p. 48.
36. This notion of learning through encounters with conflicting points of view is at the core of Jean Piaget's approach to cognitive development and, following his work, the model of learning known as constructivism. For a recent elaboration of this theory from another Swiss researcher, see Willem Doise, "The Development of Individual Competencies through Social Interaction."
37. Michael Marland, a British educator, is quoted in Joan Green and John Myers, "Conversations," p. 330.
38. Judy Clarke, "The Hidden Treasure of Co-operative Learning," p. 3.
39. Robert Bellah et al., *The Good Society,* pp. 172, 176.

40. For one discussion on this topic, see Johnson and Johnson, *Learning Together and Alone*, p. 64.

41. Webb, "Student Interaction and Learning in Small Groups," pp. 165–67.

42. For some concrete suggestions on random-assignment procedures, see Dee Dishon and Pat Wilson O'Leary, "Tips for Heterogeneous Group Selection."

43. For a thorough discussion of different kinds of learning groups, see Judy Clarke et al., *Together We Learn*, chaps. 3 and 4.

44. Johnson and Johnson, *Learning Together and Alone*, p. 146. Also see their *Circles of Learning*, pp. 80–85; Clarke et al., *Together We Learn*, chap. 5; and two papers by Nancy B. Graves and Theodore D. Graves: "Creating a Cooperative Learning Environment" and "Should We Teach Cooperative Skills as a Part of Each Cooperative Lesson?"

45. Selma Wassermann, "Children Working in Groups? It Doesn't Work!" pp. 203–204.

46. See Johnson and Johnson, *Learning Together and Alone*, pp. 58–59. For an example of research supporting the value of group processing, see Stuart Yager et al., "The Impact of Group Processing on Achievement in Cooperative Learning Groups."

47. Kipling D. Williams and Steven J. Karau, "Social Loafing and Social Compensation," p. 570.

48. Besides asking "accountable to whom?" we might ask "accountable with respect to what?" For one group of researchers, individual accountability is defined "in terms of operating in accordance with the norms of a classroom community . . . rather than in terms of performance on achievement tests" (Erna Yackel et al., "Small Group Interactions as a Source of Learning Opportunities in Second-Grade Mathematics," p. 398).

49. Thomas L. Good et al., "Using Work-Groups in Mathematics Instruction," p. 60. I am indebted to Judy Clarke for her incisive analysis of role assignments.

50. Slavin, "Cooperative Learning and Student Achievement," p. 31.

51. Johnson and Johnson, *Learning Together and Alone*, pp. 134, 143.

52. See Yael Sharan and Shlomo Sharan, "Group Investigation Expands Cooperative Learning," and virtually anything else written by either of them.

53. The best known of these programs is the Child Development Project, for information about which see Daniel Solomon et al., "Cooperative Learning as Part of a Comprehensive Program Designed to Promote Prosocial Development"; chapter 6 of my book *The Brighter Side of Human Nature;* or my article "The ABC's of Caring."

54. See, for example, Mark Brubacher et al., eds., *Perspectives on Small Group Learning*, the contributors to which repeatedly show how children learn by talking, and the work of Judy Clarke in Canada, Helen Cowie and Jean Rudduck in England, and Joan Dalton in Australia, among many others.

55. Together, in Mara Sapon-Shevin and Nancy Schniedewind, "Selling

Cooperative Learning Without Selling It Short"; separately, in Schniedewind and Ellen Davidson's excellent guidebook for teachers, *Cooperative Learning, Cooperative Lives,* and in Sapon-Shevin's "Cooperative Learning, Cooperative Visions."

56. See my article "Group Grade Grubbing versus Cooperative *Learning*" and a forthcoming book tentatively titled *Punished by Rewards.*

57. Nastasi and Clements point out that in all the studies purporting to show that rewards are necessary for learning to occur, CL was basically glued on to "traditional classroom structures which are individualistic and competitive in orientation" ("Research on Cooperative Learning," p. 123). For additional criticisms of the claim that CL yields achievement gains only if extrinsic motivators are present, see my article "Group Grade Grubbing versus Cooperative *Learning.*"

58. Spencer Kagan notes that his "structural" method of CL shares with Slavin's approach "an emphasis on specific behaviors among teachers" as opposed to "general principles" of cooperation or collaboration (Brandt, "On Cooperative Learning," p. 10). While I am not aware of any CL theorist or researcher who makes the connection explicitly, anyone who relies on extrinsic incentives to get children to cooperate might very well rely on extrinsic incentives to get teachers to use CL; concepts like merit pay are quite consistent with this paradigm.

59. Leann Lipps Birch et al., "Eating as the 'Means' Activity in a Contingency." The experimenters did not expect to find that verbal rewards would have precisely the same motivation-killing effects as tangible rewards.

60. "In STAD or TGT [two of the student team learning methods developed at Johns Hopkins University], learning and cooperating are the means; the goal is winning," observed Spencer Kagan ("Co-op Co-op," p. 439). The third edition of a book describing these methods (Robert E. Slavin, *Using Student Team Learning*) begins with the announcement that "competition between teams is no longer recommended" (p. 1). This is particularly remarkable for two reasons: first, the reason given for this shift is not a change of heart or mind on the part of the author but a growing resistance to the technique on the part of educators themselves: "The same teachers who are attracted to cooperative learning are often repelled by moving competition up to the team level" (p. 1). Second, notwithstanding this comment in the introduction, the manual proceeds to set out the rules for how "students compete" in the tournaments (p. 24; see also Slavin, *Cooperative Learning,* chap. 4).

61. Teresa M. Amabile and Judith Gitomer, "Children's Artistic Creativity." For more evidence of, and a theoretical basis for, the auspicious effects of autonomy, see the work of Edward L. Deci, including his book with Richard M. Ryan, *Intrinsic Motivation and Self-Determination in Human Behavior.*

62. Shlomo Sharan, "Cooperative Learning and Helping Behaviour in the Multi-ethnic Classroom," p. 158.

63. Yael Sharan and Shlomo Sharan, "Group Investigation Expands Cooperative Learning," p. 20.

64. These remarks were part of a speech delivered at the second annual cooperative learning conference in 1986. See Shlomo Sharan, "Cooperative Learning: Problems and Promise," p. 4. Striking a similar theme, Mara Sapon-Shevin writes that instead of wondering "What cooperative learning method will increase student test scores?" we might ask "What kinds of cooperative learning methods and practice best allow students to experience control over their own learning and learn to make meaningful decisions related to their own education and that of others?" ("Cooperative Learning, Cooperative Visions," pp. 26–27).

65. For discussions of task characteristics that tap and promote intrinsic interest, see Thomas W. Malone and Mark R. Lepper, "Making Learning Fun," and Raymond J. Wlodkowski and Judith H. Jaynes, *Eager to Learn.*

66. Elizabeth G. Cohen, *Designing Groupwork*, p. 69. Cohen emphasizes that the curriculum, besides being interesting, must be structured so that different kinds of abilities are necessary for success. This allows everyone to make a contribution, which in turn reduces the differences in status that students represent in each other's eyes. (See also Cohen, "Continuing to Cooperate.")

67. For example, Spencer Kagan has remarked that his "structural" version of CL "shares with David and Roger Johnson's approach the idea of giving teachers new methods so they can teach whatever they want to teach more successfully. It's curriculum free; the choice of a structure does not involve choice of any particular curriculum or curriculum materials." (Ron Brandt, "On Cooperative Learning," p. 10).

68. Mara Sapon-Shevin, "Cooperative Learning: Liberatory Praxis or Hamburger Helper?"

69. "I'm often depressed, however, to see these methods [Student Teams-Achievement Divisions and Teams-Games-Tournaments] applied to subjects that lend themselves more to discussion and controversy" (Robert E. Slavin, "Here to Stay — Or Gone Tomorrow?" p. 5).

70. Sapon-Shevin and Schniedewind, "Selling Cooperative Learning Without Selling It Short." Also see Eric Schaps and Catherine Lewis, "Extrinsic Rewards Are Education's Past, Not Its Future."

71. For one of many criticisms, see D. Monty Neill and Noe J. Medina, "Standardized Testing: Harmful to Educational Health." For reactions to the prospect of expanding such tests, see Susan Chira, "Prominent Educators Oppose National Tests." Some criticize these exams for various methodological flaws that limit their usefulness at doing even what they claim to do. I am more concerned with their inherent limits, the misconceived purposes for which they were designed. The only legitimate reason to evaluate students, I would argue, is to help them learn more effectively. Tests that sort children like so many potatoes — or that are intended to serve as extrinsic motivators for studying (or teaching) — ultimately interfere with a meaningful education.

72. See my book *The Brighter Side of Human Nature* and some of the more than 600 sources cited therein.

73. For that matter, the project also places special emphasis on the quality

of the curriculum and on giving students more control over their learning — all of which have moved the project's designers away from relying on punishments or rewards. For details, see the sources listed in note 53 above.

74. See my article "Caring Kids: The Role of the Schools."

75. Sapon-Shevin and Schniedewind, "Selling Cooperative Learning Without Selling It Short," p. 64.

76. Nan and Ted Graves, "Sue Smith: The Child Development Project in Action," p. 12.

77. Steven A. Gelb, "On Being Cooperative in Noncooperative Places," pp. 1–2. For a useful guide to implementing college-level CL, see David W. Johnson et al., *Active Learning*.

78. Daniel Solomon et al., "Creating a Caring Community," pp. 13, 29.

79. See Paul Cobb et al., "Assessment of a Problem-Centered Second-Grade Mathematics Project"; and Erna Yackel et al., "Small-Group Interactions as a Source of Learning Opportunities in Second-Grade Mathematics." (The quotation is from the latter article, p. 394). Children in the project classroom were also less motivated to be superior to their peers — further corroboration of the argument that excellence and competition tend to pull in opposite directions. In third grade, project students were plunged back into the conventional textbook-based approach to learning math. Nevertheless, those who had spent the preceding year in constructivist, cooperative classrooms continued to score higher than the others on conceptually challenging tasks (Paul Cobb et al., "A Follow-Up Assessment of a Second-Grade Problem-Centered Mathematics Project").

80. Most of the opposition to CL comes from individuals put off by the very idea of teaching children to cooperate. One academic psychologist told a reporter that cooperative learning should be opposed because it "goes against the American grain. . . . Education should prepare kids for life in a particular culture. In reality the name of the game is dog eat dog." (Barbara Foorman quoted in William J. Warren, "New Movement Seeks to Replace Rivalry in Class With Team Spirit.") The closest thing to organized opposition comes from advocates for special programs for "gifted" children, who bolster what they see as their underdog status by wildly overstating the popularity of CL. "In the [current] climate, marshalling an argument against cooperative learning is an unpopular, if not risky position" is how one writer prefaces her attack (Ann Robinson, "Cooperation or Exploitation?" p. 9).

81. See, for example, Samuel Totten et al., *Cooperative Learning: A Guide to Research*, and the September 1990 issue of *Cooperative Learning* magazine. The March 1987 issue of the IASCE newsletter (precursor to the magazine) is devoted to the academic roots of CL, with articles on the work of Lewin, Deutsch, Dewey, and others.

82. Scott Willis, "Coop. Learning Shows Staying Power," p. 1. The article appeared on the front page of the newsletter of the Association for Supervision and Curriculum Development.

83. Considerable research has demonstrated the academic and psychologi-

cal peril in this widespread practice. Ability grouping does not respond to differences in what children can learn so much as it *creates* differences in what they *will* learn. (The indispensable source on this topic is Jeannie Oakes's *Keeping Track*. For a summary of other empirical research, see my book *You Know What They Say . . .*, pp. 163–66, 223.) The sensible response to tracking, however, is not simply to dump students of widely varying achievement levels into one classroom but to provide the opportunity for them to engage in structured heterogeneous interaction.

84. AAAS report excerpt quoted in Susan F. Wooley et al., "BSCS Cooperative Learning and Science Program," p. 32.

85. "Small groups provide a forum for asking questions, discussing ideas, making mistakes, learning to listen to others' ideas, offering constructive criticism, and summarizing discoveries in writing" (National Council of Teachers of Mathematics, *Curriculum and Evaluation Standards for School Mathematics*, p. 87).

86. See Elizabeth Culotta, "The Calculus of Education Reform." In a cooperative and conceptual approach to teaching calculus to students at Duke University and elsewhere, "much of their grade depends on co-authored written reports," which means that "students have to collaborate during lab and outside class. And so they befriend each other" (p. 1061).

87. The recommendation quoted here is taken from a pamphlet entitled "The English Coalition Conference: Assumptions, Aims, and Recommendations of the Secondary Strand," distributed by the NCTE. The 1988 anthology, *Focus on Collaborative Learning*, was edited by Jeff Golub and the National Council of Teachers of English Committee on Classroom Practices.

88. Helen Cowie and Jean Rudduck, "Learning from One Another," p. 236.

89. For a sense of what is involved in helping teachers to become skilled in CL, see Susan S. Ellis, "Introducing Cooperative Learning," and the entire Winter 1991/1992 issue of *Cooperative Learning* magazine.

90. Ron Brandt, "On Cooperation in Schools: A Conversation with David and Roger Johnson," p. 15. For more on the subject, see the Johnsons' book *Leading the Cooperative School*.

91. Mary Male, "Cooperative Learning and Staff Development," p. 4.

92. Yisrael Rich, "Ideological Impediments to Instructional Innovation," p. 83.

93. I am borrowing, in the discussion that follows, from my article "Resistance to Cooperative Learning: Making Sense of Its Deletion and Dilution."

94. Goodlad, *A Place Called School*, pp. 239–42.

95. Rich, "Ideological Impediments to Instructional Innovation," p. 83.

96. Ibid., p. 89.

97. "The teacher in the cooperative classroom context will be more a facilitator than a director of learning. . . . Children make sense of the learning events together, within a mutually constructed experience. The teacher participates in this process, and as appropriate, models

strategies and in other ways provides scaffolding to support children's thinking until they can function independently" (Nastasi and Clements, "Research on Cooperative Learning," p. 126).

98. "Placing more emphasis on students' explanations necessarily requires teachers to relinquish some control over the direction the lesson will take. This can be a frightening prospect to a teacher who is unprepared to evaluate the validity of a novel idea that students inevitably propose" (James W. Stigler and Harold W. Stevenson, "How Asian Teachers Polish Each Lesson to Perfection," p. 44). To the extent that this process of empowering students explains much of the resistance, it may be this, rather than CL per se, that is hard to do. Sharan has argued that successful cooperative learning is no more complex or difficult to bring off well than whole-class instruction; the fact that whole-class instruction is used widely does not mean it is being done well (see Sharan, "Cooperative Learning: New Horizons, Old Threats," p. 5).

99. Sharan, "Cooperative Learning: New Horizons, Old Threats," p. 5. Likewise, a British educator writes: "Unless we are prepared to recognize that what's involved here are radical changes in our expectations of pupils, our own role in the classroom, and our method of classroom management, small group work is likely to remain just another teaching technique, rather than, as it could be, a road toward new patterns of thinking and feeling for the pupils, or new ways for them to make sense of their world" (Alan Howe, "A Climate for Small Group Talk," pp. 115–16).

100. Sören Kierkegaard, *Concluding Unscientific Postscript*, pp. 165–66.

101. Yackel et al., "Small Group Interactions as a Source of Learning Opportunities in Second-Grade Mathematics," p. 396.

102. Eric Schaps, "Cooperative Learning: The Challenge in the '90s," p. 8. Schaps describes his growing sense that something may be wrong even in smoothly functioning cooperative classrooms where children are "on task" and interacting with each other. "They aren't as careful, as serious, as probing as one would like. They are too casual and quick, and too accommodating, about deciding on their answers. And in the processing afterwards, they tend day after day to give the same, short, almost 'canned' answers: 'We shared and helped each other, and everyone got along.'" Many teachers, he continues, "seem satisfied with easy or predictable answers. Their questions do not often probe or challenge; their comments are often routine and formulaic." If teachers and students were really exploring ideas wholeheartedly, there would be "more conflict, more frustration" (p. 8).

103. For example, see Nancy Schniedewind and Ellen Davidson, *Cooperative Learning, Cooperative Lives*, and Ebba Hierta, *Building Cooperative Societies*.

AFTERWORD

1. See Lonnie Wheeler, "No-Cut Policy Prompts a Lot to Cheer About," and Michael Ryan, "Here, Everybody Gets to Play." Of course, opening

the cheerleading squad to all who are interested does not change what they are cheering about, namely, competitive triumph, but progress comes one step at a time.

2. See Joanne Kaufman, "Here She Is, Ms. Tiny Miss!" A full-page *New York Times* advertisement (on 20 September 1988) for the magazine in which this article appeared carried the banner headline: "You're never too young to learn that winning isn't everything. It's the only thing."

3. See Gary Putka, "Knowing Pi Now Could Mean a Shot at a Varsity Letter."

4. Walter Bonime, "Competitiveness and Human Potential."

5. Dale Miller, "Creative Art vs. Competitions."

6. James R. Austin, "Competition: Is Music Education the Loser?"

7. Dewitt Jones, "No Contest!"

8. *Teen Magazine*, "Compete, Don't Retreat!" The correct answers are those indicating a preference for being graded on a curve (because "it tends to motivate you to stand out from the crowd"), trying to outmaneuver friends for jobs and boyfriends, and so on. Readers who don't consistently pick these responses are chided for letting their "sense of team spirit slow [them] down."

9. Associated Press, "Students Blame Stress Problems on Competition." Also see Haibin Jiu, "Science Contest Pressures Kids Too Much," which describes the effects of intense stress brought on by the Westinghouse science competition.

10. Reuters, "Fight at Exit May Have Slowed Escape from Jet." Thirty-four people ultimately died in the crash, which took place in early 1991. A few months earlier, eight people died in another crash, this one in Detroit. The National Transportation Safety Board blamed that accident on a "lack of proper crew coordination" in the cockpit and suggested training sessions to help crews cooperate effectively (Lawrence Knutson, "Cockpit Confusion Cited as Cause of Detroit Crash"). Robert Helmreich and Dean Tjosvold, both of whose work is cited elsewhere in this book, have independently conducted research on airplane crew coordination over the last few years.

11. "Human nature being what it is," one article in *Working Woman* asserted, "experts warn against baring your soul to someone who is going after the same goals" (Holloway McCandless, "Taking the Edge Off Competition"). The psychological costs of perpetual wariness and concealment of one's emotions are conspicuously ignored here. Likewise, the possibility that a competitive work environment, rather than "human nature," could be at fault — and might be changed — is never considered.

12. John T. Lanzetta and Basil G. Englis, "Expectations of Cooperation and Competition and Their Effects on Observers' Vicarious Emotional Responses."

13. David A. Wilder and Peter N. Shapiro, "Role of Competition-Induced Anxiety in Limiting the Beneficial Impact of Positive Behavior by an Out-Group Member." In this experiment, subjects were told that they would work on projects in small groups and that their work would be evaluated by members of another group. Some subjects were told that

the other group was cooperating with them; others, that it was competing. When asked to describe one member of the other group (who had made mostly positive comments about their own group's efforts), those who thought they were competing responded more negatively to that person and were also somewhat more likely to see that person as similar to the other members of that group.

14. Kenny Hill quoted in Frank Litsky, "Aggression Necessary, Hill Says," p. D30.

15. William Zimmerman, "On Negative Ads." That was in 1986. Six years later, Susan Estrich, who had been Michael Dukakis's campaign manager, delivered an even more rousing endorsement of dirty campaigns. "You can't really blame the candidates. . . . They're doing what works" ("Let the Mud Fly").

16. Gary Edwards quoted in Paul Wilkes, "The Tough Job of Teaching Ethics," p. 24F.

17. Sheila Widnall quoted in Fox Butterfield, "Scandal Over Cheating at M.I.T. Stirs Debate on Limits of Teamwork."

18. See my brief essay on this topic, "Competition vs. Excellence."

19. Richard A. Knox, " 'Free-choice' Rhetoric Isn't the Answer."

20. James C. Robinson and Harold S. Luft, "Competition and the Cost of Hospital Care, 1972 to 1982." Their study of nearly 6,000 hospitals found that these institutions competed for patients (and doctors) by providing fancy amenities rather than by lowering their rates. A hospital admission was 26 percent more expensive (and the average patient cost per day was 15 percent higher) in hospitals located within fifteen miles of more than ten competitors. Another result of competition, the researchers suggested, is a lower patient load and therefore, in the long run, less expertise-building experience for the clinical staff. Competition in this field, therefore, may actually provide lower-quality care at higher cost for fewer people who really need it.

21. In the last few years, deregulation has bankrupted several more airlines, throwing tens or even hundreds of thousands of employees out of work, increasing the market share of the three or four remaining giants, reducing the quality of service, and raising prices on most routes. (The Department of Transportation claims that airfares, adjusted for inflation, actually have declined since the industry was deregulated in the late 1970s. But a 1990 study by the Economic Policy Institute pointed out that this change was due to a drop in the price of jet fuel. When this variable, obviously unrelated to competition, is held constant, prices increased through the 1980s.) Furthermore, airlines are free to sell their excess takeoff and landing slots at airports, but some refuse to do so, effectively reducing the number of flights available to the public just so rival carriers will not benefit. (See Bob Kuttner, "Air Fares That Reach to the Sky.") Such is the logic of competition.

22. Dean Tjosvold, *Working Together to Get Things Done*, pp. 29, 70. Tjosvold's studies appear with remarkable frequency in journals of psychology, management, and organizational studies.

23. The task was a video game with a joystick that could be performed

either individually or at cross-purposes with another player. In the latter condition, speed went up and accuracy went down. See David A. Washburn et al., "Effects of Competition on Video-Task Performance in Monkeys."

24. Deming's comments are included in an introduction to his work on videotape, a series called "The Deming Library." See volume 18, "Competition Doesn't Work, Cooperation Does."

25. For a description of the parallel deprivation of substantive opportunities for workers in the United States and the USSR to participate in making decisions, see Thomas H. Naylor, "Redefining Corporate Motivation, Swedish Style," pp. 566, 568.

26. See, for example, David Warsh, "A Financial World in Dark Until It Finds Bottom Line."

27. For welcome exceptions to this rule, see Samuel Bowles, "Economic Justice — For Us and Them," and David M. Gordon, "Do We Need to Be No. 1?" Another economist, Bob Kuttner, framed the issue well: "The need is to restore American productivity, but not at other nations' expense. . . . [We must put] the world back on a high-growth path where every economy can prosper" ("A Time for Shared Trade Growth"). This is easier said than done, of course, but first we must convince our leaders that it is a goal worth saying.

28. Teresa M. Amabile, "The Motivation to Be Creative," pp. 242–43.

29. Robert J. Vallerand et al., "Negative Effects of Competition on Children's Intrinsic Motivation."

30. Edward L. Deci and Richard M. Ryan, *Intrinsic Motivation and Self-Determination in Human Behavior,* p. 85.

31. Joan L. Duda, "The Relationship Between Goal Perspectives, Persistence, and Behavioral Intensity Among Male and Female Recreational Sport Participants." Indeed, teenagers are dropping out of organized sports in sizable numbers — partly because of the pressure to win — as is confirmed by the work of Martha Ewing and Vern Seefeldt at the Youth Sports Institute of Michigan State University.

32. UCLA Sport Psychology Laboratory, "Playing On," p. 39.

33. Deci and Ryan, *Intrinsic Motivation,* p. 325.

34. Bil Gilbert, "Competition: Is It What Life's All About?"

35. Laura Fraser, "Super Bowl Violence Comes Home."

REFERENCES

===============================◁▷===============================

Ackerman, Nathan W. *The Psychodynamics of Family Life.* New York: Basic Books, 1958.

Adams, John C., Jr. "Effects of Competition and Open Receptivity on Creative Productivity." *Catalogue of Selected Documents in Psychology* 3 (1973): 16–17.

Adorno, T. W., Else Frenkel-Brunswik, Daniel J. Levinson, and R. Nevitt Sanford. *The Authoritarian Personality.* New York: Harper, 1950.

Agnew, Spiro. "In Defense of Sport." In *Sport and Contemporary Society: An Anthology,* edited by D. Stanley Eitzen. New York: St. Martin's, 1979.

Ahlgren, Andrew, and David W. Johnson. "Sex Differences in Cooperative and Competitive Attitudes from the Second Through the Twelfth Grades." *Developmental Psychology* 15 (1979): 45–49.

Allee, W. C. *Cooperation Among Animals.* New York: Henry Schuman, 1951.

Allport, Gordon W. *Becoming: Basic Considerations for a Psychology of Personality.* New Haven: Yale University Press, 1955.

Amabile, Teresa M. "Children's Artistic Creativity: Detrimental Effects of Competition in a Field Setting." *Personality and Social Psychology Bulletin* 8 (1982): 573–78.

———. "The Motivation to Be Creative." In *Frontiers in Creativity,* edited by S. Isaksen. Buffalo, N.Y.: Bearly, 1987.

Amabile, Teresa M., and Judith Gitomer. "Children's Artistic Creativity: Effects of Choice in Task Materials." *Personality and Social Psychology Bulletin* 10 (1984): 209–15.

Ames, Carole. "Children's Achievement Attributions and Self-reinforcement: Effects of Self-concept and Competitive Reward Structure." *Journal of Educational Psychology* 70 (1978): 345–55.

———. "Competitive Versus Cooperative Reward Structures: The Influence of Individual and Group Performance Factors on Achievement Attributions and Affect." *American Educational Research Journal* 18 (1981): 273–87.

———. "An Examination of Children's Attributions and Achievement-Related Evaluations in Competitive, Cooperative, and Individualistic Reward Structures." *Journal of Educational Psychology* 71 (1979): 413–20.

Ames, Carole, and Russell Ames. "Competitive Versus Individualistic Goal Structures: The Salience of Past Performance Information for Causal Attributions and Affect." *Journal of Educational Psychology* 73 (1981): 411–18.

Archer, Dane, and Rosemary Gartner. "Violent Acts and Violent Times: A Comparative Approach to Postwar Homicide Rates." *American Sociological Review* 41 (1976): 937–63.

Aronson, Elliot. *The Social Animal.* 2d ed. San Francisco: W. H. Freeman, 1976.

Associated Press. "Students Blame Stress Problems on Competition." *Boston Globe,* 19 November 1987: 41.

Atkinson, John W. *An Introduction to Motivation.* Princeton, N.J.: Van Nostrand, 1964.

————. "The Mainsprings of Achievement-Oriented Activity." In *Motivation and Achievement,* edited by John W. Atkinson and Joel O. Raynor. New York: John Wiley and Sons, 1974.

Augros, Robert, and George Stanciu. *The New Biology: Discovering the Wisdom in Nature.* Boston: New Science Library, 1988.

Austin, James R. "Competition: Is Music Education the Loser?" *Music Educators Journal,* February 1990: 21–25.

Axelrod, Robert. *The Evolution of Cooperation.* New York: Basic, 1984.

Azrin, Nathan H., and Ogden R. Lindsley. "The Reinforcement of Cooperation Between Children." *Journal of Abnormal and Social Psychology* 52 (1956): 100–102.

Bachrach, Judy. "Rivalry in the Sisterhood." *Boston Globe,* 18 January 1984: 57–58.

Bandura, Albert. *Social Learning Theory.* Englewood Cliffs, N.J.: Prentice-Hall, 1977.

Barber, Benjamin. *Strong Democracy: Participatory Politics for a New Age.* Berkeley and Los Angeles: University of California Press, 1984.

Barnes, Hazel. *An Existentialist Ethics.* Chicago: University of Chicago Press, 1967.

Barnett, Mark A., and James H. Bryan. "Effects of Competition with Outcome Feedback on Children's Helping Behavior." *Developmental Psychology* 10 (1974): 838–42.

Barnett, Mark A., Karen A. Matthews, and Jeffrey A. Howard. "Relationship Between Competitiveness and Empathy in 6- and 7-Year-Olds." *Developmental Psychology* 15 (1979): 221–22.

Bateson, Gregory, Don D. Jackson, Jay Haley, and John Weakland. "Toward a Theory of Schizophrenia." *Behavioral Science* 1 (1956): 251–64.

Bateson, Patrick. "Cooperation and Competition." *World Press Review,* August 1984: 55.

Battaglia, Carl. "Piano Competitions: Talent Hunt or Sport?" *Saturday Review,* 25 August 1962: 31–33, 39.

Baum, Julian. "Friendship No Longer Ranks Ahead of Winning for Chinese Olympians." *Christian Science Monitor,* 26 July 1984: 1.

Baumeister, Roy F. "Choking Under Pressure: Self-Consciousness and Paradoxical Effects of Incentives on Skillful Performance." *Journal of Personality and Social Psychology* 46 (1984): 610–20.

Beane, James A. "Sorting Out the Self-Esteem Controversy." *Educational Leadership,* September 1991: 25–30.

Beisser, Arnold R. *The Madness in Sports: Psychosocial Observations on Sports.* New York: Appleton, 1967.

Belkin, Lisa. "Young Albany Debaters Resolve Who's Best." *New York Times,* 29 April 1985: A1, B4.

Bellah, Robert N., Richard Madsen, William M. Sullivan, Ann Swidler, and Steven M. Tipton. *The Good Society.* New York: Knopf, 1991.

―――. *Habits of the Heart: Individualism and Commitment in American Life.* Berkeley and Los Angeles: University of California Press, 1985.

Benedict, Ruth. *The Chrysanthemum and the Sword: Patterns of Japanese Culture.* 1946. Reprint. New York: New American Library, 1974.

Bennett, William J. "In Defense of Sports." *Commentary,* February 1976: 68–70.

Benware, Carl A., and Edward L. Deci. "Quality of Learning with an Active Versus Passive Motivational Set." *American Educational Research Journal* 21 (1984): 755–65.

Berger, Peter L. *The Sacred Canopy: Elements of a Sociological Theory of Religion.* Garden City, N.Y.: Anchor Books, 1969.

Berger, Peter L., and Brigitte Berger. *Sociology: A Biographical Approach.* 2d ed. New York: Basic, 1975.

Berkowitz, Leonard. *Aggression: A Social Psychological Analysis.* New York: McGraw-Hill, 1962.

―――. "Experimental Investigations of Hostility Catharsis." *Journal of Consulting and Clinical Psychology* 35 (1970): 1–7.

Berlage, Gai Ingham. "Are Children's Competitive Team Sports Socializing Agents for Corporate America?" In *Studies in the Sociology of Sport,* edited by Aidan O. Dunleavy et al. Ft. Worth, Tex.: Texas Christian University Press, 1982.

Bettelheim, Bruno. *The Uses of Enchantment: The Meaning and Importance of Fairy Tales.* New York: Vintage, 1977.

―――. "Violence: A Neglected Mode of Behavior." 1966. Reprinted in *Surviving and Other Essays.* New York: Knopf, 1979.

Birch, Leann Lipps, Diane Wolfe Marlin, and Julie Rotter. "Eating as the 'Means' Activity in a Contingency: Effects on Young Children's Food Preference." *Child Development* 55 (1984): 431–39.

Blau, Peter. "Cooperation and Competition in a Bureaucracy." *American Journal of Sociology* 59 (1954): 530–35.

Block, Jeanne Humphrey. "Conceptions of Sex Role: Some Cross-Cultural and Longitudinal Perspectives." *American Psychologist* 28 (1973): 512–26.

Blotnick, Srully. *Otherwise Engaged: The Private Lives of Successful Career Women.* New York: Facts on File, 1985.

Boffey, Philip M. "Rise in Science Fraud Is Seen; Need to Win Cited as a Cause." *New York Times,* 30 May 1985: B5.

Bok, Sissela. *Lying: Moral Choice in Public and Private Life.* New York: Vintage, 1979.

Bonime, Walter. "Competitiveness and Human Potential." *Journal of the American Academy of Psychoanalysis* 14 (1986): 149–66.

Boslooper, Thomas, and Marcia Hayes. *The Femininity Game.* New York: Stein and Day, 1973.

Bowles, Samuel. "Economic Justice — For Us and Them." *Harper's Magazine,* December 1988: 29–32.

Branden, Nathaniel. *The Psychology of Self-Esteem.* New York: Bantam, 1971.

Brandt, Ron. "On Cooperation in Schools: A Conversation with David and Roger Johnson." *Educational Leadership,* November 1987: 14–19.

———. "On Cooperative Learning: A Conversation with Spencer Kagan." *Educational Leadership*, December 1989/January 1990: 8–11.

Bredemeier, Brenda Jo, and David L. Shields. "Values and Violence in Sports Today." *Psychology Today*, October 1985: 23–32.

Breer, Paul E., and Edwin C. Locke. *Task Experience as a Source of Attitudes.* New York: Dorsey Press, 1965.

Brody, Jane E. "Heart Attacks: Turmoil Beneath the Calm." *New York Times,* 21 June 1983: C5.

Brownmiller, Susan. *Femininity.* New York: Simon and Schuster, 1984.

Brubacher, Mark, Ryder Payne, and Kemp Rickett. *Perspectives on Small Group Learning: Theory and Practice.* Oakville, Ontario: Rubicon Publishing, 1990.

Bryan, James H. "Prosocial Behavior." In *Psychological Processes in Early Education,* edited by Harry L. Hom, Jr., and Paul A. Robinson. New York: Academic Press, 1977.

Bryant, Brenda K. "The Effects of the Interpersonal Context of Evaluation on Self- and Other-Enhancement Behavior." *Child Development* 48 (1977): 885–92.

Buber, Martin. *The Knowledge of Man: A Philosophy of the Interhuman.* New York: Harper Torchbooks, 1966.

Butt, Dorcas Susan. *Psychology of Sport: The Behavior, Motivation, Personality, and Performance of Athletes.* New York: Van Nostrand Reinhold, 1976.

Butterfield, Fox. "Scandal Over Cheating at M.I.T. Stirs Debate on Limits of Teamwork." *New York Times,* 22 May 1991: A23.

Caillois, Roger. *Man, Play, and Games.* Translated by Meyer Barash. New York: Free Press, 1961.

Campbell, David N. "On Being Number One: Competition in Education." *Phi Delta Kappan,* October 1974: 143–46.

Caplow, Theodore. *Principles of Organization.* New York: Harcourt, Brace & World, 1964.

Carroll, Lewis. *Alice's Adventures in Wonderland.* New York: New American Library, 1960.

Chira, Susan. "Prominent Educators Oppose National Tests." *New York Times,* 29 January 1992: B9.

Chodorow, Nancy. *The Reproduction of Mothering: Psychoanalysis and the Sociology of Gender.* Berkeley and Los Angeles: University of California Press, 1978.

Christy, Pauline R., Donna M. Gelfand, and Donald P. Hartmann. "Effects of Competition-Induced Frustration on Two Classes of Modeled Behavior." *Developmental Psychology* 5 (1971): 104–11.

Clarke, Judy. "The Hidden Treasure of Co-operative Learning." *Cooperative Learning,* October 1991: 2–3.

Clarke, Judy, Ron Wideman, and Susan Eadie. *Together We Learn.* Scarborough, Ontario: Prentice-Hall Canada, 1990.

Clifford, Margaret M. "Effect of Competition as a Motivational Technique in the Classroom." *American Educational Research Journal* 9 (1972): 123–37.

Cobb, Paul, Terry Wood, Erna Yackel, John Nicholls, Grayson Wheatley, Beatriz Trigatti, and Marcella Perlwitz. "Assessment of a Problem-

Centered Second-Grade Mathematics Project." *Journal for Research in Mathematics Education* 22 (1991): 3–29.

Cobb, Paul, Terry Wood, Erna Yackel, and Marcella Perlwitz. "A Follow-Up Assessment of a Second-Grade Problem Centered Mathematics Project." *Educational Studies in Mathematics.* In press.

Cohen, Elizabeth G. "Continuing to Cooperate: Prerequisites for Persistence." *Phi Delta Kappan,* October 1990: 134–38.

———. *Designing Groupwork: Strategies for the Heterogeneous Classroom.* New York: Teachers College Press, 1986.

Cohen, Joshua, and Joel Rogers. *On Democracy: Toward a Transformation of American Society.* New York: Penguin, 1983.

Coleman, James S. "Academic Achievement and the Structure of Competition." *Harvard Educational Review* 29 (1959): 330–51.

———. *The Adolescent Society.* New York: Free Press of Glencoe, 1961.

Combs, Arthur W. "The Myth of Competition." *Childhood Education* 33 (1957): 264–69.

———. *Myths in Education.* Boston: Allyn and Bacon, 1979.

Cowie, Helen, and Jean Rudduck. "Learning from One Another: The Challenge." In *Children Helping Children,* edited by Hugh C. Foot, Michelle J. Morgan, and Rosalyn H. Shute. Chichester, England: John Wiley and Sons, 1990.

Cratty, Bryant J. *Social Psychology in Athletics.* Englewood Cliffs, N.J.: Prentice-Hall, 1981.

Crockenberg, Susan B., Brenda K. Bryant, and Lee S. Wilce. "The Effects of Cooperatively and Competitively Structured Learning Environments on Inter- and Intrapersonal Behavior." *Child Development* 47 (1976): 386–96.

Crutchfield, Will. "The Ills of Piano Competitions." *New York Times,* 16 May 1985: C25.

Csikszentmihalyi, Mihaly. *Beyond Boredom and Anxiety: The Experience of Play in Work and Games.* San Francisco: Jossey-Bass, 1975a.

———. "Play and Intrinsic Rewards." *Journal of Humanistic Psychology* 15 (1975b): 41–63.

Culbertson, John M. *Competition, Constructive and Destructive.* Madison, Wis.: Twenty-first Century Press, 1985.

Culotta, Elizabeth. "The Calculus of Education Reform." *Science* 255 (1992): 1060–62.

Cummings, William K. *Education and Equality in Japan.* Princeton, N.J.: Princeton University Press, 1980.

Currie, Elliott. *Confronting Crime: An American Challenge.* New York: Pantheon, 1985.

Darwin, Charles. *The Origin of Species.* London: John Murray, 1859.

Davidson, Henry A. "Competition, the Cradle of Anxiety." *Education* 76 (1955): 162–66.

Dawes, Robyn M., Jeanne McTavish, and Harriet Shaklee. "Behavior, Communication, and Assumptions About Other People's Behavior in a Commons Dilemma Situation." *Journal of Personality and Social Psychology* 35 (1977): 1–11.

Dawkins, Richard. *The Selfish Gene.* New York: Oxford University Press, 1976.

Deci, Edward L. "Effects of Externally Mediated Rewards on Intrinsic Motivation." *Journal of Personality and Social Psychology* 18 (1971): 105–15.

———. "Intrinsic Motivation, Extrinsic Reinforcement, and Inequity." *Journal of Personality and Social Psychology* 22 (1972): 113–20.

Deci, Edward L., Gregory Betley, James Kahle, Linda Abrams, and Joseph Porac. "When Trying to Win: Competition and Intrinsic Motivation." *Personality and Social Psychology Bulletin* 7 (1981): 79–83.

Deci, Edward L., and Richard M. Ryan. *Intrinsic Motivation and Self-Determination in Human Behavior.* New York: Plenum, 1985.

Derber, Charles. *The Pursuit of Attention: Power and Individualism in Everyday Life.* New York: Oxford University Press, 1983.

Deutsch, Morton. "A Critical Review of 'Equity Theory': An Alternative Perspective on the Social Psychology of Justice." *International Journal of Group Tensions* 9 (1979a): 20–49.

———. *Distributive Justice: A Social-Psychological Perspective.* New Haven: Yale University Press, 1985.

———. "Education and Distributive Justice: Some Reflections on Grading Systems." *American Psychologist* 34 (1979b): 391–401.

———. *The Resolution of Conflict: Constructive and Destructive Processes.* New Haven: Yale University Press, 1973.

Deutsch, Morton, and Robert M. Krauss. "The Effect of Threat Upon Interpersonal Bargaining." *Journal of Abnormal and Social Psychology* 61 (1960): 181–89.

DeVoe, Marianne W. "Cooperation as a Function of Self-Concept, Sex and Race." *Educational Research Quarterly* 2 (1977): 3–8.

Diamant, Anita. "The Women's Sports Revolution: Change for the Better? Or Only for the Best?" *The Real Paper,* 24 March 1979: 20–21, 24–25.

Directory of Intentional Communities: A Guide to Cooperative Living. 2d ed. Evansville, Ind.: Fellowship for Intentional Community, 1991.

Dishon, Dee, and Pat Wilson O'Leary. "Tips for Heterogeneous Group Selection." *Cooperative Learning,* October 1991: 42–43.

Doig, Stephen. "Ecology May Never Be the Same After Daniel Simberloff." *Science Digest,* June 1984: 17.

Doise, Willem. "The Development of Individual Competencies through Social Interaction." In *Children Helping Children,* edited by Hugh C. Foot, Michelle J. Morgan, and Rosalyn H. Shute. Chichester, England: John Wiley and Sons, 1990.

Dollard, John, Neal E. Miller, Leonard W. Doob, O. H. Mowrer, and Robert R. Sears. *Frustration and Aggression.* New Haven: Yale University Press, 1939.

Dostoevsky, Fyodor. *The Brothers Karamazov.* Translated by Constance Garnett. Revised and edited by Ralph E. Matlaw. New York: Norton, 1976.

Duda, Joan L. "The Relationship Between Goal Perspectives, Persistence, and Behavioral Intensity Among Male and Female Recreational Sport Participants." *Leisure Sciences* 10 (1988): 95–106.

Dunn, Robert E., and Morton Goldman. "Competition and Noncompetition in Relationship to Satisfaction and Feelings Toward Own-group and Nongroup Members." *Journal of Social Psychology* 68 (1966): 229–311.

Edwards, Harry. *Sociology of Sport.* Homewood, Ill.: Dorsey Press, 1973.
Eggerman, Richard W. "Competition as a Mixed Good." *The Humanist,* July/
    August 1982: 48–51.
Eichenbaum, Luise, and Susie Orbach. *Understanding Women: A Feminist Psy-
    choanalytic Approach.* New York: Basic, 1983.
Eifermann, Rivka R. "Social Play in Childhood." In *Child's Play,* edited by
    R. E. Herron and Brian Sutton-Smith. New York: John Wiley and
    Sons, 1971.
Eitzen, D. Stanley, ed. *Sport and Contemporary Society: An Anthology.* New York:
    St. Martin's, 1979.
Elleson, Vera J. "Competition: A Cultural Imperative." *The Personnel and
    Guidance Journal,* December 1983: 195–98.
Ellis, M. J. *Why People Play.* Englewood Cliffs, N.J.: Prentice-Hall, 1973.
Ellis, Susan S. "Introducing Cooperative Learning." *Educational Leadership,*
    December 1989/January 1990: 34–37.
Estrich, Susan. "Let the Mud Fly." *New York Times,* 20 March 1992: A33.
Etzioni, Amitai. "After Watergate — What?: A Social Science Perspective."
    Human Behavior, November 1973: 7–9.
Evans, Richard I. "A Conversation with Konrad Lorenz." *Psychology Today,*
    November 1974: 82–93.

Faber, Adele, and Elaine Mazlish. *Siblings Without Rivalry.* New York: Norton,
    1987.
Farber, Leslie H. "Merchandising Depression." *Psychology Today,* April 1979:
    63–64.
Festinger, Leon. "A Theory of Social Comparison Processes." *Human Rela-
    tions* 7 (1954): 117–40.
Fishman, Pamela. "Interaction: The Work Women Do." *Social Problems* 25
    (1978): 397–406.
Fiske, Edward B. "Japan's Schools Stress Group and Discourage Individual-
    ity." *New York Times,* 11 July 1983: A1, A6.
Fleming, Anne Taylor. "Women and the Spoils of Success." *New York Times
    Magazine,* 2 August 1981: 30–31.
Flew, Anthony. "From Is to Ought." In *The Sociobiology Debate,* edited by
    Arthur L. Caplan. New York: Harper & Row, 1978.
Foot, Hugh C., Rosalyn H. Shute, Michelle J. Morgan, and Anne-Marie Bar-
    ron. "Theoretical Issues in Peer Tutoring." In *Children Helping Children,*
    edited by Hugh C. Foot, Michelle J. Morgan, and Rosalyn H. Shute.
    Chichester, England: John Wiley and Sons, 1990.
Ford, Gerald R. "In Defense of the Competitive Urge." *Sports Illustrated,* 8
    July 1974: 16–23.
Foster, Gerald W., and John E. Penick. "Creativity in a Group Setting." *Jour-
    nal of Research in Science Teaching* 22 (1985): 89–98.
Frank, Lawrence K. "The Cost of Competition." *Plan Age* 6 (1940): 314–24.
Frank, Robert H. *Choosing the Right Pond: Human Behavior and the Quest for
    Status.* New York: Oxford University Press, 1985.
Frankel, Marvin E. *Partisan Justice.* New York: Hill and Wang, 1980.
———. "The Search for Truth: An Umpireal View." *University of Pennsylvania
    Law Review* 123 (1975): 1031–59.

Fraser, Laura. "Super Bowl Violence Comes Home." *Psychology Today,* January 1987: 15.

Freud, Anna. *Normality and Pathology in Childhood: Assessments of Development.* New York: International Universities Press, 1965.

Freud, Sigmund. *Civilization and Its Discontents.* Translated by James Strachey. New York: Norton, 1961.

Friedenberg, Edgar Z. *R. D. Laing.* New York: Viking, 1974.

Fromm, Erich. *Escape from Freedom.* 1941. Reprint. New York: Avon, 1965.

———. *Man for Himself: An Inquiry into the Psychology of Ethics.* 1947. Reprint. Greenwich, Conn.: Fawcett Premier, 1970.

Fultz, Jim, C. Daniel Batson, Victoria A. Furtenbach, Patricia M. McCarthy, and Laurel L. Varney. "Social Evaluation and the Empathy-Altruism Hypothesis." *Journal of Personality and Social Psychology* 50 (1986): 761–69.

Gardner, Howard. *Frames of Mind: The Theory of Multiple Intelligences.* New York: Basic, 1983.

Gaskell, George, and Robert Pearton. "Aggression and Sport." In *Sports, Games, and Play: Social and Psychological Viewpoints,* edited by Jeffrey H. Goldstein. Hillsdale, N.J.: Lawrence Erlbaum Associates, 1979.

Gaylin, Willard. *The Rage Within: Anger in Modern Life.* New York: Simon and Schuster, 1984.

Gelb, Steven A. "On Being Cooperative in Noncooperative Places." Paper presented at the annual meeting of the American Educational Studies Association, Chicago, October 1989.

Gilbert, Bil. "Competition: Is It What Life's All About?" *Sports Illustrated,* 16 May 1988: 86–100.

Gilligan, Carol. *In a Different Voice: Psychological Theory and Women's Development.* Cambridge, Mass.: Harvard University Press, 1982.

Glasser, William. *Schools Without Failure.* New York: Harper & Row, 1969.

Goldman, Irving. "The Bathonga of South Africa." In *Cooperation and Competition Among Primitive Peoples,* edited by Margaret Mead. Boston: Beacon, 1961.

———. "The Zuñi Indians of New Mexico." In *Cooperation and Competition Among Primitive Peoples,* edited by Margaret Mead. Boston: Beacon, 1961.

Goldman, Morton, Joseph W. Stockbauer, and Timothy G. McAuliffe. "Intergroup and Intragroup Competition and Cooperation." *Journal of Experimental Social Psychology* 13 (1977): 81–88.

Goleman, Daniel. "Great Altruists: Science Ponders Soul of Goodness." *New York Times,* 5 March 1985: C1–2.

Gonzales, Lawrence. "Airline Safety: A Special Report." *Playboy,* July 1980: 140–42, 148, 150, 205–22.

Good, Thomas L., Barbara J. Reys, Douglas A. Grouws, and Catherine M. Mulryan. "Using Work-Groups in Mathematics Instruction." *Educational Leadership,* December 1989/January 1990: 56–62.

Goodlad, John I. *A Place Called School: Prospects for the Future.* New York: McGraw-Hill, 1984.

Gordon, David M. "Do We Need to Be No. 1?" *The Atlantic,* April 1986: 100–108.

Gorney, Roderic. "Cultural Determinants of Achievement, Aggression, and Psychological Distress." *Archives of General Psychiatry* 37 (1980): 452–59.

———. *The Human Agenda.* New York: Simon and Schuster, 1972.

Gould, Stephen Jay. "Biological Potential vs. Biological Determinism." In *The Sociobiology Debate,* edited by Arthur L. Caplan. New York: Harper & Row, 1978.

———. "The Nonscience of Human Nature." In *Ever Since Darwin: Reflections in Natural History.* New York: Norton, 1977.

Graves, Nancy B., and Theodore D. Graves. "Creating a Cooperative Learning Environment: An Ecological Approach." In *Learning to Cooperate, Cooperating to Learn,* edited by Robert Slavin et al. New York: Plenum, 1985.

———. "Should We Teach Cooperative Skills as a Part of Each Cooperative Lesson?" *Cooperative Learning,* October 1989: 19–20.

———. "Sue Smith: The Child Development Project in Action." *Cooperative Learning,* March 1990: 10–14.

Green, Joan, and John Myers. "Conversations: Observations on the Implementation of Interactive Learning." In *Perspectives on Small Group Learning: Theory and Practice,* edited by Mark Brubacher, Ryder Payne, and Kemp Rickett. Oakville, Ontario: Rubicon Publishing, 1990.

Green, Mark, and John F. Berry. "Corporate Crime II." *The Nation,* 15 June 1985: 731–34.

Gross, Jane. "Against the Odds: A Woman's Ascent on Wall Street." *New York Times Magazine,* 6 January 1985: 16–27, 55, 60, 68.

Grossack, Martin M. "Some Effects of Cooperation and Competition Upon Small Group Behavior." *Journal of Abnormal and Social Psychology* 49 (1954): 341–48.

Haines, Donald Bruce, and W. J. McKeachie. "Cooperative Versus Competitive Discussion Methods in Teaching Introductory Psychology." *Journal of Educational Psychology* 58 (1967): 386–90.

Haley, Jay. "The Art of Being a Failure as a Therapist." In *The Power Tactics of Jesus Christ and Other Essays.* New York: Avon, 1969.

Halliwell, Wayne. "Instrinsic Motivation in Sport." In *Sport Psychology: An Analysis of Athlete Behavior,* edited by William F. Straub. Ithaca, N.Y.: Movement Publications, 1978.

Hardin, Garrett. *Promethean Ethics: Living with Death, Competition, and Triage.* Seattle: University of Washington Press, 1980.

———. "The Tragedy of the Commons." *Science,* 13 December 1968: 1243–48.

Harragan, Betty Lehan. *Games Mother Never Taught You: Corporate Gamesmanship for Women.* New York: Warner, 1978.

Harrington, Michael. *The New American Poverty.* New York: Holt, Rinehart and Winston, 1984.

Harvey, John, J. St. G. C. Heath, Malcolm Spencer, William Temple, and H. G. Wood. *Competition: A Study in Human Motive.* London: Macmillan and Co., 1917.

Hechinger, Fred. "Experts Call a Child's Play Too Serious to Be Left to Adults." *New York Times,* 21 October 1980: C4.

Heller, Joseph. *Something Happened.* New York: Ballantine, 1975.

Helmreich, Robert L. "Pilot Selection and Training." Paper presented at the annual meeting of the American Psychological Association, Washington, D.C., August 1982.

Helmreich, Robert L., William Beane, G. William Lucker, and Janet T. Spence. "Achievement Motivation and Scientific Attainment." *Personality and Social Psychology Bulletin* 4 (1978): 222–26.

Helmreich, Robert L., Linda L. Sawin, and Alan L. Carsrud. "The Honeymoon Effect in Job Performance: Temporal Increases in the Predictive Power of Achievement Motivation." *Journal of Applied Psychology* 71 (1986): 185–88.

Helmreich, Robert L., Janet T. Spence, William E. Beane, G. William Lucker, and Karen A. Matthews. "Making It in Academic Psychology: Demographic and Personality Correlates of Attainment." *Journal of Personality and Social Psychology* 39 (1980): 896–908.

Hendin, Herbert. *The Age of Sensation: A Psychoanalytic Exploration.* New York: Norton, 1975.

———. *Suicide in America.* New York: Norton, 1983.

Henry, Jules. *Culture Against Man.* New York: Vintage, 1963.

Herman, Ellen. "Toward a Politics of Self-Esteem?" *Z Magazine,* July–August 1991: 42–46.

Hewstone, Miles. *Attribution Theory: Social and Functional Extensions.* Oxford, England: Basil Blackwell, 1983.

Hierta, Ebba. *Building Cooperative Societies: A Curriculum Guide for Grades 6–9 on Social and Economic Cooperation.* Ann Arbor: Michigan Alliance of Cooperatives, 1984.

Hinds, Michael deCourcy. "Private Schools: The First Steps." *New York Times,* 14 November 1984: C1.

Hirsch, Fred. *Social Limits to Growth.* Cambridge, Mass.: Harvard University Press, 1976.

Hoch, Paul. *Rip Off the Big Game: The Exploitation of Sports by the Power Elite.* Garden City, N.Y.: Anchor Books, 1972.

Hoffman, Martin L. "Is Altruism Part of Human Nature?" *Journal of Personality and Social Psychology* 40 (1981): 121–37.

Hofstadter, Douglas R. "Irrationality Is the Square Root of All Evil." 1983. Reprinted in *Metamagical Themas: Questing for the Essence of Mind and Pattern.* New York: Basic, 1985.

Hofstadter, Richard. *Social Darwinism in American Thought.* Revised edition. Boston: Beacon, 1955.

Holland, Bernard. "The Well-Tempered Tenor." *New York Times Magazine,* 30 January 1983: 28–29, 44–45, 51–54.

Holt, John. *How Children Fail.* Revised edition. New York: Delacorte, 1982.

Horn, Jack C. "Fan Violence: Fighting the Injustice of It All." *Psychology Today,* October 1975: 30–31.

Horner, Matina S. "Femininity and Successful Achievement: A Basic Inconsistency." In *Feminine Personality and Conflict,* edited by Judith M. Bardwick et al. Belmont, Calif.: Brooks/Cole, 1970.

———. "The Measurement and Behavioral Implications of Fear of Success in Women." In *Motivation and Achievement,* edited by John W. Atkinson and Joel O. Raynor. Washington, D.C.: V. H. Winston and Sons, 1974a.

———. "Performance of Men in Noncompetitive and Interpersonal Competitive Achievement-Oriented Situations." In *Motivation and Achievement*, edited by John W. Atkinson and Joel O. Raynor. Washington, D.C.: V. H. Winston and Sons, 1974b.

———. "Sex Differences in Achievement Motivation and Performance in Competitive and Noncompetitive Situations." Ph.D. dissertation, University of Michigan, 1968.

Horney, Karen. "Culture and Neurosis." 1936. Reprinted in *Theories of Psychopathology and Personality*, edited by Theodore Millon. 2d ed. Philadelphia: W. B. Saunders, 1973.

———. *Neurosis and Human Growth: The Struggle Toward Self-Realization.* New York: Norton, 1950.

———. *The Neurotic Personality of Our Time.* New York: Norton, 1937.

Howe, Alan. "A Climate for Small Group Talk." In *Perspectives on Small Group Learning: Theory and Practice*, edited by Mark Brubacher, Ryder Payne, and Kemp Rickett. Oakville, Ontario: Rubicon Publishing, 1990.

Huizinga, Johan. *Homo Ludens: A Study of the Play Element in Culture.* Reprint. Boston: Beacon, 1955.

Hymowitz, Carol. "Five Main Reasons Why Managers Fail." *Wall Street Journal*, 2 May 1988: 27.

Jacoby, Russell. *Social Amnesia: A Critique of Contemporary Psychology from Adler to Laing.* Boston: Beacon, 1975.

Jahoda, Marie. *Current Concepts of Positive Mental Health.* New York: Basic, 1958.

Jiu, Haibin. "Science Contest Pressures Kids Too Much." *New York Times*, 19 February 1992: A20.

Johnson, David W., and Brenda Bryant. "Cooperation and Competition in the Classroom." *Elementary School Journal* 74 (1973): 172–81.

Johnson, David W., and Roger T. Johnson. *Cooperation and Competition: Theory and Research.* Edina, Minn.: Interaction Book Co., 1989.

———. "Instructional Goal Structure: Cooperative, Competitive, or Individualistic." *Review of Educational Research* 44 (1974): 213–40.

———. "The Internal Dynamics of Cooperative Learning Groups." In *Learning to Cooperate, Cooperating to Learn*, edited by Robert Slavin, Shlomo Sharan, Spencer Kagan, Rachel Hertz Lazarowitz, Clark Webb, and Richard Schmuck. New York: Plenum Press, 1985.

———. *Leading the Cooperative School.* Edina, Minn.: Interaction Book Co., 1989.

———. *Learning Together and Alone: Cooperative, Competitive, and Individualistic Learning.* 3d ed. Englewood Cliffs, N.J.: Prentice-Hall, 1991.

———. "Motivational Processes in Cooperative, Competitive, and Individualistic Learning Situations." In *Research on Motivation in Education*, vol. 2, edited by Carole and Russell Ames. Orlando, Fla.: Academic Press, 1985.

———. "The Socialization and Achievement Crisis: Are Cooperative Learning Experiences the Solution?" In *Applied Social Psychology Annual 4*, edited by L. Bickman. Beverly Hills, Calif.: Sage, 1983.

Johnson, David W., Roger T. Johnson, and Edythe Johnson Holubec. *Circles of Learning: Cooperation in the Classroom.* Rev. ed. Edina, Minn.: Interaction Book Co., 1986.

Johnson, David W., Roger T. Johnson, Jeanette Johnson, and Douglas Anderson. "Effects of Cooperative versus Individualized Instruction on Student Prosocial Behavior, Attitudes Toward Learning, and Achievement." *Journal of Educational Psychology* 68 (1976): 446–52.

Johnson, David W., Roger T. Johnson, and Geoffrey Maruyama. "Interdependence and Interpersonal Attraction Among Heterogeneous and Homogeneous Individuals: A Theoretical Formulation and a Meta-analysis of the Research." *Review of Educational Research* 53 (1983): 5–54.

Johnson, David W., Roger T. Johnson, and Linda Scott. "The Effects of Cooperative and Individualized Instruction on Student Attitudes and Achievement." *Journal of Social Psychology* 104 (1978): 207–16.

Johnson, David W., Roger T. Johnson, and Karl A. Smith. *Active Learning: Cooperation in the College Classroom.* Edina, Minn.: Interaction Book Co., 1991.

Johnson, David W., Roger T. Johnson, and Margaret Tiffany. "Structuring Academic Conflicts Between Majority and Minority Students: Hindrance or Help to Integration?" *Contemporary Educational Psychology* 9 (1984): 61–73.

Johnson, David W., Roger T. Johnson, Margaret Tiffany, and Brian Zaidman. "Cross-Ethnic Relationships: The Impact of Intergroup Cooperation and Intergroup Competition." *Journal of Experimental Education* 78 (1984): 75–79.

Johnson, David W., Geoffrey Maruyama, Roger Johnson, Deborah Nelson, and Linda Skon. "Effects of Cooperative, Competitive, and Individualistic Goal Structures on Achievement: A Meta-Analysis." *Psychological Bulletin* 89 (1981): 47–62.

Johnson, Roger T., Charlotte Brooker, James Stutzman, Donald Hultman, and David W. Johnson. "The Effects of Controversy, Concurrence Seeking, and Individualistic Learning on Achievement and Attitude Change." *Journal of Research in Science Teaching* 22 (1985): 197–205.

Johnson, Roger T., and David W. Johnson. "Cooperation in Learning: Ignored But Powerful." *Lyceum* 5 (1982): 22–26.

———. "Science and Cooperative Learning." Unpublished manuscript, n.d.

———. "Structuring Conflict in Science Classrooms." Paper presented at the annual meeting of the National Association of Research in Science Teaching, French Lick, Ind., April 1985.

Johnson, William O. "From Here to 2000." In *Sport and Contemporary Society: An Anthology,* edited by D. Stanley Eitzen. New York: St. Martin's, 1979.

Jones, Dewitt. "No Contest!" *Outdoor Photographer,* April 1992: 18–21.

Jourard, Sidney. *Disclosing Man to Himself.* New York: Van Nostrand Reinhold, 1968.

———. *The Transparent Self.* Rev. ed. New York: D. Van Nostrand, 1971.

Kagan, Jerome. *The Nature of the Child.* New York: Basic, 1984.

Kagan, Spencer. "Co-op Co-op." In *Learning to Cooperate, Cooperating to Learn,* edited by Robert Slavin et al. New York: Plenum, 1985.

Kagan, Spencer, and George P. Knight. "Cooperation-Competition and Self-

Esteem: A Case of Cultural Relativism." *Journal of Cross-Cultural Psychology* 10 (1979): 457–67.

Kagan, Spencer, and Millard C. Madsen. "Cooperation and Competition of Mexican, Mexican-American, and Anglo-American Children of Two Ages Under Four Instructional Sets." *Developmental Psychology* 5 (1971): 32–39.

———. "Experimental Analyses of Cooperation and Competition of Anglo-American and Mexican Children." *Developmental Psychology* 6 (1972): 49–59.

Kagan, Spencer, G. Lawrence Zahn, Keith F. Widaman, Joseph Schwarzwald, and Gary Tyrrell. "Classroom Structural Bias: Impact of Cooperative and Competitive Classroom Structures on Cooperative and Competitive Individuals and Groups." In *Learning to Cooperate, Cooperating to Learn,* edited by Robert Slavin et al. New York: Plenum, 1985.

Kant, Immanuel. *Religion Within the Limits of Reason Alone.* Translated by Theodore M. Greene and Hoyt H. Hudson. New York: Harper Torchbooks, 1960.

Kaufman, Joanne. "Here She Is, Ms. Tiny Miss!" *People,* 26 September 1988: 46–49.

Kelley, Harold H., and Anthony J. Stahelski. "Social Interaction Basis of Cooperators' and Competitors' Beliefs About Others." *Journal of Personality and Social Psychology* 16 (1970): 66–91.

Kierkegaard, Sören. *Concluding Unscientific Postscript.* Translated by David F. Swenson and Walter Lowrie. Princeton, N.J.: Princeton University Press, 1941.

Kilpatrick, William H. "The Project Method." *Teachers College Method* 19 (1918): 319–35.

King, Gillian A., and Richard M. Sorrentino. "Psychological Dimensions of Goal-Oriented Interpersonal Situations." *Journal of Personality and Social Psychology* 44 (1983): 140–62.

Klaidman, Stephen. "TV's Collusive Role." *New York Times,* 27 June 1985: A23.

Knowles, John. *A Separate Peace.* New York: Bantam, 1966.

Knox, Richard A. " 'Free-choice' Rhetoric Isn't the Answer." *Boston Globe,* 17 February 1991: 75.

Knutson, Lawrence. "Cockpit Confusion Cited as Cause of Detroit Crash." *Boston Globe,* 26 June 1991: 11.

Kohn, Alfie. "The ABC's of Caring." *Teacher Magazine,* January 1990: 52–58.

———. *The Brighter Side of Human Nature: Altruism and Empathy in Everyday Life.* New York: Basic Books, 1990.

———. "Caring Kids: The Role of the Schools." *Phi Delta Kappan,* March 1991: 496–506.

———. "Competition vs. Excellence." *New York Times,* 26 April 1991: A29.

———. "Cooperation: What It Means and Doesn't Mean." In *Cooperation: Beyond the Age of Competition,* edited by Allan Combs. Philadelphia: Gordon and Breach, 1992.

———. "Existentialism Here and Now." *The Georgia Review* 38 (1984): 381–97.

———. "Group Grade Grubbing versus Cooperative *Learning.*" *Educational Leadership,* February 1991: 83–87.

———. "It's Hard to Get Left Out of a Pair." *Psychology Today*, October 1987: 52–57.

———. "Resistance to Cooperative Learning: Making Sense of Its Deletion and Dilution." *Journal of Education*, forthcoming.

———. "Soccer Riot: Competition Is the Villain." *Los Angeles Times*, 5 June 1985: II/5.

———. "Stop!" *Boston Magazine*, September 1985: 109–17.

———. "That Loving Feeling — When Does It Begin?" *Boston Globe*, 28 April 1986: 45, 47.

———. "Why Competition?" *The Humanist*, January/February 1980, 14–15, 49.

———. *You Know What They Say . . .: The Truth About Popular Beliefs*. New York: HarperCollins, 1990.

Korsh, Nina B. "Effects of Preaching, Practice, and Helpful Evaluations on Third Graders' Collaborative Work." In *Children in Cooperation and Competition: Toward a Developmental Social Psychology* by Emmy A. Pepitone. Lexington, Mass.: Lexington Books, 1980.

Kroll, Walter, and Kay H. Petersen. "Study of Values Test and Collegiate Football Teams." *The Research Quarterly* 36 (1965): 441–47.

Kropotkin, Petr. *Mutual Aid: A Factor of Evolution*. 1902. Reprint. Boston: Extending Horizons Books, 1955.

Kuttner, Bob. "Air Fares That Reach to the Sky." *Boston Globe*, 10 February 1992: 15.

———. "A Time for Shared Trade Growth." *Boston Globe*, 16 March 1987: 15.

Lanzetta, John T., and Basil G. Englis. "Expectations of Cooperation and Competition and Their Effects on Observers' Vicarious Emotional Responses." *Journal of Personality and Social Psychology* 56 (1989): 543–54.

Lappé, Frances Moore, and Joseph Collins. *Food First: Beyond the Myth of Scarcity*. Revised. New York: Ballantine, 1978.

Lasch, Christopher. *The Culture of Narcissism: American Life in an Age of Diminishing Expectations*. New York: Warner, 1979.

Lauterbach, Albert. *Man, Motives, and Money: Psychological Frontiers of Economics*. Ithaca, N.Y.: Cornell University Press, 1954.

Lear, Norman. "Bottom Linemanship." *New York Times*, 20 May 1984: E23.

Lentz, Theo. F., and Ruth Cornelius. "All Together: A Manual of Cooperative Games." Photocopy. Attitude Reseach Laboratory, St. Louis, Mo., 1950.

Leonard, George B. *Education and Ecstasy*. New York: Dell, 1968.

———. *The Ultimate Athlete*. New York: Viking, 1975.

———. "Winning Isn't Everything. It's Nothing." *Intellectual Digest*, October 1973, 45–47.

Lepper, Mark R., and David Greene, eds. *The Hidden Costs of Rewards*. Hillsdale, N.J.: Lawrence Erlbaum, 1978.

Lerch, H. J., and M. Rubensal. "Eine Analyse des Zusammenhangs zwischen Schulleistungen und dem Wetteifermotiv." *Psychologische Beitrage* 25 (1983): 521–31.

Levin, Jenifer. "When Winning Takes All." *Ms.*, May 1983: 92–94, 138–39.

Lewis, C. S. *Mere Christianity*. New York: Macmillan, 1952.

Lewis, Sinclair. *Babbitt.* New York: Harcourt Brace, 1922.

Lewontin, R. C., Steven Rose, and Leon J. Kamin. *Not in Our Genes: Biology, Ideology, and Human Nature.* New York: Pantheon, 1984.

Lifton, Robert Jay. *The Life of the Self: Toward a New Psychology.* New York: Touchstone, 1976.

Light, Richard J. *The Harvard Assessment Seminars: Explorations with Students and Faculty about Teaching, Learning, and Student Life.* 2d report. Cambridge, Mass.: Harvard University, 1992.

Lindsey, Robert. "Airline Deregulation Stranding Some Towns." *New York Times,* 25 November 1983: A1, B19.

Litsky, Frank. "Aggression Necessary, Hill Says." *New York Times,* 22 January 1987: D25, D30.

Lüschen, Günther. "Cheating in Sport." In *Social Problems in Athletics: Essays in the Sociology of Sport,* edited by Daniel M. Landers. Urbana: University of Illinois Press, 1976.

———. "Cooperation, Association, and Contest." *Journal of Conflict Resolution* 14 (1970): 21–34.

———. "The Interdependence of Sport and Culture." *International Review of Sport Sociology* 2 (1967): 127–41.

Maccoby, Eleanor Emmons, and Carol Nagy Jacklin. *The Psychology of Sex Differences.* Stanford, Calif.: Stanford University Press, 1974.

Madsen, Millard C. "Developmental and Cross-Cultural Differences in the Cooperative and Competitive Behavior of Young Children." *Journal of Cross-Cultural Psychology* 2 (1971): 365–71.

Male, Mary. "Cooperative Learning and Staff Development." *Cooperation in Education* (newsletter of the International Association for the Study of Cooperation in Education), May 1989: 4–5.

Mallick, Shahbaz Khan, and Boyd R. McCandless. "A Study of Catharsis of Aggression." *Journal of Personality and Social Psychology* 4 (1966): 591–96.

Mallone, Thomas W., and Mark R. Lepper. "Making Learning Fun: A Taxonomy of Intrinsic Motivations for Learning." In *Aptitude, Learning, and Instruction,* vol. 3: *Conative and Affective Process Analyses,* edited by Richard E. Snow and Marshall J. Farr. Hillsdale, N.J.: Lawrence Erlbaum, 1987.

Mansbridge, Jane J. *Beyond Adversary Democracy.* Chicago: University of Chicago Press, 1983.

Marcuse, Herbert. *One-Dimensional Man.* Boston: Beacon, 1964.

Martens, Rainer. "Competition: In Need of a Theory." In *Social Problems in Athletics: Essays in the Sociology of Sport,* edited by Daniel M. Landers. Urbana: University of Illinois Press, 1976.

Marwell, Gerald, and David R. Schmitt. *Cooperation: An Experimental Analysis.* New York: Academic Press, 1975.

Maslow, Abraham. *The Farther Reaches of Human Nature.* New York: Penguin, 1976.

———. *Motivation and Personality.* 2d ed. New York: Harper & Row, 1970.

———. *Religion, Values, and Peak-Experiences.* New York: Viking, 1964.

———. *Toward a Psychology of Being.* 2d ed. New York: D. Van Nostrand, 1968.

May, Mark A. "A Research Note on Cooperative and Competitive Behavior." *American Journal of Sociology* 42 (1937): 887–91.

May, Mark A., and Leonard Doob. *Cooperation and Competition.* New York: Social Science Research Council, 1937.

May, Rollo. *The Meaning of Anxiety.* Rev. ed. New York: Norton, 1977.

Mays, Bruce. "In Fighting Trim." *New York Times Magazine*, 2 September 1984: 28.

McCandless, Holloway. "Taking the Edge Off Competition." *Working Woman*, September 1989: 110.

McClintock, Charles G. "Development of Social Motives in Anglo-American and Mexican-American Children." *Journal of Personality and Social Psychology* 29 (1974): 348–54.

McElwaine, Sandra. "On the Couch in the Capital." *New York Times Magazine*, 22 May 1983: 58–63.

McKee, John P., and Florence B. Leader. "The Relationship of Socio-Economic Status and Aggression to the Competitive Behavior of Preschool Children." *Child Development* 26 (1955): 135–42.

McLanahan, Jack, and Connie McLanahan, eds. *Cooperative/Credit Union Dictionary and Reference.* Richmond, Kent.: Cooperative Alumni Association, 1990.

Mead, George Herbert. *Mind, Self, and Society from the Standpoint of a Social Behaviorist.* Vol. 1 of *Works of George Herbert Mead*, edited by Charles W. Morris. Chicago: University of Chicago Press, 1934.

Mead, Margaret. Introduction and "Interpretative Statement" in *Cooperation and Competition Among Primitive Peoples*, edited by Margaret Mead. Boston: Beacon, 1961.

Meggyesy, Dave. *Out of Their League.* Berkeley, Calif.: Ramparts Press, 1970.

Meislin, Richard J. "Mexico City Gets Too Big a Million Times a Year." *New York Times*, 8 September 1985: E26.

Messé, Lawrence A., and John M. Sivacek. "Predictions of Others' Responses in a Mixed-Motive Game: Self-Justification or False Consensus?" *Journal of Personality and Social Psychology* 37 (1979): 602–7.

Michener, James A. *Sports in America.* New York: Random House, 1976.

Miller, Anthony G., and Ron Thomas. "Cooperation and Competition Among Blackfoot Indian and Urban Canadian Children." *Child Development* 43 (1972): 1104–10.

Miller, Dale. "Creative Art vs. Competitions." *Guitar Player*, February 1989: 10.

Mills, C. Wright. *Power, Politics, and People: The Collected Essays of C. Wright Mills.* New York: Ballantine, n.d.

Mintz, Alexander. "Non-adaptive Group Behavior." *Journal of Abnormal and Social Psychology* 46 (1951): 150–59.

Minuchin, Salvador. *Family Kaleidoscope.* Cambridge, Mass.: Harvard University Press, 1984.

Mirsky, Jeannette. "The Dakota." In *Cooperation and Competition Among Primitive Peoples*, edited by Margaret Mead. Boston: Beacon, 1961.

Montagu, Ashley. *Darwin, Competition and Cooperation.* 1952. Reprint. Westport, Conn.: Greenwood Press, 1973.

———, ed. *Man and Aggression.* 2d ed. New York: Oxford Univ. Press, 1973.

Moore, Robert A. *Sports and Mental Health*. Springfield, Ill.: Charles C. Thomas, 1966.

Morgan, George W. *The Human Predicament: Dissolution and Wholeness*. New York: Delta, 1970.

Moulton, Janice. "A Paradigm of Philosophy: The Adversary Method." In *Discovering Reality*, edited by Sandra Harding and Merrill B. Hintikka. Dordrecht, Holland: D. Reidel, 1983.

Moyer, K. E. *The Psychobiology of Aggression*. New York: Harper & Row, 1976.

Munroe, Robert L., and Ruth H. Munroe. "Cooperation and Competition Among East African and American Children." *Journal of Social Psychology* 101 (1977): 145–46.

Nance, John J. *Blind Trust*. New York: William Morrow, 1986.

Nastasi, Bonnie K., and Douglas H. Clements. "Research on Cooperative Learning: Implications for Practice." *School Psychology Review* 20 (1991): 110–31.

National Council of Teachers of Mathematics, Working Groups of the Commission on Standards for School Mathematics. *Curriculum and Evaluation Standards for School Mathematics*. Reston, Va.: NCTM, 1989.

Naylor, Thomas H. "Redefining Corporate Motivation, Swedish Style." *The Christian Century*, 30 May–6 June 1990: 566–70.

Neill, D. Monty, and Noe J. Medina. "Standardized Testing: Harmful to Educational Health." *Phi Delta Kappan*, May 1989: 688–97.

Nelson, Janice D., Donna M. Gelfand, and Donald P. Hartmann. "Children's Aggression Following Competition and Exposure to an Aggressive Model." *Child Development* 40 (1969): 1085–97.

Nelson, Linden L., and Spencer Kagan. "Competition: The Star-Spangled Scramble." *Psychology Today*, September 1972: 53–56, 90–91.

Nicholls, John G. *The Competitive Ethos and Democratic Education*. Cambridge, Mass.: Harvard University Press, 1989.

Norem-Hebeisen, Ardyth A., and David W. Johnson. "The Relationship Between Cooperative, Competitive, and Individualistic Attitudes and Differentiated Aspects of Self-Esteem." *Journal of Personality* 49 (1981): 415–26.

NOVA. "Nomads of the Rainforest." Transcript from the WGBH-TV program broadcast, 26 November 1984.

Novak, Michael. *The Joy of Sports: End Zones, Bases, Baskets, Balls, and the Consecration of the American Spirit*. New York: Basic, 1976.

Oakes, Jeannie. *Keeping Track: How Schools Structure Inequality*. New Haven: Yale University Press, 1985.

Ogilvie, Bruce C., and Thomas A. Tutko. "Sport: If You Want to Build Character, Try Something Else." *Psychology Today*, October 1971: 61–63.

Orlean, Susan. "Taking It to the Limit." *Boston Globe Magazine*, 19 June 1983.

Orlick, Terry. *The Cooperative Sports and Games Book*. New York: Pantheon, 1978b.

———. *The Second Cooperative Sports and Games Book*. New York: Pantheon, 1982.

————. *Winning Through Cooperation: Competitive Insanity, Cooperative Alternatives.* Washington, D.C.: Acropolis Books, 1978a.

O'Roark, Mary Ann. " 'Competition' Isn't a Dirty Word." *McCall's,* January 1984: 66, 121.

Orwell, George. "The Sporting Spirit." In *Shooting an Elephant and Other Essays.* New York: Harcourt, Brace and World, 1950.

————. "Such, Such Were the Joys." In *A Collection of Essays by George Orwell.* New York: Harcourt Brace Jovanovich, n.d.

Parenti, Michael. *Democracy for the Few.* 2d ed. New York: St. Martin's, 1977.

Patten, William. *The Grand Strategy of Evolution: The Social Philosophy of a Biologist.* Boston: Gorham Press, 1920.

Patterson, C. H. *Humanistic Education.* Englewood Cliffs, N.J.: Prentice-Hall, 1973.

Pepitone, Emmy A. *Children in Cooperation and Competition: Toward a Developmental Social Psychology.* Lexington, Mass.: Lexington Books, 1980.

Percy, Walker. "Questions They Never Asked Me." 1977. Reprinted in *Conversations with Walker Percy,* edited by Lewis A. Lawson and Victor A. Kramer. Jackson: University Press of Mississippi, 1985.

Pertman, Adam. "Media Observers Say News Coverage Is Pressuring U.S. to Act." *Boston Globe,* 26 June 1985: 14.

Piaget, Jean. *The Moral Judgment of the Child.* Translated by Marjorie Gabain. New York: Free Press, 1965.

Pilbeam, David. "An Idea We Could Live Without: The Naked Ape." In *Man and Aggression,* edited by Ashley Montagu. 2d ed. New York: Oxford University Press, 1973.

Pillsbury, Fred. "Bus Industry Slips Into a Lower Gear." *Boston Globe,* 15 September 1985: A1.

Pines, Maya. "Good Samaritans at Age Two?" *Psychology Today,* June 1979: 66–77.

Pugh, George Edgin. *The Biological Origin of Human Values.* New York: Basic, 1977.

Putka, Gary. "Knowing Pi Now Could Mean a Shot at a Varsity Letter: Even Kindergarteners Vie in Academic Contests; Healthy or Demoralizing?" *Wall Street Journal,* 23 March 1990: A1, A9.

Quain, B. H. "The Iroquois." In *Cooperation and Competition Among Primitive Peoples,* edited by Margaret Mead. Boston: Beacon, 1961.

Quanty, Michael B. "Aggression Catharsis: Experimental Investigations and Implications." In *Perspectives on Aggression,* edited by Russell G. Geen and Edgar C. O'Neal. New York: Academic Press, 1976.

Raush, Harold L. "Interaction Sequences." *Journal of Personality and Social Psychology* 2 (1965): 487–99.

Rensberger, Boyce. "What Made Humans Human?" *New York Times Magazine,* 8 April 1984: 80–81, 89–95.

Reston, James. "Politics and Taxes." *New York Times,* 16 December 1984: E21.

Reuters. "Fight at Exit May Have Slowed Escape from Jet." *Boston Globe,* 7 February 1991: 12.

Rheingold, H. L., and D. F. Hay. "Prosocial Behavior of the Very Young." In *Morality as a Biological Phenomenon: The Presuppositions of Sociobiological Research.* Chicago: University of Chicago Press, 1980.

Rich, Yisrael. "Ideological Impediments to Instructional Innovation: The Case of Cooperative Learning." *Teaching and Teacher Education* 6 (1990): 81–91.

Riesman, David. "Football in America: A Study in Culture Diffusion." In *Individualism Reconsidered and Other Essays.* Glencoe, Ill.: Free Press, 1953.

Roberts, Joan I. *Scene of the Battle: Group Behavior in Urban Classrooms.* Garden City, N.Y.: Doubleday, 1970.

Robinson, Ann. "Cooperation or Exploitation: The Argument against Cooperative Learning for Talented Students." *Journal for the Education of the Gifted* 14 (1990): 9–36.

Robinson, James C., and Harold S. Luft. "Competition and the Cost of Hospital Care, 1972 to 1982." *Journal of the American Medical Association* 257 (1987): 3241–45.

Rogers, Carl R. *On Becoming a Person.* Boston: Houghton Mifflin, 1961.

———. "A Theory of Personality." 1959. Reprinted in *Theories of Psychopathology and Personality,* edited by Theodore Millon. 2d ed. Philadelphia: W. B. Saunders, 1973.

Romney, Kimball, and Romaine Romney. *The Mixtecans of Juxtlahuaca, Mexico.* Six Cultures Series, edited by Beatrice B. Whiting, vol. 4. New York: John Wiley and Sons, 1966.

Rose, I. Nelson. "Litigator's Fallacy." *Whittier Law Review* 6 (1984): 85–98.

Rosenberg, Morris. *Society and the Adolescent Self-Image.* Princeton, N.J.: Princeton University Press, 1965.

Ruben, Harvey L. *Competing.* New York: Pinnacle Books, 1981.

Rubin, Lillian B. *Just Friends: The Role of Friendship in Our Lives.* New York: Harper & Row, 1985.

Rubinstein, Ruth P. "Changes in Self-Esteem and Anxiety in Competitive and Noncompetitive Camps." *Journal of Social Psychology* 102 (1977): 55–57.

Russell, Bertrand. *The Conquest of Happiness.* New York: Horace Liveright, 1930.

———. *Why I Am Not a Christian.* New York: Touchstone, 1957.

Rutherford, Eldred, and Paul Mussen. "Generosity in Nursery School Boys." *Child Development* 39 (1968): 755–65.

Ryan, Frank. *Sports and Psychology.* Englewood Cliffs, N.J.: Prentice-Hall, 1981.

Ryan, Michael. "Here, Everybody Gets to Play." *Parade Magazine,* 15 March 1992: 10.

Sadler, William A., Jr. "Competition Out of Bounds: Sports in American Life." In *Sport in the Sociocultural Process,* edited by Marie Hart. 2d ed. Dubuque, Ia.: William C. Brown, 1976.

Sage, George H. "American Values and Sport: Formation of a Bureaucratic Personality." *Journal of Physical Education and Recreation,* October 1978: 42–44.

Sagotsky, Gerald, Mary Wood-Schneider, and Marian Konop. "Learning to Cooperate: Effects of Modeling and Direct Instruction." *Child Development* 52 (1981): 1037–42.

Sahlins, Marshall D. "The Origin of Society." *Scientific American,* September 1960: 76–87.

———. *The Use and Abuse of Biology: An Anthropological Critique of Sociobiology.* Ann Arbor: University of Michigan Press, 1976.

Salmans, Sandra. "Women Dressing to Succeed Think Twice About the Suit." *New York Times,* 4 November 1985: A1, D4.

Sapon-Shevin, Mara. "Cooperative Instructional Games: Alternatives to the Spelling Bee." *Elementary School Journal* 79 (1978): 81–87.

———. "Cooperative Learning, Cooperative Visions." *Holistic Education Review,* Winter 1991: 25–28.

———. "Cooperative Learning: Liberatory Praxis or Hamburger Helper?" *Educational Foundations* 5 (1991): 5–17.

Sapon-Shevin, Mara, and Nancy Schniedewind. "Selling Cooperative Learning Without Selling It Short." *Educational Leadership,* December 1989/ January 1990: 63–65.

Sassen, Georgia. "Sex Role Orientation, Sex Differences and Concept of Success." Master's thesis, University of Massachusetts, 1981.

———. "Success Anxiety in Women: A Constructivist Interpretation of Its Source and Its Significance." *Harvard Educational Review* 50 (1980): 13–24.

Sattel, Jack W. "Men, Inexpressiveness, and Power." In *Language, Gender and Society,* edited by Barrie Thorne, Cheris Kramarae, and Nancy Henley. Rowley, Mass.: Newbury House, 1983.

Schaps, Eric. "Cooperative Learning: The Challenge in the '90s." *Cooperative Learning,* June 1990: 5–8.

Schaps, Eric, and Catherine Lewis. "Extrinsic Rewards Are Education's Past, Not Its Future." *Educational Leadership,* April 1991: 81.

Schmitt, David R. "Performance Under Cooperation or Competition." *American Behavioral Scientist* 24 (1981): 649–79.

Schniedewind, Nancy, and Ellen Davidson. *Cooperative Learning, Cooperative Lives.* Dubuque, Iowa: William C. Brown, 1987.

Schoen, Elin. "Competition: Can You Bear It When Your Friends Get Ahead?" *Mademoiselle,* April 1981: 210–11, 244–46.

Schumacher, E. F. *Small Is Beautiful: Economics as if People Mattered.* New York: Harper Perennial, 1975.

Seeley, John R., R. Alexander Sim, and Elizabeth W. Loosley. *Crestwood Heights: A Study of the Culture of Suburban Life.* New York: Basic, 1956.

Serrin, William. "How Deregulation Allowed Greyhound to Win Concessions from Strikers." *New York Times,* 7 December 1983: A22.

Shaffer, Thomas L. "The Unique, Novel, and Unsound Adversary Ethic." *Vanderbilt Law Review* 41 (1988): 697–715.

Shapira, Ariella, and Millard C. Madsen. "Between- and Within-Group Cooperation and Competition Among Kibbutz and Nonkibbutz Children." *Developmental Psychology* 10 (1974): 140–45.

———. "Cooperative and Competitive Behavior of Kibbutz and Urban Children in Israel." *Child Development* 40 (1969): 609–17.

Sharan, Shlomo. "Cooperative Learning: A Perspective on Research and

Practice." In *Cooperative Learning: Theory and Research*, edited by Shlomo Sharan. New York: Praeger, 1990.

———. "Cooperative Learning and Helping Behaviour in the Multi-ethnic Classroom." In *Children Helping Children*, edited by Hugh C. Foot, Michelle J. Morgan, and Rosalyn H. Shute. Chichester, England: John Wiley and Sons, 1990.

———. "Cooperative Learning: New Horizons, Old Threats." *The International Association for the Study of Cooperation in Education Newsletter*, December 1987/January 1988: 3–6.

———. "Cooperative Learning: Problems and Promise." *The International Association for the Study of Cooperation in Education Newsletter*, December 1986: 3–4.

———. "The Group Investigation Approach to Cooperative Learning: Theoretical Foundations." In *Perspectives on Small Group Learning: Theory and Practice*, edited by Mark Brubacher, Ryder Payne, and Kemp Rickett. Oakville, Ontario: Rubicon Publishing, 1990.

Sharan, Yael, and Shlomo Sharan. "Group Investigation Expands Cooperative Learning." *Educational Leadership*, December 1989/January 1990: 17–21.

Sherberg, Ellen. "The Thrill of Competition." *Seventeen*, June 1982: 73.

Sherif, Carolyn. "The Social Context of Competition." In *Social Problems in Athletics: Essays in the Sociology of Sport*, edited by Daniel M. Landers. Urbana: University of Illinois Press, 1976.

Sherif, Muzafer, O. J. Harvey, B. J. White, W. R. Hood, and C. W. Sherif. *Intergroup Conflict and Cooperation: The Robbers' Cave Experiment*. Norman, Okla.: University Book Exchange, 1961.

Shirk, Susan L. *Competitive Comrades: Career Incentives and Student Strategies in China*. Berkeley and Los Angeles: University of California Press, 1982.

Simmons, John, and William Mares. *Working Together*. New York: Knopf, 1983.

Simon, Irving. "A Humanistic Approach to Sports." *The Humanist*, July 1983: 25–26, 32.

Simpson, George Gaylord. *The Meaning of Evolution*. New Haven: Yale University Press, 1949.

Singer, Robert N., and Richard F. Gerson. "Athletic Competition for Children: Motivational Considerations." *International Journal of Sport Psychology* 11 (1980): 249–62.

Sipes, Richard G. "War, Sports and Aggression: An Empirical Test of Two Rival Theories." *American Anthropologist* 75 (1973): 64–86.

Slater, Philip. *The Pursuit of Loneliness: American Culture at the Breaking Point*. Boston: Beacon, 1970.

Slavin, Robert E. "Cooperative Learning and Student Achievement." *Educational Leadership*, October 1988: 31–33.

———. "Cooperative Learning and the Cooperative School." *Educational Leadership*, November 1987: 7–13.

———. *Cooperative Learning: Theory, Research, and Practice*. Englewood Cliffs, N.J.: Prentice-Hall, 1990.

———. "Group Rewards Make Groupwork Work: Response to Kohn." *Educational Leadership*, February 1991: 89–91.

————. "Here To Stay — Or Gone Tomorrow?" *Educational Leadership*, December 1989/January 1990: 5.

————. *Using Student Team Learning*. 3d ed. Baltimore: Johns Hopkins Team Learning Project, 1986.

Slusher, Howard S. *Man, Sport and Existence: A Critical Analysis*. Philadelphia: Lea and Febiger, 1967.

Smith, Karl, David W. Johnson, and Roger T. Johnson, "Can Conflict Be Constructive? Controversy Versus Concurrence Seeking in Learning Groups." *Journal of Educational Psychology* 73 (1981): 651–63.

Sobel, Jeffrey. *Everybody Wins*. New York: Walker & Co., 1982.

Solomon, Daniel, Marilyn Watson, Eric Schaps, Victor Battistich, and Judith Solomon. "Cooperative Learning as Part of a Comprehensive Classroom Program Designed to Promote Prosocial Development." In *Cooperative Learning: Theory and Research*, edited by Shlomo Sharan. New York: Praeger, 1990.

Solomon, Daniel, Marilyn Watson, Victor Battistich, Eric Schaps, and Kevin Delucchi. "Creating a Caring Community: A School-Based Program to Promote Children's Sociomoral Development." Paper presented at the International Symposium on Research on Effective and Responsible Teaching, Fribourg, Switzerland, September 1990.

Sommerlad, Elizabeth A., and W. P. Bellingham. "Cooperation-Competition: A Comparison of Australian, European, and Aboriginal School Children." *Journal of Cross-Cultural Psychology* 3 (1972): 149–57.

Spence, Janet T. "The Thematic Apperception Test and Attitudes Toward Achievement in Women: A New Look at the Motive to Avoid Success and a New Method of Measurement." *Journal of Consulting and Clinical Psychology* 42 (1974): 427–37.

Spence, Janet T., and Robert L. Helmreich. "Achievement-related Motives and Behavior." In *Achievement and Achievement Motives: Psychological and Sociological Approaches*, edited by Janet T. Spence. San Francisco: W. H. Freeman, 1983.

Stark, Elizabeth. "Women's Tennis: Friends vs. Foes." *Psychology Today*, July 1984: 17.

Stautberg, Susan Schiffer. "The Rat Race Isn't for Tots." *New York Times*, 9 August 1984: 23.

Steigleder, Michele K., Robert Frank Weiss, Susan Siclari Balling, V. L. Wenninger, and John P. Lombardo. "Drivelike Motivational Properties of Competitive Behavior." *Journal of Personality and Social Psychology* 38 (1980): 93–104.

Steigleder, Michele K., Robert Frank Weiss, Robert Ervin Cramer, and Richard A. Feinberg. "Motivating and Reinforcing Functions of Competitive Behavior." *Journal of Personality and Social Psychology* 36 (1978): 1291–1301.

Stent, Gunther S. "You Can Take the Ethics Out of Altruism But You Can't Take the Altruism Out of Ethics." Review of *The Selfish Gene*, by Richard Dawkins. *Hastings Center Report* 7 (1977): 33–36.

Stigler, James W., and Harold W. Stevenson. "How Asian Teachers Polish Each Lesson to Perfection." *American Educator*, Spring 1991: 12–20, 43–47.

Stock, Robert W. "Daring to Greatness." *New York Times Magazine*, 11 September 1983: 142.

Strick, Anne. *Injustice for All*. New York: Penguin, 1978.

Sullivan, Harry Stack. *The Interpersonal Theory of Psychiatry*. New York: Norton, 1953.

Suttie, Ian D. *The Origins of Love and Hate*. New York: Julian Press, 1952.

Talentino, Arnold V. "The Sports Records Mania: An Aspect of Alienation." Photocopy, n.d.

"Team Play Drawback for Young." *New York Times*, 24 July 1984: C2.

Teen Magazine. "Compete, Don't Retreat!" May 1991: 12, 36.

Thayer, Frederick. "Can Competition Hurt?" *New York Times*, 18 June 1979: 17.

Thomas, Lewis. *The Lives of a Cell: Notes of a Biology Watcher*. New York: Bantam, 1975.

Tjosvold, Dean. *Working Together to Get Things Done*. Lexington, Mass.: Lexington Books, 1986.

Tjosvold, Dean, David W. Johnson, and Roger Johnson. "Influence Strategy, Perspective-Taking, and Relationships Between High- and Low-Power Individuals in Cooperative and Competitive Contexts." *Journal of Psychology* 116 (1984): 187–202.

Totten, Samuel, Toni Sills, Annette Digby, and Pamela Russ. *Cooperative Learning: A Guide to Research*. New York: Garland Publishing, 1991.

Traub, James. "Goodbye, Dr. Spock." *Harper's*, March 1986: 57–64.

Tresemer, David. "The Cumulative Record of Research on 'Fear of Success.'" *Sex Roles* 2 (1976): 217–36.

Trippett, Frank. "Local Chauvinism: Long May It Rave." *Time*, 20 August 1979: 34.

Tutko, Thomas, and William Bruns. *Winning Is Everything and Other American Myths*. New York: Macmillan, 1976.

UCLA Sport Psychology Laboratory. "Playing On: Motivations for Continued Involvement in Youth Sport Programs." Unpublished manuscript. 1990.

Underwood, John. "A Game Plan for America." *Sports Illustrated*, 23 February 1981: 66–80.

————. *Spoiled Sport*. Boston: Little, Brown and Co., 1984.

Vallerand, Robert J., Lise I. Gauvin, and Wayne R. Halliwell. "Negative Effects of Competition on Children's Intrinsic Motivation." *Journal of Social Psychology* 126 (1986): 649–56.

Vance, John J., and Bert O. Richmond. "Cooperative and Competitive Behavior as a Function of Self-Esteem." *Psychology in the Schools* 12 (1975): 225–29.

Vanderzwaag, Harold J. *Toward a Philosophy of Sport*. Reading, Mass.: Addison-Wesley, 1972.

Veroff, Joseph. "Social Comparison and the Development of Achievement Motivation." In *Achievement-Related Motives in Children*, edited by Charles P. Smith. New York: Russell Sage Foundation, 1969.

Wachtel, Paul L. *The Poverty of Affluence: A Psychological Portrait of the American Way of Life.* New York: Free Press, 1983.

Wagner, Lilya. *Peer Teaching: Historical Perspectives.* Westport, Conn.: Greenwood Press, 1982.

Walker, Stuart H. *Winning: The Psychology of Competition.* New York: Norton, 1980.

Warner, Gary. *Competition.* Elgin, Ill.: David C. Cook, 1979.

Warren, William J. "New Movement Seeks to Replace Rivalry in Class With Team Spirit." *New York Times,* 4 January 1989: B11.

Warring, Douglas, David W. Johnson, Geoffrey Maruyama, and Roger Johnson. "Impact of Different Types of Cooperative Learning on Cross-Ethnic and Cross-Sex Relationships." *Journal of Educational Psychology* 77 (1985): 53–59.

Warsh, David. "A Financial World in Dark Until It Finds Bottom Line." *Boston Globe,* 20 October 1987: 34.

Washburn, David A., William D. Hopkins, and Duane M. Rumbaugh. "Effects of Competition on Video-Task Performance in Monkeys (*Macaca mulatta*)." *Journal of Comparative Psychology* 104 (1990): 115–21.

Wassermann, Selma. "Children Working in Groups? It Doesn't Work!" *Childhood Education,* Summer 1989: 201–5.

Watzlawick, Paul. *The Situation Is Hopeless, But Not Serious.* New York: Norton, 1983.

Wax, Joseph. "Competition: Educational Incongruity." *Phi Delta Kappan,* November 1975: 197–98.

Webb, Noreen M. "Peer Interaction and Learning in Small Groups." *International Journal of Educational Research* 13 (1989): 21–39.

———. "Student Interaction and Learning in Small Groups." In *Learning to Cooperate, Cooperating to Learn,* edited by Robert Slavin et al. New York: Plenum, 1985.

Weingold, Harold P., and Ronald L. Webster. "Effects of Punishment on a Cooperative Behavior in Children." *Child Development* 35 (1964): 1211–16.

Weisman, Mary-Lou. "Jousting for 'Best Marriage' on a Field of Hors d'Oeuvres." *New York Times,* 10 November 1983: C2.

Weisskopf, Walter A. "Industrial Institutions and Personality Structure." *Journal of Social Issues* 7 (1951): 1–6.

Wheeler, Lonnie. "No-Cut Policy Prompts a Lot to Cheer About." *New York Times,* 6 November 1991: A18.

Whiting, Beatrice B., and John W. M. Whiting. *Children of Six Cultures: A Psycho-Cultural Analysis.* Cambridge, Mass.: Harvard University Press, 1975.

Whittemore, Irving C. "The Influence of Competition on Performance: An Experimental Study." *Journal of Abnormal and Social Psychology* 19 (1924): 236–54.

Wiens, John A. "Competition or Peaceful Coexistence?" *Natural History,* March 1983: 30–34.

Wilder, David A., and Peter N. Shapiro. "Role of Competition-Induced Anxiety in Limiting the Beneficial Impact of Positive Behavior by an Out-Group Member." *Journal of Personality and Social Psychology* 56 (1989): 60–69.

Wilkes, Paul. "The Tough Job of Teaching Ethics." *New York Times*, 22 January 1989: F1, F24.

Williams, Kipling D., and Steven J. Karau. "Social Loafing and Social Compensation: The Effects of Expectations of Co-Worker Performance." *Journal of Personality and Social Psychology* 61 (1991): 570–81.

Willis, Scott. "Coop. Learning Shows Staying Power." *ASCD Update*, March 1992: 1–2.

Wilson, Edward O. *On Human Nature*. New York: Bantam, 1979.

Winer, Frank. "The Elderly Jock and How He Got That Way." In *Sports, Games, and Play: Social and Psychological Viewpoints*, edited by Jeffrey H. Goldstein. Hillsdale, N.J.: Lawrence Erlbaum Associates, 1979.

Winsten, Jay. "Science and the Media: The Boundaries of Truth." *Health Affairs*, Spring 1985: 5–23.

Wlodkowski, Raymond J., and Judith H. Jaynes. *Eager to Learn*. San Francisco: Jossey-Bass, 1990.

Wodarski, John S., Robert L. Hamblin, David R. Buckholdt, and Daniel E. Ferritor. "Individual Consequences Versus Different Shared Consequences Contingent on the Performance of Low-Achieving Group Members." *Journal of Applied Social Psychology* 3 (1973): 276–90.

Wolff, Robert Paul. *The Ideal of the University*. Boston: Beacon, 1969.

Wooley, Susan F., Terry G. Switzer, Gail C. Foster, Nancy M. Landes, and William C. Robertson. "BSCS Cooperative Learning and Science Program." *Cooperative Learning*, April 1990: 32–33.

Workie, Abaineh. "The Relative Productivity of Cooperation and Competition." *Journal of Social Psychology* 92 (1974): 225–30.

Wynne-Edwards, V. C. *Animal Dispersion in Relation to Social Behaviour*. Edinburgh, Scotland: Oliver and Boyd, 1962.

Yackel, Erna, Paul Cobb, and Terry Wood. "Small-Group Interactions as a Source of Learning Opportunities in Second-Grade Mathematics." *Journal for Research in Mathematics Education* 22 (1991): 390–408.

Yager, Stuart, David W. Johnson, and Roger T. Johnson. "Oral Discussion, Group-to-Individual Transfer, and Achievement in Cooperative Learning Groups." *Journal of Educational Psychology* 77 (1985): 60–66.

Yager, Stuart, Roger T. Johnson, David W. Johnson, and Bill Snider. "The Impact of Group Processing on Achievement in Cooperative Learning Groups." *Journal of Social Psychology* 126 (1986): 389–97.

Yamauchi, Hirotsugu. "Sex Differences in Motive to Avoid Success on Competitive or Cooperative Action." *Psychological Reports* 50 (1982): 55–61.

Yarrow, Marian Radke, Phyllis M. Scott, and Carolyn Zahn Waxler. "Learning Concern for Others." *Developmental Psychology* 8 (1973): 240–60.

Yarrow, Marian Radke, and Carolyn Zahn Waxler. "The Emergence and Functions of Prosocial Behaviors in Young Children." In *Readings in Child Development and Relationships*, edited by Russell C. Smart and Mollie S. Smart. 2d ed. New York: Macmillan, 1977.

Zillmann, Dolf, Jennings Bryant, and Barry S. Sapolsky. "The Enjoyment of Watching Sport Contests." In *Sports, Games, and Play: Social and Psychological Viewpoints*, edited by Jeffrey H. Goldstein. Hillsdale, N.J.: Lawrence Erlbaum Associates, 1979.

Zimbardo, Philip G., Craig Haney, W. Curtis Banks, and David Jaffe. "The Psychology of Imprisonment: Privation, Power, and Pathology." In *Theory and Research in Abnormal Psychology*, edited by David Rosenhan and Perry London. 2d ed. New York: Holt, Rinehart and Winston, 1975.

Zimmerman, Don H., and Candace West. "Sex Roles, Interruptions, and Silences in Conversation." In *Language and Sex: Difference and Dominance*, edited by Barrie Thorne and Nancy Henley. Rowley, Mass.: Newbury House, 1975.

Zimmerman, William. "On Negative Ads." *New York Times*, 13 November 1986: A31.

Zubin, Joseph. *Some Effects of Incentives*. New York: Teachers College, 1932.

Zuckerman, Miron, and Ladd Wheeler. "To Dispel Fantasies About the Fantasy-Based Measure of Fear of Success." *Psychological Bulletin* 82 (1975): 932–46.

INDEX

316

Bruns, William, 25, 93, 160,
    165–66, 266n.32, 269n.32
Bryan, James H., 258n.23, 269n.22
Bryant, Brenda, 149–50
Buber, Martin, 90, 137–40
Burt, Cyril, 12
Business competition. *See* Economic
    competition
Butt, Dorcas Susan, 126–27,
    256n.12

Caillois, Roger, 16, 80
Campbell, David N., 31, 59
Camus, Albert, 90
Capitalism. *See* Economic compe-
    tition
Catharsis theory, 144–47
Cheating, 27, 58, 158–67, 239
Chesterton, G. K., 81
Child-rearing styles and competi-
    tion, 27–29, 36–37, 38, 119–20,
    185–86, 234–35
Child Development Project, 224,
    225, 231–32. *See also* Develop-
    mental Studies Center
Chinese, 37, 66, 188, 251n.52
Chodorow, Nancy, 251n.52,
    274–75n.28
"Choking," 121
Cities, competition among, 154, 155
Clarke, Judy, 211
Clifford, Margaret, 47, 59
Cohen, Elizabeth, 222
Coleman, James S., 16
Collective action for social change,
    67, 131, 189–92, 195–96,
    256n.23, 260n.85
Color War, 146
Combs, Arthur W., 77, 129,
    161–62, 249n.21
Common enemy, 128, 152–55
Commons, tragedy of the, 67
Communication, 150
Comparison, social: and low self-
    esteem, 100–101; as unnecessary

for identity, 41–42, 184; without
competition, 42–43, 184n.
Competition: among animals,
19–24, 244; as cause of conformity, 78, 128–31, 211; as cause of
either/or thinking, 127–28; as
cause of external locus of control,
107; as cause of goal orientation,
125–27; as cause of hostility, 9,
135, 143–48, 186; caused by hostility, 143; caused by psychological need, 97–106, 113; caused by
social norms, 97, 102–3; as damage control, 101–2; defined, 3–5,
9; difficulty of eliminating, 43,
182–83, 237–38; distinct from
conflict, 156–57; distinct from success, 6, 45–46, 55–61, 77, 100–
101, 117, 171–72, 239; distinct
from survival, 8, 195; effect of,
on children vs. adults, 115–16; effect of, on relationships, 9, 115,
132–57, 204, 207, 238; as extrinsic motivator, 59–61, 206, 218,
242; felt to be undesirable, 31–
32, 62–65, 79, 89n., 91–92, 96;
intergroup vs. intragroup, 5, 7,
48–49, 152–55, 204, 220n.; as
learned, 24–33; associated with
lower moral standard, 163, 239,
273n.21; mixed messages regarding, 117–18; moderate vs. excessive, 103–5, 158–67; moderate
vs. radical criticism of, 9–10, 93,
159–67, 237–39; myths of, 8,
186, 194; with oneself, 6, 89; in
other cultures, 33–39; as perpetuating inequity, 72–73, 76–77,
196; prevalence of, 1–3, 7, 236–
38; "process" version of, 86–87,
184; psychological impact of,
96–97, 106–31, 237; as public
event, 105–6, 120; and quantification, 85–86; as rarely examined, 1, 3; reactions to criticisms

"We have been in prison from wrong teaching. By perceiving that cooperation is the answer, not competition, Alfie Kohn opens a new world of living. I am deeply indebted to him."

— W. Edwards Deming,
management consultant

"A really impressive piece of work. Challenging and thoughtful, it reaches to the heart of many problems of our social life and the ideology that constrains and distorts it."

— Noam Chomsky,
professor of linguistics,
Massachusetts Institute of Technology

"A brilliant debunking of America's most sacred cow. Kohn demolishes the myths of competition decisively and irrefutably."

— Philip Slater, sociologist,
author of *The Pursuit of Loneliness*

"Well-researched and sound, *No Contest* exposes erroneous assumptions about the inevitability and value of competition. This book . . . deserves our attention."

— Carl Rogers, psychologist

"Alfie Kohn marshals the evidence that [competition] is not the mainspring of achievement in industry, the arts, education, or games."

— Dr. Benjamin Spock, pediatrician

"*No Contest* has already changed the way many of us think about competition. The second edition is even better, with a new chapter on cooperation in the classroom that is thorough, informative, even brilliant. Anyone who cares about education and children will find reading this book a necessity; it will reframe the educational debate. Even people with years of experience as educators and researchers will be challenged by this book — as I was."

— David W. Johnson,
Cooperative Learning Center,
University of Minnesota